Storytelling Sovereignty

Storytelling Sovereignty

Indigenous Peoples and the Media

EDITED BY CRISTINA L. AZOCAR
AND META G. CARSTARPHEN

University of Oklahoma Press : Norman

Financial support for publication was provided from the University Libraries, the Office of the Vice President for Research and Partnerships, and the Office of the Provost, University of Oklahoma.

Library of Congress Cataloging-in-Publication Data

ISBN 978-0-8061-9718-0 (hardcover)
LCCN 2025054286

The paper in this book meets the guidelines for permanence and durability of the Committee on Production Guidelines for Book Longevity of the Council on Library Resources, Inc. ∞

The manufacturer's authorized representative in the EU for product safety is Mare Nostrum Group B.V., Mauritskade 21D, 1091 GC Amsterdam, The Netherlands, email: gpsr@mare-nostrum.co.uk.

For the storytellers of the Upper Mattaponi Indian Tribe
Cristina L. Azocar

For mi familia
Meta G. Carstarphen

In honor of John P. Sanchez (Yaqui/Apache) 1954–2026

Explanation of the art by James Kwaksistala

The book cover depicts a young eagle holding onto pieces of traditional Kwakwaka'wakw culture, representing the importance of imparting knowledge and wisdom to the youth.

In one claw, there is a salmon, the primary food source of many coastal native peoples throughout history; in the other claw, hemlock branches, a symbol of grace and blessing.

The copper shield on the eagle's chest is a symbol of great wealth. And the sun above the eagle's head represents life-giving, creativity, and benevolence. Back when the Kwakwaka'wakw people lived a simpler life, before European colonization overtook the native people of the coast, their media was not as vast and accessible as it is today.

Life has evolved exponentially in ways of communication and understanding. Although the times are always changing, I think it is important to recall how life has evolved throughout history to better understand the current affairs of today. Their media of the past was storytelling, and mainly passed down from generation to generation. They did not read or write; their only means of communicating knowledge was verbally and physically.

In reflecting on the history of Native culture, I have become very drawn to the simplicity of how these people once lived. It highlights the importance of life. The main focus of their culture back then was hunting, eating, singing, dancing, all in the midst of the community. Without each other, we have no purpose and could do very little. But with each other, we are strong, and our wealth lies in love.

Contents

Preface xi
Meta G. Carstarphen

Acknowledgments xv

Introduction: A Framework for Storytelling Sovereignty *1*
Cristina L. Azocar

Part One: News

1 Media and Indigenous Standpoint Theory *9*
Cristina L. Azocar

2 "Indigenous Knowledge Is Rooted in Community" *23*
Interview with Shondiin Silversmith

3 A Yakama Story Revisited: Sustaining Indigenous Science and Environmental News *28*
Ryan N. Comfort

4 "I Will Never Retire from Native Media" *41*
Interview with Joseph Orozco

5 The News Coverage of Unmarked Graves at Indian Residential Schools by the Canadian Broadcasting Corporation *46*
Dennis Foung

6 "You Don't Have to Explain Why It's a Story. It's Implicit" *57*
Interview with Mark Trahant

7 Indigenizing Free Expression in Oklahoma *62*
Kevin R. Kemper and Litzy Galarza

8 "If You're Not at the Table, You're Probably Part of the Menu" *77*
Interview with Paul DeMain

9 The News Media and the Indian Child Welfare Act *82*
Nancy Marie Spears

10 "We're Getting More of Our Stories out from That Native Perspective" *96*
Interview with Patty Talahongva

Part Two: Multimedia

11 Emergent Sources Supporting Sovereignty on Social Media: Three Supreme Court Cases *103*
Sarah Liese, Victoria LaPoe, Benjamin LaPoe, and Taylor Orcutt

12 "It's Time to Collectively Rise, Rebuild, and Support One Another" *117*
Interview with Brian Bull

13 The *Kuleana* of Culture–Nature Relationships in *Moana* and *Waikiki* *122*
Colby Y. Miyose

14 "We're the Original Storytellers" *136*
Interview with Taietsarón:sere Leclaire

15 The Power of Positionality in Indigenous Nonfiction Film *141*
Tsanavi Spoonhunter

16 "One of the First Images Captured Was of Native People" *155*
Interview with Colleen Thurston

Part Three: Persuasion

17 Lights, Camera, Activism! How Three Tribal Teens Helped Stop a Mine *163*
Patty Loew

18 Promoting *Bad Press*: A Documentary Film from Indian Country and a Model for Public Relations *176*
Sarah Liese, Shondiin Silversmith, Benjamin LaPoe, Victoria LaPoe, and Taylor Orcutt

19 "The Struggle of the Freedmen Is Part of Tribal History" *186*
Interview with Marilyn K. Vann

20 Flipping the Script: How Deb Haaland Used Instagram to Question Indigenous Stereotypes *193*
Newly Paul

21 "We Prayed and Danced in Our Own Ways" *206*
Interview with LiL Mike and Funny Bone

22 Still Buying into Racism: Beyond Using American Indian Icons in Product Marketing *212*
Victoria E. Sanchez

23 "Indigenous Media . . . Are Our Acts of Resistance" *232*
Interview with Candace Hamana

Bibliography *237*
List of Contributors *277*
Index *283*

Preface

Meta G. Carstarphen

Indigenous Peoples and the Media is a book that builds on the success of its predecessor, a previously published University of Oklahoma Press volume titled *American Indians and the Mass Media.* With its new title and expanded commitment to foregrounding Indigenous storytelling and media, this book revises the legacy of the previous volume primarily by centering Indigenous voices and ways of knowing even more strongly in the media analyses it offers. *Storytelling Sovereignty: Indigenous Peoples and the Media* explores Indigenous achievements and extends our understanding of the fluidity of forms of news telling, entertainment, and community building in the digital age.

American Indians and the Mass Media, edited by Meta G. Carstarphen and John P. Sanchez and published in 2010, broke new ground in terms of both publishing concept and scope. That book, conceived as a project to counter the invisibility of Indigenous people in the media, enlisted the talents of fifteen contributors to help tell this story. Skilled authors representing academic scholars and practicing journalists embraced this enormous task and produced what is a comparatively slim volume. The resulting publication, while well-received, challenged the notion of what a "scholarly" collection should look like in light of its assortment of distinctive voices. Scholars of journalism and media topics blended their perspectives with media-makers and practitioners to provide insights honed by data, observation, and, most importantly, the lived experiences of Indigenous news-makers.

There had been few precursors to *American Indians and the Mass Media* that studied both mass media and Indigenous life in North America, resulting in fragmented outcomes whereby Indigenous media was unevenly or not completely accurately covered. For example, a significant edited volume in the late 1990s compiled analyses of the uneven reporting and coverage of Native Americans as part of a sweeping review of communities of color.[1] That book led with a section about Native Americans, incorporating a broad sweep of events and analyses that framed their media footprint as that of a racial minority. However, this framework obscured their lived realities as sovereign communities. The framework, which repeated itself throughout the book in relation to other communities of color, illustrated a core deficiency in portraying the nature of Indigenous media. This deficiency also exposed central questions and complexities. If Indigenous nations are sovereign, how do their media expressions connect with the nontribal societies in which they are embedded? In this book, *Indigenous Peoples and the Media*, the context of sovereignty centers on an understanding and appreciation of Indigenous nations and their histories, and so the evolution of their ownership of and participation in mass media becomes clearer.

During the latter half of the twentieth century and through the early decades of the twenty-first century, the number of scholarly works that have re-examined the meaning of "Indian-ness" has increased. Collectively, the sum of these works helped create momentum for more Native American studies programs in colleges and universities, as well as in other educational spaces. Still, a gap remained for works that centered on the role of Indigenous people in creating and distributing their own media. One early effort to address this absence was made by scholars James E. Murphy and Sharon M. Murphy, whose 1981 work analyzed inaccurate and biased portrayals of Indigenous subjects in the news, and also documented in some detail the publishing successes and struggles for early Native newspapers in the United States.[2]

More often than not, subsequent scholarly attention has focused on the interconnectedness of Indigeneity and media, documenting the near invisibility of Native nations as subjects covered or occasionally as active participants in the centuries-old practices of media in the United States. Then, in 2005, Patty Loew (Bad River Band of the Lake Superior Ojibwe) published a significant study that shifted the scholarly gaze from Native nations as merely consumable subjects to creators in their own right.[3] Her work encouraged more comprehensive works in the same vein, including *American Indians and the Mass Media*.

Co-editor of the 2010 volume, John Sanchez (Yaqui and Apache) was pivotal in crystallizing the position of this first collection. He focused on showcasing Indigenous contributors whose experiences would be central to the integrity and tone of the book. Professor and journalist Mark Trahant (Shoshone-Bannock), for instance, captured the rich oral history of the formation of national organizations for Indigenous journalists, beginning with the American Indian Press Association and going through to the founding of the Native American Journalists Association.[4] Veteran newsmaker Paul DeMain (Oneida and Ojibwe) blended personal narrative, memoir, storytelling, and intellectual grit in his challenge to readers to think about the paradox of Native sovereignty in the Americas.[5] Scholars and professors Stacey J. T. Hust and Debra Merskin combined their research efforts, using feminist sensibilities and historical fact to confront the too-casual media use of a slur meant to denigrate Native women.[6] And, on the edge of unseen breakthroughs in new media emerging in the early years of the twenty-first century, Roy Boney Jr. (Cherokee) described the nascent efforts the Cherokee Nation was making to adapt its language to digital spaces, including YouTube and Facebook.[7]

The editors of the reimagined successor volume, *Storytelling Sovereignty: Indigenous Peoples and the Media*, have been intentional about assembling content that speaks to contemporary media representations while centering on the varied experiences of Indigeneity. In an elevated approach, we have combined scholarly chapters with brief, transcribed interviews with Indigenous news-makers, media influencers, and significant media creators. These direct conversations weave in and out of the scholarly chapters, amplifying the chorus of Indigenous voices and perspectives that shape this volume. Reflecting on the digital impact on all forms of mediated communication, we have reimagined the media content into three parts: News, Multimedia, and Persuasion.

This volume will expand on previous work, thanks to the formidable talents of co-editor Cristina L. Azocar (Upper Mattaponi). Her professional, academic, and scholarly achievements have consistently focused on advocating for and elevating Indigenous media and those who create these vital channels of communication and culture.[8] Azocar's introduction, "A Framework for Storytelling Sovereignty," explains this conceptual framework.

Part 1, "News," examines news-gathering about Indigenous communities. Azocar opens this part with "Media and Indigenous Standpoint Theory": an exploration of Indigenous Standpoint Theory and its relevance to representation and identity, which leads our examination by more specifically linking media with Indigenous identity. Nine more chapters and interviews contextualize familiar journalism practices, with culturally specific examples of reporting, editing, and significant legal cases important to Indigenous communities.

The second part, "Multimedia," reflects perspectives about the convergence of media technologies and approaches that mark contemporary information gathering and diffusion. The six chapters and interviews in this part spotlight key Indigenous perspectives about social media, radio, television, and filmmaking.

Finally, the third part, "Persuasion," explores diverse forms of media and how Indigenous thought leaders and practitioners use them for strategic purposes. These seven chapters and interviews feature a diverse array of media producers and scholars, including those from documentary filmmaking, social media, rap artistry, advertising, public relations, and social activism. All these examples show the various ways Indigenous identities use media to reflect authentic experiences and reject harmful stereotypes.

With a respectful nod toward the past, including the predecessor of this new book, *Storytelling Sovereignty: Indigenous Peoples and the Media* seeks to break new ground. Intentional in its inclusion of new voices, this volume is committed to its focus on understanding Indigenous-produced media. Historical perspectives sit side by side with contemporary and emerging media performances, to honor the ever-presence of Indigenous tradition and experience.

Notes

1. See Beverly Ann Deepe Keever, Carolyn Martindale, and Mary Ann Weston, 1970, *U.S. News Coverage of Racial Minorities: A Sourcebook, 1934–1996*, foreword by Oscar Gandy Jr. (Westport: Greenwood Press).

2. See James Emmett Murphy and Sharon Murphy, 1981, *Let My People Know: American Indian Journalism, 1828–1978*, foreword by Jeannette Henry, 1st ed. (Norman: University of Oklahoma Press).

3. See Patty Loew and Kelly Mella, 2005, "Black Ink and the New Red Power: Native American Newspapers and Tribal Sovereignty," *Journalism & Communication Monographs* 7, no. 3: 99–142.

4. See Mark Trahant, 2010, "American Indians at Press: The Native American Journalists Association," in *American Indians and the Mass Media*, eds. Meta G. Carstarphen and John P. Sanchez (Oklahoma: University of Oklahoma Press), 213–21. In 2023, the Native American Journalists Association officially changed its name to the Indigenous Journalists Association.

5. See Paul DeMain, 2010, "The Notion of Somebody Sovereign: Why Sovereignty Is Important to Tribal Nations," in *American Indians and the Mass Media*, eds. Meta G. Carstarphen and John P. Sanchez (Norman: University of Oklahoma Press), 169–84.

6. See Stacey J. T. Hust and Debra Merskin, 2010, "The 'S' Word: Activist Texts and Media Coverage Related to the Movement to Eradicate 'Squaw,'" in *American Indians and the Mass Media*, eds. Meta G. Carstarphen and John P. Sanchez (Oklahoma: University of Oklahoma Press), 128–49.

7. See Roy Boney Jr., 2010, "Cherokeespace.com: Native Social Networking," in *American Indians and the Mass Media*, eds. Meta G. Carstarphen and John P. Sanchez (Norman: University of Oklahoma Press), 222–26.

8. See Cristina Azocar, 2022, *News Media and the Indigenous Fight for Federal Recognition* (New York: Lexington Press).

Acknowledgments

A book project of this scope needs many hands to carry it to fruition. We take this moment to thank and acknowledge the people who carried this book.

First, we would like to thank John Sanchez, who co-edited the first iteration of this book, *American Indians and the Mass Media* (2012). His commitment to empowering as many Indigenous voices as possible through his work laid the groundwork for this reimagined and expanded volume.

Storytelling Sovereignty: Indigenous Peoples and the Media has more than doubled the number of contributions compared to the 2012 volume. We are grateful to each of the 33 contributors in this volume—listed in our table of contents—for the scholarship, professional experience, and knowledge they share in these pages. We are excited that our book cover features the original art of James Kwaksistala, a young, emerging Kwakwaka'wakw artist based in Campbell River, British Columbia.

Coordinating and polishing the broad yet interconnected content in this volume required the expertise of interview transcribers, proofreaders, indexers, and copy editors. We thank Ian Gaerlan, B. Narr, Dolissa Medina, and University of Oklahoma Press–affiliated staff Riley E. Hines and Estelle Lloyd for their input and support.

This project was fortunate to receive financial support for writing, illustrations, and production costs. We are grateful for a grant from James Wagstaffe, which helped fund writers, conference presentations and some production aspects of this book. Financial support was also provided by the University of Oklahoma Libraries' Open Access Fund. Both editors received valuable support from their respective academic institutions, San Francisco State University and the University of Oklahoma, in the form of course release time, financial assistance, and sabbatical leave. This support enabled them to draft, edit, and refine the manuscript over nearly four years. We sincerely appreciate the feedback, encouragement and helpful suggestions we received from our external reviewers at various stages throughout this process.

None of this would have been possible without the steady and wise guidance of University of Oklahoma Press Senior Acquisitions Editor Alessandra Jacobi-Tamulevich. We sincerely appreciate her unwavering support for our project.

Finally, we dedicate this book to the enduring presence of Indigenous peoples around the globe, and to all readers who embrace media in all its forms and influences.

Introduction

A Framework for Storytelling Sovereignty

Cristina L. Azocar

Wingapo, and welcome to *Storytelling Sovereignty: Indigenous Peoples and the Media*. Elizabeth Cook-Lynn wrote in *New Indians, Old Wars*: "It is a great responsibility to be an Indian in America."[1] Indigenous storytellers are the custodians of their communities' histories, languages, traditions, values, and knowledge systems. Indigenous media-makers provide a platform for Indigenous voices, perspectives, and cultural expressions, ensuring that traditional knowledge, language, and values are safeguarded and revitalized. Indigenous storytellers have a great responsibility. We, as editors, have a great responsibility in this book to set an agenda that orients the work toward Indigenous self-determination.

Media affects every part of life for Indigenous people. It influences how others see us and often how we see ourselves. Article 16 of the Declaration of Rights of Indigenous Peoples states: "Indigenous peoples have the right to establish their own media in their own languages and to have access to all forms of non-Indigenous media without discrimination." The General Assembly of the United Nations adopted this statement in 2007, almost twenty years ago. The intention behind these words shows what may happen when Indigenous people gain control of the media. Indeed, in 2025, the United Nations Permanent Forum on Indigenous Issues recommended that the United Nations Educational, Scientific and Cultural Organization conduct a study concerning Indigenous peoples and the media. The foreword to that study states: "In a world increasingly influenced by media narratives, the representation of Indigenous Peoples in the media has far-reaching implications for their rights, cultural and linguistic preservation, economic empowerment, well-being and inclusion in society. Access to information and media content that is tailored to Indigenous audiences enables them to make informed decisions and fully participate in society."[2]

We will not be replaced, and we will not be erased.

Storytelling Framework

Since the publication in 2012 of Meta G. Carstarphen and John Sanchez's *American Indians and the Media*, significant changes in the media landscape have made it easier for Indigenous peoples to tell our stories from our perspectives. *Storytelling Sovereignty: Indigenous Peoples and the Media* honors how our current storytellers take responsibility for the new environments in which our stories emerge. Digital and social media platforms have empowered Indigenous voices to connect, mobilize, and share stories internationally, and have facilitated opportunities to share Indigenous movements widely, thus fostering solidarity and awareness among Indigenous and non-Indigenous audiences. This new environment has also allowed Indigenous media to become part of a global network of resistance, reclamation, and community, which was never possible under legacy media. It is now much easier to bypass the traditional media gatekeepers who have long tried to ignore or silence us. This change has been transformative, and it has created an even greater responsibility for the storytellers because the mediated sharing of our stories provides insight to those who only know us through mass media. Authentic representation profoundly affects public perception, public policy, and social attitudes toward Indigenous communities, which has led to changes in policies, public opinion and the fostering of allyships. Examples of Indigenous-led media campaigns that have led to worldwide visibility include the Dakota Access Pipeline protests on the Standing Rock Sioux Tribe reservation, the Land Back movement, Missing and Murdered Indigenous People, and the legacy of American Indian boarding schools. We want this book to contribute more accurate, diverse, and nuanced portrayals of these examples of our lived experiences.

Indigenous people have always used storytelling to remind us of the past, guide the present, and help us navigate the future. Stories connect us and help us understand coming changes, foreseeable or not. That is the vision for this book: to move forward and promote what I am calling "storytelling sovereignty." Storytelling sovereignty means that we decide how to share and steward our stories. It also recognizes Indigenous media's diversity, uniqueness, and complexity, reflecting different Indigenous communities' varied languages, cultural practices, media needs, and structures. Storytelling sovereignty affects cultural preservation, autonomy, and resistance among Indigenous people. It protects sacred knowledge, upholds cultural protocols, and challenges external misrepresentations.

Storytelling Sovereignty: Indigenous Peoples and the Media aims to showcase the diversity and resilience of Indigenous storytelling across various media forms and contexts, promoting an understanding of media as a powerful tool for cultural expression and political agency. Our vision is to unite the voices of academics, journalists, filmmakers, public relations professionals, artists, and other media-makers. In this book, we document experiences, analyze representations, spotlight Indigenous voices, and provide a platform for dialogue about how mass media can lead us toward social justice. The legacy radio and print mediums remain crucial for connecting Indigenous people, because many still lack broadband access. In regions where digital infrastructure is limited or inaccessible, radio and print provide a lifeline for information and empower Indigenous communities to maintain autonomy over their narratives and resist the marginalization and homogenization that can often occur in broader media landscapes.

This book will not compare Indigenous and non-Indigenous media. The concept of making comparisons comes from an anthropological perspective, which does not work in this context. However, some chapters will reference non-Indigenous media. They will foreground Indigenous voices and show how non-Indigenous people can learn from, collaborate with, and see through an Indigenous lens.[3] Non-Indigenous allies in media can support Indigenous media by amplifying Indigenous-led narratives, respecting intellectual property, and working collaboratively. This is reminiscent of Martin Nakata's "cultural interface theory"—that is, how we work "in the metaphoric space where Indigenous knowledge and cultures interact with other cultures and ways of being."[4] Recalling our core narratives, we are at the center of the world, and the rest are at the margins.[5]

We also envision *Storytelling Sovereignty: Indigenous Peoples and the Media* as a "living archive" that preserves and respects the legacy of Indigenous media, while adapting to ongoing shifts in technology, policy, and cultural exchange. Such a collection reinforces the idea that this book is a living document that is part of an ongoing, dynamic movement.

The academy needs more Indigenous scholars. There is an increasing recognition that Indigenous expertise can influence the direction humanity is headed in ways that were not previously possible, as Indigenous presence is being felt like never before. Mainstream society is beginning to realize that the knowledge carried within Indigenous stories can help turn humanity away from the brink of environmental destruction, before it is too late.

When the editors were assembling *American Indians and the Media* in 2012, Indigenous journalism was beginning to ascend in the public consciousness. Then social media, streaming platforms, and other interactive mediums proliferated; Indigenous voices and reporting became more accessible. For example, in 2012, the Change the Mascot campaign and advocacy from Native groups sought to pressure teams like the Washington Red***** (now the Washington Commanders) to change their names. Journalism plays an essential role in Indian Country, and readers of this book will find several Indigenous journalists who will amplify truth-telling and bring integrity to what the world knows about us. Almost every journalist interviewed in this book mentions the influence that the Native American Journalists Association (now the Indigenous Journalists Association) had on their career and their understanding of the importance of training the next generation. Expanding access to accurate news and information is essential for creating an informed citizenry and a healthy democracy across tribal, local, state, and national levels. For more than forty years, Indigenous journalists across the United States and Canada have worked to support and sustain the Native American Journalists Association/Indigenous Journalists Association (NAJA/IJA).

Although the number of Indigenous journalists is increasing, there need to be more to cover the richness of Indigenous life, and the ones who are currently working are very busy. There are even fewer Indigenous scholars working in the broad field of communication. Although new Indigenous media scholars are entering the academy, few are working in communication studies and related fields like journalism and public relations. Many more are in American Indian, Indigenous, Native American, and other fields because these fields are more likely to value Indigenous voices, methods, and research; the fields respect an Indigenous point of view. However, these disciplines are also less likely to be able to exert their influence on the Indigenous experience and in turn influence larger fields such as anthropology, history, and literature. These same fields foreground theories and methods that denigrate Indigenous voices and help continue the legacy of colonialism. Media influences everyone, but media studies are also steeped in colonialism.

My chapter on Indigenous Standpoint Theory (chapter 1) seeks to address the legacy of colonialism and move toward an Indigenous viewpoint by showing how the research from fields based on Indigenous research and methods can change perspectives and directions in research. However, this chapter promotes advocacy, rather than necessarily a theory or methodology. My understanding of Indigenous Standpoint Theory has evolved since I wrote that chapter, particularly from interviewing scholars like Martin Nakata, a leading Indigenous academic in Australia and the first Torres Strait Islander to hold a doctorate in philosophy.

Interviewing allows us to part the veil of colonialism and hear the stories that are so important firsthand. This is why, in some chapters, we have turned to ethnographic interviews to offer a purer form of storytelling that broadens the range of contributions to this book. We encouraged some nonacademics, like seasoned journalists Tsanavi Spoonhunter and Nancy Marie Spears, to add their voices and stories. There were other voices we wanted, but we also knew that, as media professionals, they would not have the time to write a book chapter. Mark Trahant is celebrating his fiftieth year as a journalist. Taietsarón:sere Leclaire is an actor and writer. LiL Mike and Funny Bone are Pawnee rappers. Indigenous storytelling speaks across generations, honoring elders while inspiring youth. Indigenous media bridges traditional knowledge and contemporary expression, passing down values and encouraging young storytellers to continue shaping Indigenous narratives.

The interviews, edited for brevity, are stories that twist and turn. They are not linear; they are conversations. For example, the answer to the question "What does Indigenous media mean to you?" took Paul DeMain back to his birth. We asked each interviewee to review their words so that the stories resonated in their voices, including their richness, diversity, experience, history, resilience, and humor. The themes that emerged from our conversations show how Indigenous people learn from and rely on each other through storytelling. The interviews provide evidence of the growing interest in the ways Indigenous storytelling can change the human trajectory.

Our ethnographic interviewees all answered the same core questions:

- *Introduce yourself.*
- *What does Indigenous media mean to you?*
- *Describe your work. What compels you to do it?*
- *Why is it important to have Indigenous people tell their own stories?*
- *What does the future hold for your work, in your view?*
- *What should the next generation consider? Why is this work important?*
- *Is there anything else you would like to add?*

Of course, more voices could have been included in the book to show the richness and expansiveness of Indigenous media, but the medium of book publishing only allows so much. We hope that what you read encourages you to seek out other voices and think about Indigenous sources first when looking for stories about Indigenous people.

Including Indigenous voices in media helps preserve culture, advocate for rights, and combat stereotypes, while fostering a more truthful and comprehensive understanding of our lives, histories, and resilience. Indigenous media serves as a tool for reconnecting with cultural identity and healing from historical traumas by reclaiming narratives that have often been misappropriated or silenced. Media ownership by Indigenous people allows Indigenous communities to assert their histories, reclaim cultural practices, and offer paths toward intergenerational healing.

People do not trust the media in general. However, Indigenous people do tend to trust Indigenous media. We have always told stories about ourselves, but the most well-known ones are those told about us. Shondiin Silversmith tells us that such stories could save us all.

Finally, we encourage non-Indigenous readers to support Indigenous media by following Indigenous creators, consuming media through an Indigenous-centered lens, and questioning mainstream narratives about Indigenous communities. Change is easier when responsibility is shared.

How should you read this book? Although there appear to be many moving pieces—parts, chapters, and ethnographic interviews—they often overlap and touch on more than one designated topic. So choose a story. There's no beginning and no end.

Notes

1. Elizabeth Cook-Lynn, 2007, *New Indians, Old Wars* (Champaign: University of Illinois Press), 5.
2. UNESCO, 2025, *Indigenous Peoples and the Media* (Paris: UNESCO), https://unesdoc.unesco.org/ark:/48223/pf0000393487.
3. M. Greene-Blye and T. Finneman, 2023, "The Influence of Indigenous Standpoint: Examining Indian Country Press Portrayals of Native Women in Politics," *Newspaper Research Journal*, 394–95 and 401–2, https://doi.org/10.1177/07395329231155195.
4. Cristina L. Azocar, interview with Martin Nakata, June 23, 2023.
5. Martin Nakata, 2007, "The Cultural Interface," *The Australian Journal of Indigenous Education* 36, Supplement: 7–14, https://doi.org/10.1017/S1326011100004646.

PART ONE

NEWS

1

Media and Indigenous Standpoint Theory

Cristina L. Azocar

Media research continues to legitimize theories developed by dead white men over those of scholars of color, even though such theories often perpetuate inaccurate stereotypes of people of color, focus on negative social issues, and adopt a pathological lens of our communities (Thambinathan and Kinsella 2021). Perhaps this is one of the reasons why there are so few Indigenous media scholars in academia. If the goal of theory is to provide meaning to and predict the reasons for events, it must be done in a way that doesn't damage those it purports to understand and direct, or damage the few Indigenous academics who use it. It's time to decolonize media theory.

Kessi et al. (2020) argued that the term decolonization "is best understood as a verb that entails a political and normative ethic and practice of resistance and intentional undoing—unlearning and dismantling unjust practices, assumptions, and institutions—as well as persistent positive action to create and build alternative spaces and ways of knowing" (271).

Although widely used in different disciplines around the world to replace Eurocentric models, many of which have had detrimental effects on Indigenous communities, decolonizing theories are largely absent from media research, particularly from research examining Indigenous media and Indigenous issues in media within the United States. Grounding media research by employing decolonizing theories, and the methods that support them, provides a foundation from which to actively resist current media theories that are rooted in the paradigm of dead white men whose goals were to support the colonial structures that put them in power (Sheehan 2001).

Media produced about Indigenous people, from which the theories eventually developed, were based on stories created about us that were intended to erase and other us: "Travellers' stories were generally the experiences and observations of white men whose interactions with

Indigenous 'societies' or 'people' were constructed around their own cultural views of gender and sexuality" (Smith 2012, 9). These stories are more than five hundred years old, but research on US media about Indigenous issues using decolonization theories only began in 2021, when the first study analyzing American journalism using Indigenous Standpoint Theory (IST), "Indigenous Communities and COVID-19: Reporting on Resources and Resilience," was published (Azocar et al. 2021). This study sought to understand the impact of the loss of gaming revenue on Indigenous communities when tribal gaming operations were shuttered because of COVID-19. The study was also used in my book *News Media and the Indigenous Fight for Federal Recognition* (Azocar 2022), which examined news media coverage of the federal recognition of tribes. It found that coverage perpetuated ignorance and stereotypes about tribal sovereignty, prioritized gaming over sovereignty, and interfered with tribes' ability to be federally recognized. The study "Mothers Are Medicine: U.S. Indigenous Media Emphasizing Indigenous Women's Roles in COVID-19 Coverage" (Olson et al. 2022) showed how Indigenous journalism acts as a community forum that can help reinforce cultural values and languages. Although these were the first studies to use a decolonizing theory, Curran and Park's study laid the groundwork for this by encouraging media scholars to reconsider theories, epistemologies, methods, and empirical research approaches, particularly media research focused on the Global South (Curran and Park 2018).

These initial works argued that predominant approaches from the United States couldn't address issues in the Global South (Latin America, Asia, Africa, the Middle East, and the Arab world) because of the prevalence of differing contexts and epistemologies (Rao 2011). They did not take into account the differing contexts and epistemologies of Indigenous people in the United States. IST, therefore, is a more appropriate theory to utilize in media research that examines issues such as Indigenous media use, Indigenous media production, portrayals of Indigenous people and issues, and the effects of coverage of Indigenous issues and people in the United States.

IST contextualizes content into meaningful cultural and social perspectives to which Indigenous communities can relate. It privileges the work of Indigenous scholars because of our ability to understand the complexities of Indigenous communities and the issues we face.

Decolonizing Theories: Roots and Practices

Linda Tuhiwai Smith's *Decolonizing Methodologies: Research and Indigenous Peoples* (2012) was a groundbreaking book that showed how

Western research formed from an imperialist structure that was maintained to colonize the Maori people of New Zealand. Smith's central thesis is that an international Indigenous peoples' movement must protect and restore Indigenous traditions and reject the West, and so the second part of her book is devoted to examples of how Indigenous movements have used Indigenous, decolonizing research to protect their communities. The book concludes with suggestions for how Indigenous researchers can decolonize research for their own communities, because we have the opportunity to examine the many meanings, contradictions, and opportunities in the formation, messaging, and reception of aural, visual, textual, and other representations found in the media (Deloria 2003). IST is just one theory that can be applied to many areas of media research.

The Global South (Oglesby 1969) includes regions that tend to be politically and culturally marginalized because of their economic positions in relation to the Global North—that is, Western regions that hold the majority of the world's wealth and power. "The term Global South functions as more than a metaphor for underdevelopment. It references an entire history of colonialism, neo-imperialism, and differential economic and social change through which large inequalities in living standards, life expectancy, and access to resources are maintained" (Dado and Connell 2012, 13). The goal of doing research from the perspective of the Global South is to destabilize and ultimately reject perspectives from the Global North. Indigenous worldviews that draw from Indigenous epistemologies and ontologies are key to this revolution. Although the Indigenous people of the United States are not generally included in definitions of the Global South, decolonizing research that examines the Global South can be beneficial for Indigenous research practices that come from an Indigenous view of the world.

Seven principles of Indigenous worldviews provide underlying principles for Indigenous research practices (Simpson 2000): 1) knowledge is holistic, cyclic, and dependent on relationships and connections to all things; 2) there are multiple truths that are dependent upon individual and collective experiences; 3) everything is alive; 4) everything is equal; 5) the land is sacred; 6) the relationship between people and the spiritual world is central; and 7) human beings are the least important part of everything (Hart 2010).

The term "epistemology" encompasses the holistic aspect of knowledge formation, including who creates it, where it comes from, what it looks like, how it is verified, and how it is passed on (e.g., Gageo 2001; Goldman 1986, 1999; Fuller 1988; Landesman 1997; Audi 1998). Epistemology is concerned with who can be a knower, what can be known, what constitutes knowledge, and how that knowledge is constructed and verified, as well as the role of knowledge in all aspects of life. Indigenous epistemologies refer to the way in which Indigenous people theorize and construct knowledge and then encode it and gift it to the next generation (Gageo 2001). Conducting research in an Indigenist manner corresponds with the United Nations Declaration on the Rights of Indigenous Peoples, which states: "Indigenous peoples have the right to maintain and strengthen their distinct political, legal, economic, social and cultural institutions, while retaining their right to participate fully, if they so choose, in the political, economic, social and cultural life of the State" (United Nations 2007, Article 5, 5).

Ontology describes how people are in the world and their way of being. Spirituality and reciprocity (Rice 2005) are underlying factors of Indigenous ontologies. Spirituality is the recognition by Indigenous people that spiritual and physical realms are interconnected (Cajete 2000; Meyer 2008; Rice 2005). Reciprocity is the understanding that we receive from those who give us knowledge, and that knowledge must also be offered to others and should not be gained solely for the benefit of the person who is acquiring it.

Considering Indigenous worldviews, epistemologies, and ontologies leads to research that "must, therefore, be conducted in a way that fully captures and honors the voices and perspectives of Indigenous peoples but, more importantly, emanates from an Indigenous ontological and epistemological basis. This is Indigenist research. It ensures that Indigenous Knowledges, experience, and wisdom are captured, applied, and disseminated in ways that resonate with Indigenous ways of knowing, being, and doing" (Rix et al. 2019, 15).

Indigenous Standpoint Theory

IST is grounded in Indigenous ontology and epistemology. It contextualizes content into meaningful cultural and social perspectives that Indigenous communities can relate to (Foley 2003; Rigney 1999). It privileges the work of Indigenous scholars because of our ability to understand the complexities of Indigenous communities and the issues that we encounter (Rigney 1999) in our everyday lives. It provides a framework for Indigenous scholars to define research, methodologies and the interpretation of results in a culturally appropriate way (Rigney 1997), because of our lived reality.

IST has the following characteristics, according to Martin and Mirraboopa (2003):

- honors social mores "through which we live, learn, and situate ourselves" in our own lands and the lands of others
- emphasizes the "social, historical, and political contexts which shape our experiences, lives, positions, and futures"
- privileges Indigenous voices, people, and lands
- identifies "our worldviews, our knowledges, and our realities as distinctive and vital to our existence and survival" (205), as US Indigenous communities, including a complex array of beliefs, values, systems, practices, and traditions that are difficult for outsiders to understand (Choy and Woodlock 2007).

Collectively decided group knowledge provides marginalized groups with a system to examine and positively change the oppressive structures that shape our lives. These "standpoints" are not individual perspectives, which are often considered the gold standard for academic research, but community perspectives created from "situated location" (Bailey 2021).

Indigenous researchers share a common experience of colonization by Europeans, but we are not a homogeneous group. Foley (2003) provides guidelines for using IST in research. He notes that IST should be flexible enough for many Indigenous communities to find it applicable, and it must not replicate existing Western theories but rather free itself from them. As such, IST strives to include the principles described below (Foley 2003, 50). Although these are principles to strive for, in many cases it will not be possible to reach them all. Possible challenges to including all of the principles are mentioned when applicable:

- The practitioner must be Indigenous. If the researcher has supervision, the supervisor or supervisors should also be Indigenous. If the practitioner is not Indigenous, they must be advised by an Indigenous researcher, even if they must go outside their discipline to do so.
- The practitioner must be well versed in social theory, critical sociology, post-structuralism, and postmodernism. This is not so the Indigenous researcher may reproduce them but so they may be acutely aware of the limitations of these discourses in order to ensure that Indigenous research is not tormented by or classified in the physical and metaphysical distortions of these Western approaches.
- Some media uses quantitative methods or mixed methods. Social theory, critical sociology, and post-structuralist and postmodernist theories may not necessarily be applicable to quantitative methods,

but the researcher should understand the implications of quantitative research for Indigenous communities, and potentially supplement it with other methods.

- The Indigenous research must not be done for the benefit of the researchers, but for the community or the wider Indigenous community and/or an Indigenous research community. The epistemological approach from an Indigenous standpoint enables knowledge to be recorded for the community, not the academy. The participants are the owners of the knowledge. Researchers are gifted the knowledge from the community and must return it to them for their benefit. This reciprocity principle is the most important one and cannot be put aside.
- Wherever possible, the traditional language should be the first form of recording. English interpretation is the second form of recording. Unfortunately, many Indigenous languages were stolen from their people, so following this principle is not possible in many research situations. Research should not be discounted if the Indigenous language is not available, because it could leave important communities out of the discourse. However, Indigenous voices should be the most apparent and take precedence over all other voices.

Indigenous Standpoint Theory in Non-Media Research

IST has only been used a few times in media research and only recently, as described in the Introduction (Azocar et al. 2021; Azocar 2022; Carter et al. 2022). But Indigenous approaches to methodological research have been adopted in other areas of academic inquiry for at least twenty-five years, because Indigenous scholars in the areas described below realize that "Indigenous peoples have been, in many ways, oppressed by theory" (Smith 2021, 38). In climate and environmental studies in particular, the knowledge accumulated by Indigenous societies has provided a deeper understanding of the relationship between humans and the environment and can be used to understand how to better use resources and alleviate the environmental impact of humans (Kempton 2001).

Walker et al. (1995) used IST to center ethical concerns about participation and power, and to recognize that Indigenous knowledge is a powerful source of understanding in research about agroforestry—agriculture that incorporates the cultivation and conservation of trees. Hellier et al. (1999) examined the usefulness of rapid surveys of Indigenous knowledge for assessing trends in biodiversity in Chiapas, Mexico. Srinivasan (2004) advocated for adopting "socially benign and culturally appropriate adaptation policies" to document and understand local strategies in India for coping with climate change.

Indigenous Standpoint Pedagogy (ISP) has been used in educational research, although almost exclusively in Australia, in response to the limits of Western scientific constructs (Foley 2003). ISP focuses on the integration of Indigenous knowledge into educational programs and can be described as a pedagogy that "fundamentally acknowledges and embeds Indigenous community participation in the development and teaching of Indigenous standpoints and perspectives and is a multifaceted process" (Winslett and Phillips 2005, 731).

For example, Choy and Woodlock (2007) used ISP to integrate Indigenous knowledge into vocational education and the training curriculum, in order to make it more relevant to Indigenous people by providing a way for them to engage and collaborate with their communities.

Phillips (2019) used an ISP framework to develop critical tools for students in Australia to understand the epistemic forces that empower their worldviews and behaviors. Taking an Indigenist standpoint shifts the framing in learning spaces from trying to discern what students should know about Indigenous people and their experiences to understanding where their knowledge comes from, the purpose of that knowledge, and how that knowledge affects how they relate to and form understandings about Indigenous experiences.

Cox et al. (2021) examined how using IST in social science research related to Indigenous health can help interpret how historical loss, structural violence, colonial trauma, social isolation, cultural context, and tribal identities are linked to larger structural forces and health outcomes.[1] The process of decolonizing social science begins by integrating Indigenous knowledges into social science.

The areas of climate and environment, education, and health are also stereotypically reserved for studying Indigenous people, because they focus on loss. The study of loss is often reserved for marginalized groups like Indigenous people, but these are often spaces of resilience within Indigenous communities (Azocar et al. 2021). Other areas of inquiry have profound effects on societies and can benefit from adopting Indigenous-centered theories. As stated above, media studies in this area have only just begun to consider IST as a way of informing this type of research.

Decolonizing Media Research

Only a handful of studies consider decolonization frameworks for media research. A recent study used feminist standpoint epistemologies in Argentina; it analyzed the online content of *LatFem* and *Diario Digital Femenino*, two feminist Argentine news outlets, and examined how feminist standpoint epistemologies shaped the news production process. It showed that these two feminist newsrooms provided the journalists with the space to consider their own position in the community, to contextualize their journalistic practices, and to question when systemic discrimination had occurred (Cabas-Mijares 2022). The implications for journalism point to the need to rethink the notion that journalism can be objective, and to consider the role of journalism in democracies.

A study critiquing articles from the *Weekend Australian* newspaper (Rothwell 2001; Toohey 2001) found that the dominant culture perpetuated its agenda of sustaining the moral righteousness of the "white centre," while abrogating Indigenous Aboriginal culture as a factor in the perpetuation of crime and abuse (Sheehan 2001). The author, Norm Sheehan, refers to this as an "Imagined Moral Centre," which is really a mask for racism under the guise of ensuring the preservation of the imagined morality of white people. Sheehan's research shows that this type of reporting focuses on the worthiness of Indigenous culture, with the ultimate goal of drumming up support for the assimilation of Indigenous people into modern society and the need to modernize Indigenous culture. In the groundbreaking 2012 book *Decolonizing Methodologies: Research and Indigenous Peoples*, Linda Tuhiwai Smith supports this premise: "These are the procedures by which Indigenous peoples and their societies were coded into the Western system of knowledge" (Smith 2012, 43).

Media theories evolved from white men's need to preserve this system of knowledge. They have developed predominantly from a white male standpoint. IST makes contextualizing the differences between mainstream journalism and Indigenous journalism possible when considering how these media theories evolved. Although work in communication studies has examined decolonization within the context of Africana communications, there is scant research on Indigenous communications and Indigenous issues in communication in the United States (e.g., Langmia 2018; Langmia and Lando 2020). Three recent studies analyzing US media compared Indigenous journalistic practices and considerations in opposition to these old theories.

Indigenous journalism may provide more meaningful cultural and social perspectives for its audience than mainstream journalism can (Azocar et al. 2021), which enables Indigenous journalists to address problems at a level (Nataka 2004) that encourages ownership of issues and leads to social responsibility (Srinivasan 2004).

The first news media research in the United States that used an IST framework looked at the difference between mainstream and Indigenous news coverage of the COVID-19 crisis in Indigenous communities in the United States. The findings revealed the ways economic inequality and non-Indigenous people's misunderstandings of tribal gaming operations led to stereotypical news coverage of Indigenous communities during the early months of the COVID-19 pandemic in 2020. The findings showed how mainstream media used "parachute reporting" to create a one-sided view of the pandemic's impact on Indigenous communities, particularly when it came to industries like tribal casinos, which are necessary to fund indispensable tribal operations. IST foregrounded the differences in these narratives and showed the differences in the ways that Indigenous journalists tell their stories, in contrast to non-Native media reporters and non-Native media companies. The findings highlighted how non-Indigenous reporters failed to connect gaming operations to the core structure of Indigenous people's lives and mostly focused on loss of resources, government tensions, and chronic, disproportionate struggle.

IST provided a path to highlight the differences in how Indigenous people tell their stories in contrast to how non-Native reporters and their media outlets do this. Other theories would not have allowed the researchers to use their own cultural knowledge to interpret the results in a way that didn't further demonize Native communities that use casinos as sources of economic restoration.

A second study published in 2022 (Olson et al.) also focused on reporting during COVID-19. IST allowed for a decolonization of the academic discussion on the role of the matriarchy in replicating and strengthening cultures. It provided a space for the researchers to highlight the ways that elder women's knowledge provided the best response to COVID-19. The study showed that Indigenous women use social media, digital news outlets, and other media to reinforce and teach about their culture and its resilience to international audiences.

The book *News Media and the Indigenous Fight for Federal Recognition* (Azocar 2022) examined forty years of news media coverage of the process of federal acknowledgment of tribes. The book closes with the chapter "Indigenous Standpoint Journalism for Non-Indigenous Journalists," which asks that non-Indigenous journalists move away from considering Indigenous communities as deficient and instead understand that they have developed ways to collect and disseminate knowledge through journalism for hundreds of years. Instead of reporting *on* communities, journalists need to report *for* them, including working proactively in support of Indigenous peoples by understanding their issues instead of just covering them.

Future Paths for Media Scholars Using Indigenous Standpoint Theory

In the article "Bilchiinsi Philosophy: Decolonizing Methodologies in Media Studies," Wunpini Mohammed (2021) called for a paradigm shift in knowledge building in media studies and communication studies: "Decolonizing how we do research must first look to Indigenous African epistemologies and knowledge systems to support knowledge production in communication studies and media studies" (8). Although specifically focusing on Indigenous Africans, the call holds true for Indigenous communities in the United States. IST can provide both Indigenous and non-Indigenous researchers with a way to actively resist the colonized thinking that continues to dominate the field.

IST can make it possible to contextualize how the mainstream news views and covers Indigenous issues, and how Indigenous journalists and journalism outlets view and cover them in journalism research. "News created by Indigenous journalists may provide more meaningful cultural and social perspectives for its audience than mainstream journalism can" (Azocar 2022, 55).

At its core, journalism is storytelling. Both the ethics and the accountability of the storyteller need to be considered when using IST as a framework for media research. The researcher is also a storyteller, and so their ethics and accountability also need to be considered during the research process.

As a starting point, therefore, it's important to restate the principles that need to be applied before the research process begins. First, Indigenous knowledge cannot be undertaken merely for profit (Nakata 1998). Second, Indigenous people hold collective rights to their knowledge (United Nations Declaration on the Rights of Indigenous People 2007). Third, the researcher must situate themselves within the context of their community and the context of the research, and recognize their privileges as a researcher and their responsibility to the community they are doing research for. Fourth, research must be *for* a community, not *on* a community.

Why Should Research Using IST Be Undertaken?

Although Smith doesn't refer to IST in her book, she succinctly sums up why theories like it should be considered for doing research up in the chapter "Imperialism, History, Writing and Theory": "It helps make sense of reality. It enables us to make assumptions and predictions about the work in which we live. It contains within it a method or methods for selecting and arranging, for prioritizing and legitimating what we see and do . . . it gives us a space to plan, to strategize, to take greater control over our resistances" (2012, 38).

The world is organized around structural inequalities stemming from Western colonial practices. Indigenous journalism is a means to disseminate information to our communities so that we can understand the world we live in, and to show how Indigenous communities can resist these colonial practices. The world could benefit from understanding this resistance in all our forms of media—from newspapers to social media, to other Indigenous forms of news dissemination.

But Indigenous knowledge is often co-opted for the benefit of the colonial pocketbook. It is also expected to solve some of the world's problems (e.g., the climate emergency), and when it cannot, it is considered deficient (Wohling 2009). Therefore, any media research undertaken using IST must be done with the knowledge that media produced by Indigenous people and for Indigenous channels is done for the benefit of the community and it may not translate to other communities, Indigenous or not. Inherent in this is the notion of pan-Indigeneity—the idea that there is homogeneity among Indigenous people and Indigenous thought. Western notions of research do not always consider that Indigenous people, even those in similar regional areas, are very different. It should be acceptable to do research that benefits a small group of people and does not translate to a larger group.

Indigenous People Hold Collective Rights to Their Knowledge

The right of Indigenous people to collectively hold the rights to their knowledge is in opposition to the Western ideal that the researcher holds the rights to their research. Article 31, Section 1, of the United Nations Declaration on the Rights of Indigenous Peoples (2007, Article 31, 22) states:

> Indigenous peoples have the right to maintain, control, protect and develop their cultural heritage, traditional knowledge and traditional cultural expressions, as well as the manifestations of their sciences, technologies and cultures, including human and genetic resources, seeds, medicines, knowledge of the properties of fauna and flora, oral traditions, literatures, designs, sports and traditional games and visual and performing arts. They

> also have the right to maintain, control, protect and develop their intellectual property over such cultural heritage, traditional knowledge, and traditional cultural expressions.

Once the research is complete, it needs to be given to the community to hold. And the community must be part of the dissemination at every step of the research process. Each time the research is shared, the community needs to be informed of how it is being shared and why, and how it is being used to inform other research. The researcher must situate themselves and recognize their privileges as a researcher and their responsibility to the community they are doing research for.

Research Must Be for *a Community, Not* on *a Community*

I have been privileged since the publication of *News Media and the Indigenous Fight for Federal Recognition* (Azocar 2022) to lead a number of workshops and present the findings of my book, particularly for professional journalists. As someone who does research on the intersection of race and journalistic practice, I intend my work to have an impact on how journalists do their job. I'm always happy when I'm asked to share the knowledge I gathered while working on this book—or any other research I've conducted—given that many of us produce work that only gets shared among other academics.

Part of the decolonization process should be to promote our work, not for self-aggrandizement but to ensure that the norms and practices that have harmed Indigenous and other marginalized groups end. When it comes to translating my work, I ask that journalists incorporate one simple premise: they should go into a story with the mindset not of reporting *on* a community, but of reporting *for* a community, because it is their responsibility as journalists to do so. This does not create biased journalism; it creates ethical, fair, accurate journalism that reflects the communities that news organizations serve, not profit from.

Indigenous news organizations recognize their responsibility to their community and state it in their missions. For example, Indian Country Today's mission states: "Indian Country Today is a spacious channel that serves Indigenous communities with news, entertainment, and opinion" (Indian Country Today website n.d.a). The mission of the *Navajo Times*, or *Diné bi Naltsoos*, is to inform the Navajo people of events, news, and issues that are of importance to them, whether from within the boundaries of the Navajo Nation or throughout the United

States (*Navajo Times* website). Media scholars using IST must begin their research with the underlying premise that the first responsibility of their scholarship is to the community, not to themselves or their institution.

As of 2025, there are a handful of university-affiliated North American Indigenous media scholars working in the United States: Patty Loew (Bad River Band of Lake Superior Ojibwe) at Northwestern University, John Sanchez (Apache) at Pennsylvania State University, Victoria LaPoe (Cherokee) at Ohio University, Melissa Green-Blye (Miami Nation) at the University of Kansas, Ryan Comfort (Keweenaw Bay Indian Community Ojibwe) at Indiana University Bloomington, and myself at San Francisco State University. This means that Indigenous media scholarship falls on very few of us, so we are at risk of being further marginalized, tokenized, overlooked, and overworked. IST is predicated on the idea that Indigenous scholars will be the ones who use it. However, because there are so few Indigenous media scholars, and because of the structural issues that keep Indigenous knowledge and scholarship on the margins, this is often not the case. I therefore hope to provide some direction for how non-Indigenous media scholars can advocate for and be allies of Indigenous media scholarship.

Tuck and Yang maintain that "too-easy adoption of decolonizing discourse" can play out in a way that ultimately serves to "reconcile settler guilt and complicity, and rescue settler futurity" (Tuck and Yang 2012, 3). Decolonizing research "may do more to help alleviate the guilt of white academics and to ensure their continued prominence in academia than it does to meaningfully contribute to decolonial struggles" (Matthews 2021, 1113). White academics do not have an Indigenous standpoint. They therefore cannot engage in research that employs IST, but they can teach IST research in their classrooms, cite it in their own research, promote it in their academic and research circles, and ensure their Indigenous students have access to it. They can accept our findings as a valid interpretation of what has occurred (Smith 2021).

Decolonizing media research has just begun, and the few Indigenous scholars using IST and other decolonizing theories must be given the space, time, and resources—that is, the structural support—to continue their work. Indigenous media scholars can provide alternative ways of understanding media through the theories and methodologies we develop and the findings we share. More Indigenous scholars need to be given the opportunity to teach theory and research courses. Only in this way can the centuries-long scholarship that denigrates Indigenous people as relics of the past be countered. Only in this way will we even begin to consider that we are moving toward justice.

Discussion Questions

1. What can you do to ensure that you are following the principles of decolonizing research in your work?
2. How might your identity or positionality help or hinder your work?
3. What Indigenous resources are available that might guide how you work?

Note

1. For a review of these health disparities, see Cox et al. (2021).

2

"Indigenous Knowledge Is Rooted in Community"

Interview with Shondiin Silversmith

Shondiin Silversmith is an award-winning journalist from the Navajo Nation who has covered Indigenous affairs for more than fourteen years. She is Editorial Director for the Diné College Press. She currently focuses on Arizona's twenty-two federally recognized tribal nations. Silversmith earned a master's degree in journalism from Northeastern University in Boston and is pursuing a PhD at Arizona State University. She is a member of the Indigenous Journalists Association and is committed to amplifying Indigenous voices and storytelling through journalism. She has made it a point in her career to advocate for, pitch, and produce stories about Indigenous communities in every newsroom she's worked in.

Please introduce yourself.

Yá'át'ééh. Shí éí Shondiin Silversmith yinishyé. Hónágháahnii nishłį Kinyaa'áanii bashishchiin bilagáana dashicheii Todích'íi'nii dashinalí.

My name is Shondiin Silversmith. I am "One Who Walks Around Clan and Born for Towering House People Clan." That is who my mother and my father are. I always make an effort and a point to introduce myself traditionally in Navajo and to show people who I am as a Diné woman.

Introducing yourself, especially on the Navajo Nation, is customary with Navajo people so you can always tell who you are in terms of your clan—so people can make that connection of whether or not you are clan related, or at least get an understanding of who this person is. As I get older, I respect why this is so important and why it is customary for us to do it, because people need to know who you are. And us being able to introduce ourselves traditionally, or in the way that is connected to who we are as Indigenous people, is really, really powerful.

Fig. 2.1. Shondiin Silversmith. Author photo.

Describe your work. What compels you to do it?

I've been a journalist for nearly fifteen years now, and I've focused on writing and storytelling about Indigenous people and Indigenous communities. I started out in my own community on the Navajo Nation. That's why I wanted to become a journalist in the first place—I think storytelling is such an important part of who I am and how I grew up. But also, I just think storytelling is an important part of Indigenous communities.

I didn't know I wanted to be a journalist until I actually got to write for the first time. A close friend already knew she wanted to be a journalist. One day she asked, "Do you wanna write an article with me?" She was gonna pitch it to the *Navajo Times*. Going through the entire process of it, I was like, "This is what I wanna do!" I dropped out of the nursing program I was in and switched my major to fine arts, so I could get the fundamentals of what I would need to be a journalist.

I was taking a communication class and when the teacher, Pamela Stovall, found out that I wanted to be a journalist, she zoned in on me and was like, "You wanna be a journalist? I wanna help you do that." She ran the student newspaper at UNM Gallup called the *Campus Voice*. She introduced me to the Native American Journalists Association and the American Indian Journalists Institute. She let me believe that I did not just have to be a journalist—I could be an Indigenous journalist. I could write stories about the community and about people.

I got my first internship at the *Farmington Daily Times*. Then I became the editor of the *Campus Voice*. The following summer I applied to the *Navajo Times*, and when I graduated they transitioned me to full time. I left the *Navajo Times* to get my master's degree at Northeastern University in Boston, Massachusetts. I was introduced to one of the directors of that program. She said that it was a master's program in media innovation, but the whole point was to be able to help journalists who were already a little bit seasoned.

It was a very fundamental point in my life because it solidified my views and my thought process as an Indigenous journalist. I introduced myself to the director of the program and told him how I wanted to be able to utilize everything I was learning in the program to be a better Indigenous journalist, to be a better Diné journalist. He said, "I don't want you to be an Indigenous journalist. I just want you to be a journalist."

I'm a rez kid. I grew up on the Navajo Nation. The furthest I had moved away from the Navajo Nation was to Gallup, and that's a border town to the Navajo Nation. I was surrounded by Navajo people all the time. I was around my culture all the time, so it was very comfortable.

I made it a priority to pitch stories that I was working on that focused on Indigenous communities. And it was the first time I experienced non-Native editors and teachers saying, "That's not a story." It cracks me up when I think about it now, because I was the only person in my cohort who got a story published in the end—and it was about the Wampanoag Tribe!

What does Indigenous media mean to you?

Because I worked for the *Navajo Times*, I saw how important a tribal newspaper is for its community. This experience showcased how Indigenous communities and tribal nations have the power to share their own stories and uplift their own voices.

It's so important for media to pay attention to tribal communities and tribal nations, because they have been dealing with misrepresentation by mainstream media for generations. We're in this unique time where more people are paying attention to Indigenous communities. We're in this unique space where the Indigenous communities have more control and power over their stories than ever before.

Why is it important to have Indigenous people tell their own stories?

Indigenous people have always highlighted the importance of community and how you connect with it, and you connect with other people in order to not only build community but uplift it. For Indigenous journalists, having that fundamental understanding of what community means—not only for their own tribes, but for tribal nations in general—is beneficial because it allows them to make that basic connection. Approaching journalism from an Indigenous perspective falls back on that connection of humanity and community.

What should the next generation consider? Why is this work important?

This journalism work falls back on that foundation of storytelling. Storytelling is such an important part of Indigenous communities. It's an important part of being an Indigenous person. And I think when people see quality storytelling, they recognize quality storytelling.

Young Indigenous people who want to come into this field should ask themselves what they hope to achieve, but also what type of stories they are trying to tell, because journalism is such a hard industry to begin with. If I didn't identify that that was the type of journalism I wanted to do in the beginning, my journey would have been a lot harder and probably would have stopped way before I got started.

Young Indigenous journalists should be aware that there are people who want to help them. I can guarantee if they find an Indigenous journalist they like and the work they appreciate from these journalists, they'll be able to connect with them right away.

In terms of how my work has evolved, it adjusts to the platforms that I'm working for. Before I started at the *Arizona Mirror*, I was working for *The Arizona Republic*, and that environment for journalism was a lot different because *The Arizona Republic* is a sister paper of *USA Today*, which is owned by Gannett Co. Inc. Their goals and outlooks for what type of storytelling you're going to do and the way they share their stories online is very corporate.

By contrast, the *Arizona Mirror*, which is a non-profit newspaper, operates under a Creative Commons framework, so people are allowed to use my stuff anywhere. I think working under Creative Commons is kind of how my work has been evolving for me these past couple of years. A big part of the challenge when I became the Indigenous affairs reporter for *The Arizona Republic* is that I often had to advocate for my stories not to be put behind paywalls.

I wrote a series about the Navajo code talkers. At the time I started writing it, there were five code talkers left. Writing those stories was one of my highlights of my career at *The Arizona Republic*. I got to meet with those code talkers and their families in their own homes, and I got to sit there and talk to them and just hear them telling their stories. This is why I do what I do, to be able to let them tell their own stories.

Is there anything else you would like to add?

Now that I've come into this academic world of journalism, I do believe that the way that journalism is taught can benefit from Indigenous knowledge because of how much Indigenous knowledge is rooted in community and rooted in people. Coming into this PhD program reaffirms why I hold Indigenous knowledge and viewpoints so tightly, because they align with my own. Indigenous journalism is so important because it showcases how Indigenous journalists and Indigenous media networks still fundamentally focus on uplifting community voices and uplifting their own communities.

Indigenous knowledge and the way that Indigenous people approach journalism and research is so valuable and important, and Western media can learn something from it.

—Interviewed by Cristina L. Azocar

3

A Yakama Story Revisited

Sustaining Indigenous Science and Environmental News

Ryan N. Comfort

Native stories often move in circles. We begin and end in roughly the same place, but only after a journey. A short story might involve one circle; a long story might involve many. At least, this is what I and two other Native scholars, Chris Teuton and Jeff Corntassel, mused while sketching story arcs on a bar napkin somewhere in Tahlequah, Oklahoma. I still have the napkin. We ventured that there is a "return" in Native stories because many of our cultures value reciprocity and sharing what we have learned with people in our communities. Central characters often return to tell the story of their journey and what they learned. The act of sharing stories honors those who have helped us on our journeys to learn and grow. This practice grounds our research in longer Indigenous intellectual traditions. So . . . I have a story for you.

In Toppenish, Washington, a narrow sidewalk flanked by an eight-foot-tall, razor wire–topped chain-link fence led to the windowless front door of the *Yakama Nation Review*. The tribal paper, founded in 1970 and currently helmed by editor and tribal member Ronnie Washines, lives in a vacated portion of the Yakama Nation's police building. While some Indigenous nations enshrine press freedoms in their constitutions, others restrain the ability of the Indigenous press to act as watchdogs of tribal government (Shearer et al. 2022). I wondered what had characterized the relationship between the *Review* and tribal government throughout the paper's life. I wondered about the paper's vulnerability to censorship, distribution in the digital age, relationships with local news outlets, and vision for the future. All these questions percolated, but the main ones were about the relationships between the paper, the tribal council, and the natural resources department. Environmental issues have always been a cornerstone of the tribal press (Loew and Mella 2005), but the ability of Indigenous journalists to cover these crucial issues can be highly contingent on tribal government policy. As I took in the scene, I wondered what social and political forces affected the paper's ability to tell the Nation's environmental stories, and how the history and culture of the Nation shaped journalists' access to science and environmental stories unfolding within the reservation's boundaries.

Another story returned to me as I stood in the hot, dry summer air. The first edition of this book, *American Indians and the Mass Media*, began with a foreword by Patty Loew (see also chapter 17 in this book). Around the same time Loew penned her introduction, she invited me to lunch at a Thai restaurant in Madison, Wisconsin to talk about my future. I was working on multimedia projects with Wisconsin Public Television and the Wisconsin Educational Communications Board and saw the potential to tell striking visual stories about Indigenous science, sovereignty, and environmental management. These stories might reduce public prejudice toward treaty-reserved hunting and fishing rights, but I didn't know how to start telling these stories through my own lens. Patty and I sat in her office after lunch. She showed me which graduate schools had won awards for visual storytelling. She pushed me to think about Indigenous environmental journalism and apply to one of these graduate schools. I did. I wouldn't have been in Toppenish, Washington, chuckling about the optics of putting tribal journalists behind razor wire, if it weren't for her guidance. One of my first questions for Ronnie at the *Review* was, "Do you happen to know Patty Loew?" His eyes lit up.

A Complex Problem: "Their Job Isn't Based on Talking to the Press"

We should use mass media channels to broadcast stories of Indigenous environmental and scientific work far and wide, but this belief may arise from the history and culture of my peoples (Anishinaabe) and my journey. In the 1980s, violent and racist conflicts erupted in Wisconsin after a series of federal court decisions affirmed the rights of Ojibwe peoples to hunt and fish off reservation (Nesper 2002). Wisconsin and other states eventually passed unfunded mandates designed to prevent these types of conflicts from happening through better public education (Leary 2018). I helped implement this mandate in the University of Wisconsin–Madison's teacher education program, but I found few media resources showing our land and contemporary resource science save a small handful of stories produced by Native journalists.

Like many Ojibwe citizens, I enjoy reading the *Mazina'igan*, a quarterly newsletter produced by the Great Lakes Indian Fish & Wildlife

Commission. The publication contains pictures and news articles about issues like superfund site cleanups, pending environmental legislation, and water quality, along with obituaries, recipes using traditional foods, and language learning puzzles for children and adults. In some ways, it's the newspaper of record for the Great Lakes Ojibwe. As I moved away from Wisconsin and spoke with other Indigenous people, I learned how rare and important it was to have this contemporary communication channel devoted to science and environmental news. I learned two things in interviews with other Indigenous people living in the US Native diaspora. First, Ojibwe peoples frequently cited the *Maz* as a major, if not primary, source of environmental news and information. Second, other Indigenous people in the diaspora were hungry for environmental news and media about their nations, but often lacked knowledge of a comparable nation-specific source (Comfort 2022a).

It's easy to assume that mistrust of non-Indigenous media outlets, lack of funding for news and other communication work, or a host of other deficit-based reasons led to this perception. But the issue seemed to be thornier.

The biggest factor against the broader use of media to tell Indigenous science and environmental stories seemed to be uncertainty over what information could be shared via media channels (Comfort 2022b). Environmental professionals working for Native nations reported desiring to better use social media, understand their tribal audiences, and receive media relations training. However, uncertainty regarding the boundaries of cultural knowledge sharing and the political ramifications of oversharing manifested in ambivalent attitudes about speaking to media outlets and producing their own tribally specific media.

"I get why they are gun-shy," said Ronnie when asked about access to tribal government staff. "They got jobs, and their job isn't based on talking to the press," he chuckled. Here, in a cinder-block office lined with yellowed copies of back editions of a newspaper partially funded by the Nation, the silver-haired editor explained by telling a story: "One of our council members was visiting Washington, DC, and he saw a copy of our tribal paper in a senator's office. He came back worried that they knew all about what we were doing out here." The tribal leader seemed concerned, and not without reason, that information published about the tribe could easily be used against them.

Throughout the early to mid-1900s, state and federal policies repeatedly eroded the Yakama's ability to exercise treaty-reserved rights to hunt, fish, and gather (Wilkinson 2005, 157–65). Only after hydroelectric dam projects destroyed hundreds of miles of salmon habitat, though, did US federal courts begin upholding treaty rights in Washington state. The Yakama played a central role in court cases that reaffirmed Indigenous rights to use and manage natural resources. Tensions between state citizens and tribal members erupted in conflict (Grossman 2017, 35–78). State game wardens frequently targeted tribal peoples with aggressive and violent tactics, often refusing to recognize and uphold court rulings (Wilkinson 2005, 169).

In Washington, Wisconsin, and states across the country, legislators hoped public education would reduce bias toward tribal people exercising treaty-reserved hunting and fishing rights (Leary 2018). However, once public schooling ends, US citizens primarily turn to news and specialty media sources for their science and environmental information needs (Funk et al. 2017). Herein lies one major problem: mainstream media sources frequently and repeatedly offer problematic framing and portrayals of Indigenous peoples (Greene-Blye 2020; Carstarphen and Sanchez 2012; Weston 1996; Miller and Ross 2004; LaPoe et al. 2018; Azocar et al. 2021; Leavitt et al. 2015). Indigenous peoples rarely appear as contemporary scientists, thoughtfully and purposefully stewarding lands and resources. Perhaps outlets cater to expectations. Maybe the routines of journalistic news production steer narratives into predictable story paths before journalists shoot the first video frame (Tandoc Jr. and Duffy 2019), and journalism practice therefore needs decolonizing before accurate and authentic stories can be told (McCue 2022).

If we want our stories told and told accurately, we need to tell them ourselves. Indigenous peoples excel at using new media to advance our goals. One need look no further than the history of the Aboriginal Peoples Television Network in Canada (Roth 2005), the growth and digitization of Native news in the United States (LaPoe and LaPoe 2017), and the role of Indigenous film in advocating for policy change in Australia (Wilson and Stewart 2008). Indigenous media covers environmental stories about the challenges faced by the Inuit Circumpolar Council (Alia 2010). When the COVID-19 pandemic required rapid health information dissemination, Indigenous media filled news gaps by providing our communities with specific, balanced coverage and proactive health information (LaPoe et al. 2022c).

The current mass and social media ecosystem challenges Indigenous peoples' ability to control information. Some advocate for stricter controls on Indigenous ecological information due to legacies of appropriation and misuse (Walter 2021). These trends raise questions about information boundaries and the future of Indigenous media. Journalists covering tribal governments already struggle for editorial independence (Shearer et al. 2022), and negotiating information politics may become another source of tension. The task for media scholars like myself is to better understand the sociopolitical forces within Indigenous communities so we can collectively increase the visibility of Indigenous environmental issues, science, and cultural values that underpin our environmental governance rights and responsibilities.

Theories in media sociology offer routes to understanding the sociopolitical dynamics of Indigenous science and environmental communication. Shoemaker and Reese's (2014) classic "hierarchy of influences" model places news and media products at the center of concentric circles of influence, structured by different levels of social organization, moving from the individual level to the level of the broadest social systems. Fisher Liu and Horsley (2007) centered government communicators, such as public information officers, and proposed a model of the social and political factors that might affect the communication decisions of such actors, ranging from legal frameworks to a mandate to serve the public good. Scholars cannot take the same social structures and associated influences for granted in Indigenous communities, as different cultures, value orientations, and histories of colonization have shaped them. These forces shape contemporary politics and information policies. They also influence the ability of Indigenous communities to sustain a science and environmental news beat. This chapter aims to provide an example of the complexity of such influences and their potential effects on one Indigenous Nation's science and environmental media work.

The Authority to Share: "I Don't Know Who This Is Really Helping"

This story is a media ethnography designed to explore the key cultural and sociopolitical influences on environmental media production in the Yakama Nation. In Indian Country, this research is a "survivance" story—a narrative reinforcing our persistence, our environmental sovereignty, and our continued cultural survival (Vizenor 2008). Anishinaabe scholar Kimberly Blaeser (2013) writes, "Storytelling is both harvest and reseeding . . . somewhere there is intersection between the motion of stories, the motions of life, and the mobile centers of meaning." For many Indigenous scholars, doing research is about weaving together scholarship and story to interpret our world and experiences (Tachine et al. 2022). Understanding Indigenous methodologies requires understanding Indigenous storytelling as data collection and a means of analysis with equal validity to Western ethnographic methods (Iseke 2013). So, let's return to the story.

"What do you need help with?" I asked Michael Beckler, the lead biologist for the Yakama Nation Aviary. "Everything," he responded. "How do we talk about a program that might be controversial? How do we talk to the public?" A non-Native and former trainer of mine-hunting dolphins for the US Navy (ask him about it sometime), Michael was hired by the Yakama Nation to expand the nascent aviary. Like many across Indian Country, Michael was hired for his scientific knowledge and expertise, but he suddenly found himself in an intercultural public relations role. "I don't know about all that, I just feed the birds and go home," he would joke when I ventured too far into strategic communication research and theories. Biologists employed by Indigenous nations can be important sources of science and environmental news for both the tribal and nontribal presses, so helping Michael answer his questions would help me understand the systems influencing his public communication work.

Both research and reporting share foundational requirements of trust and reciprocity. Reporters from the neighboring non-Native paper sometimes contact Ronnie Washines to ask how to gain better access to tribal government sources. His response doesn't change: "You need to spend time with them. They need to see your face, your smile. You need to joke with them. You need to break bread with them . . . I don't know if they ever did that." He recalled pointedly telling one reporter, "I don't know who this is really helping, you or them [the tribal people]." Themes of trust, relationship building, and reciprocity echo throughout scholarship on Indigenous research methodologies (Smith 2012). They are the reason Indigenous-centered research takes longer and requires community input before settling on questions and methodology.

Following conversations with Michael, I adopted a participant-observer ethnographic methodology, with the twist that I would help with media production in the Nation to explore the systems in which tribally employed scientists and journalists construct their media. While traditional participant-observer studies maintained more "objective" separation between the researcher and interlocutors, modern methodologists acknowledge the need to spend time with communities and to participate in nontraditional ways to help balance the power dynamics (Mannik and McGarry 2017, 34). The partnership we established in this project meant I would be answering questions about a website redesign, shooting video, and taking on a photographic assignment for the tribal paper. It also meant checking for equipment that bounced out of the truck bed the day before, and using a blowtorch to help separate pipes. After nearly four weeks in the Yakama Nation, a common theme emerged.

"I can't tell you everything . . ."

—A former Yakama council member

"We've been well disciplined in what we are allowed to share and not share," explained an elder. "I would certainly describe our culture as closed," said a Yakama cultural leader. "I feel the Yakama Nation is pretty apprehensive about sharing," said a Yakama citizen and tribal employee.

The first time I visited the Yakama Nation, I felt it. When meeting someone new in Indian Country, I often share stories about history, culture, or politics from my own corner of the Indigenous world. Usually, sharing is reciprocated and we learn about each other's people. But sometimes Yakama citizens would sometimes respond with silence or a polite "That's interesting." Sometimes citizens would simply *be* closed. It felt like some big cultural force was looming, but I couldn't see it. After a few interviews, I brought up this cultural difference in sharing and asked what my present interlocutor thought contributed to it. "Ah, you might be running into the *unwritten law*," they said. There it was. In my field notes, I circled the words with question marks and exclamation points.

Ask five people what the unwritten law means to them and you'll get five different answers. Broadly speaking, the law encompasses the deep cultural knowledge of the Nation and how that knowledge should be treated. Knowing something also means knowing the rules about communicating that knowledge. As revered Yakama elder Virginia Beavert writes, "The laws are strict in our Indian way of life" (Beavert 2017, 3). When I asked about publishing photographs of traditional plants and using the Ichishkíin language to label them (a recent hot-button issue caused by a social media post), one elder explained, "The unwritten law forbids us to show. It's for your own tradition and culture. The only place it's supposed to be recorded is your heart and mind. Not on media." Several elders and cultural leaders argued that cultural knowledge, such as the Yakama language, should be shared in spaces and places only accessible to Yakama citizens. A few said that cultural knowledge should only be shared within the family. One recounted an argument among elders in which someone suggested that "the language shouldn't ever be written or recorded."

Even the land is closed on the Yakama Reservation. The Nation maintains a "Closed Area" reserved for the exclusive use of tribal citizens "to hunt and gather without distraction from the outside world," as one staff member described it. Nontribal members require a special permit to enter the Closed Area. The Closed Area protects many plant and animal beings key to Yakama culture. One elder recounted: "[The Closed Area] is supposed to be sacred and protected. My mom would say, 'The foods, they are going to leave you if we don't protect them.'" Multiple people shared stories about tourists from Portland and Seattle coming over the Cascades and decimating fields of wild huckleberries in the Closed Area. According to the elders, natural resources staff, and cultural leaders, knowledge of the Closed Area is itself potentially protected cultural knowledge. One staff member explained that, even to other Yakama citizens, "There are people who won't tell you where to go [to collect roots] in the Closed Area." Another elder expressed concern: "Lots of people are putting pictures of our first foods and where to find them on social media, and it's scary."

Concerns over sharing ecological information are strongly tied to the politics and processes of colonization. One citizen explained: "We learned to be creatively protective. Don't tell them everything. We are the people of the Yakama, we are the people of the land, but don't tell the government that. These kinds of secrets are useful. That's why we don't share everything even though we are proud of it. We learned not to tell the government everything."

One staff member suggested people might be afraid of sharing too much because "the federal government might think that maybe the tribe isn't fulfilling its grants properly . . . and then use that information to terminate the tribe." All Indigenous people have had similar (though to be clear, not identical) experiences of colonization and conflict, which explains at least part of our closed orientation to information sharing. Still, this history seemed to collide with and amplify an existing wave of protectionist cultural orientations in the Yakama Nation.

Yakama orientations toward protecting land and protecting cultural information parallel each other (for many Indigenous peoples, land and culture are inseparable), but the Nation's policies speak to how culture influences access to information and ecosystems. Indigenous communities and peoples might rest on a continuum between "open" and "closed" information-sharing value orientations, which influence media and communication practices and policy. History, politics, and deep culture affect the position of an Indigenous community on this spectrum, as evidenced by the collective memory of colonization in the Yakama Nation. Like all value orientations, these positions are relatively stable but can change over time. They affect the ability of people working for Indigenous governments to share their environmental stories with tribal and nontribal journalists. The point of this section is not to suggest a value judgment—for example, that the Nation needs to be more open—but rather to argue that sustaining environmental media requires working with, not against, these value orientations.

Almost all the elders, employees, and leaders I spoke with recognized the tension between a closed culture and the need to use media for cultural revitalization and other Nation-building purposes, like environmental communication and tribal journalism. One elder I spoke with wanted to create a language app and had visited a friend to ask permission to do so. To greatly paraphrase the story, they discussed the app while sitting down to dinner with the friend's grandchildren. The grandchildren remained buried in their phones while the friend recounted stories and talked about the Ichishkíin language. Frustrated with the lack of attention from the children, the friend finally exclaimed, "Fine! Make your app. Maybe if my voice is in there [pointing to the phones], then they'll listen to me."

Cultural Capital and the Authority to Share

The "closed" orientation of the Yakama Nation naturally begs the question: how can journalists gain access to tribal government sources and be trusted to publish environmental stories? The work relies on having access to personnel, lands, and information. How do environmental scientists like Michael Beckler become "well disciplined" in the boundaries of knowledge? Would it even be appropriate to do so given the unwritten law? Again, maybe it's my bias as an Anishinaabe from the Midwest, but the ability of tribal biologists to explain to the media the cultural importance of their environmental science and management actions seems key to maintaining and improving environmental governance outcomes. Could or should the Yakama Nation Department of Natural Resources publish something like the *Maz*? It turns out they have.

Carol Craig works as a reporter for the *Yakama Nation Review*. Before sharing the razor wire–encircled *Review* building with Ronnie Washines, Carol was the public information manager in the Nation's fish and wildlife program. In 1995 she published the first edition of the *Sin-Wit-Ki*, a print newsletter featuring photographs and stories about the Nation's natural resources work. "These resources that can't speak for themselves, we need to speak for them," explained Carol. Trained as a journalist, she used the monthly publication to highlight the Nation's environmental work and put their efforts into context within state, regional, and national news. In the first edition, you'll find stories about tribal fisheries management projects, cooperative ecological restoration agreements with the State of Washington, policy disputes with federal agencies, and a new fishing net design pioneered by a tribal member. Looking back through the newsletter's twelve-year run, you'll find pictures of tribal members preparing traditional foods and stories about the cultural importance of some plants and animals. You might even find harvesting tips. When I brought up the *Sin-Wit-Ki* in the fish and wildlife program offices, some long-time staff remembered the publication fondly and recounted stories of having read it cover to cover. Its last issue was published in 2007.

Carol lent me copies of the publications, pamphlets, and newsletters she produced in her former role. Upon showing the publications to newer program staff, one exclaimed, "I could never publish something like that!" Another staff member explained that, now, "we steer away from anything using the language. . . . As far as cultural information, we steer clear. People are scared it'll get abused like everything else. People are scared it'll be too easy to access." After Carol's departure, it seems the department reverted to a more protectionist orientation. Sustaining environmental news and communication required something Carol brought to the table.

The best explanation I can muster for how Carol was able to publish the *Sin-Wit-Ki* to popular acclaim is based on two factors: her journalism training and her cultural capital. Carol earned a bachelor's degree in journalism from Portland State University, and after graduation she worked for the Columbia River Inter-Tribal Fish Commission (CRITFC) for eight years. When Carol returned to the Yakama Nation, she brought the knowledge and experience of applying a journalist's lens to Indigenous natural resources work. Given current attitudes toward information sharing, I asked Carol how she could have published the *Sin-Wit-Ki*.

"It's important to get our message out, to get our history out . . . that's what I was telling [the council] when I started back here," she explained. "You need someone to get out there and work with the nontribal public. It's letting people know what we are doing because they don't think we do anything." The way Carol tells it, she received broad support from both the department and elders on the council, but it seemed that this was contingent upon her cultural capital and the fact that she was well disciplined in the unwritten law. "If you know it [cultural knowledge], you can share it, but there's also personal choice and judgment," she explained.

On my last day in Toppenish, I swung by the *Review* office to apologize for skipping out on a staff lunch we had planned so I could catch an earlier flight home. As usual, the quick stop turned into an hour-long chat about the day's news. Carol told me she was off to take photographs of a group of Yakama citizens gathering roots. "Wait a minute," I said, "I thought folks were against taking pictures of the first foods? Didn't someone at

CRITFC just get into hot water for that?" Both Carol and Ronnie jumped in to explain what I can best describe as the *unwritten editorial law*. The gathering was taking place at an old US military bombing range, so the coverage didn't risk revealing the location of plants in the Closed Area. There's still some debate over what plants can be pictured and how, but this story was focused on the gathering. Ultimately, the timeliness of the issue (many people were gathering for feasts at that time of the year) and the news value of showing the resilience of seasonal cultural practices won out.

Conclusion: "Reaching Our Hands Back"

> *"To get the kids back to the culture, we need to include something modern, we need to include science. It's hard to blend the culture into the future . . . but working past that is our generation's duty. To reach our hand back and bring our culture into the future."*
>
> —*A Yakama elder*

When an elder spoke these words during a six-hour interview, what struck me with force wasn't that an elder spoke to these themes, but that there was a recognition of their duty to help the culture grow and modernize. The intergenerational transfer of knowledge remains a key part of many tribal epistemologies, and a core component of traditional ecological knowledge processes (Berkes et al. 2000). Sustainability isn't simply a buzzword among environmentally conscious folks, it's a useful concept for thinking about the way in which we tend to Indigenous science and environmental communication. What could make environmental media sustainable within our communities? What can help modernize this centuries-old practice and bring it into a heavily mediatized future? Doing the work and fulfilling that intergenerational duty requires a deep understanding of the social, political, cultural, and historic influences on media work within Indigenous communities and Nations.

To partially answer these and Michael Beckler's original questions, sustaining science and environmental media in the Yakama Nation requires building both cultural authority and media capacity. At present, professionals like Michael can gain approval from tribal council committees to do media work, but that process has left some feelings of uncertainty about information boundaries. Some staff in the Nation's Fisheries program reported working closely with the council on media projects and topics, while others felt uncertain about how or when to approach the council. Here and across Indian Country, the politics of ecological knowledge protection have created an uncertain environment for some science communicators. In an ideal world, there would be many tribal citizens well trained in culture, knowledge boundaries, environmental science, and communication to fill all the needs of our nations, but the present reality means hiring Native and non-Native staff who aren't always versed in one or more of these areas.

Sustaining environmental media work within our current media ecosystem while protecting and revitalizing cultural knowledge will require creative thinking and collective decision making. It will require elders and tribal leaders to discuss how this work should be done, who should do it, and where information boundaries lie. For Michael, this might mean hiring a tribal member with cultural authority who is well trained in what to share and what not to share. For the natural resources department, it might mean working with elders or cultural revitalization experts to host training focused on cultural knowledge and knowledge boundaries. For Ronnie, it might mean treating the *Yakama Nation Review* staff like a cultural family and helping the next generation build journalistic knowledge and cultural authority (which I'm sure he already does). I can't tell the Nation what to do, but their decisions about how to bring Yakama culture into the future will certainly affect scientists, journalists, and outsiders like me as we work to elevate stories of Indigenous environmental science and sovereignty.

In that spirit, I want to yield the final few words to another "Yakama story."

Over a lunch of chile verde (yes, we're always eating while sharing stories), Carol told me about a group of agitated fishermen who approached her while she and other staff were stocking salmon in one of the local rivers. Recall the history of fisheries conflicts from the beginning of the chapter? The fishermen likely believed the biased and erroneous narrative that Indigenous peoples were given "unfair" rights and would decimate fisheries. I thought I knew what came next in Carol's story: the fishermen would throw rocks and racist slurs, if not shoot at them. "What are you doing?" the fishermen asked aggressively as they advanced toward Carol and her colleagues. Reaching her hand back, the unflappable journalist kindly responded, "I'm so glad you asked. Come here and let me show you." Within a few minutes the formerly agitated fishermen were lifting buckets themselves, helping the tribal staff stock the river.

Come here and let us show you there's power in creating stories together.

Discussion Questions

1. Why might Indigenous peoples feel protective of their cultural and environmental knowledge?
2. How does journalistic access to science and scientists differ in Indigenous communities?
3. What are the risks and rewards of using media to communicate about Indigenous science?
4. What other social, political, cultural, or historic factors may influence the visibility of Indigenous environmental science in media?

4

"I Will Never Retire from Native Media"

Interview with Joseph Orozco

Joseph Orozco is board vice chair to the Pacifica Association of Affiliates. From 1970 to 1981, he was the editor of *Common Sense*, the only independent newspaper in Hoopa Valley. In 1980 when KIDE-FM Hoopa Tribal Radio started, Orozco served as a board member. He was hired as the station manager in 1988, and stepped aside in 2020. From 1992 to 1996, Orozco served two terms on the National Federation of Community Broadcasters Board. He also helped negotiate the American Indian Radio on Satellite in 1994. In 2005, he co-produced with his wife *Dying for Water: Indians, Politics and Dead Fish in the Klamath River Basin.* Currently, he is a board member of the Hoopa Tribal Education Association.

Please introduce yourself.

I am Joseph Orozco. I am a member of the Hoopa Valley Tribe and I am also of Hopi descent.

Describe your work. What compels you to do it?

I have been involved in Native media since before I knew I was involved in Native media. I was introduced to radio when I was helping prepare a dance ground for a Sun Dance. The guy I was sharing my tent with was building a ten-watt radio station for DQ University [a tribal college founded in 1970 in Davis, California, which closed in 2005]. I told my mom when I was five years old, "One day I'm going to come home [to Hoopa]." I love these mountains.

Many years later, I came home and I went to the post office. And who did I run into? That same guy. I said, "What are you doing here?" He said the Hoopa Education Committee hired him to build that radio station. I went with him to an Education Committee meeting and they sent us both to the NFCB [National Federation of Community Broadcasters]. At

Fig. 4.1. Joseph Orozco. Author photo.

a regional conference in Fresno, I met a lot of people who were very experienced in noncommercial educational FM radio, and I thought, *Wow, this is what Hoopa needs, people need to be able to talk.*

Before that, I was always writing. People said, "Hey, you got to be a newspaper editor," so they got funds to start an independent newspaper I named *Common Sense*. That's what I did for a couple of years, and that's how I got to know the community, 'cause that's what media does—you listen to a lot of stories.

I wrote editorials, and people wondered why they didn't do that. So that changed the whole concept of the tribal council looking at media. Anyway, that's how I got started in getting to know the community, and them getting to know me and my liking of media.

Then came the radio station, and I was on the board of directors there. We thought, *Wow, let's start this whole telecommunications corporation, and we'll structure it so that we will be the directors over any way the Hoopa Tribe communicates*. That's why we called ourselves the Telecommunications Corporation. The radio station started December 16, 1980. There are only three people at the station now and there are no producers.

I will never retire from Native media. I'll always have some way to be involved with it. I'm gonna start my own web station. Web radio has fewer restrictions and you don't have to broadcast every day. I am the license owner of KWDR.org and .net. It stands for "Wolf Den Radio."

What does Indigenous media mean to you?

It means taking control and taking responsibility to speak to truth from our perspective about our lives and the things that are influencing our lives. We get to respond to the non-Native community and government, and also respond to our own people in our government. What we do is the same thing that non-Native media does with the non-Natives, but we do it on our own terms and for our own understanding, and to address the things that we understand and don't understand.

I think that's the value of Native media: to share that information and build. I don't think there's a place in this world where we don't have some kind of connection with people different than ourselves.

What does the future hold, in your view?

When we first started the radio station, we owned it. It was ours, and that was very attractive to our people. We had funding for it, but not very much, and we didn't understand how the media operates. Nowadays, people don't embrace radio. You got social media. But radio still has that value—I've come across articles analyzing how young people get news, and they're still connected to radio. I'm finding out that if you don't use the word "radio" anymore and say "media," then what you have is Indigenous people in the media.

I'm looking at other forms of media. It's not necessarily just the technology that people need to understand, it's getting them to understand that there's a use for it. This is a tool. Maybe they'll never be in radio, but learning how to do radio as a stepping stone is the foundation for how you communicate in the rest of your life. Whether you're being a DJ or applying for a job, you'd better be able to tell a good story. But it's not just telling a good story. You still have to learn how to do the research.

I've got this iPad that I'm talking on right now, and this came from a tribal organization in the health department who had this grant to teach broadcast, which is a video program. They wanted to put elders and young people together during COVID so that we could start talking—getting stories from one another and learning how to use this technology.

I always shied away from doing video. But I see the similarities and the patterns of how this technology works, and it just takes a little more learning. I thought what I would do is give tribal departments a proposal to do five-minute interviews with their staff. I want to know why people are doing what they're doing. That's how I can fund myself into some employment over the long term. We'll see if I can pull it off and help fund KWDR, and then I can get on the internet and go even further.

What should the next generation consider?
Why is this work important?

Well, I would like people to learn that there's a value in sharing stories. Somebody has to tell these stories, and we Native people just have thousands them. And we like to talk and tell people those stories. How you get to know other people's stories is by having a way to put them in these electronic envelopes and send them out to people. It's a living archive. It's very valuable. And in order to do that, not only do you need to have the skills, you have to have that sense of responsibility, that sense of ownership. We're very good media consumers, but we're very poor owners.

We don't understand, and we take on the responsibility and do the diligence to take full responsibility for how that system is used, how it is financed, and for journalistic integrity. Part of that responsibility is to figure out how it integrates into the media system of America. As ethnic groups, we are siloed. It's important that we talk with one another, but it's far more important, or as important, that others understand us from our perspectives.

Is there anything else you would like to add?

The government gave us trust responsibilities like water, health, law enforcement, and education, but they didn't acknowledge communication. In fact, they didn't want us to communicate. The federal government needs to step forward and start to figure out how they can meet the needs of our sovereign nations, which are equal to theirs.

The self-governance tribes should band together and negotiate a subsidy for media. That is reasonable. I say $600,000 a year for every medium [radio, newspaper, internet] that is developed on our terms, not federal terms. We've always had trouble with communications. Our female spiritual leader told me this story:

We lived on two rivers. We had villages, but only two rivers, and you got the news as fast as the river traveled, unless you could run faster than the river, then you got the news sooner. That's what we had. We had people from all of the tribes. We had three tribes along two rivers, and villages along both those rivers. There was a whole society of ridge runners, and their job was to run along the ridges, drop down into the villages along the rivers, and share the news and gather the news and run on. All three tribes had different languages, so these people had to be multilingual.

Now we have electronic communications. But we haven't figured it out. How do we really hold on to new technologies and still grab the tradition of the ridge runners? That's what I'm thinking. Now we need some ridge runners. Let's develop this whole web of ridge runners through the electronic medium.

Can you imagine if we had this telecommunication system in 1491? The whole world would have been different.

—Interviewed by Cristina L. Azocar

5

The News Coverage of Unmarked Graves at Indian Residential Schools by the Canadian Broadcasting Corporation

Dennis Foung

In 2021, amid the hardships caused by the COVID-19 pandemic in Canada, the discovery of the unmarked graves of 215 children in Kamloops, British Columbia touched the heart of every Canadian and others around the world. The story started on May 21, 2021 with a statement issued by the Tk'emlups te Secwepemc chief, Rosanne Casimir, concerning the discovery of the remains of 215 students from the Kamloops Indian Residential School (Casimir 2021). It developed further on May 31, when Canadian prime minister Justin Trudeau ordered Canadian flags to be lowered to honor the Indigenous children (CBC News 2021a). In June and July 2021, more unmarked graves were subsequently discovered in other former residential school sites in British Columbia and across Canada, including Saskatchewan and British Columbia Southern Interior. Alongside an increasing number of news stories about the discovery of further unmarked graves (Eneas 2021; Migdal 2021a), other news stories included:

- the cancellation of Canada Day celebrations in response to the discoveries (Courtney 2021);
- local events to honor the missing children (Monkman 2021);
- Prime Minister Trudeau's visits on the first National Day for Truth and Reconciliation (Maloney 2021);
- the responses from (and vandalism of) local Catholic churches (CBC News 2021b); and
- an apology from Pope Francis (CBC News 2022), which was only given in 2022.

The Canadian Broadcasting Corporation (CBC) is a publicly funded broadcasting agency that has a mandate to connect local communities with all Canadians (Canadian Broadcasting Corporation, n.d.). At such a somber time for Canada, CBC's handling of the news of the discovery of these unmarked graves was critical in helping Canadians to react, heal, and most importantly, support one another. Although CBC is a mainstream, non-Indigenous media outlet, it acted as the official channel to give space to Indigenous communities as part of its mandate to connect communities. In practice, how CBC revealed the truth of these discoveries to its audience—and gave a voice to Indigenous peoples and survivors of the Indian residential schools and their families—affected how Canadians reacted.

Indigenous Peoples in Canada

In Canada, there are three categories of Indigenous peoples as recognized by the Canadian government: First Nations, Inuit, and Métis. Among the First Nations peoples, there are more than 630 communities in Canada. Based on the Canadian census in 2021, 1.8 million people identified themselves as Indigenous (5 percent of the Canadian population). The Indigenous peoples, as suggested by the Canadian government, govern their own territory (Malone and Chisholm 2016).

Indian Residential School Context

The Indian residential school system can be understood as a means of "cultural invasion," aimed at eradicating the home culture (Haig-Brown 2022). Sadly, as part of colonization practices, such systems were common in the 1800s to the 1960s in the United States (Reyhner 2018) and Australia (Norman-Hill 2019), as well as in Canada. According to Haig-Brown (2022), residential schools started with European traders bringing "better" lifestyles or practices to their new territories. Native peoples became aware of these practices, such as farming methods, and were forced to adopt them for survival, or starve. The Canadian government later saw a need to "civilize" the Indigenous peoples to "help" them survive. It first introduced a school system to promote "civilized" culture, before deciding that Indigenous children should be removed from their families and placed in residential schools, distancing them completely from their home culture. The residential schools imposed harsh discipline (Haig-Brown 2022; Hoerig 2002); accounts of abuse and death were common among survivors (Haig-Brown 2022), as was loneliness (Woolford

2021). While Norman-Hill (2019) sees differences between the residential school systems of Australia, the United States, and Canada, common factors included cultural invasion and punishment. Accounts from Haig-Brown (2022) show that residential schools had an intergenerational impact on Indigenous peoples. For example, parents who had attended residential schools were more likely to impose an authoritarian or disciplinary approach on their Indigenous children, which in turn affected the mental well-being of those children. Reyhner (2018) confirms the intergenerational impact from the US residential school context, finding that, due to the shame that parents experienced when speaking their native language in residential schools, subsequent generations feel ashamed of speaking their own language. Alongside the deaths of residential school children, the effect of the mental abuse on subsequent generations cannot be underestimated.

Understanding Trauma: A Historical Trauma Approach

The deaths of children in residential schools, along with the mental abuse inflicted on survivors, have resulted in long-term intergenerational historical trauma. "Western" understanding of trauma labels or diagnoses the trauma of a victim based on symptoms and/or causes. A common example is post-traumatic stress disorder after experiencing a traumatic event (American Psychiatric Association 2013). Generally, the treatment and diagnosis rely on the victim's own experience of an event. For example, it is possible to address the post-traumatic narrative that the victim believes themselves to be responsible for the traumatic event, and this is key to treatment (Fast and Collin-Vézina 2010). However, traumas such as those caused by residential schools have been argued to extend beyond personal experiences; here, simply examining personal experience is not an effective way to understand trauma (Duran et al. 1998).

Recent literature promotes the framework of "historical trauma" to understand trauma that is experienced by an entire group (Fast and Collin-Vézina 2010). Brave Heart-Jordan (1995) argues that, in seeking to understand the trauma of the Indigenous peoples, one should extend an understanding of trauma to the entire cultural group. The traumatic experience of a victim's parents or grandparents can be transmitted to the victim, and therefore having an understanding of intergenerational trauma and its transference process is important. For example, parents may have been traumatized by their experiences in the residential schools—such as being forbidden to speak their native language—and, being unable to handle this trauma, they may transfer the traumatic experience to their children, making them feel ashamed to speak their own language. The effect of such traumatic experiences can be amplified when the entire cultural group has the same experience. While historical trauma theory has a strong psychiatric basis and applications (see Brave Heart et al. 2011), a historical trauma experience is very similar to the intergenerational impact described by the residential school scholars above. This study will, therefore, attempt to understand news frames with reference to the historical trauma framework.

Analysis of News Frames and News Sponsors

A news frame is the "central organizing idea or story" that helps readers understand the news. It is an attempt not to deceive or mislead readers, but rather to highlight certain elements so that readers can digest the story more easily (Gamson and Modigliani 1989). Frame analysis is not new; previous studies have compared the frames of health news used in Indigenous and mainstream media (LaPoe et al. 2022c), as well as those of reconciliation in Indigenous politics (Budd 2021) and the coverage of Indian residential schools (Nagy and Gillespie 2015).

News sponsor analysis is another common strategy used in the analysis of media coverage. It is often used to examine the voices, both internal (from news organizations) and external (from the public), that build news content (Tanner and Friedman 2011). Following earlier efforts in frame analysis and frame sponsor analysis, recent frame analysis conducted on the news coverage of the pandemic has started to make use of computational approaches (e.g., Hubner 2021), which provide additional perspectives to the human-based coding adopted by earlier frame-analysis studies. The emergence of news articles on the discovery of unmarked burial sites in Kamloops offered researchers opportunities to examine coverage of the story using news frame analysis.

Exploring the Frames and Frame Sponsors

This study explores the frames and frame sponsors in online CBC News articles published from May to December 2021. To detect news frames, a mix of text analytics and manual coding was performed. Generally, manual coding means that researchers read and examine stories and assign a label each story with its assigned frame. Text analytics methods computerize these manual processes and automatically assign a frame based on the words used in each story. This chapter argues that manual coding has advantages over computer-only coding. While computers can identify general patterns in the use of common words, frames depend on how humans read the headlines and sub-headlines. Also, in this study we adopt a human-based interpretative approach to the frame sponsors. While only one is first quoted in the news article, how readers interpret or classify the role of that person can vary, and thus a manual coding methodology is appropriate in an interpretivist approach.

While past studies have used ProQuest Newsstand for similar purposes, to find news stories, this study found that news from CBC could be better identified through Google searches. Therefore, a Google search was conducted on June 17, 2023, using the keywords "Kamloops," "residential schools," and "unmarked graves," with the specification that the results should be news articles from "cbc.ca" between May 1 and December 31, 2021. More than 500 articles were identified through this process, and duplicate articles and articles irrelevant to the topic were removed. The final dataset included 425 articles. To allow comparison between Indigenous and non-Indigenous writers, this study examined the self-introduction of each writer and identified the writer as Indigenous if they identified themselves as a member of the First Nations. Among the 425 articles, eighteen authors of eighteen articles identified themselves as members of an Indigenous community.

Both a computing coding and a manual coding approach was adopted. This study at first included only the headline, lead, first, second, and third paragraphs (following Hubner 2021) in the dataset, and removed the stop words, punctuation, numbers, and other unnecessary words. Readers can refer to earlier sections of this chapter for a more in-depth discussion and further references. The total number of topics (or frames) to be included was decided using the lda package in R library (Chang 2024). This depended on the statistical parameters (coherence score) and interpretability, as suggested by Blei et al. (2003). After deciding the number of frames, a frame was assigned to each article based on popular words in the dataset. Next, the author manually examined each frame together with the keywords to decide whether it was necessary to reorganize the frame structure and/or reassign certain articles to different frames. It was not possible to employ a second coder, so the author completed one round of manual coding and then revisited the data three days later to ensure that the framing process was validated more than once.

These categories were tagged for each article. It is possible that a source could belong to more than one category: for example, a source could be an Indigenous leader (i.e., a person from both the Indigenous leader and Indigenous people categories) who also identifies as a residential school survivor.

Toward Truth and Reconciliation

Upon further examination, it was found that, while some stories were written by professional Indigenous journalists, others were written by Indigenous leaders, including Daisy House, chief of the Cree Nation of Chisasibi (House 2021), and Willie Sellars, chief of the Williams Lake First Nation of the Secwepemc Nation (Sellars 2021). These people were identified as Indigenous writers or authors throughout, not as Indigenous journalists.

The frames assigned to these articles were first examined using a text analytics approach. Based on the coherence score, the analytics applications determined that there were either two frames or eleven frames across the whole dataset. Upon further examination of the keywords provided by the text analytics, eleven frames were used. Based on a closer examination of the frames assigned to each article, some frames were reassigned and one new frame was produced to better describe the data. The names, distribution, and respective keywords of ten frames are presented in table 5.1. The table includes the percentages of frames from all stories and stories from Indigenous authors. The principle of topic modeling considers both statistical constructs and interpretability, and the frames that were assigned complied with the principle.

The most prevalent frame was "healing/mourning" (22%), which describes articles about the efforts and events to mourn the 215 missing children across Canada, including marches (Cox 2021) and memorials (CBC News 2021c). The second most prevalent frame was "further search" (14%), which includes articles that describe the radar technology used to search for more graves (Gollom 2021) or calls for further searches on other residential school sites across Canada (Taekema 2021). The third most common frame was "church reaction" (11%), which covers stories on how local churches apologized or the Pope's response to the unmarked graves (and other burial sites), such as CBC News (2021b). Other prevalent frames included descriptions of what happened or the need to know what happened (9%), the implications of lowering flags or having holidays for the National Day of Truth and Reconciliation (8%), cancelling Canada Day celebrations (7%), and resources or funding for further searches, education, or mourning events (7%). Frames relating to the intergenerational impact account for only 7% of all stories.

The differences in the proportions of frames in stories written by Indigenous and non-Indigenous writers were examined. There were no obvious differences regarding the frames "what happened," "resources/ funding," "healing/mourning," and "further search." However, "further

Table 5.1. Frame sponsors in news stories, as seen in all stories (left column) vs. stories from Indigenous authors (right column).

Frame	Percentage: All stories (n=425)	Percentage: Stories from Indigenous authors (n=18)	Keywords from text
What happened	9%	11%	records, trying, happened
Resources/funding	7%	6%	million, funding, expert
Healing/mourning	22%	22%	vigil, shoes, honor
Further action	6%	22%	support, seek, beginning
Intergenerational impact	7%	17%	children, trauma, talk
Further search	14%	17%	radar, search, uncovered
Flag lowering/ having national days	8%	0%	flags, statutory, half-mast
Renaming/ removing symbols of colonialism	9%	0%	Ryerson, statue, name
Canada Day	7%	0%	celebration, Canada, cancel
Church reaction	11%	6%	archbishop, church, apology

Note: Totals may exceed 100% due to rounding.

action" (+16%) and "intergenerational impact" (+10%) were adopted by Indigenous writers more often than non-Indigenous writers, while "flag lowering/having national days" (–8%), "church reaction" (–5%), "Canada Day" (–7%), and "renaming/removing symbols of colonialism" (–9%) were more frequently adopted by non-Indigenous writers. Overall, the overarching differences were significant. Indigenous authors emphasized themes focused on community harms and ways of healing more than non-Indigenous authors did. At the same time, non-Indigenous journalists used common "symbolic" or "performative" frames that ignored intracommunity harms.

To understand who was quoted in the articles as the frame sponsor, each story was manually examined and the sponsor was identified when the first instance of a person or organization was directly quoted in the story. A preliminary examination of the sources quoted identified six

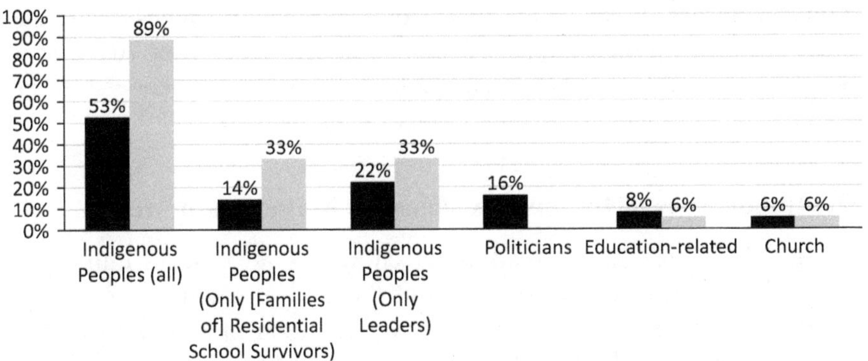

Figure 5.1. Frames adopted by news stories (a sponsor may belong to more than one category). Dark gray: all stories; light gray: stories from Indigenous authors.

common categories: Indigenous peoples, education-related individuals, government officials, survivors of residential schools or their families, the church, and Indigenous leaders. It should again be noted that there were duplications across these categories, but these classifications are generally helpful in understanding how sources were quoted. Figure 5.1 shows the percentage of quotations from specific categories of sponsors.

Overall, it is pleasing to see that 53 percent of all sources quoted were from Indigenous categories, and that they were given space to present their perspectives on the stories. In particular, 14 percent of all sources were survivors of residential schools or their families. Indigenous voices were present in frames related to healing or mourning—for example, CBC News (2021d) narrated how family members who went missing or died after attending a residential school were mourned. A substantial 22 percent of all sources were Indigenous leaders, who were usually quoted when calling for further searches to be conducted at other residential school sites (Taekema 2021). They also played a role in explaining their perspectives on other stories, such as CBC News (2021e). Interestingly, despite the role played by the Catholic Church, it was only quoted in 6 percent of all sources, and only 16 percent of all sources were quotes from government officials.

Interestingly, in some examples of stories relating to an apology from a local church, the quote given was from Indigenous peoples; that is, the apology was presented as a paraphrase of a First Nations member (CBC News 2021b). Similarly, when a story started with the prime minister's remarks, the quote was from an Indigenous person, not the prime minister himself (Migdal 2021b). Education-related quotes, such as those from parents, teachers, or school districts, were presented in frames that relate to the intergenerational impact of residential schools (Fraser 2021). Stories also covered the need for a curriculum review on Indigenous history from education-related Indigenous voices (e.g., Ann 2021).

The Importance of Indigenous Voices in Mainstream Media

While it is distressing to read about children's remains in unmarked graves, it is promising that over half of the sources quoted were Indigenous. Indigenous voices were especially common in stories using the "healing/mourning" frame. They were categorized as belonging to Indigenous communities in general, or residential school survivors or their families. Promoting Indigenous voices in the media allows people to grieve. With carefully crafted frames, such as "healing/mourning," mainstream media outlets like CBC may help Indigenous people understand that they neither have to face this trauma alone nor bear responsibility for it. Understanding is an important part of the long-term healing process.

One way to frame these stories is to include the voices of residential school survivors. For example, Lenard Monkman (2021), an Indigenous journalist, quoted survivor Sue Caribou, who spoke at a public mourning event about how "emotional" and "heavy" the news was for the community. Such an approach can connect Indigenous and non-Indigenous communities and facilitate the healing process. In addition, employing frames to promote healing can help people move forward with their grief. This may include participation in mourning activities (such as those introduced by Monkman) or performances by Indigenous artists (CBC News 2021f), such as Freddy Taylor, who was quoted as saying that art promotes a "healing world." By including voices from Indigenous communities, the mainstream media can become a resource that provides all Canadians with a way to grieve and heal.

Indigenous writers used news frames and sponsors differently from non-Indigenous writers. Generally, Indigenous writers were more forward-looking and interested in future generations (i.e., intergenerational trauma and actions to be taken). They also saw the value of telling these stories through an Indigenous lens and thus quoted Indigenous people more often. They seemed less interested in changing the past (e.g., national days, changing symbols of colonialism, quoting politicians), which may suggest that Indigenous communities are focused on moving forward rather than looking back. For example, Angela Sterritt is a professional Indigenous journalist who worked with a non-Indigenous writer (Bridgette Watson) to develop an interactive story on "reclaiming

Indigenous culture" as a way to move forward (Watson and Sterritt 2021). Another example is a story (Sterrit 2021) that claimed that the main reason to acquire residential school records is to identify the missing children (not to find out what happened, as in other frames). Indigenous people were quoted in both stories, which shows the importance of these issues to these communities. One way to grieve and navigate the complex path to truth and reconciliation is to look forward.

Historical Trauma Is "Generational"

The trauma experienced by victims of residential schools is intergenerational, as explained in the historical trauma framework (Brave Heart et al. 2011). This was reasonably represented in the media in this case: many of the survivors' children described how they were affected by these experiences (CBC News 2021d). One example of a news story about the intergenerational impact was written by Melanie Ferris (2021), an Indigenous journalist. She described the importance of the granddaughter of a residential school victim understanding intergenerational trauma and starting a conversation with her mother about it. Such stories show the prolonged impact of residential schools. They typically rely on the historical trauma framework and help educate the general public about the intergenerational effect of trauma in Indigenous communities.

Some stories also covered how parents (both Indigenous and non-Indigenous) can talk to their children about the discovery of the unmarked graves (e.g., Fraser 2021). One news story, written by Hiawatha First Nation journalist Rhiannon Johnson (2021), described how a member of the Indigenous community, Joseph Pitawanakwat, took gradual steps to teach his child about the history of residential schools and use art to "honour lost life," which could help younger children understand how to manage historical trauma. There were also pieces produced by CBC dedicated to helping children understand residential schools (e.g., CBC Kids News 2021). As these stories were specifically crafted for children, using colorful layouts and narratives by other children, this allowed young people to heal and promote truth and reconciliation.

This study examined the frames and sponsors employed in news stories by CBC on the unmarked children's graves discovered in Kamloops, British Columbia, Canada. The analysis shows that the most prevalent frame was "healing/mourning," followed by "further search." There were differences in the news frames used by Indigenous and non-Indigenous writers. Indigenous voices accounted for over half of the sponsors in the news stories; they were more common in stories written by Indigenous writers. In addition to exploring the impact of intergenerational trauma, the news stories also described various strategies for navigating historical trauma with children by considering the views of Indigenous parents and younger generations. This study argues that Indigenous voices are crucial for the healing process of Canadians. Further studies could explore more attributes of this healing process, as well as delineate more specifics about these stories and the roles Indigenous journalists play.

Discussion Questions

1. What strategies can be used to encourage Indigenous communities to contribute to the media (i.e. the first person on CBC)?
2. What strategies encourage Indigenous professional journalists to contribute to mainstream media outlets, on top of Indigenous media outlets?
3. How effectively or ineffectively do computational approaches (e.g. topic modeling) explore the coverage of topics in news media articles?

6

"You Don't Have to Explain Why It's a Story. It's Implicit"

Interview with Mark Trahant

Mark Trahant is a managing innovator at IndiJ Public Media and an editor-at-large at ICT (formerly *Indian Country Today*). Trahant was hired to revive ICT after it went out of business in 2017. The success of this revival has been phenomenal. The digital site now reaches 700,000 people a month and the broadcast is carried on two dozen public television stations. Trahant is a member of the American Academy of Arts and Sciences and has held endowed chairs at the University of North Dakota and University of Alaska Anchorage. He is a citizen of the Shoshone-Bannock Tribes.

Please introduce yourself.

I'm a citizen of the Shoshone-Bannock Tribes, as well as Fort Peck Assiniboine. I've been working in both mainstream and tribal media for fifty years.

Describe your work. What compels you to do it?

I think I always wanted to be a journalist. When I was about eight years old, I made a crayon newspaper and distributed it around the neighborhood, so I think it was pretty inevitable. And my grandparents were great storytellers; I loved hearing their stories.

I had two first jobs in journalism. I was working for a little radio station doing play-by-play for basketball tournaments, and the BIA [Bureau of Indian Affairs] education officer got me a small contract to do a video story on the Shoshone-Bannock Festival, so I was running around taping different dancers and talking to people.

I started at *Sho-Ban News* and took a brief detour to work for the BIA. Then I went to the *Salt Lake Tribune*, covering the Navajo elections, and ended up the editor of *Navajo Times*. Then *The Arizona Republic*, *Salt Lake Tribune*, *Navajo Nation Today*. After that *Moscow-Pullman*

Fig. 6.1. Mark Trahant. Author photo.

Daily News, *Seattle Times*, Maynard [The Maynard Institute], and *Seattle Post-Intelligencer*. I also taught for a while at universities in Colorado, Alaska, and North Dakota. Then, finally, *Indian Country Today*.

What does Indigenous media mean to you?

For me it is community. *Sho-Ban News* was (and is) a weekly, and it really connected with community. One of the things I like about Indigenous journalism is that you can't hide behind the First Amendment—you've got to sit down and talk to people. And if they don't like it, they're gonna have coffee with you the next day. Those conversations, I think, are really helpful.

It's amazing how many really remarkable stories I have witnessed. Some are intertwined with my life. When I would go fishing with my dad, it was pre-Boldt [a Supreme Court decision that upheld treaty fishing rights], and then the Supreme Court case that directly impacts Sho-Ban was the Tinno decision that protected the Tribe's right to fish. When I was a kid, my dad would say, "I'm going to get arrested," and we had to look out for game wardens. By the time I was in my twenties, the right to fish was understood as protected treaty rights. Yet all of that happened about the same time as there was real pressure on the survival of the salmon resource, so it was almost a Pyrrhic victory in the sense that, yeah, the treaty right is there, but the salmon are in great danger.

For some of the stories I've been on in my long career, I've just been totally lucky to be in the right place at the right time.

Why is it important to have Indigenous people tell their own stories?

I think the biggest reason is context. When folks parachute into a story, they might write about that particular event, and it might even be as accurate as possible, but the problem is, they don't have the context. They don't know what happened fifty years before, or one hundred years before that—and adding that context to the story is essential to getting it right.

I think representation matters in general, that you cannot have any kind of reflection without having some sort of representation of the constituency you purport to represent. So many stories would just be lost without that representation.

What does the future hold, in your view?

Technology has changed the most. Much of our broadcast is done on an iPhone. The technology is so good that you don't need to have a studio. Just in the last two years, what's been dramatic is the change in social media. We used to rely probably way too much on social media for our audience, and like everybody in the media, we felt it was just so easy. Now, the algorithms have all changed and Twitter is gone. You don't have the same ability to reach a large audience for social media. You really have to work for every reader.

I think with digital you have the ability to be a daily. I remember trying to be a daily with the *Navajo Times*, and the challenges we had with that were logistical. We had to try to serve the Navajo Nation and, given the geography, we would print the paper about 11:30 p.m. and use the rest of the night to get it out. The Navajo Nation goes from southern Utah to western Arizona, parts of New Mexico. We had to use an airplane every night and load it up with newspapers and do a big loop.

Now we can reach a national audience, essentially Indian Country, without leaving our office. One of the things I really like about that is it ties the whole country together in a way that we didn't have before; even *Indian Country Today* as a print publication didn't have the same breadth that we do in that sense. And we get data. We know so much more about our readership than we ever have before.

At ICT, we're making some pretty dramatic changes—that's just this week. We're shifting the show to a weekly. Part of it is, we just couldn't afford the studio space anymore. But one of the real challenges for us has been "time-appointed" television. People don't watch TV the way they did, and one of our hopes with a weekly is that we can do a lot more shorter things on YouTube, which is now building a pretty good audience, and stuff other than a half-hour show.

We're just at the beginning of this technological revolution. You see it every day, how fast it's changing. AI and the ability for machine learning is going to be really dramatic. On the positive side, imagine taking every database that's ever existed about Missing and Murdered Indigenous Women and Girls and then coding that into a machine-learning process, having the machine sort the information in new ways. A negative perspective is, imagine machines taking every ceremony that's ever existed and turning it into something else. How do you control that? As it is, writers are not able to control our own content.

What should the next generation consider? Why is this work important?

The big one is to chase metaphors. Don't just look at the day-to-day story; look at the big picture. What does it all mean? Pull back and look for how things are connected in a bigger way. I don't think we do enough of that.

When you think about this climate of fascism, Indian Country has dealt with that before. Look at what happened to the Cherokee Nation in Georgia—it was brutal.[1] So having that perspective of time, I think, is really important. You think about where we were a century ago: poverty, disease, people barely survived. Now, in 2024, there's this incredible pool of talent doing amazing things, whether it be on climate or economic development or sovereignty, or coming up with a way to have a future for children. That is really remarkable.

One of those big stories is the depth of talent in Indian Country.

Is there anything else you would like to add?

One area I hope will be next for tribal media is more expertise. Wouldn't it be great to have folks who understand economics, who understand hard sciences, and who particularly understand health care?

For example, what is missing from the overall media narrative, and is so crucial, is that when the Indian Health Care Improvement Act was passed in 1976, the average age of death for native people was forty years old. We have had the most amazing, stunning turnaround in health statistics compared to any population in the country. We're now two years behind the general population. So instead of focusing on the disparity, which is real and needs to be addressed, the idea is that we've had this amazing program that's worked. Instead, the dominant worldview just misses the whole picture, when in fact, we have had the only cohesive healthcare system in the United States.

I think more expertise maybe means we need to receive more journalism education. There's a tendency to learn the craft in journalism school, but maybe now it requires extra to make sure you get a specialty, whether that be law or health or whatever.

I think one of the exciting things is the more international aspects of indigeneity. We are connected to Greenland and New Zealand, and places that we have never been connected to before, and that's really a good thing. It's made the world a lot smaller and it's also made journalism a lot smaller and more efficient.

We need institutions like ICT. It's essential that we have an institutional home for journalism. One of the things I think is so great about working at ICT, but really at any tribal medium, is the idea that you don't have to explain why it's a story. It's implicit.

—Interviewed by Cristina L. Azocar

Note

1. For more in-depth information, see Robert J. Conley, The Cherokee Nation: A History, Albuquerque, University of New Mexico Press, 2005.

7

Indigenizing Free Expression in Oklahoma

Kevin R. Kemper[1] and Litzy Galarza

"Everybody, whether it's our tribe or other tribes, [has] talked about improving communication and transparency," said Alexandria Harjo (Iowa, Pawnee, Muscogee) when she ran for the office of chairperson of the Iowa Tribe of Oklahoma (Herrera 2013a). More and more frequently, Indigenous peoples are speaking their truths in their own way while being protected by their own laws. The Iowa Tribe of Oklahoma, or the Bah Kho-Je, the People of the Grey Snow, has a constitution that explicitly and implicitly protects free speech and press. That does not mean there are no pressures and challenges; it simply means the Ioway people have legal protections. However, tribes vary in how much protection they have for free expression. There are numerous examples of repression and censorship of Indigenous media across Indian Country. Tribes in Oklahoma provide some essential examples of this, and they expose a delightful and difficult truth: a media practitioner, another communicator, or a lawyer representing anyone in these tribal courts in Oklahoma can use at least one law from almost every tribe to argue that there is free expression for that tribe, and some tribes have more protections than others, thanks to statutes or more detailed language in their constitutions. This chapter explores how Indigenous nations in Oklahoma have protected and even expanded free expression so that media practitioners know how to exercise this fundamental liberty, while at the same time honoring the inherent sovereignty of each of those nations.

Still, the fight for free expression in Indian Country continues. For instance, November 2018 brought darkness instead of light to the Muscogee[2] (Creek) Nation and its people in Oklahoma. The National Council, with the smallest of majorities, decided to repeal the tribe's Free Press Act, which codified press rights that were not explicit in the Muscogee Constitution of 1979. This raised serious concerns and alarm across Indian Country, especially among Indigenous journalists and advocates who believe that free press and speech are essential to the well-being of tribes (NAJA Executive Director 2018). The Constitution did not use the words "press" or "speech," like one would find in the First Amendment of the United States Constitution. Instead, there were already implicit protections for free expression in place. For instance, in Article II, Section 2 of the Muscogee Constitution of 1979:

> This Constitution shall not abridge the rights and privileges of individual citizens of the Muscogee (Creek) Nation enjoyed as citizens of the State of Oklahoma and of the United States of America.

To strengthen those inherent rights of the Muscogee people, whose reservation sits in east central Oklahoma, Indigenous journalists and advocates, like those with the IJA (formerly known as the Native American Journalists Association), fought until free press came back to the tribe. On July 23, 2020, the National Council unanimously restored free press with a revised statute, NCA 20–037, which included a measure of editorial independence for the tribe's media outlet, Mvskoke Media. This fight was featured in the documentary film *Bad Press* (2023), which was at the Sundance Film Festival and won the Special Jury Award for Freedom of Expression.

That is a story from one tribe about one major issue, but there are hundreds of similar stories across Indian Country about how best to protect and promote free press. For instance, Mandan-Hidatsa-Arikara leaders in North Dakota fired Jodi Rave Spotted Bear (Mandan-Hidatsa-Arikara) from her position as publisher of the *MHA Times*, because she reported about the tribal budget and criticism of the leadership (Scott 2021). Among Oklahoma tribes, some people think the tribes have few, if any, free press or speech rights, though most tribal constitutions protect those. The legal realities are more complicated and even promising.

Free expression remains the cornerstone of a free society and the media and other communicators operating within it; the legal protections of constitutions and statutes are, therefore, essential for anyone communicating within and outside of Indian Country. In this chapter, we dig into some of the details about how tribes in Oklahoma protect free press and speech in unique ways (or not). We researched and analyzed the available constitutions of thirty-eight federally recognized tribes in Oklahoma to find any explicit references to free press, speech, and expression, as well as implicit guarantees through other rights like due process and equal protection. We also looked for references to the Indian Civil Rights Act of 1968, 25 USC § 1302, which purports to protect these freedoms. Our findings prove an essential point: tribal nations protect rights for free expression in their own ways and with more depth and breadth than imagined in their sovereignty. In ways that reflect responsible sovereignty, almost all federally recognized tribes in Oklahoma have some kind of explicit and/or implicit protection for free expression in their constitutions or corporate charters, though a handful add strong free press statutes.

Storylines and Interpretations

Late in the last century, after years of battling for free press, noted Indigenous journalist Richard LaCourse claimed that only sixty-four tribes had free press provisions in their constitutions, but he had primarily looked for expressions that mirrored exactly the First Amendment of the US Constitution (LaCourse 1998). There remains a pervasive storyline that there is not free press or speech in Indian Country, thanks to true anecdotes about violations of free press and speech there. One would be hard-pressed to go to an IJA convention without finding panels and programs devoted to advocating for free press in Indian Country. The IJA's leaders also promote statutes to protect free press, like those of the Osage Nation, the Cherokee Nation of Oklahoma, the Muscogee (Creek) Nation in Oklahoma, and the Confederated Tribes of Grand Ronde in Oregon (najanewsroom.com). Most of these also have statutes that protect access to public records and freedom of information.

The extent of free expression protections across Indian Country is not, in our experience, well known. The IJA conducted surveys of Indigenous journalists, media practitioners, and consumers through its Red Press Initiative and found that "the freedoms of speech and press are valued" and "press freedom in Indian Country is inconsistent." Academic research has reported an essential point: Indigenous journalism and its protections need to be rooted in Indigenous culture and sovereignty. An emerging and influential idea is Indigenous Standpoint Theory, which has been used by Indigenous media scholars like Azocar (2022) to argue that Indigenous nations and peoples need to be the basis of knowledge about those nations and peoples. For example, Azocar et al. (2021, 443) explained how news reporting by Indigenous journalists and media outlets about COVID-19 was less likely to misrepresent Indigenous peoples:

> From a journalistic perspective, [Indigenous Standpoint Theory] therefore makes it possible to contextualize the differences between the goals of mainstream journalism and those of Indigenous journalism. News created

by Indigenous journalists may provide more meaningful cultural and social perspectives for its audience than mainstream journalism can.

In 2012, I looked at how the interstices of culture create complicated relationships with media, Indigenous or not (Kemper 2012). In 2010, I noted how certain Indigenous journalists have worked in the field to support and protect their own people (Kemper 2010). Also, in 2013, I explained how media practitioners need to familiarize themselves with laws and boundaries about information gathering and reporting among tribes (Kemper 2013). Attorneys have also been fighting for tribal press freedom by providing basic knowledge about media laws in Indian Country (Cappetta and Matthews n.d.), like those with the Reporters Committee for Freedom of the Press. However, that kind of detailed legal discussion is largely absent from academic literature and professional publications.

The literature about the resurgence of tribal norms and desires in the media needs to be synthesized with another truth. Tribal nations and peoples are situated in proximity to nontribal people and governments, meaning that they cross over, collide, and conflict with each other. One of the more powerful examples is *McGirt v. Oklahoma*, 140 S. Ct. 2452 (2020), where the US Supreme Court held that Congress had not eliminated or "disestablished" the reservation boundaries of the Muscogee (Creek) Nation. That meant that a Native American or Alaska Native committing a major crime within a tribal reservation, or "Indian Country," should be prosecuted in tribal or federal court. Later, the court in *Oklahoma v. Castro-Huerta*, 142 S. Ct. 2486 (2022), held that non-Indians committing crimes in Indian Country could be prosecuted in state court, too. The implication is that tribal, state, and federal governments have to figure out how to cooperate to protect the rights of all. It is one thing to protect free expression for tribal members in a tribal constitution, but it is another to protect the free expression of anyone interacting with and reporting about that tribe, which would mean being a responsible neighbor, whether or not the person is a citizen of that tribe, and it exercises sovereignty in a more collaborative and responsible way.

Responsible sovereignty means recognizing that actions carried out by tribes affect both members and nonmembers, so tribes in their sovereignty can seek ways to protect the rights of everyone as much as possible. Bauder and Mueller (2021) encouraged Indigenous sovereignty over Westphalian (or statecentric) sovereignty as an antidote to "colonial oppression" of Indigenous peoples, reminding us that the 2007 United Nations Declaration of Rights of Indigenous Peoples can serve as a liberating guidepost for Indigenous nations. In fact, that declaration incorporates the rights under the United Nations Declaration of Human Rights, which protects free expression. Thus, while tribes have the sovereignty to express *how* they protect rights, they do not have the sovereignty under international law to deprive people of certain basic human rights. Too often, sovereignty is a carte blanche excuse by tribal governments for censoring expression.

Geddert (2021) recently applied the idea of responsible and Indigenous sovereignty to protecting the environment in Canada. He argued that respecting tribal stewardship of the environment is preferable to state control by Canada. Other scholars have examined the tensions between group and individual needs. For instance, Mao and Bu (2016) argued that conceptualizing responsible sovereignty can be seen through both communitarian and libertarian viewpoints across the world. Fodder (2012) attempted to reconcile both critical race theory and libertarianism to contribute to the evolving framework of Indigenous rights. That is, individual rights *and* communal rights all matter in the Indigenous context. Further, the rights of each individual and each community—Indigenous or not—should be considered by sovereign tribal nations if they want to support their internal and external expectations for human rights like free expression. In our view, that is exercising responsible sovereignty that respects everyone.

Legal Foundations: How Do Tribes Have to Deal with the Federal Government?

The key to sorting out any legal issue in Indian Country is tribal sovereignty and the laws promulgated by each tribe. Indigenous tribes in North America have governed themselves since time immemorial. During the colonization process, US law began treating tribes as "domestic-dependent nations," meaning they have a level of autonomy and sovereignty, tempered by the oversight of the federal government (*Cherokee Nation v. Georgia*, 30 US [5 Pet.] 1 [1831]). Lately, the federal and state governments have been deferring more and more to what tribes want to do for themselves. One example is the Indian Self-Determination and Education Assistance Act of 1975, Public Law 93–638, 25 USC § 5301 *et seq.*, which recognizes more tribal autonomy in implementing federal contracts than there was before the Act.

The best path toward protecting free expression in Indian Country is *not* primarily the US Constitution and *especially not* state constitutions. Rather, the laws and customs of tribes in North America contain the answers. Tribes are sovereign governments and their members are their citizens. While some people are legitimately descended from tribal ancestors and derive ethnic identity from a tribe or tribes, by definition under federal law an American Indian or Alaska Native is primarily an enrolled member of a federally recognized tribe, though some state-recognized tribes still exist.

Over time, Indigenous peoples in North America organized (whether forced to or not) into specific and distinct tribes and governed themselves, bound together by a common language, culture, and ancestors. Federally recognized tribes generally have their own laws and court systems. After the European invasion, countries like Great Britain, France, and Spain superimposed their governments upon the Indigenous peoples. The result was genocide of people, language, and culture. Not all tribes were extinguished or exterminated, though some were.

Today's 575 federally recognized tribes usually have constitutions or articles of incorporation that are organic documents for defining and outlining the laws for those nations. The Navajo Nation in New Mexico, Arizona, and Utah has an unwritten constitution based upon the traditional customs and laws of the Diné people. Each tribe has a distinct set of traditional customs and laws that guides how it governs its own people. However, Congress passed the Indian Reorganization Act of 1934, otherwise known as the Wheeler–Howard Act (73 PL 383, 48 Stat. 984, 73 Cong. Ch. 576, 73 PL 383, 48 Stat. 984, 73 Cong. Ch. 576):

> To conserve and develop Indian lands and resources; to extend to Indians the right to form business and other organizations; to establish a credit system for Indians; to grant certain rights of home rule to Indians; to provide for vocational education for Indians; and for other purposes.

This led to numerous constitutions being forced upon tribes, rather than allowing for earlier constitutions to emerge directly from those tribes. This is because Congress asserts plenary power over tribes under US law (*Lone Wolf v. Hitchcock*, 187 US 553 [1903]).

Today, tribes do have a process by which they can amend or even replace their constitutions, though the federal Bureau of Indian Affairs has to approve it before it becomes effective (25 USCS § 5123):

> Any Indian tribe shall have the right to organize for its common welfare, and may adopt an appropriate constitution and bylaws, and any amendments thereto, which shall become effective when—
>
> **(1)** ratified by a majority vote of the adult members of the tribe or tribes at a special election authorized and called by the Secretary under such rules and regulations as the Secretary may prescribe; and
>
> **(2)** approved by the Secretary pursuant to subsection (d) of this section.

Again, Congress asserts plenary power over tribes, meaning that resolving certain constitutional issues (*Morton v. Mancari*, 417 US 535, 551–52, 94 S. Ct. 2474, 2483 [1974]):

> turns on the unique legal status of Indian tribes under federal law and upon the plenary power of Congress, based on a history of treaties and the assumption of a "guardian-ward" status, to legislate on behalf of federally recognized Indian tribes. The plenary power of Congress to deal with the special problems of Indians is drawn both explicitly and implicitly . . . from the Constitution itself. Article I, § 8, cl. 3, provides Congress with the power to "regulate Commerce . . . with the Indian Tribes," and thus, to this extent, singles Indians out as a proper subject for separate legislation. Article II, § 2, cl. 2, gives the President the power, by and with the advice and consent of the Senate, to make treaties. This has often been the source of the Government's power to deal with the Indian tribes.

The fundamental basis of the relationship between the federal government and each tribal government is the existing treaty between the parties. Those treaties survive even when the territories where tribes are located are granted statehood, as explained in *Herrera v. Wyoming* (139 S. Ct. 1686 [2019]).

Legally, the bottom line is that US tribes, as "domestic-dependent nations," have sovereignty to do what they want with their own laws, though that is tempered for most of them by their treaty relationships with the US government and their unique situations after initial colonization. Many tribes across the country do not have treaties, however. The more time passes, the more tribal laws develop unique characteristics and increasing authority.

Findings: More and More, Tribes Protect Free Expression

As mentioned above, almost all tribes in Oklahoma have some kind of legal protection for free expression. Most of the 575 federally recognized tribes of Indigenous peoples across the United States also assert their sovereign rights and responsibilities to protect fundamental human rights and liberties like freedom of expression. An earlier legal analysis of at least 477 constitutions and/or articles of incorporation of tribes across the United States found that 367 tribes have at least some constitutional protections for press and speech (Kemper and Galarza 2016)—that is 76.3 percent of the total. If that percentage reflects the total numbers of federally recognized tribes, then we would hope to see that at least 438 of

575 federally recognized tribes protect free expression in their constitutions in some way. That has not yet been confirmed.

Of the thirty-eight federally recognized tribes in Oklahoma, almost all have at least some type of explicit and/or implicit protection for free expression in speech and/or press (table 7.1). The authors believe that a quantification of tribal free expression like speech and press would present a more accurate picture of the status of these rights. We developed the scale that we used to score the rankings of press freedom within each constitution or document system to identify any explicit or implicit mention of free expression. The scoring system works as follows:

- References to protections of speech, speaking, or expression generally received one-half point.
- Protections of press, publishing, or writing generally received one-half point.
- Protections of meeting or assembly received one-half point.
- Protections of associating or association received one-half point.
- Protections for redress of grievances or filing grievances received one point.
- Protections of general rights of tribal members as citizens of the state and the United States received one point.
- Protections of rights under the Indian Civil Rights Act received one point.

Explicit references to free expression–like speech and press could have been treated as one total point, as no tribe mentioned one without the other. Assembly and petition rights were included because they facilitate communication about public issues.

Regrettably, Scott (2021) and Mintzer (2023) make it sound as if there is little, if any, free press in Indian Country. This is a dangerous overgeneralization and a stereotype. First, it implies an underlying presumption that there are no legal protections for free expression (primarily press and speech), but as table 7.1 shows, there is only one tribe without constitutional protections of any kind for free expression (press or speech): the Quapaw Nation. As of 2023, this nation has been in the process of creating a constitution to update its business resolution (Quapaw Nation n.d.).

The Ottawa Tribe of Oklahoma, the Pawnee Nation of Oklahoma, and the Seneca-Cayuga Nation are the only tribes with a perfect score of 5. Part of the reason that Oklahoma was selected as a case study is because three of five known tribes with any free press statutes—Cherokee Nation,

Table 7.1. Native American tribal free press ranking using the freedom scale.

Native American Tribal Constitution	Kemper–Galarza Freedom Scale Score
Absentee Shawnee Tribe of Indians	3
Alabama Quassarte Tribal Town	1
Apache Tribe of Oklahoma	4
Caddo Nation	4
Cherokee Nation	3
Cheyenne and Arapaho Tribes	2.5
Chickasaw Nation	4
Choctaw Nation of Oklahoma	2.5
Citizen Potawatomi Nation	3
Comanche Nation	3
Delaware Nation	4
Delaware Tribe of Indians	3
Eastern Shawnee Tribe of Oklahoma	3
Fort Sill Apache Tribe	4
Iowa Tribe of Oklahoma	4
Kaw Nation	3
Kialegee Tribal Town	3
Kickapoo Tribe of Oklahoma	4
Kiowa Tribe of Oklahoma	3
Miami Tribe of Oklahoma	2
Modoc Tribe of Oklahoma	2
Muscogee (Creek) Nation	1
Osage Nation	2.5
Otoe-Missouria Tribe of Indians	2
Ottawa Tribe of Oklahoma	5
Pawnee Nation of Oklahoma	5
Peoria Tribe of Indians	2
Ponca Tribe of Indians of Oklahoma	3
Quapaw Nation	0
Sac and Fox Nation	3
Seminole Nation of Oklahoma	1
Seneca-Cayuga Nation	5

Native American Tribal Constitution	Kemper–Galarza Freedom Scale Score
Shawnee Tribe	1
Thlopthlocco Tribal Town	3
Tonkawa Tribe of Indians of Oklahoma	3
United Keetoowah Band of Cherokee Indians	3
Wichita and Affiliated Tribes	3
Wyandotte Nation	3

Osage Nation, and Muscogee (Creek) Nation—are within that state's boundaries. However, the Cherokee Nation's Constitution scored only 3, the Osage Nation scored 2.5, and the Muscogee (Creek) Nation scored only 1. This means that their statutes are all the more important for protecting free press, though they were not factored into our scoring system. One could argue that the Cherokee Nation, Osage Nation, and Muscogee (Creek) Nation have stronger systems for free press, but this study simply measured free expression in tribal constitutions. It is important to state that tribes are political entities that change over time, so our findings are based on the situation at the time of this research. Those interested in updating the information should reach out to each tribe to verify whether its constitution or governing document has changed.

The Cherokee Nation Independent Press Act of 2009 is an example of how statutes have been needed to strengthen tribal free press. That statute was birthed in the first years of the twenty-first century to answer long-standing issues about censorship of the *Cherokee Phoenix*, among other issues (Kemper 2002). In 2000, the Cherokee Nation passed an Independent Press Act following a political and constitutional crisis in 1997 that affected press freedom (Tallent and Dingman 2011).

Later, the Osage Nation's Civil Code, Title 15, Chapter 12, strengthened protections for an independent press. It even codified open records protections in Title 15, Chapter 8. More than once, *Osage News* has been successful in open records litigation in Osage Nation courts, thanks in part to the Reporters Committee for Freedom of the Press. These statutes generally set up a process to create distance between the tribal government and the media, as well as means for resolving differences between tribal governments and media if possible. Of note is how the Osage Nation codifies tribal and federal constitutional protections (Title 15, § 12–103):

> It is the policy of the Osage Nation to respect the civil rights of Osage people set forth in the Osage Constitution. Article II of the Osage Constitution by reference, incorporated and adopted the federal Indian Civil Rights Act of 1968, 25 U.S.C. § 1302, to apply to all Osages. Therefore, the Constitution of the Osage Nation provides that the principles of free speech and free press, the rights of the people to assemble and petition for redress of grievances shall not be abridged.

Note this does not reference the rights of non-Osages who may come under Osage jurisdiction.

Some tribes still have codes that restrict or even punish certain expression. For instance, the Defamation Act for the Cheyenne and Arapaho Tribes (16 CAC § 16.100) codifies how to bring civil actions for defamation and invasion of privacy. While the Act allows for punitive damages, there are protections for privileged and true communications. The Act is somewhat similar to state statutes about defamation, as in Title 12, § 1441 *et seq.*, of the Oklahoma Revised Statutes.

One of the largest and most influential tribes in Oklahoma is the Chickasaw Nation, which roughly covers most of south central Oklahoma. It has both implicit and explicit protections in Article IV of its Constitution:

> Nothing in this Constitution shall be interpreted in a way which would change the individual rights and privileges the tribal members have as citizens of the Chickasaw Nation, the State of Oklahoma, and the United States of America. . . .
>
> Every citizen shall be at liberty to speak, write, or publish his opinions on any subject, being responsible for the abuse of that privilege, and no law shall ever be passed curtailing the liberty of speech, or of the press.

The problem, however, is that no explicit waiver of sovereign immunity can be found in any Chickasaw law. This means that no one can sue the Chickasaw government easily, if at all. It is an open legal question as to whether a Chickasaw citizen would have the legal standing to sue the Chickasaw government for violating rights to free press and speech. By contrast, the Choctaw Nation's Council approved the Claims and Immunities Act of the Choctaw Nation of Oklahoma in 2021, which authorizes a limited waiver of sovereign immunity for suits against the tribal government. The Choctaw and Chickasaw Nations are neighbors in southern Oklahoma, as well as cultural and linguistic relatives, so this distinction about sovereign immunity illustrates how one tribe protects certain rights through the courts and one does not.

Some might think that the federal government would guarantee these rights of free expression, as Congress made it clear with plain language in the Indian Civil Rights Act of 1968 (25 USC § 1302) that tribes may not violate freedoms of press or speech:

> No Indian tribe in exercising powers of self-government shall . . . make or enforce any law prohibiting the free exercise of religion, or abridging the freedom of speech, or of the press, or the right of the people peaceably to assemble and to petition for a redress of grievances. . . .

This idea of self-government respects all branches of tribal government:

> "*powers of self-government*" means and includes all governmental powers possessed by an Indian tribe, executive, legislative, and judicial, and all offices, bodies, and tribunals by and through which they are executed, including courts of Indian offenses; and means the inherent power of Indian tribes, hereby recognized and affirmed, to exercise criminal jurisdiction over all Indians. . . .

Again, given this plain language, one might assume that the federal government has the means and intention to enforce all of those provisions. However, the US Supreme Court held ten years later that Congress deliberately chose not to create a mechanism for the federal government to enforce this mandate. In *Santa Clara Pueblo v. Martinez* (436 US 49 [1978]), a tribal member sued under Title 1 of Indian Civil Rights Act 1968 over Santa Clara Pueblo in New Mexico denying her children membership in that federally recognized tribe. By holding that Title 1 did not have an enforcement provision, the court implied two relevant points. First, because they are under Title 1, there is no federal enforcement mechanism for press and speech protections. Second, it is presumed that those claiming their civil rights have been violated must first go to the tribe for some kind of legal remedy. This is consistent with the idea of "powers of self-government," as tribes govern themselves.

This idea of expecting tribes to decide these issues supports larger ideas and ideals about respecting tribal sovereignty. This practically and philosophically means that measuring free press and speech in Indian Country happens at the tribal level. The problems arise when the tribal government either does not enforce its own protections of free speech or press, or simply when it does not have explicit protections. That is the space wherein journalists and other communicators are censored and restrained without any way of legally stopping it.

Consider again the story about the Muscogee (Creek) Nation, which has had enormous publicity around its fight for free press during the twenty-first century. The Muscogee (Creek) Nation repealed the 2015 Free Press Act in November 2018 without debate or public notice, and folded the tribe's independent media into the executive branch's Department of Commerce (Krehbiel-Burton 2018a; Mvskoke Media 2023). In response, Mvskoke Media led the fight for free press: over a dozen news service employees resigned in protest, and the statute guaranteeing press freedom was restored (Caruso 2023; Mintzer 2023). The editorial independence of the tribe's media outlets, including the newspaper, radio show, and weekly TV show, was reinstated when the council reseated the independent three-member editorial board and the tribe's unamended Free Press Act (Krehbiel-Burton 2018b). However, the fight for press freedom continued into the subsequent election cycle for principal chief, and some candidates voiced support for (and others, opposition to) public demand for enshrining a free press statute into the tribe's constitution. The implications of such a fight for press freedom, where governance politics and a lack of independent news media collide, are succinctly summarized as "the perfect illustration of what happens when you dismantle the Fourth and Fifth Estates and wind up putting democracy in peril" (Mintzer 2023).

The Thlopthlocco Tribal Town, which is politically and culturally connected with the Muscogee (Creek) Nation, has the following expression in its Bill of Rights, Article VII, Section 1, in its 1936 Constitution:

> All members of this town shall enjoy without hindrance, freedom of worship, conscience, speech, press, assembly and association.

Note two important issues: 1) this applies to members and not nonmembers, and 2) the phraseology differs somewhat from the words of the First Amendment to the US Constitution.

The Constitution and Bylaws of the Kialegee Tribal Town of Oklahoma, which is also politically and culturally related to the Muscogee (Creek) Nation, include a common provision in Article IX, Section 2:

> This Constitution and Bylaws shall not in any way alter, abridge, or otherwise jeopardize the rights and privileges of the members of this Town as citizens of the State of Oklahoma and the United States.

Those rights include free expression, as guaranteed by Article 2, Section 22, of the Oklahoma Constitution, and the First Amendment to the US Constitution. The Thlopthlocco Tribal Town, in Article VII, Section 2, goes further by also promising not "to alter, abridge or otherwise jeopardize the rights and privileges of the members of this town as citizens of Creek Nation." Therefore, it can be argued that the free press laws of the Muscogee (Creek) Nation also apply to the Thlopthlocco Tribal Town.

When the Indian Reorganization Act was implemented in 1934, tribal entities like the Thlopthlocco Tribal Town and Kialegee Tribal Town were often forced to accept similar language to certain provisions in the US Constitution, including the First Amendment. However, tribes phrase their views about expression in unique ways.

Consider the Constitution of the Cheyenne and Arapaho Tribes of Oklahoma, which is a tribal government that the federal government forced upon two separate tribes and cultures: the Cheyenne and the Arapaho. The preamble expressly embraces the tribes' mandate "to sustain and promote [their] cultures, languages, and way of life." The Chickasaw Nation maintains a council house at the Chickasaw Cultural Center in Sulphur, Oklahoma, which shows how citizens would sit together as clans around a common fire to talk about important national matters. This is a concrete representation of the cultural norm of allowing voices to be heard. It is not correct to think or say that tribes have never protected free expression. In fact, they have protected and practiced it since time immemorial. Anecdotal evidence of tribal censorship of journalists and other media practitioners should never be used as a sweeping generalization, which is a logical fallacy. Tribes and their governments care more about these issues than one might think. Still, more work needs to be done by tribes so that the rights of everyone—Indigenous or not—are protected in the context of the tribal nations.

Conclusion: It Keeps Getting Better

Sovereign tribes, in responsible ways, can and do protect the free expression and communication desired by so many in Indian Country. In Oklahoma, there are laws for almost every tribe that can be used to build an argument in court for free expression that protects the media and other communicators. Similar research involving other tribes across the United States needs to be carried out and published. But there still are far too many hurdles, even for tribes with constitutional protections in place. Judges are often appointed by those tribal executives who may censor the press; such judges may not feel free to decide for the press and against the ones who appointed them. Some tribes, like the Chickasaw Nation, refuse to waive sovereign immunity, meaning that it is impractical and perhaps impossible to sue to enforce constitutional provisions. Other tribes, like the Osage, Cherokee, and Muscogee (Creek) Nations, had to pass press laws to support any constitutional protections.

This is not a zero-sum game whereby free expression is either entirely free or entirely nonexistent, which means that more protections exist than are known. The decision for each person wanting to express freely in Indian Country is to know the laws, respect the sovereignty of the tribe, and do what is best for everyone, especially tribal citizens. Indigenous journalists have been practicing free expression for years, despite some obstacles. However, tribes would be more responsible neighbors if they included more specific language that extended and applied their protections to nonmembers, too.

Still, the bottom line is that there are more tribal laws protecting free expression than the casual observer might think. The less someone knows about a tribe, its laws, and its culture, the more likely they are to misunderstand free expression protections for that tribe. More work needs to be done, and that work primarily belongs to the tribes themselves as sovereign nations.

Discussion Questions

1. In what ways do the tribes in Oklahoma protect freedom of expression for tribal citizens? For others?
2. What are some of the ongoing challenges to protecting freedom of expression for Indigenous citizens in Oklahoma?
3. How does Indigenous Standpoint Theory support the practice of free expression for citizens and journalists?
4. Which tribes offer the most protection for freedom of expression? How do they serve as a model for other tribes seeking to codify greater protections for freedom of expression for their citizens?
5. How can any Indigenous tribe anywhere in North America apply these principles to its own sovereignty and situation regarding free expression?

Notes

1. Kevin R. Kemper is a licensed attorney in state, federal, and numerous tribal courts in Oklahoma, and nothing in this chapter is legal advice or creates a attorney–client relationship.

2. Spellings vary in the text—Muscogee, Muskogee, and Mvskoke—to reflect differences in historical usage.

8

"If You're Not at the Table, You're Probably Part of the Menu"

Interview with Paul DeMain

Paul DeMain (Skabewis) is a citizen of the Oneida Nation of Wisconsin and the Bear Clan, and of Ojibwe descent. He lives near Hayward, Wisconsin on the Lac Courte Oreilles Ojibway Reservation, and he summers on Madeline Island, the historic capital of the Ojibwe Nation. He is the former and now retired editor of *News from Indian Country* and the *Ojibwe Akiing*, and he has produced video programming for IndianCountryTV.com and FNX cable news. DeMain was also a past president of the Native American Journalists Association, UNITY Coalition of Journalists of Color, and the Navajo Times Publishing Company.

Please introduce yourself.

My English name is Paul DeMain. My friends and relatives in my Indigenous community call me Skabewis, which essentially translates to "the messenger," a shorter version of the name Oshkabewis—a title in the Medicine Lodge and in ceremonial activities. Old man Pipe Mustache gave me that name, and he said, "We gave you that name so you couldn't get away from it."

I'm a citizen of the Oneida Nation of Wisconsin and I'm of Ojibwe descent, with relatives at Red Lake, Grand Portage, and pretty much all the reservations in the Great Lakes region because of some Scottish explorers from the Clan Morrison. I am a member of the Bear Clan and so I try to work within the confines of what Bear Clan members are also supposed to know.

Describe your work. What compels you to do it?

My journalism teacher asked what I was going to do when I graduated from high school. I said, "I'm going to own my own newspaper someday."

Fig. 8.1. Paul DeMain. Author photo.

And I did. What was interesting to me was engaging with people and learning from them. I wanted to tell the story of Indigenous people.

I wanted to write more about American Indians. I refined my skills as best I could, went to LCO [Lac Courte Oreilles], and got asked to start their tribal newspaper, the *Lac Courte Oreilles Journal American.* Within three months of becoming editor of the newspaper, I decided we ought to drop that "American." I dropped it. The tribal chair saw me in a bar and he said, "You're fired. You didn't ask me if you could change the name." I said I didn't know I needed the chair's permission to change the name of the newspaper.

I had a day where I saw that the FBI had arrived at the tribal office and they were loading files from the accounting department into a van. I was peeking out another tribal office window and I was going, "Oh my god, there's a raid!" The chair came back and said, "I want you to write a news release." I was both public information officer and news editor. I wrote a faxed news release denying that the FBI was there raiding the tribal government office. I wrote, "according to Rick Baker, he's denying that the FBI is blah blah" and sent it out. Then I wrote another one: "Federal Bureau of Investigation is at the LCO Tribal Office loading accounting files." I signed it as LCO Journal Editor and sent another press release out. I didn't get fired that time, because that [what I wrote] was the truth.

The *Lac Courte Oreilles Journal* turned into *News from Indian Country* around 1982, just before I took some time off for another job. I had also started the Great Lakes Indian News Bureau, a private business, in part because I was tired of being fired or feeling like I was going to be fired from the tribal editor's job. I started that freelance writing service compiling information from the Great Lakes states and reselling it, and writing stories for several different newspapers in the Great Lakes region and a few other larger publications—even a magazine called *Nations* that lasted a couple of issues.

That was 1986. I went back to the LCO reservation, and the *LCO Journal* was being operated out of the tribe's radio station, WOJB-88.9 FM, which made news-gathering sense. But the radio station didn't want to be responsible for publishing a newspaper that had in the past exposed wrongdoing by local elected tribal officials; they were thinking about putting it to bed. We made a bid on the newspaper and that was the beginning of *News from Indian Country*.

I said I wanted to own a newspaper someday. I did, and I wanted it to be editorially independent of tribal governments, and we were. We covered a lot of stories, and some tribal elected officials we covered were jailed for crimes committed. We need to look for those traditional principles to provide the community with a truthful, transparent review of what their governments are doing.

What does Indigenous media mean to you?

Indigenous media to me includes asking questions in places that you can't fear. We need to cover the Missing and Murdered Indigenous Women crisis, and also the responsibilities we have in our own community around those unsolved murders, and we need to hold officials accountable for investigating them.

There are tons of issues and stories in every community. There's no way any one person, one publication, one entity could cover even part of what's going on in our Indigenous communities. I see media as covering all these things in terms of talking, speaking, ledger work, birch bark scrolls, wampum strings, and petroglyphs that allow people to recite history by remembering certain major events, the winter count on the teepees.

We started *News from Indian Country* with a regional approach, but we wanted it to be something that served a much broader community as we watched it grow. At one point we had subscribers in all fifty states, ten Canadian provinces, and twenty-seven foreign countries. We found out that there are American Indians all over the world and they are hungry for Indian Country news.

Why is it important for Indigenous people to tell their own stories?

Partly because when you tell a story in front of a camera and they take it back to cut it up, it ends up being: "The Indians sing pretty. The Indians dance pretty. The Indians are upset about this. The Indians want to do that, and it's going to stop these jobs, and it's going to stop this development, et cetera." You have editors who may not understand the full story. We really need to tell our own story from front to back.

It's important that we have a voice. If you're not at the table, you're probably part of the menu, and so we need to be there to be able to defend ourselves and correct people with misperceptions, even kind people with misperceptions about history. They tell you that Christopher Columbus discovered America in 1492, and that this is the date "Indians" came across the Bering Strait, and then science destroys it. Scientists push that theory back, and you find out that Christopher Columbus was lost and, thank God, he wasn't looking for Turkey!

Our responsibility as journalists, in addition to telling the truth, is to challenge the community. The earth is a lot dirtier. The earth is out of balance. If I were to give advice to people in the media and communications, it's to keep building awareness.

Instead of asking, "Is there anything else you would like to add?" I would like to ask you to talk about your chapter on sovereignty in the first edition of this book.

There's got to be responsible use of sovereignty. The definition of sovereignty in some areas sometimes bothers me. You have the right to sell untaxed cigarettes, cheap cigarettes on the reservation. You have a right to engage in gambling. You have a right, because you're sovereign, to charge 300 percent or more on a short-term payday loan, bankrupt people, and take the money.

The LCO Community College said, because of educational sovereignty, they had a right to sponsor a charter school in Waukesha County, hundreds of miles from the reservation, the reddest county in the State of Wisconsin, to charter a curriculum that's devoid of Indigenous history. In other words, they want to avoid discussing the genocide of Native peoples by settlers, so they choose to leave out Indigenous history altogether. On the other hand, the exercising of that sovereignty means that we have a right to clean resources, and we protect those rights through hunting and fishing taxation, licenses, and monitoring those resources. We don't want polluting entities like sulfur-based mines and oil lines running through our pristine watersheds, because we know it's not a matter of will it leak, but *when* will it leak?

I was sitting next to Archie Mosey out in the woods at a Midewiwin lodge dance recess one day. He was in his nineties. I said, "Man, there's days when I wake up and just barely have any hope. You got hope for the future?" He said, "*Gaween*" (no). He said, "Wait a minute. I got to change that because I went there in a vision (during a fast)." He said he was watching things after the next flood: "I was floating up above the earth and looking down and thinking it is so beautiful, so peaceful. The rivers are so blue, the birds are all around the forest in music, leaves are colorful." He continued, "I have hope for the earth. But what I didn't see . . . I didn't see any human beings below; I saw there was no human beings. After I was thinking about that, I thought, *Geez! There is hope for the earth. It's going to be beautiful again after the next flood, but I don't know if man himself is going to make it. They've had their chance.*"

Miigwetch.

—Interviewed by Cristina L. Azocar

9

The News Media and the Indian Child Welfare Act

Nancy Marie Spears

"At the risk of stating the obvious, Indian commerce is hard to maintain if there are no Indian communities left to do commerce with," wrote Justice Neil Gorsuch. He had just finished a sweeping, first-of-its-kind statement in the US Supreme Court majority opinion on July 15, 2023, outlining the history of Indigenous boarding schools and why that history makes it even more important to uphold the law in question in the *Brackeen v. Haaland* case: the Indian Child Welfare Act (ICWA).

Some may view this ruling and the justice's statements as positive signs of improvement in our judicial system. However, the question remains: What does the decision mean for media literacy, and for journalists and scholars who monitor and seek to improve our country's information ecology? Legal challenges, artificial intelligence, and numerous disinformation campaigns constantly attack this tentative balance.

This chapter seeks to educate journalists, scholars, and media consumers on the history of the ICWA—a federal law governing states' involvement in tribal child welfare cases—including why the ICWA became law, and the media's role in its public perception, success in court, and level of public importance. This is also an investigation of the compounding factors in the media landscape that I believe may result in or contribute to the inadequate coverage of Indigenous child welfare in mainstream media. Congress passed the ICWA in 1978. Scholars may be aware of what caused the need for the law; journalists may or may not know that history. However, one thing is certain: the ICWA is usually not consistently represented in mainstream coverage.

The most recent—and, for the first time, unsuccessful—challenge to the ICWA in the US Supreme Court is the *Brackeen v. Haaland* case. Before this, the most recent challenge to the law was in 2013 and was known as *Adoptive Couple v. Baby Girl*. A comparison of these cases has two intentions: 1) to explain what is known and what is "fair" in tribal child welfare spaces, and the effects of colonization on social problems and Indigenous child welfare generally; and 2) to remind media consumers of the ever-growing need for self-awareness.

To give context to this research, I am an enrolled citizen of the Cherokee Nation of Oklahoma, who was born and raised in the state to which my family was forcibly removed. In addition to being part of one of the nation's largest tribes, I work full time for the only nonprofit news outlet in the country that focuses on child welfare and youth justice. To my knowledge, I am the only enrolled Indigenous person on the staff of my national newsroom; I am also one of the youngest. I cover Indigenous children and families, with a focus on both the ICWA and the boarding school era. I write about many topics, including tribal child welfare best practices and how Indigenous communities are healing from state child welfare systems.

In recent years, I have seen a movement across Indigenous media coverage by Indigenous-owned, local, and mainstream outlets. I call it the "WASH" movement—an influx of messages about Indigenous peoples that say, "We are still here." These increasingly positive (and more importantly, factually accurate) narratives in media coverage surrounding Indigenous peoples and issues complement narratives where Indigenous voices are not invisible.

Amid the WASH movement of improved Indigenous narratives in the media, journalists still contend with the idea of "whitewashing"—no pun intended—in some areas of coverage. My "Indigenized" framework uses a journalistic, and indeed feminist, lens to outline how media literacy must improve in child welfare coverage so Indigenous nations can uphold and protect their sovereignty and their legal and moral right to care for their children.

There are three pillars to this framework. First and foremost, media literacy approaches must center on the needs of Indigenous people because of their disproportionate representation in the child protection and juvenile justice systems (Fable 2021). This is especially true for coverage documenting lived experiences of Indigenous women and children, who have historically been viewed under a "white savior" umbrella of shame—something that comes up over and over again in child welfare proceedings (Selleck et al. 2023; Eveleigh 2023). It is necessary to look at child-rearing through an Indigenous feminist lens in order to authentically report on Indigenous families and their chances at reunification through the ICWA or other tribal-traditional methods, like customary adoptions (Lindschouw 2024).

Second, the media—whether it be television, advertising commercials, or written news coverage—has long been a driving force behind the fetishization of Indigenous women, girls, and LGBTQ+ people (Elliott 2016; Morton 2018). This is additionally concerning when discussing the mainstream coverage of Missing and Murdered topics, which again consistently boxes women into orientations of vulnerability or violence, including often forcing Indigenous women and children into erotic and pornographic contexts (Mackay 2020; Vogel 2022). Using a media literacy approach to understand why Missing and Murdered Indigenous People has not made it into the national news landscape as a child welfare concern is a glaringly missed opportunity in both journalistic and scholarly work.

Third, very little mainstream media coverage focuses on the Indigenous father in child welfare cases—at least, none that I have seen. There is a deep need for resource awareness in media literacy as it relates to all individuals in an Indigenous family unit. The intense focus only on what mothers need negates the lived experience and the importance of Indigenous fathers and male figures in children's lives.

It is of great importance that journalists and scholars remain wary of these three pillars and what they represent for the larger colonizing projects against Indian Country. Recall that the news media of the colonial-settler days would run ads in the paper promoting forcibly taking Native lands, and it has perpetuated racist stereotypes for sports mascots. The history of the ICWA and its mainstream coverage underscores a particularly nuanced type of perceptual violence waged against tribal people by the media. Such perceptual violence supports the idea that Native people are unfit to raise their children and handle their own legal affairs when it comes to foster care, guardianship, and adoption. The ICWA should profoundly concern anyone who cares about children and consumes, produces, or studies the media.

History of the ICWA: Boarding Schools and Child-Rearing

It is difficult, in terms of both research and practicality, to pinpoint the exact date when the concept of child welfare began to affect the livelihoods and safety of tribes and their languages, cultures, and lands. How does one begin to detail the history of hundreds of nations of people who all pre-dated the founding and formation of the United States?

The easiest place to start is with a lesser-known fact about American history. Technically, the United States' longest war was not the conflict in Afghanistan or World War I or II; it was the Indian Wars: 313 years of decimation between the seventeenth and twentieth centuries (Meuers 2021), all over became the United States. These conflicts started and were sustained mainly over land control, but they grew to have a very different goal: assimilation. Eventually, President James Monroe realized it would be financially cheaper to stop fighting with Native peoples and begin assimilating them into white, Christian society. "President Monroe believed that if the Native American population were to have access to education, it would prepare them for successful assimilation into white society. Many of the societies that were involved with the assimilation efforts were often Christian missionaries" (Lcrawfor 2022). This period of religious outreach is what scholars and journalists should consider to be the historical starting point for the trackable patterns of the Western concept of child welfare against Indigenous peoples that culminated in policies meant to "civilize" them, like the Indian Civilization Fund Act of 1819 and the Indian Removal Act of 1830 (Nesterak 2019). Imagine enduring three centuries of war only to discover that, by 1926, nearly 83 percent of children across the remaining Native communities were forced to attend boarding schools (National Native American Boarding School Healing Coalition 2019). What did the children and their families miss?

Two key federal policies enacted during the Indian Wars were key to initiating and successfully sustaining the American Indian boarding school movement. The systematic removal of children began with the Indian Civilization Fund Act of 1819 and the Peace Policy of 1869, according to the National Native American Boarding School Healing Coalition. Then, in the late nineteenth century, with the establishment of the Carlisle Industrial School in 1879, the United States, in partnership with several denominations of the Christian church, also formally adopted an American Indian boarding school policy to support "Indian education," to solve the "Indian problem," as federal officials called it, by stripping culture from American Indian and Alaska Native children.

Many scholars may be aware of how the ICWA's federal statute identifies "Indian" children as "wards" of states or tribes if the custody proceeding is appropriately transferred to a tribal court. What may not be as well understood is that this is the same concept—and nearly the same language—used in the federal assimilative policies of the church and federal government when Congress began and sustained its various boarding school and assimilation policies (National Native American Boarding School Healing Coalition 2019; Nesterak 2019). Congress began categorizing the students it was housing as "delinquent independents" in order to receive treaty and trust funds from the federal government to operate the schools both on and off the reservation. There is significant connective tissue that tethers the Western world's nuclear family view of child welfare to the ways it perpetuated its forced assimilation policies against the First Peoples of this country. Historically, the family unit in tribal communities includes "extended" members beyond the typical nuclear family. This arrangement might consist of a family structure with more communal child-rearing practices, which are often matriarchal, in direct contrast with the patriarchal worldview of Western culture (Bucko 2006; Spring 2012). Particularly in the Choctaw Nation, the boarding schools consciously worked to change gender roles to transform the Choctaws from a matrilineal clan system to a patrilineal nuclear family, suggesting that the boarding school era influenced the shifting dynamics in determining what exactly comprises and controls an Indigenous family (Byers 2010).

It is essential to frame the boarding school issue in its global context. This is not an issue of a distant and historical past, and neither is it solely a Native American (Pannett 2021) or a First Nations issue (OHCHR 2023). Instead, it is an issue of textbook colonization, terrorism, and control. Indigenous communities in Canada, New Zealand, and Australia have continued to grapple with the same experience and the long-term implications for child welfare policy and practice in those countries (Engel et al. 2012). How can one group of people effectively bring another group to their knees and keep them under-resourced and constantly struggling with social challenges? Separate them from their children. Colonial control relies on separating children from their birth families, and the loss of children is defined as genocide, according to the United Nations Convention on the Prevention and Punishment of the Crime of Genocide, which states that "forcibly transferring children of a group to another group" is one of many acts that constitute genocide (United Nations Genocide Convention 1948). Another method, as seen in the case of *Brackeen v. Haaland* and *Adoptive Couple v. Baby Girl*, is to start chipping away at the tribe's legal rights to raise them (Spears 2023a).

Tribes went from the horrors of the boarding school era in the 1800s to the 1960s—which, according to the Department of the Interior's volume for its first ever investigation into the government's policies, included "rampant physical, sexual, and emotional abuse; disease; malnourishment; overcrowding; and lack of health care" (Federal Indian Boarding School Initiative Investigative Report 2022)—to an even more blatant weaponization of child welfare best practices, when the federal government passed the Indian Adoption Project. The Indian Adoption Project was a federal effort in conjunction with the Bureau of Indian

Administration (now known as the Bureau of Indian Affairs) and the Child Welfare League of America. These entities created an alliance between 1958 and 1967 to exact policies that prioritized and financially incentivized the removal of Native children from their tribal homelands and kin by white and often Christian people. A report from the Bureau of Indian Affairs released in April 1967 states: "Since the Indian Adoption Project began in 1958, there have been 276 Indian children placed, the great majority in non-Indian homes" (Bureau of Indian Affairs 1967). In the eleventh hour of the 95th Congress on October 24, 1978, the ICWA was passed, despite monumental opposition from entities including the Bureau of Indian Affairs.

Indigenous media scholar Cristina Azocar's work cites IST—a term popularized in 2003 and 2006 by Dennis Lance Gordon Foley of the University of Canberra—which supports the idea that everything is connected, and hinges around the central idea that Indigenous researchers are best positioned to research Indigenous people (Foley 2006). It is difficult to claim to an Indigenous woman that this is anything but true. As my journalistic work demonstrates, acknowledging generational trauma is imperative to providing ethical coverage of Indigenous communities and their child welfare needs. Moreover, as Azocar said in an interview about IST, "To understand truth for Indigenous communities . . . means [having] awareness of who has written history to this date and what rights are afforded to whom and by whom under what condition (e.g., broken treaties). For those not used to IST, it may seem that going back to past historical points is not needed or not connected to our research questions, but it is" (Biswas 2022).

I believe that there is a connection between the ability of mainstream media to cover Indigenous women and children ethically, and the nonexistent coverage of Indigenous child-rearing practices—which cuts to the heart of why the ICWA is so generationally important. Media literacy requires many things from the consumer, including being aware of previous perpetuations of stereotypes by the media and considering how they may influence coverage in other areas. Such is the case for Indigenous women's coverage and the intersection with child welfare coverage.

One scholarly work found that boarding schools have had a generational effect on child-rearing practices. Researcher Rosalyn Ing (1990, ii) wrote that boarding schools:

> caused psychological and cultural losses in self-esteem, child-rearing patterns, and Native Indian language. New and different behaviors had to be learned by the children in middle childhood to cope and exist in a parentless

> environment where no feelings of love or care were demonstrated by the caretakers and the speaking of Cree and other Native languages was forbidden. . . . These experiences will presumably be transmitted in some form to the next generation, thereby affecting the way Natives view themselves.

The amount of research about this has increased in recent years. Jihan Gearon stated that Indigenous feminism is fundamentally about generational decolonization. "However, patriarchy isn't just entwined with the systems of colonization, white supremacy, and capitalism. Colonization, white supremacy, and capitalism need patriarchy to work" (Gearon 2021). Additionally, in traditional Aboriginal communities, researchers found that historical and intergenerational trauma inflicted by boarding schools affected the quality of parenting of those who had attended them (Muir and Bohr 2019), and the boarding school era also contributed to the disruption of traditional child-rearing practices that damaged their ability to parent (Child 2018).

Myths and misconceptions abound regarding the framing that media uses around Indigenous mothers' and fathers' ability to parent safely. Often in child welfare proceedings—like the Adoptive Couple and Brackeen cases—the arguments for taking Indigenous children into non-Indigenous homes are couched in ideas of financial or housing stability, according to the numerous *amicus* briefs, oral arguments, and hearings from both Supreme Court cases. Chippewa grandmother Robyn Bradshaw, a defendant in *Brackeen v. Haaland*, was almost barred from obtaining full custody of her granddaughter because of a decades-old criminal charge, which had been expunged (Spears 2022).

In 2021, a study demonstrated that there are often negative clichés and stereotypes in thought processes surrounding how Indigenous parents operate (McKinley et al. 2021). Using a strengths-based framework known as the "Framework of Historical Oppression, Resilience, and Transcendence," the researchers looked at data from 436 members of two Indigenous tribes in the southeast. They uncovered the following themes in Indigenous child-rearing mindsets: 1) "'Your Kids Come First': Prioritizing Children's Needs," 2) "'They Should Enjoy their Childhood': Sheltering Children from Family Stressors," 3) "'I Have to Watch Them Closely': Closely Monitoring Children," and 4) "'There's No Drinking at My House': Preventing Children's Exposure to Substance Abuse." These results demonstrate that Indigenous parents are indeed child-centric and "protect their children from the potentially harmful environments created through historical oppression" (McKinley et al. 2021, 2952).

Post-1978: What Does Indigenous Child Welfare Look Like Now?

Having such varied and conflicting levels of government oversight in things like education funds, healthcare resources, land and water management, and, yes, child welfare law means that tribes are not truly exercising their rightful sovereignty over these issues. Because of this, some advocates believe the ICWA has been less effective than it could have been due to a lack of state compliance and social worker bias.

As of July 2024, sixteen more states (Turtle Talk 2024) have their own codifications of the federal ICWA statute than did at the time of the ICWA's inception. This trend took off especially recently, as the nation witnessed the Supreme Court's historic decision in the latest constitutional challenge, *Brackeen v. Haaland.* Beginning in 2018, at the start of the Brackeen case, a flurry of state ICWA laws were passed in preparation for the potential upending of the law. However, since then, little data has been collected around compliance with the law showing efficacy in keeping Indigenous families together. States are not required—though they are encouraged—to maintain data on ICWA case compliance and outcomes (Fort and Smith 2023). Recall that 25–35 percent of Indigenous children were put in state custody prior to the ICWA's enactment, and Native children are still three times more likely than their non-Native peers to be put into foster care or out-of-home placements, despite the legal protections that the ICWA is supposed to provide (National Indian Child Welfare Association 2018). So, regardless of the existence of the ICWA, Indigenous children are one of the most overrepresented groups in social services investigation, intervention, and removal.

A 2023 study found that 87 percent of ICWA-based appeals came from an Indigenous parent, and 40 percent of all such cases were sent back to lower courts or reversed. "These data indicate that agencies and courts are still struggling with the first step in an ICWA case—whether they have an ICWA case at all" (Fort and Smith 2023).

ICWA Coverage Comparisons and the Intersectional Erasure of Missing and Murdered Indigenous Women (MMIW) and Fatherhood

Although many states have folded the federal ICWA into their child welfare codes, some are giving mixed signals about their commitment to the ICWA's values. Unlike the Adoptive Couple case, the Brackeen case is significant because it was the first time multiple states requested that the

Supreme Court review the law. The *Adoptive Couple v. Baby Girl* case, which was decided by the nation's highest court in 2013, and the *Brackeen v. Haaland* case, which began in 2018 and was upheld in favor of the ICWA in 2023, are the focus of this analysis. How the media covered the 2013 case, and how that coverage affected the outcome, reveals what we as scholars, journalists, and media consumers can learn from the more recent challenge.

The way the media covers topics can influence the public's perception in areas such as federal recognition, which is an important factor in Indian child welfare. Tribes that are federally recognized can access federal and state dollars in order to operate independent child welfare programs in their tribally specific community. Only fourteen of today's 575 recognized tribes can access Title IV-E funds, the largest pot of federal funds to go toward child welfare needs. Only 150 tribes outside that provision can access Title IV-B funds, a smaller and less flexible set of funds. All other tribes—even if they are federally recognized—are unable to operate their own child welfare system. This provision means it is practically impossible for a nonrecognized tribe to have the sovereign ability to keep their children within their families, because of the lack of funding and the high costs of conducting social services in tribal and remote areas around the country.

Azocar (2022) notes the problematic concept of blood quantum—the amount of "Indian blood" in one's body that, among some tribes, determines if you are eligible for citizenship—and the irony that it is someone other than an Indigenous person who gets to decide who is and is not, for lack of a better phrase, "Indigenous enough." The same goes for determining a child's eligibility for the ICWA in state courts; as we have seen in the number of ICWA cases that have made it to the Supreme Court alone, this is often decided by someone other than the tribe. A key example is how blood quantum affected the Adoptive Couple case. Prior to the 2013 ruling, mainstream media displayed an apparent obsession with baby Veronica's "blood quantum"; the term was mentioned four times in the Supreme Court decision, and consistently false assertions were made that Veronica was three-256ths Cherokee even though her father was one-eighth—which would have made her one-sixteenth—and the Cherokee Nation itself does not even require a degree of blood quantum to enroll its citizens (Indianz.com 2013). The level of speculation by the media as to the child's Indigeneity had a noticeable impact on how both the general public and the justices of the Supreme Court perceived the case. Justice Samuel Alito wrote for the majority of five justices who sided with the white adoptive couple. The opinion's first sentence was that Veronica "is classified as an Indian because she is 1.2 percent (3/256) Cherokee." Alito then rejected the lower court's interpretation of the ICWA that sided with Veronica's biological family, stating that not allowing the adoptive couple, the Capabianocos, to adopt would discourage non-Native adoptive couples and keep the Indigenous child out of "a permanent and loving home" (Supreme Court of the United States 2013).

Missing and Murdered Indigenous Women

"Modern colonialism has evolved from outright barbary to more covert forms of violence which are exacerbated by extractive capitalism, structural racism, and fetishization of Indigenous bodies in mainstream media" (Heckes 2021). More Indigenous peoples, and particularly Indigenous women, are reported missing and murdered than any other demographic. For years, scholars and some government agencies agreed the epidemic was urgent; however, US-based coverage did not start to take off until a series of successful campaigns by activists on social media that used hashtags like #MMIW, #NoMoreStolenSisters, and #RedDressDay. Scholars have coined the term "Pocahontas paradox" to explain "the underlying frameworks" that create and contribute to the fetishization of Indigenous women. The paradox, in essence, places Indigenous women into one of two boxes: either powerful, dangerous, and strong, or beautiful and lustful. "The duality which presents itself within these identities, causes a false depiction of Indigenous women, thus causing fetishization. . . . The fetishization of Indigenous women could also be a potential contributing factor to the MMIW crisis" (Vogel 2022, 10).

The literature is far scarcer when determining the needs of Indigenous fathers from a media literacy approach. According to 2022 research, "It is in the best interests of children if men are proactively supported in their transition to fatherhood as early as possible to promote a positive impact on their children's development and future wellbeing" (Wright et al. 2022). We as a society need not only more resource awareness around Indigenous peoples generally, but to better advocate for all women and all men, biological or not. To fail to include Indigenous fathers and Two Spirit people as parents is to fail to address the inconsistencies in how the media portrays our communities and how we view and portray ourselves.

The media strategies involved in covering Indian child welfare cases seem to be ethically ambiguous at best and damaging to Indian families at worst, according to another study looking at media coverage of the

Adoptive Couple case: “Like abusive procedural practices, abusive media strategies are difficult to remedy. No attorney has ever been sanctioned or disciplined for revealing confidential information about Indian children. Because it is so effective, it will continue to occur” (Fletcher 2022, 1795).

Analysis of the Most Recent ICWA US Supreme Court Ruling and New Challenges

Thankfully, the media landscape and information ecology around the ICWA have improved. There is undoubtedly more fair and pro-tribe coverage of the law and its newest constitutional challenges, as well as a marked increase in the number of Indigenous journalists who have been empowered to cover the most recent case. Further, more non-Native outlets are beginning to see Indigenous affairs as a priority in the new legal landscape, as opposed to an afterthought or something not to be considered at all. *The Imprint*, the only national nonprofit news outlet in the United States covering child welfare and youth justice, launched a first-of-its-kind full-time reporting position emphasizing coverage of the ICWA and Indigenous child welfare (Fostering Media Connections 2022). Media as a whole seems to want to shine a slightly stronger spotlight on the attacks on tribal sovereignty, especially in child welfare spaces.

Another important distinction between the circumstances around the Adoptive Couple case and the Brackeen case lies in the makeup of the Supreme Court itself. The Supreme Court's appointments have changed significantly since 2013. At that time, Ruth Bader Ginsburg was still alive and had been appointed by the Democratic Barack Obama administration, which also appointed Justices Stephen Breyer, Sonia Sotomayor, and Elena Kagan. But the court is purple no longer. The Donald Trump administration responded in earnest, stacking the Supreme Court with conservative, right-wing idealogues of justice. Neil Gorsuch, Amy Coney Barrett, and Brett Kavanaugh are all Republicans with little to no experience or background in federal Indian law or child welfare law. They miraculously decided in favor of the ICWA, even though three of the nine justices are Catholic or international adoptive parents. Chief Justice John Roberts already has a history of dissenting from the ICWA, as seen in his statements in the Adoptive Couple case decision (Supreme Court of the United States 2013).

While I am not a legal scholar, the heart of my coverage lies in understanding the ICWA and how it is designed to uphold tribal sovereignty. I come to this analysis of the *Brackeen v. Haaland* Supreme Court decision with years of ICWA coverage under my belt, along with multiple public and global speaking opportunities educating the public, and my other work. My analysis of the Brackeen decision is three-fold: 1) yes, the door has been firmly shut, or so it seems, on various arguments against the ICWA; 2) no, that does not mean opportunities to chip away at the law do not still exist; and 3) just because the specific justices in the majority may be surprising does not mean there is a solid line of judicial defense for the law's intentions.

In this case, the plaintiffs' constitutional challenges to the law were myriad. Ultimately, they unsuccessfully argued that the ICWA is unconstitutional because Congress did not have the authority to enact the ICWA in 1978, or to continue to enforce it forty-five years later, because it "commandeers" states to adhere to federal law, and because it violates equal protection due to the ICWA's alleged "race-based" nature. The law was meant to prevent erroneous removals of Indigenous children from Indigenous homes—a key colonizing tactic in the boarding school and Indian adoption eras—but allegedly created unfair legal obstacles for white families to adopt Indigenous children, according to the plaintiffs.

In a methodically laid-out decision that surprised many (Spears 2023b), the justices rejected each argument by a 7–2 ruling and upheld the ICWA in its entirety. The court fully rejected most of the plaintiffs' challenges and made clear that they lacked standing in several instances to bring those challenges.

However, what is key to note is the questions the court answered: the challenge about plenary powers and commandeering were both rejected with a full explanation. The most dangerous question—the one regarding the "race-based" nature of the ICWA's placement preferences—was left hanging by the justices. They did not issue an opinion on whether the ICWA violated the equal protection rights of the white adoptive couples, as the majority outlined the parties' lack of standing as grounds for dismissal without a ruling.

Justice Kavanaugh, whom experts typically view as the "wild card," flipped and ultimately sided with the majority of justices to uphold the ICWA. However, he did this with the caveat that, should another defendant come up with better grounds for what they were attempting to do, he would be interested in re-examining the case (Supreme Court of the United States 2023). "Under the Act, a child in foster care or adoption proceedings may in some cases be denied a particular placement because of the child's race—even if the placement is otherwise determined to be in the child's best interests," Kavanaugh wrote, adding that the race-based scenario would be the same for a prospective foster or adoptive parent. "Those scenarios raise significant questions under bedrock equal protection principles and this Court's precedents."

The two dissenting justices, Samuel Alito and Clarence Thomas, wholly disagreed with the majority's defense of the ICWA as being within the "plenary powers" of Congressional authority, which they said should be limited to the issue of commerce. To make clear the ongoing desire to dismantle the law, the Arizona-based conservative think tank Goldwater Institute stated, "It is at least gratifying that the Court left open the door to future lawsuits challenging the race-based injustices caused by ICWA" (Spears 2023b).

Suppose these statements by anti-ICWA proponents are not prominent enough to delineate just how committed certain folks are to striking down the law. In that case, some judicial activity in areas outside the nation's highest court may be more convincing. Opportunities for chipping away linger—for example, in multiple state-level supreme courts, essential aspects of the ICWA are being questioned. When the Brackeen decision came down, there was a flurry of coverage from all major outlets, then radio silence the following week when it was determined that there were no more threats to the ICWA and everyone should go home happy. That is not the case, as my coverage—and only my coverage—can show. Even though the Brackeen decision firmly rejected certain arguments, state-level challenges continue to move through lower courts across the country with "varying degrees of success" (Spears 2023c). I've more recently reported on another unsuccessful constitutional challenge to ICWA in Minnesota's Supreme Court, for example.

Ultimately, understanding the legal, political, and assimilative histories of the ICWA will prove critical as journalists and scholars continue to follow constitutional challenges to and state-level appeals of the law. Communication and education disciplines—all intersectional in journalism and scholarship—will only benefit by acquiring a more in-depth knowledge of the ICWA. These professions must provide better awareness of the effects of the colonizing history that led to the ICWA's enactment and the effects it continues to have on parents across Indian Country. To begin to address this, media consumers, as well as scholars and journalists, must acknowledge and make clear in their work the ways that child welfare services as a system originally existed to suppress Indigenous cultures and oppress Indigenous families. This trauma from child protective services and the assimilative intentions of erasure by the media continue in the present day.

Discussion Questions

1. Regarding the media narrative movement that the author coined "WASH" or "We are still here," what are other areas

of media coverage where students see this increased messaging? Why do students think that is, especially in non-Native communities?

2. In coverage of all types of Indigenous peoples—for example, from foreign countries, or those indigenous to certain regions in the states, including rural and urban Natives—what are the harms of whitewashing national stories or "othering" groups in any way when it comes to media practices?
3. Why is the inclusion of legal precedence important to national or local news stories related to legislation generally (not necessarily just the ICWA) and/or systems-involved policy and practice? This includes the incarceration, juvenile justice and child protection, healthcare, and law systems, and other areas of society where marginalized groups may be overrepresented in the systems but underrepresented in media coverage of those systems.

10

"We're Getting More of Our Stories out from That Native Perspective"

Interview with Patty Talahongva

Patty Talahongva is a journalist with more than forty-five years of experience covering the news. She is Hopi and comes from the Corn Clan. Her Hopi name is White Spider. Patty was the first Native American to anchor a national news program; *Village America* aired on PBS stations nationwide from 2000 to 2004. She's also produced for CBS News. Patty has served in leadership roles at *Native America Calling, National Native News*, and *Indian Country Today.* She is a past president of the Native American Journalists Association and won its Medill Milestone Achievement Award in 2016. Her story "Alaska's Vanishing Native Villages" aired in 2025 on the PBS program *Frontline.*

Please introduce yourself.

I'm Patty Talahongva and I'm Hopi from First Mesa, specifically the villages of Walpi and Sitstomovi. I've been a journalist since I was fifteen.

Describe your work. What compels you to do it?

I got my first job as a journalist when I was attending the Phoenix Indian School and I became a reporter for the *Teen Gazette*. I was a correspondent from my high school and I wrote about things that were happening at Phoenix Indian. The *Teen Gazette* had never had a correspondent from Phoenix Indian before. It was great because we got paid. So, I started out in print.

I transferred to Flagstaff High School for my senior year and got my first job in television news at the local station. I wasn't covering Indian Country per se, we were covering the local news, but I saw how our local news could influence the national news.

Fig. 10.1. Patty Talahongva. Author photo.

I went to work for a CBS affiliate in Phoenix—the letters were KOOL, and they would answer the phone, "It's KOOL in Phoenix." There I was asked to cover stories on the reservations, so that's when I started bringing news crews out to the reservations. I covered a couple of tribal elections. The station would put you on their private plane and fly you up to the assignment. There's no driving five or six hours to get to the rez!

I got to cover our tribal election when Hopi first voted on whether to go into Indian gaming. It was my day off and I was packing up my little baby and preparing to do a nine-hour day of driving, literally to drive up to the rez and vote and then drive back home. There were no off-site voting sites. My station called and said, "Can you go up there?" I flew up in the helicopter instead. The first thing I did when we landed was go inside and vote. Then I came back outside and started doing my interviews.

It's important to tell those stories, to cover Indian Country. People would assume in my newsrooms that I knew every Native American anywhere. It got to be a joke with my son's father. He said, "I'm going to make you a card, and it's going to say: Patty Talahongva, she knows every single Indian."

Why is it important to have Indigenous people tell their own stories?

Context. It's so important to understand federal Indian law and how it affects some stories. When the Fort McDowell Yavapai Nation was fighting for their right to go into Indian gaming, federal agents came in and shut down their casino. That caused a standoff between the tribe and the State of Arizona. There were faxes going back and forth between the governor and the state attorney general. One fax mentioned the president of Fort McDowell; his name was Clinton Pattea. One of the producers in the newsroom said, "Oh my god, they're calling in President Clinton." And I'm reading it going, no, they're calling in Clinton Pattea, the president of Fort McDowell. They didn't know tribal sovereignty. They didn't understand the jurisdictional issues and they didn't even know the name of the tribal president.

I had to fight to get some coverage of Indian Country. I think people don't realize commercial TV news can be very cutthroat. You might be on the same team, but you're fighting for airtime, story angles, the length of your story. As a producer, you're juggling everything back and forth to make sure you keep to your total running time. But when I was young, I loved it.

A funny thing happened when some inmates were transported to the state hospital in Phoenix in the mid-1990s.[1] The driver left the engine running and went into the hospital. One inmate managed to crawl into the front seat and drove away. I got dispatched with my videographer to cover that story. All the media was down there and everybody was trying to get an eyewitness. There was a big Indian sitting at the end of the sidewalk, drinking soda and watching everything. I said, "Hey, what tribe are you?" He said, "Oh, I'm Pima." I said, "Oh, I'm Hopi. Have you been out here a long time? What did you see?" He's like, "Oh, man. That guy just left the van running and he went into the hospital." I said, "Can I get a camera here and can you tell me that on camera?" I got the eyewitness that everyone else just walked by. Nobody talked with him. Prejudice, you know.

What does Indigenous media mean to you?

I used to think it was media that was primarily owned and operated by tribes. There were few independent news outlets operating on reservations for Indian communities that were not supported by the tribe. In some cases, they became the mouthpiece for the tribe. I think that's changed, because with social media there are so many more outlets, and people may not have a huge news crew, but they do have a following and they are reporting news. Now we're getting more of our stories out from that Native perspective.

What should the next generation consider? Why is this work important?

I think people are interested in more in-depth content. We just don't get it on our regular news. Consultants have ruined this for us too because they survey focus groups, but those groups never include Native Americans, so how can that be a good focus group? With *Frontline*, I'm being given a year to produce one program. I've never had that luxury. But even when I was doing documentaries, you still have less than a year to produce something. The topic is climate change. I think we need to understand and truly embrace climate change on a daily basis. I want to say that we should all be running out of our houses every morning, saying, "We're on fire, we're on fire! What are we going to do today to stop the fire? Because it is happening and we're ignoring the signs."

Everyone has a website, every newsroom has social media. So they have to feed their own work to social media and maybe the news outlet's social media, and then file whatever story they're going to do. It's a lot of work and the pay has not improved. I think that drive to tell stories that journalists care about, that are relevant to their community, is still there. I would hope that they would continue to look at context and historical knowledge.

Identity is also an issue, such as being a "Rez Indian" or an "Urban Indian." My generation, I think, is pretty much the last generation of full-bloods. When it comes to identity, it's becoming more and more blurred. You know what makes you Indian? I think all of that is changing.

What does the future hold, in your view?

We are all so different in how we consume and use media. I got my first job in the city and my career has always been with the mainstream. I have written for my tribal paper, I have gone into national Native media outlets, but a lot of my work has been done with mainstream media. That used to be an issue. It was like, you're the Urban Indian. You're the city girl. You're the mainstream journalist. You're not tribal media. I'm glad that there's social media today where you don't have those hard-drawn lines. And also, mainstream news is not always bad.

Is there anything else you would like to add?

Being involved in every form of the media is the only way we're going to grow as a Native community of journalists. That's why I spent all those years at NAJA [the Native American Journalists Association] running the TV program and helping mentor students. When I left mainstream news, my newsroom no longer had a Native person there, and so I felt it was my responsibility to help populate other newsrooms with people from a perspective they didn't have and with experiences they could draw on.

I've loved my career. I've been able to sustain this for all these decades. And jeez, you know I'm an old lady now, and I don't think I will ever retire, unless AI takes over writing. I appreciate all the skills I have to do the work I've done, and I don't take any of that for granted. So how can I help the next generation? How can I help guide them and talk to them?

—Interviewed by Cristina L. Azocar

Note

1. Incidents such as these were often considered local police matters and usually did not generate major national or regional headlines. Talahongva's vivid account represents an "insider" account showing a creative way journalists often developed sources before the era of social media and widespread mobile phone use.

PART TWO

MULTIMEDIA

11

Emergent Sources Supporting Sovereignty on Social Media

Three Supreme Court Cases

Sarah Liese, Victoria LaPoe, Benjamin LaPoe, and Taylor Orcutt
(All authors contributed equally.)

Aren't we getting tired of protesting and fighting for rights we've already been granted, rights that are backed by federal and international law, rights that our ancestors fought and died for?

—Switters (2022)

The answer to the above rhetorical question, posed by JR Switters (Lakota and Dakota) on his TikTok page, is of course a resounding "Yes!" Indigenous erasure and Indigenous efforts to survive this erasure are nothing new. This chapter posits an emergent source process based on an observation model (see figure 11.1). Emergent sources are actors, collectives, or communicative formations that arise organically within evolving sociopolitical contexts to articulate, legitimize, and mobilize claims for rights and sovereignty. In other words, our research analyzes how news sources become prominent in stories, which validates their authority and prominence. Our observations from this research seem to illustrate a continued struggle between Indigenous and non-Native sources for authority and credibility on Native topics. We observed this tension between the authority of Indigenous sources vs. non-Native sources while analyzing the discourse on three US Supreme Court cases surrounding "body sovereignty." This emergent source process provides a lens that theorists and practitioners may use to "view" how sources work in the Indigenous struggle for rights. The sourcing of information for activists is critical. We followed Indigenous news sources, organizations, entertainers, politicians, and tribes, among others, by taking advantage of the visual format of Instagram to discuss body sovereignty (LaPoe et al. 2022c).

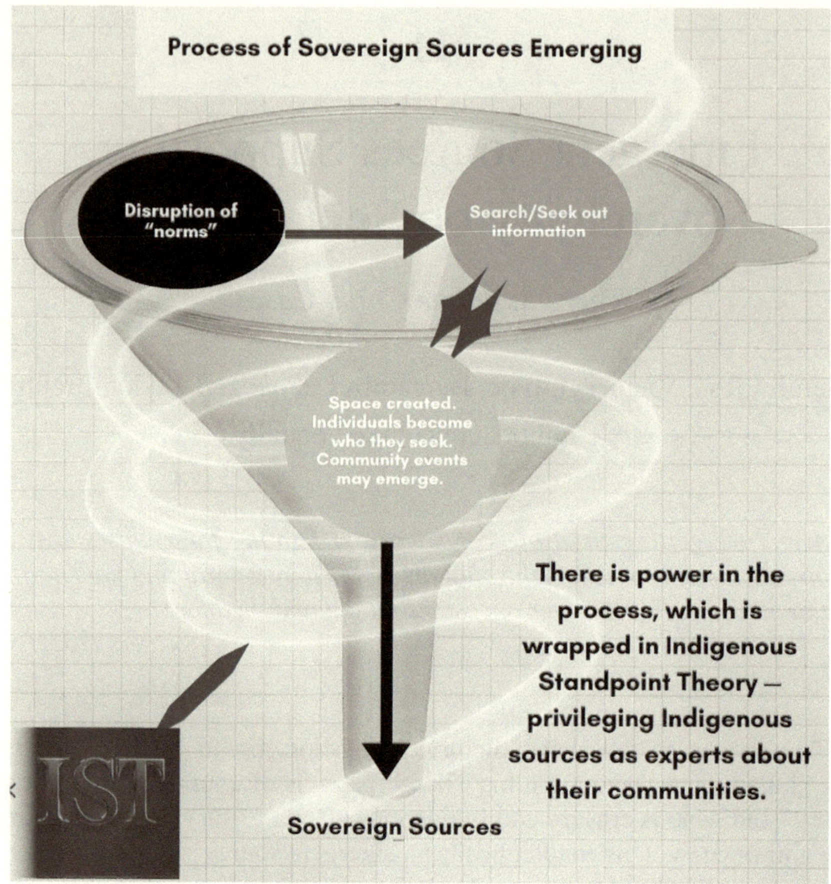

Fig. 11.1. A diagram of the process centering indigenous voices.

In the summer of 2022, the US Supreme Court, with a male and conservative majority (Snodgrass 2022), overturned *Roe v. Wade*, a piece of legislation that protected women's right to privacy and right to have an abortion (*Roe v. Wade* 1973). In this chapter, we will also discuss the Supreme Court cases *Oklahoma v. Castro-Huerta* and *Brackeen v. Haaland*, both of which are also referred to as Indian Child Welfare Act (ICWA) decisions (Azocar et al. 2021; LaPoe et al. 2021; Carter Olson et al. 2022). The ICWA focuses on tribal sovereignty and protecting children from abuse (see chapter 9).

Repeal of *Roe v. Wade*

The result of the anti-abortion ruling to repeal *Roe v. Wade* in 2022 affected women nationwide, and especially Indigenous women, transmen,

Two Spirit, and gender nonconforming people, who are "two to three times more likely to die as a result from pregnancy than white women," according to the US Centers for Disease Control and Prevention (2022), which also pointed out that "this disparity increases with age" (Centers for Disease Control and Prevention 2019).

Indigenous people have long distrusted the government and understand the need to protect the sovereignty of the female body. In addition to the significant health risks associated with Indigenous pregnancies, medical professionals working for the Indian Health Service forced sterilization upon Indigenous women, without consent, in the 1970s. The Government Accounting Office released a report entitled "Investigation of Allegations Concerning Indian Health Service" in 1976, which showed that the Indian Health Service had performed 3,406 sterilizations from 1973 through 1976 at four locations: Aberdeen, Albuquerque, Oklahoma City, and Phoenix (US Government Accountability Office 2023). The Indian Health Service did not list these forced sterilizations as "voluntary or therapeutic" (US Government Accountability Office 2023).

Thus, the Supreme Court's 2022 decision in *Dobbs v. Jackson Women's Health Organization*, which ended *Roe v. Wade*, caused outrage among Indigenous people (Denetclaw 2022), as it resulted in Indigenous women not having the fundamental right to reproductive choice that comes with not only being a mother, but also with being a child (Hodison 2022). Sarah Deer (Muscogee [Creek] Nation), a leading legal scholar and advocate against violence against Native women (Win 2021), said in an article in *The Lawrence Times*, "For us, reproductive justice is not just about abortion, but the right to have children and the right to raise children and the right to have the resources to raise children" (Hodison 2022).

Social media platforms provided a space for Indigenous people to express their opinions about the topic after the Dobbs decision. Montana's Senate Bill 419, which banned TikTok for residents within the state's "territorial jurisdiction," highlighted the importance of keeping these platforms accessible to Indigenous communities to have open discourse about the law and its effects. Indigenous residents questioned if the ban encroached on digital and data sovereignty, which is integral to protecting tribal sovereignty. Maranda Compton, a citizen of the Delaware Tribe of Indians and adjunct law professor at the University of Montana, said, "Tribes need to be a part of the conversations when dealing with laws and policies that may overreach jurisdiction" (Wagner and KickingWoman 2023).

Our observation of the social media posts, largely from Twitter and Instagram, found that during this critical historical moment, social media amplified Indigenous changemakers as sources of stories, resources, knowledge, advocacy, and shared experiences (LaPoe et al. 2022a). Jana Schmieding (Lakota), an actress featured on the television series *Rutherford Falls* and *Reservation Dogs*, started a weekly Instagram event in July 2022 called "Beading Our Bodies Sovereignty" for her more than 32,000 Instagram and 37,000 Twitter (now X) followers. Her goal was to raise awareness about reproductive care and health care for Indigenous people, specifically those seeking abortions. Each of her Instagram stories featured guests talking about their work in connection with body sovereignty and reproductive rights, and the discussion often overlapped with themes of land sovereignty and the idea of consent. By the end of the month, she had raised about $2,500 for the Indigenous Women Rising's abortion fund—one of the only resources for Indigenous women seeking abortions (Schmieding 2022). Schmieding became the positive embodiment of an Indigenous woman who embraces herself unapologetically while helping others do the same.

Nonprofit organizations also took to social media to express their empathy toward people who can conceive, while taking action to provide resources for those seeking access to safe abortions. The Changing Woman Initiative is one nonprofit organization working to restore Indigenous sovereignty by providing Indigenous communities with safe and decolonized birth practices. It made the following post on Instagram on December 16, 2022: "Reclaiming our Indigenous medicine and teachings around health and wellness is our human right. We should not face criminalization for making every effort to decolonize healthcare" (Changing Woman Initiative 2022). Their platform allowed them to inform Indigenous women, provide their services as resources, and express the importance of decolonized health practices. The Dobbs decision caused uncertainty for individuals who are able to conceive. The help of people like Schmieding and organizations like the Changing Woman Initiative allowed Indigenous people to receive support and access to safe pregnancy and abortion healthcare options without fear.

A crew of Indigenous women also harnessed social media to spread awareness about abortion, including Lieutenant Governor of Minnesota Peggy Flanagan (White Earth Nation), Tara Houska (Couchiching First Nation), and Caitlin Newago (Bad River Band of Lake Superior Chippewa). These leaders hold different roles within their communities: Peggy Flanagan is a politician, Tara Houska is a lawyer and activist, and Caitlin Newago is an artist. Their voices merged on social channels to communicate that Indigenous women are sacred, as are their decisions, especially when it comes to their own bodies.

The Indian Child Welfare Act

Our initial search of social media posts about the ICWA began in the fall of 2022 and was intended to showcase raw Indigenous narratives in response to the central court cases included in our analysis. Our keyword searches were built around the Supreme Court, also commonly referred to as "SCOTUS" on social media, as well as words and phrases pertaining to each specific court case. Most of the social media posts referenced in our research originally came from Twitter because of the (then easy) searchability of hashtags and keywords, and the ability to scroll from post to post (LaPoe et al. 2022a; LaPoe et al. 2022b).

On October 27, 2022, Twitter was plagued by executive dysfunction when Elon Musk transitioned to CEO after acquiring the company for $44 billion (Vanian 2023). Even through its 2022 change of ownership, Twitter's search functions were not substantially affected. The Twitter posts we found contributed to the larger narrative of Indigenous reactions to the Supreme Court cases and the ripple effects these cases had on Indian Country.

Since the first European contact in the region currently labeled "North America," actions to assimilate Indigenous peoples and institute a Eurocentric, Christian-focused narrative have molded the country now known to many as the "United States of America." Within the United States, there are 575 federally recognized tribal nations (US Government, n.d.) and sixty-three state-recognized nations (National Conference of State Legislatures 2016). US public school education frequently does not teach students about the vast number of tribal nations in the United States, furthering "institutionalized ignorance" that continues today (Hammersley et al. 2022, 24). US "land decision-makers" have often received public school or Christian education that promotes "Manifest Destiny"—the American expansionist movement that framed the conquest of North America as "divinely ordained" (Solomon 2009, 81). Those decision-makers directly affect all citizens in America, especially those residing in tribal nations.

As part of the Federal Indian Boarding School Initiative, the US Department of the Interior released a report that found that, between 1819 and 1969, 408 federal boarding schools operated across thirty-seven states, including twenty-one schools in Alaska and seven schools in Hawaii (Department of the Interior 2022). "At least 500 children died" at nineteen of these boarding schools, and further investigation may reveal more casualties (Herald 2023). Within the walls of these boarding schools, students "endured abuse and illness," thinly veiled by religion, particularly Catholicism (Herald 2023).

Like US boarding schools, Canadian residential schools (see chapter 5) caused significant emotional and physical harm to generations of First Nations children (Denetclaw 2023a). Most of these residential schools (reportedly 70 percent) were Catholic-operated until the Canadian government took control of them in 1964 (Mansoor 2022). Scholars have estimated that "between ten thousand and fifty thousand children never returned home" after enduring these residential schools, the last of which did not close until the 1990s (Mansoor 2022).

Not one Supreme Court justice is a member of a tribal nation, and most of them are men. The law firm Gibson, Dunn, and Crutcher, which represented Brackeen, also represented Maverick Gaming in *Maverick Gaming LLC v. United States*, a case that challenged the Indian Gaming Regulatory Act (Denetclaw 2023a). Still, the Supreme Court justices also had the power to make a salient decision about women's bodies, and the bodies of everyone who could conceive, during the overturning of *Roe v. Wade*. Thus, despite gatherings held, speeches given, and steps taken by Indigenous changemakers, political progress toward the betterment of Indigenous peoples' well-being happens sparingly. This halting progress causes Indigenous people to carve out channels to amplify their voices.

On June 28, 2002, writer and storyteller Alfred Walking Bull (Sicangu Lakota Oyate) tweeted: "If #SCOTUS says prayer in school is fine, I say: SAGE THE F*** OUT OF EVERYTHING AND CALL THOSE ANCESTORS INTO YOUR CLASSROOM TO DROP SOME #INDIGENOUS WISDOM" (Walking Bull 2022). We highlight this Twitter post because it summarizes Walking Bull's anxious anticipation while awaiting the Supreme Court's decision on the *Oklahoma v. Castro-Huerta* case; he tweeted this message the day before the decision was made. His tweet suggests doubt about the Supreme Court's decisions and implies that prayer must include other spiritualities as well as Christianity, including Indigenous ways of praying, such as using sage. Walking Bull is not a politician or a famous actor, but his voice garnered five retweets and seventeen favorites because of his perception and opinions. This is the power of social media. If used correctly, messages and posts can reach many people despite geographical distance. Social media provides platforms for creative expression, resource sharing, and virtual communities. Users, alone or together, can raise awareness about issues and educate followers.

In 2020, the Native American Journalists Association (NAJA)—now known as the Indigenous Journalists Association (IJA)—tweeted their guide "So You Need an Indigenous Expert" to provide a process for finding sources in their reporting. Through social media, creators can inform, correct, and reinvigorate the Indigenous narrative to shed their distinct light on the truth, as stated by Schmieding on Instagram: "Our power is and has always been in our love for each other, our love for this land, and—through telling our own stories and pursuing autonomy—our love for ourselves. On this extraordinarily sad day of remembrance, I want to remember our power" (Schmieding 2020).

Schmieding's Instagram post responded to tweets by Nick Estes (Lower Brule Sioux), who reminded his Twitter audience of the complexities of Indigenous people and the history they come from (Schmieding 2020). Both Estes' and Schmieding's posts were made on December 29, 2020 to commemorate ancestors murdered during the Wounded Knee Massacre. Further examples of the power taken back into the hands of Indigenous people is evident in Indigenous media such as the television shows *Reservation Dogs* and *Rutherford Falls*, the news organization *ICT* (formerly *Indian Country Today*), and on social media platforms where Indigenous people can make their own statements about today's issues.

While support for Indigenous representation in the entertainment industry has increased (IllumiNative 2022), writers' wages have decreased and lost value. As Diné writer Sierra Ornellas shared with *Indian Country Today*, "It's pretty ironic; they started letting Brown and Black people make television right when they decided to stop paying us" (Schulman 2023). Thus, respect for Indigenous stories and Indigenous representation in the media remains an uphill battle, one that Indigenous writers are still fighting to have their voices heard.

Media must have connections to a community to report on it with context. Covering an issue or including a quote from an official interview in a strategic communication campaign is easy, the journalistic version of shooting fish in a barrel. But the "watchdog journalism" that keeps elite officials in check needs to happen more in mainstream media, or else incorrect information will appear (Bennett et al. 2008, 186–88). Individuals in positions of power, such as Supreme Court justices, are historically elusive to journalists and reclusive in their decision-making. "They don't want a reporter asking any more questions that may raise doubt about the Court's decision," say Slotnick and Segal (1998), and this is seen in the case of the historic overturning of *Roe v. Wade*. However, social media (and leaked information amplified on social media) provides opportunities for information on Supreme Court decisions, such as the leaked Dobbs opinion, to circulate swiftly through citizen journalism, professional news organizations, and changemakers. The hashtag #roevwade had been viewed 5.6 billion times and #scotus one billion times on TikTok as of September 25, 2024. Information that was circulated quickly through social media gave Indigenous changemakers time to process, organize, question, and respond to the Supreme Court decisions this chapter focuses on.

The overarching aim people have when they go to social media is to find connection. Moreover, people turn to social media to satisfy a need for interaction, reassurance, and an empathetic connection to others, particularly those with shared identities (LaPoe et al. 2022a). Social media allows creators and users to foster a sense of belonging within their community's support (LaPoe et al. 2017). A testament to this is TaNeel Filesteel (Aaniiih Tribe of the Fort Belknap Indian Reservation), who said in an article in *Indian Country Today* that she uses social media to connect with others by documenting her experiences as a mother and a Native law student (Wagner and KickingWoman 2023). Furthermore, social media is a tool to support those isolated from or by mainstream discourse, such as Indigenous women and Indigenous members of various 2SLGBTQIA+ communities (LaPoe et al. 2017). In this way, social media is invaluable for community protection and intracommunity connection and support. To support their communities, people may use social media to stimulate sociopolitical advocacy, discourse, and advancement.

The concision of social media platforms like Twitter and TikTok removes "de-motivating barriers" to communication (LaPoe et al. 2022b, 241). The hashtag—perhaps one of social media's most complex yet effective and powerful tools—was created in response to this concise nature (LaPoe 2022). The parameters of these platforms' content and the power of hashtags "assisted with encouraging understandable information . . . increasing the likelihood of not alienating audiences due to cognition limitations," which further promotes connectivity within communities and between communities and support systems (LaPoe et al. 2022b, 241).

Oklahoma v. Castro-Huerta

> *All of y'all who were so vocal about Native Nations being a loophole for abortions, where's the same outrage as the Supreme Court just took another swing at our tribal sovereignty by granting states jurisdiction over crimes committed by non-Natives on tribal lands #CastroHuerta*
>
> —*BlackDeer (2022)*

The *Oklahoma v. Castro-Huerta* decision[1] did not garner as much attention as the Dobbs case did, as Autumn Asher BlackDeer (Tsistsistas) voiced in her Twitter post above. She tweeted this on the same day as the Supreme Court justices decided the *Oklahoma v. Castro-Huerta* case, showing her watchdog role as an Indigenous person and changemaker. We chose to analyze this tweet because BlackDeer is a prominent voice in the Twitter community as a social work professor and "Indiqueer." The frustration in BlackDeer's message echoed in Indian Country because of the lack of media coverage and discussions about the impact of this court ruling.

The main reason for the lack of non-Indigenous media publicity is that the case did not directly affect most non-Indigenous people residing in America. However, the decision was huge for Indian Country. The president of the National Congress of American Indians, Fawn Sharp, said, "We all felt the pain of that decision. We all felt the pain of what that might mean for our collective futures, so we knew that tribal nations had to come together. . . . Because we have been working for centuries, for decades, to ensure that our futures are secure, to ensure that our inherent rights to govern our land, territories, and peoples exclusively belong to us" (National Congress of American Indians 2022).

It is imperative to discuss the history of the events that occurred in the 1830s to explain why this case is important. During this time, southern states were hungry for Indian land, and in this particular case, the State of Georgia desperately desired to inhabit and control Cherokee land. Georgia prohibited non-Indigenous people from being on Cherokee land without the state's approval, which is how it asserted jurisdiction over Indian Country as a way to dispel the allyship between non-Native missionaries and the Cherokee. The Cherokee Nation fought back and challenged that law in the Supreme Court, ultimately winning and releasing the state's control over their lands. *Worcester v. Georgia* (1832) granted the federal government exclusive power to oversee relations with Native nations. Georgia did not comply with the ruling and sent in troops. The result pressured the Cherokee to sign a treaty, which moved them to present-day Oklahoma, but that treaty included an agreement that the state would never have control over Cherokee land (Ablavsky and Hidalgo Reese 2022).

Worcester v. Georgia established that Native nations are distinct sovereign political communities and that the federal government holds exclusive authority over relations with them, sharply limiting state power within Indian Country. In contrast, *Oklahoma v. Castro-Huerta* (2022) held that states share concurrent jurisdiction with the federal government to prosecute non-Native defendants who commit crimes against Native victims in Indian Country. While *Worcester* emphasized federal exclusivity and tribal autonomy, *Castro-Huerta* expanded state authority, reflecting a significant shift in the Court's approach to tribal sovereignty and the balance of power among federal, state, and tribal governments.

An editorial by Mary Kathryn Nagle (Cherokee) for *Indian Country Today* questioned the integrity of the Supreme Court, as suggested by this tweet: "OP-ED: The Supreme Court's decision in *Oklahoma v. Castro-Huerta* is not an application of the law. It is an outcome-determinative decision designed to satisfy the governor of Oklahoma's multi-million dollar campaign to undermine McGirt" (*Indian Country Today* 2022). This tweet is a snippet from Nagle's story, which traces her perspective on the Supreme Court from her experience as a little girl, to why she went to law school, to her disappointment following the *Castro-Huerta* decision. As Nagle put it, "*Worcester* was not a misunderstanding. It was, and continues to be, an example of what the Supreme Court can be, if and when it decides to look past prejudice and simply apply the law" (Nagle 2022).

The *Castro-Huerta* case awarded the state of Oklahoma jurisdiction over tribal lands, muddying the waters for tribal nations and breaking the treaty agreed upon two centuries before. Moreover, it meant that, when a non-Indigenous person committed a crime against a tribal citizen, there was now tribal jurisdiction, state jurisdiction, and federal jurisdiction. Jurisdiction is defined as "the power and authority a government has over its people and land" (Garrow and Deer 2015, 75). To provide context, Ablavsky and Hidalgo Reese (2022) wrote an opinion piece in *The Washington Post* and summed up the ruling as "an act of conquest. And it could signal a sea change in federal Indian law, ushering in a new era governed by selective ignorance of history and deference to state power."

A wave of responses flooded social media platforms from users wishing to express their opinions and their personal and tribal stakes in the decision. Regardless of the status of the users, the decision created a social media sea of empathy across Indigenous people and communities, and across tribal nations and affiliations. It showed a culmination of emotions, with many people worrying about the future, especially given that the people in power had suggested they did not have knowledge of or respect for the land, Indigenous history, or sovereignty.

An example of one of these responses is a tweet by Twyla Baker (@Indigenia), an enrolled member of the Mandan Hidatsa, Arikara Nation: "I am not a legal expert by any means, just a Tribal citizen. I do believe, though, that decisions like today's are continuing to chip away at Tribal sovereignty, which will keep on until we reach the point of dissolution of Tribes and Tribal lands. That's BEEN the goal" (Baker 2022).

Another tweet by Elizabeth Hidalgo Reese (Yunpovi) (@yunpovi) outlines why the decision was harmful to all Indigenous people in the United States: "For those wondering, 'Why is it bad that states can prosecute, too?' Three answers: 1-States/Tribes have a long history of animosity. Fair treatment isn't a fair assumption. 2-Tribes want to make different laws for their land than states. 3-Many resources are a zero-sum game" (Hidalgo Reese 2022).

Hidalgo Reese and Baker's tweets were posted to Twitter on June 29, 2022, the same day as the Supreme Court's decision. We included Twitter posts in our analysis, including those that were also disseminated across other social media platforms and reported in news coverage. On Twitter, Indigenous people took the initiative to relay the justices' decisions in their own words and to inform Indigenous and non-Indigenous audiences alike.

Brackeen v. Haaland

Before the ICWA, Native children were systematically separated from their families and communities by state and private adoption agencies, without evidence of harm or neglect (Western Native Voice 2023). Indigenous children were unjustly stolen from their homes and often forced to live with non-Indigenous families, depriving the youth of their cultures and traditional teachings. When the ICWA became law in 1978, one-third of Indigenous children had been taken from their homes (National Indian Child Welfare Association 2019, 3). When Congress passed the ICWA, tribes had the right to intervene in an Indigenous child's case "regarding removal and placement of Indian children in foster care, guardianship, or adoptive homes" (The Indian Child Welfare Act 2021, 1). The Supreme Court upheld the ICWA in 2023.

Despite the essential protections the ICWA provides for Indigenous children and tribal nations, its constitutionality has faced challenges. Thus, Indigenous changemakers "nurture and empower new native leaders" through focused "support and encourage Native community members to step up and be a voice for their families and communities through the civic engagement process and public policies" (Western Native Voice n.d.). The nonprofit Western Native Voice states that it has relationships with all seven reservations in Montana, including 50 percent of tribal members off the reservation (Western Native Voice n.d.).

As Western Native Voice explained, the ICWA emerged to stop historical trauma from deepening further. The organization aims to inspire Indigenous leaders to raise their voices, just as they did in their Twitter posts, and to speak out on social media about the injustices of life before the ICWA and the importance of the ICWA for tribal nations and Indigenous futures.

"Native kids have been the tip of the spear in attacks on Tribal sovereignty for years," journalist and activist Rebecca Nagle (Cherokee) explained on the May 2023 episode of National Public Radio's (NPR's) *Code Switch*, in an interview with NPR journalist B. A. Parker (IllumiNative 2023). IllumiNative, an Indigenous nonprofit organization empowering Indigenous creatives and communities, posted this quote on Twitter in May 2023.[2] The program focused on Nagle's episodic podcast *This Land*. In the first season of the podcast, Nagle journeyed back in time: "back to the Trail of Tears—the story of how my people came to Oklahoma—to the story of my family, the treaty they signed, and why they were killed for our land" (IllumiNative 2023). The second season of *This Land* examined the *Brackeen v. Haaland* case, including details about the prosecution team that may seem minor on the surface but that uncover broader truths. The podcast alludes to the idea that Indigenous children were collateral damage both throughout US history—as implied by Western Native Voice's tweet—and now in the present with the *Brackeen* case, and highlights the colonized way of thinking that ignores the best interests of these children because of more prominent, greedier pursuits. This case arises from three separate child custody proceedings governed by the ICWA, a federal statute that aims to keep Indian children connected to Indian families. The ICWA governs state court adoption and foster care proceedings involving Indian children. Among other things, the Act requires placement of an Indian child according to the Act's hierarchical preferences, unless the state court finds "good cause" to depart from them.

Nagle questioned whether striking down the ICWA as racial discrimination could jeopardize other federal Indian laws and institutions, such as the Indian Health Service, tribal gaming, and even tribal sovereignty itself. The concern was that if the ICWA were deemed race-based rather than grounded in tribal political status, the reasoning could threaten the broader legal framework supporting Native nations. However, Nagle argued that this sweeping outcome would not be legally or factually accurate, maintaining that the ICWA is based on the political relationship between tribes and the federal government, not race, and therefore would not automatically undermine other areas of federal Indian law.

Native Western Voice, IllumiNative, and Rebecca Nagle all emphasized the importance of Indigenous children because they were at the heart of the *Brackeen v. Haaland* case and they are the future of Indian Country. The social media posts regarding *Brackeen v. Haaland* were made to produce change, because what is at stake is invaluable to Indigenous people. If Indigenous children are again taken from their families and placed into non-Indigenous homes, the outcomes could be harmful not only to tribal nations but to the battles Indigenous people are fighting, like climate change. The cases mentioned in this chapter may seem separate, but the link binding them together is sovereignty; the same link binds the social media posts we have shared throughout our findings.

Conclusion

A key element in the emergent source process is understanding that Indigenous voices are the knowledge system that should be the privileged source. This approach is essential to providing ethical coverage of Indian Country (Azocar et al. 2021; LaPoe et al. 2021). The 171 social media posts we gathered show how voices can emerge in spaces created around issues such as Supreme Court cases, and how they can serve as sources for how these cases affect the lives of Indigenous communities. They can act as reminders about historical events, emotions, and milestones reached, as well as blooming Indigenous resilience. However, even more than that, these sources—emerging changemakers—create their own spaces through their standpoints, advocacy, and agency, justifying and lending importance to Indigenous voices regardless of politics, occupation, class, or education. This allows for a more detailed embodiment of the struggles and triumphs to come forward from an array of Indigenous perspectives.

Social media can be an excellent tool for weaving together narratives and using them as launchpads for discussion. Whether a message is posted under the name of an individual or an organization, the potential the message carries is substantial. When used responsibly, social media can uplift and empower Indigenous people to reclaim their voices as instruments of change and power. Suppose, years from now, the education system continues to suppress narratives showcasing Indigenous leaders and history. People will still be able to use social media to allow the voices of Indigenous people far and wide to culminate into a well-sourced history, with context.

This study is not exhaustive, but it amplifies understanding of the emergent source process. To date, on TikTok alone, the general population of users has viewed the hashtag #indigenous 9.1 billion times, #indigenoustiktok 5.0 billion times, #indigenouswomen 228.3 million times, #icwa 85.4 million times, #indigenouspolitics 36,100 times, and #indigenouswomeninpolitics 6,530 times. The digital traffic these hashtags garner indicates that there is a more significant sociopolitical conversation around Indigenous topics to be had.

Discussion Questions

1. In what ways can journalists, communicators, and teachers understand and articulate the importance of sourcing?
2. What steps and processes help students become aware of who they are considering as a source and why they are a good source for that topic? And why are these steps helpful?
3. How can the realities of Indigenous communities not being monolithic be amplified?
4. What resources from organizations like the IJA help examine how to find and choose sources, and raise awareness of who is speaking for what community and with what possibly in mind?

Notes

1. In the case of US Supreme Court *Oklahoma v. Castro-Huerta 2022*, Victor Manuel Castro-Huerta, a non-Native, was convicted in Oklahoma state court of child neglect, and he was sentenced to 35 years. The victim, his stepdaughter, is Native American, and the crime was committed within the Cherokee Reservation.
2. IllumiNative ceased operations in 2025 after seven years.

12

"It's Time to Collectively Rise, Rebuild, and Support One Another"

Interview with Brian Bull

Brian Bull is an enrolled member of the Nez Perce Tribe, and he has been working as a broadcast journalist for nearly 30 years. He's worked at NPR, as well as South Dakota Public Radio, Wisconsin Public Radio, WCPN in Cleveland, and KLCC in Eugene, Oregon. He's also a longtime mentor on the NPR Next Generation Project, and he was recently a professor of journalism at the University of Oregon. He's freelanced for Underscore Native News and National Native News. More recently he's become a senior reporter for Buffalo's Fire, and he is a substitute host for National Native News, helping listeners keep up on the latest on Indian Country.

Please introducce yourself.

Ta'c méeywi.

I am an enrolled member of the Nez Perce Tribe, or as we call ourselves, the *Nimiipuu*. I'm also a member of the IJA. I've worked in public broadcasting for 27 years—just a little more than half my life working at NPR stations, affiliates, and networks, and at NPR headquarters itself.

What does Indigenous media mean to you?

I see Indigenous media as an offshoot of oral narrative, as we knew it well before the missionaries arrived in the 1800s and introduced ways to write out and publish our language. Our people and pretty much all Native people across the continent relied heavily on oral narrative to convey the tribe's history, values, and stories from one generation to the next.

Going by the calendar, we're just moving out of winter. This time of year was usually a time for people to gather in lodge houses and other dwellings as a community and tell stories and exchange accounts and information. So it was paramount that every speaker who passed on

Fig. 12.1. Brian Bull. Author photo.

knowledge did so with accuracy and authenticity, which to me is very similar to my work as a journalist. It's very important to convey things accurately and make sure that all perspectives are accounted for. Going into radio was a natural move for me, I just felt inherently drawn to that form of communication.

Describe your work. What compels you to do it?

I got involved with media journalism after some very bad encounters in my childhood. I put up with a lot of racism in a pulp mill town called Lewiston, Idaho, across the river from Clarkston, Washington. Those communities are named for Lewis and Clark, the explorers who came through the area and were, in fact, saved by the Nez Perce as they were starving. There were hostile, aggressive, and potentially threatening, even violent encounters that I dealt with.

In time, I thought, *Well, if there's ignorance, then maybe I can share stories that will help others be more informed about Native people.* I like to think that, in some immeasurable form, my voice and the sharing of Native voices, articles, and stories helps alleviate some of that ignorance and prejudice. So that's what has compelled me to share Native voices and go in-depth with Native coverage.

Native media is doing very well lately. I think there's more and more of an appreciation of it, with the rebirth of *Indian Country Today* and programs [like] *Native America Calling* still going strong. I still see a lot of misunderstanding, racism, and prejudice in the world, so I'm not naive enough to think that my work or that of other Native journalists is solving the world's ills, but it's certainly alleviating and addressing them. If we keep silent, it only reinforces the notion that we're either extinct or passive, silent. Many Natives and allies choose to fight and speak out so we have representation, rights, and respect.

Why is it important to have Indigenous people tell their own stories?

Authenticity is a big one. It's fine if a non-Indian wants to tell a Native story, but they should incorporate Natives' input and participation.

One example involves the geographical name changes happening all across the United States. There was one small group of non-Natives who decided they were going to rename a creek or small mountain or something, and they chose a name they assumed was respectful and honorable, but they didn't consult anyone from the tribe. The tribe got offended because they had other ideas for a place name. So here were some non-Natives who'd put on their superhero capes and felt they were doing a grand thing, but in turn ended up offending the very people they were supposedly trying to honor.

It's important that people incorporate tribal input. You can't just assume that because you feel you're doing the right thing, you're going about it right. That's why it's important we tell our stories. We have the perspective, the history, and the background many non-Natives don't know about.

What does the future hold, in your view?

We've seen Native media rise, especially over the last fifty, sixty years. Almost every tribe has a newspaper. Many have radio stations. A number of tribes are exploring video platforms such as YouTube as a way to communicate and share programs. Native TikTok apparently is huge. We're seeing social media become a new platform for today's journalists to venture into and share their stories.

Prior to the internet, I figured I was going to get into broadcasting easy-peasy. I'd record my sound and get my story on the terrestrial broadcast that people catch on their breakfast table radio or their car stereo, and call it a day. But with the internet came so many options that any journalist who's worth their salt needs to be a multimedia specialist now. So, in addition to getting that sound, I have to get good photos, and maybe I'll also shoot video if I think that there's some activity that sound just can't capture alone or a still photo won't do justice to. Then we also have to do a digital build-out—a web story—so that the online audience has a richer experience.

I welcome all of this because it lets me do more creative storytelling. It's built on my photography, videography, and online writing skills. That's just where the audience has gone to. If you're a serious journalist, you need to go where the audience goes. There's just no escaping it.

I'm hopeful that the next generation of journalists, especially Native journalists, will run with it and become innovative with how they use mediums like TikTok and YouTube, and whatever else is around the corner. I call these folks "evolutionaries" because they're always growing and adapting new skills with the times.

What should the next generation consider? Why is this work important?

I think Native people will continue to innovate and find ways to get their message across. On TikTok, you see history, Native cooking, language lessons, and comedy. Are you familiar with The 1491s? They have a huge slew of videos. They got rolling on YouTube and are now involved with major projects like *Rutherford Falls* and *Reservation Dogs.*

Despite the toxicity of social media, we're seeing the rise of Native influencers and performers. A lot of Native news gets disseminated through TikTok, YouTube, and Facebook. It's a great time to see who we are and promote our culture.

Is there anything else you would like to add?

We must remember that for 500 years we've been invaded. We've been oppressed. We've dealt with war and the reservation system. Termination. And now the horrors and abuses of boarding schools are coming more to light. We've had generations of elders who were shamed and prevented from practicing their culture and their language. Since those eras, we've just begun to regain our footing. There are Natives who don't know their complete history or language, or who grew up in a city as opposed to a reservation. I don't think those are things we need to divide ourselves on, because we're all trying in our own respective ways to understand and support our Indigeneity. We're all working to come to terms with who we are and how we are keepers of our culture and traditions, so it doesn't benefit any of us to constantly compare and tear ourselves down.

We also gotta shake imposter syndrome, which I know many people feel. Not that there aren't "pretendians" to look out for, or those who otherwise exploit, misrepresent, or appropriate Native culture. I just feel like we need to acknowledge that Natives—as a people—have been through so much. It's time to collectively rise, rebuild, and support one another. Every effort, big or small, to honor, practice, and preserve our culture is the defining quality we should honor, in my view.

Finally, we need to recognize how colonization has affected us. I've seen old Eurocentric and Judeo-Christian perspectives feeding prejudice against certain Natives by other Natives. Two Spirits and LGBTQ individuals used to be accepted, even celebrated, prior to colonization. Now many are trying to find acceptance again in our tribal communities. Others are trying to bridge differences between religions, politics, and opinions about who we should kiss goodnight.

This all circles back to sharing stories and amplifying voices that need to be heard. It's why I've stuck with journalism as long as I have. I may never know the full effect my reporting has had in the last three decades, but if it all means one less Native kid gets rocks thrown at them by some seething, purple-faced bigot, then I'll call it good.

—Interviewed by Cristina L. Azocar

13

The *Kuleana* of Culture–Nature Relationships in *Moana* and *Waikiki*

Colby Y. Miyose

Hawai‘i's statehood, granted in 1959, is often construed as a major turning point in its history, but it did little to change the conditions of ownership on the islands. For instance, one-quarter of Oahu's land is still in military possession and one-fifth of the population serves in the military (Teaiwa 2016). It also did not change Hawai‘i's ideological representation in cinema. A major step has been taken to support Kānaka Maoli (Native Hawaiians) in recent years: the state of Hawai‘i signed the Native Hawaiian Recognition Bill in 2011, granting Indigenous rights to Native Hawaiians and their descendants. But although Indigenous rights are strengthening, the question of who creates the representation of Hawaiians in film, and to what extent Hawaiians are involved in the process, is still a widely concerning issue. The most important sources of discourse for a representational makeover of Hawai‘i against Hollywood's fantasy of an idealized whiteness subsuming non-White, Native Hawaiian culture are decolonial or anticolonial voices from Native Hawaiians in the film industry.

Films such as *Princess Kaiulani* (2009) and *The Descendants* (2011) address the overlooked question of land rights and critically engage with Hawai‘i's annexation and occupation. *Princess Kaiulani* revisits the struggle of asserting independence and avoiding annexation in the final days of the Hawaiian Kingdom. *The Descendants* looks toward the future of a Hawai‘i trying to curb the growing expansion of tourism and construction and return the islands to an ecological balance. These films also portray the complexity of Kānaka identity. Both Princess Kaiulani and Matthew King constantly struggle with negotiating who they are. Princess Kaiulani has a formal Western education, yet attempts to use this to build a bridge between Hawai‘i and the West. Matthew's lineage is both Indigenous and colonizer, and he faces a pinnacle moment when he is pressured to sell land to corporations that will degrade his Hawaiian legacy.

Though the storylines take a more empathetic approach to the Hawaiian experience than previous films, in attempting to empathize or connect with Native Hawaiians' historical colonization and contemporary oppression, what is upsetting is the cast members who represent these "Hawaiians." White actors such as George Clooney (*The Descendants*) and Emma Stone (*Aloha* 2015) are effortlessly cast as "Hawaiian," allowing them to "go native," since no Hawaiian identifiers are necessary in a white-dominated onscreen Hawaiʻi. In reality, whites remain a minority in Hawaiʻi, making up only 24 percent of the population (Sasaki 2016). In addition, Q'orinanka Waira Qoiana Kilcher, the actress who portrayed Princess Kaiulani, is Quechua-Huachipaeri, but all Indigenous cultures are not a monolith, where one Indigenous person represents all. In recent years, there has been a shift toward casting Pasifika/Pacific Islanders in these roles and hiring Pasifika/Pacific Islander writers and producers (i.e., *The White Lotus* 2021; *Finding 'Ohana* 2021; *Dougie Kameāloha* 2021; *Lilo and Stitch* 2024; *Moana* 2016). But who decides how Native Hawaiians are represented? This chapter will look at two films to see how Pacific Islanders, especially Hawaiians, are represented: *Moana* (2016)—which means "wide expanse of water"—hired a diversity council to inform the filmmakers about Pacific culture; and *Waikiki* (2020) was the first feature-length film to be directed by a Native Hawaiian.

Past literature pertaining to Pacific Islander media representations have homed in on the many negative stereotypes perpetuated in mainstream media, such as the idea that Oceanic people are lazy and apathetic, but few have commented on the positive messages that can be garnered from these films and television shows (Konzett 2017). Furthermore, within the sparse literature, few studies have analyzed these specific films' representations of Pacific culture (Cheu 2013). Those that have done so have evaluated the specific intricacies of how Pasifika culture is misrepresented, such as pointing out the inaccuracies in the depiction of Maui in *Moana* (Leslie 2017). However, when evaluating Pasifika values on a "big-picture" level, *Moana* and *Waikiki* encapsulate the importance of a culture–nature relationship in many Pacific Islanders' lifestyles. Using Hawaiian culture as an example, this chapter analyzes *Moana*'s and *Waikiki*'s portrayal of the connection between nature and culture, and the possible consequences of severing this. These films also demonstrate the importance of including Indigenous voices on screen and behind the scenes.

Misrepresentation of Hawaiians in Film and Television

As Edward Said wrote in *Orientalism*, "the Orient was almost a European invention, and had been since antiquity a place of romance, exotic beings, haunting memories and landscapes, remarkable experiences" (Said 1978, 1). Such narratives of Hawai'i were a Western invention. In an orientalized version of Hawai'i, benevolent Hawaiians provide the "aloha spirit" for tourists, rather than the spiritual belief grounded in centuries of theology (Antinora 2017). White American tourists are targeted as consumers, while Native Hawaiians are largely consumed. Further, Native Hawaiians are largely absent from any positions of power in the production of touristic "Hawaiian" culture. Instead, "the orientalization of Hawaiiana (Hawaiian culture) silences or marginalizes Native Hawaiians, while simultaneously freezing them in a romanticized past" (Antinora 2017, 19).

While making *Moana*, directors Ron Clements and John Musker formed the Oceanic Story Trust (OST), a group of Pasifika experts who guided the project in an attempt to ensure it would be culturally respectful. This group consisted of people from many walks of life: academics, archeologists, anthropologists, linguists, historians, cultural practitioners, tattoo artists, master navigators, elders, and artists (Sciretta 2016). It was named the Oceanic *Story* Trust because its members shared knowledge and stories with the production team, and their stories were incorporated in the film. The OST was involved in "guiding the film's narrative beyond a fixation on paradise and toward a perspective that is infused in meaningful ways with Pacific histories and epistemologies" (Tamaira and Fonoti 2018, 298). "Every name in the movie either comes from or was approved by the Oceanic Story Trust. . . . Every draft of the script, every little change, was sent to the Oceanic Story Trust to vet" (Sciretta 2016). However, *Moana* is still an animated fantasy version of Polynesian life steered by two non-Polynesian men. Thus, there remains a vital need for Native Hawaiians and Pacific Islanders to be involved in the entire filmmaking process. Adopting the lens of postcolonial film theory provides a path toward ensuring this process is culturally authentic.

Postcolonial Film Theory

Shohat and Stam (1994) assert that the global process of decolonization takes place through the creation of anticolonialist media. It involves raising Indigenous voices and creating self-controlled media that asserts Indigenous identity, culture, and experiences. It involves contesting Western narratives of Indigenous history, ethnography, and sociology.

Filmmakers attempt to break down stereotypes of Indigenous cultures established by Western media within these works of anticolonialist media (Knopf 2008). The creation of anticolonialist media requires Indigenous filmmakers to be involved in both production and distribution.

Settler colonialism, a system of oppression whereby one group takes control of all the land and resources of another and claims that land as their own, operates predominantly through the oral, written, and visual texts that make up colonial discourse, which have historically produced collective identities alienated from Indigenous roots, and continue to do so. Postcolonial theory addresses textual works that create counter-discourses that respond to colonial discourses. Spivak has suggested employing a strategic essentialism to combat cultural hegemonies and oppressive systems: "You pick up the universal that will give you the power to fight against the other" (Danius et al. 1993, 29). It is necessary to combine a critical application of "classical" tools for film analysis with postcolonial theory for postcolonial film analysis. Classical film analysis here serves to study technical (camera work, salient methods, lighting), structural (narrative features, motifs, form), and stylistic features. Post-colonial theory needs to be employed for the assessment of these features and for the analysis of content (Knopf 2008).

Postcolonial filmmaking is driven by the need to differentiate itself from mainstream filmmaking, but the binary reception or separation of postcolonial film from the Western Hollywood model of filmic practice needs to be dissolved and hybrid filmic practices introduced. Hybrid film practice can be understood in the Bhabhian sense of creating a third space—what others propose as a braided approach (Bhabha 2012). Here, Western film technology and conventions are woven together with Indigenous usage, infused with content that derives from various Indigenous constructions of cultural meaning, structures, styles, and techniques that are informed by Indigenous cultural practice and expression. Using Western technologies, however, does not necessarily mean assimilating into Western conventions and philosophies, but rather that video is a tool for cultural preservation and expression (Ginsburg 1991).

There is also the issue of language usage. According to Fanon (2008), colonialism restricts Indigenous languages, destroying cultures and creating cultural alienation. He says that speaking the colonial language implies an acceptance of colonialist consciousness and values. The colonized subject becomes assimilated into the colonizers' culture and alienated from their own. Knopf (2008) argues that Indigenous filmmakers have the choice to employ either their own language or the language of the colonizers. Each choice has its advantages and drawbacks. Films made in English or other European languages can reach a larger audience than films made in the respective Indigenous language. On the other hand, using an Indigenous language means a higher degree of self-determination and decolonization in the filmmaking process and in the end product.

Arguably, to truly adopt a braided approach to filmmaking would mean using *both* Western and Indigenous languages. For example, Pidgin Hawaiian in Hawai'i is neither fully English nor fully Hawaiian. When immigrants from European countries like Portugal and Great Britain, as well as from Asian countries like Japan, China, and the Philippines, started populating Hawai'i, there was a dire need for a common language. "[Pidgin] has a rich linguistical history based on the need for a common language among a diverse group of people who spoke different languages. It also has a dark side based on plantation domination and American English hegemony" (Hargrove et al. 2014). Pidgin is the hybrid language born out of combining different languages and it showcases an "and/all" perspective instead of an "either/or" mentality.

The films *Moana* and *Waikiki* adopt a hybridized approach to film production by fusing Western film technique with Pacific Islander culture. The two films are specific to Native Hawaiian culture in their storylines and address current Indigenous issues, such as land and water rights, sustainability, and houselessness. As an animated studio product, *Moana* must also fit into the larger Disney business model, which demands that profits be made, but there is still potential in *Moana*'s ability to showcase Pasifika performativity on screen. *Moana* and *Waikiki* portray the significance of the relationship between nature and culture, and the consequences when either one of those things is neglected.

Culture–Nature Relationship in the Pacific Islands

The Pacific Islands are home to the world's most diverse range of Indigenous cultures, but due to colonialism, these cultures have continued to struggle to sustain many ancestral lifeways. The fewer than 6.5 million people of the Pacific Islands possess a vast ocean of cultural traditions (Lindstrom 2010). For example, Papua New Guinea alone is home to one-third of the world's languages, with more than 800 distinct vernaculars (Lindstrom 2010). Oceania thus may have the most to lose culturally from the pressures of globalization and environmental erosion (Sasaki 2016). Pasifika people occupy an array of environments across a vast expanse of the Pacific, from Papua New Guinea's massive mountains to Auckland, New Zealand's urban jungles. About 85 percent of the population is rural and often nearly self-sufficient, planting their own crops and tending their own livestock. Still, over one-quarter of the more than two million Micronesians, Melanesians, and Polynesians live in cities or have moved to metropolitan centers (Sasaki 2016).

Despite their diversity, all Pacific societies are small and vulnerable. A typical Native group consists of only a few thousand people, and this has drastic consequences for cultural survival (Lindstrom 2010). An estimated one million Native Hawaiians lived in the Hawaiian archipelago before contact with the West in 1778; this number had diminished to 40,000 by 1892 (Dudley and Agard 1993). In 1990, there were a mere 8,244 "full-blooded" Native Hawaiians left (Dudley and Agard 1993). This decline in the Native Hawaiian population threatens the legacy of Hawaiian identity, culture, and livelihoods. Environmental forces also pose a major threat to island communities. In Fiji and Samoa, major storms, from Cyclone Winston in 1979 to Cyclone Ana in 2021, have caused significant damage to villages and national infrastructure that will take years to rebuild (Sasaki 2016).

To the Pasifika, culture and nature are intertwined in a distinct relationship where, if one suffers, so does the other. This culture–nature relationship was embedded at the inception of Pacific culture. For example, Hawaiians cherish a value called *aloha ʻāina* (caring for the land), which is spiritually recognized during the course of life and death. Hawaiian cultural historian and practitioner Haunani Trask (1999, 112) states, "we are children of Papa (earth mother), and Wakea (sky father) who created the sacred lands of Hawaiʻi Nei. From these lands come the taro, and from the taro came the Hawaiian people." Trask educates and reminds the Indigenous people of the commitment their ancestors made to the land, and that the land made to its *ʻohana* (family). Hawaiians consider the land to be an entity that works in harmony with life. "Hawaiians, therefore, did not regard land as a lifeless object to be used or discarded as one would treat any ordinary material thing. As part of the great earth, land is alive—it breathes, moves, reacts, behaves, adjusts, grows, sickens, dies" (Kanahele 1992, 187). *Aloha ʻāina* is the spirit that connects the land to Kānaka Maoli. As nature dissipates, so does culture, but also as culture dissolves, so then is the land neglected. This relationship is displayed in *Moana* and *Waikiki*.

Culture–Nature Relationship in *Moana* and *Waikiki*

On the Thanksgiving weekend of November 23, 2016, *Moana* splashed into the hearts of young children as Disney's latest princess movie, grossing $683 million to date. The film takes place about 2,000 years ago, after the goddess of nature, Te Fiti, has had her heart stolen. Blight has overcome the islands, devastating the vegetation and fish supply and endangering the livelihood of the people. Moana, the film's protagonist, is called by the ocean to return Te Fiti's heart and restore balance to the islands. As her journey proceeds, she encounters many who want Te Fiti's heart for their own personal gain.

The people of Motunui, where Moana resides, live in harmony with their natural surroundings. "Consider the coconut," they sing, celebrating the fruit that supplies food and liquid for their nutritional needs, as well as fiber from the shell, which can be used to make netting and other useful tools. The coconut tree supplies shelter from the weather, and its palms can be used as a building material. Chief Tui strongly believes that the island supplies the islanders with all they need to live rich and fulfilling lives. But there are signs that this form of living on the land might be in trouble. The villagers are catching fewer fish than they used to, and the coconuts on the island are starting to decay. Later in the film, Moana has visions of her island becoming rotten and black, with her people hungry and struggling. Even though Moana is drawn to the ocean and longs to learn about what is beyond the reef, her father is firm. The island is their home, and the reef is their safety barrier. No one sails beyond it.

During the film, a hidden secret is unveiled in a cave. There are depictions of islanders sailing very large boats, much larger than the small fishing boats that the people of Motunui use inside the reef. Moana has a vision of people who look like those who live on Motunui, but who roam the ocean, using stars for navigation. She hears them sing: "We are explorers. . . . We tell the stories of our elders in a never-ending chain." Moana learns that people stopped exploring the seas at the same time that Te Fiti's heart went missing. They found a safe island and stayed there. Moana sets out on a journey to find Te Fiti's heart, which she eventually restores, and the goddess starts to repair the destruction that has spread throughout the lands. Green leaves emerge and quickly start to reinvigorate the blackened, dying islands. As Motunui rediscovers a luscious version of itself, its inhabitants also rediscover their past and their desire to voyage beyond the reef. As the islanders celebrate Moana's return, and the regreening of their island, they drag the voyaging boats out of the cave. Finally, we see the islanders sailing the boats in the open ocean. Te Fiti's heart has been restored, the oceans are safe again, the islands are healing, and the people of Motunui have embraced their ancestors' natural penchant for exploration.

Moana justly represents the culture–nature relationship. The people of Motunui were once voyagers who used the stars to navigate and explore from one island to another. They tended to these new lands, but when they stopped, their environment slowly degraded. The land no longer provided for them because they no longer tended to the land. Thus, it was Moana's calling to rebuild this severed relationship by returning the heart of Te Fiti.

A similar but more visceral narrative can be seen in *Waikiki*. Written and directed by Native Hawaiian and Sundance Institute Native Lab fellow Christopher Kahunahana, *Waikiki* premiered in 2020 at the Los Angeles Asian Pacific Film Festival and the Hawaiʻi International Film Festival, winning top awards at both. Audiences and film critics lauded *Waikiki*'s cinematography and narrative, calling it arguably the most important film ever made by a Native Hawaiian. Gallichio (2020) asserted that *Waikiki* is "offering a literal behind-the-scenes glimpse of the iconic tourist spot. . . . *Waikiki* is a succinct emotional dive into the complex intergenerational trauma that plagues many Native Hawaiians."

The film follows the events in one week of the life of Kea (Danielle Zalopany), a Native Hawaiian who works as a hula dancer at a Waikiki restaurant, a nightclub hostess, and a teacher at a Hawaiian immersion school, while living out of her van and saving up to rent an apartment for low-income residents. Her current living situation is the result of having moved out of an apartment she shared with her abusive boyfriend (Jason Quinn). One night, she flees an altercation she has with him in a parking lot. While driving erratically, she hits a homeless man, Wo (Peter Shinkoda). Distraught, Kea puts Wo in her van, eventually shuttling him around as she attempts to maintain her life and her jobs. Their developing friendship is soon shattered when her van is towed away, leaving her and Wo shelterless. Her desperation triggers past trauma, driving her toward insanity. All the while, tourists walk by and judge her for being dirty, poor, and mentally incapable. The only redeeming quality, as one passerby says about her, is that "she looks pretty." *Waikiki* serves as an allegory for the contemporary issues Native Hawaiians face, including mental illness, physical abuse, homelessness, and most importantly, the loss of their land and Hawaiian identity. Kea learns to find peace in the chaos by turning back to what she learned from her ancestors, returning to the land—to a culture–nature relationship.

In the opening scene of the film, Kea performs with a troupe of hula dancers at a restaurant for tourists, against the backdrop of Diamond Head. She is adorned in stereotypical "hula girl" attire: coconut bra, sarong (linen cloth skirt), a lei around her neck, and a flower haku lei (headpiece). They dance to the melodic "Hawaiian" song "Waikiki" by Andy Cummings (2007), which extolls an idyllic vision of a bygone era in Hawai'i's 1950s golden age, showcasing Waikiki as a heavenly escape from routine life. As they dance, the lyrics state:

Waikiki, my whole life is empty without you
I miss that magic about you
Magic beside the sea
Magic of Waikiki

This first scene immediately portrays an idyllic vision of Hawaii. But in fact, it is an orientalized oasis from reality stuck in a pristine and peaceful past.

This imagery is strengthened by the following scene. Kea must hustle to her hostess job at a nightclub after being ogled by tourists. One group has the privilege to gaze, while the other is objectified as the gazed-upon to make ends meet. At the nightclub, Kea sits close to an older white man and sings "Waikiki," the song she performed to earlier as a hula dancer. As she sings, the man slowly brushes his hand against her leg and hands her a large monetary tip. Kea, looking uncomfortable, goes along with it because she really needs the money. From being merely an object for tourists to gaze at, she quickly becomes an object for them to handle. This supports Trask's (1999, 140) argument that Hawaiians become cultural prostitutes for the tourist industry: "The prostitute is a woman who sells her sexual capacities . . . the pimp is the conduit of exchange, managing the commodity that is the prostitute while acting as the guard at the entry and exit gates, making sure that the prostitutes behave." In this scene, Kea is not just figuratively made to be a prostitute, as Trask contends; she is literally sexually harassed by a white tourist and becomes a real object of subjugation. She has no choice but to comply or risk losing her job, which she desperately needs to survive.

Kea's van is eventually towed while she is working at the nightclub. She becomes fully homeless in this instance. In the days and nights that follow, she looks for her van and sleeps on the sidewalks of Waikiki, while tourists pass by her with glaring eyes. Having once been gazed upon for her exotic beauty, she is now gazed upon for being dirty, perhaps primitive. In one incident, police escort her away from a popular tourist site. This is an inherent symbol of the continued aftermath of settler colonialism in Hawai'i: Hawaiians are pushed out of their living spaces. It also portrays the immense institutional power the tourist industry has. If a Kānaka does not behave in the orientalizing vision created by tourism, they are symbolically annihilated.

Kea continues to have flashbacks to her more peaceful childhood while living on sidewalks and searching for her van. She remembers being with her grandma in the forest and in the ocean. She remembers learning to sing *mele* (songs) in *'ōlelo* (Hawaiian language), and dancing hula to those songs. She remembers her grandmother leading by example, teaching her the Hawaiian culture. Kea copes with her current struggles through her memories. Though the film does not provide a resolution to Kea's homelessness and objectification, the last scene shows her at a beach at Waikiki, kneeling and tossing the sand around while dancing hula and singing in *'ōlelo.* This scene stands in stark opposition to the first two scenes of the film, where she performs for the pleasure of tourists by dancing and singing to a "Hawaiian" English song written by a white person. In this final scene, she is not performing for a person, but is singing and dancing hula in front of the ocean—she is performing for the *'āina.* She finds solitude in the brief moment of returning to the culture and *'āina,* even while her homelessness and other challenges persist.

Waikiki's conclusion is drastically different from *Moana*'s. *Moana* offers viewers a cheerful optimism about the culture–nature relationship in Pacific Islander cultures, and the need to return to such a connection. *Waikiki*'s ending, on the other hand, does not resolve any of Kea's struggles, and in a sense presents the viewer with a more realistic view of the fate of Native Hawaiians in a largely white, colonized, militarized, and tourist-driven institution. Instead of optimism, it provides a dystopic outlook for all Native Hawaiians should we continue to live in such conditions. We see the struggle of sustaining culture and environments across the Pacific Islands. For example, in Hawai'i, recent attempts to build a telescope on top of the mountain Maunakea or Mauna O'Wakea have sparked Native Hawaiians to protest construction on that sacred ground (Brown 2016). In order to maintain culture and reestablish the Kānaka Maoli connection to *'āina,* it is our *kuleana* (responsibility) to make sure the next generation of Hawaiians learns this. The responsibility of providing for the next generation is apparent in both *Moana* and *Waikiki.*

Kuleana

Moana and *Waikiki* showcase the inherent role of *kuleana* in continuing the beliefs, traditions, and legacy of Pacific Island culture. *Kuleana* is extremely important for Hawaiians. According to Pukui and Elbert (1986, 179), *kuleana* means "right, privilege, concern, responsibility." *Kuleana* referred to a plot of land an individual person or family was charged with maintaining and caring for in traditional society (Kame'eleihiwa 1992), so this idea of responsibility is culturally grounded within Oceanic tradition. *Moana* and *Waikiki* display different levels of *kuleana*: to the self and to the community.

Understanding one's own purpose helps illuminate our personal responsibilities toward Pasifika culture. Understanding our own role, not just physically but also spiritually, is *kuleana* to the self. In finding oneself, we then understand our connection to the land and the people, and our responsibility to them. It is our responsibility to learn and understand our own identity and the importance of preserving the culture and *'āina*. Moana questions her identity and purpose at the outset of the film. Her father is adamant that no one travels beyond the reef because the island will provide all that is needed. Her calling, according to Chief Tui, is to follow in his footsteps and lead the people of Motunui. Instead, an inner inkling tells Moana that she is meant to do more, that she should go beyond the reef to find her identity and her true calling. This tension between being the person her father wants her to be and trying to find out who she is meant to be is displayed in her song "How Far I'll Go":

I've been staring at the edge of the water
Long as I can remember, never really knowing why
I wish I could be the perfect daughter
But I come back to the water, no matter how hard I try . . .
But the voice inside sings a different song
What is wrong with me?
See the light as it shines on the sea?
It's blinding
But no one knows
How deep it goes
And it seems like it's calling out to me

When Moana discovers her ancestors were explorers, she finds her own purpose and responsibility to the people of Motunui and to the land. She is able to pass on her legacy to her family and community when she finds herself.

Similarly, in *Waikiki*, Kea struggles with her identity. She is well-versed in Hawaiiana, yet she is lost in how she should use her knowledge. At the beginning of the film, we see her use her hula skills to appear as an exotic object for the tourist gaze. Though she finds displeasure in her performance, her culture and her body are appropriated and objectified for the colonizers' pleasure. As the film progresses and nostalgic memories of better days spending time in nature, caring for the *'āina*, and learning from her grandmother fill her head, she finds moments of relief from her current struggles. This reaches its pinnacle in the final scene, where Kea dances hula and sings on the beach—in nature. It is when she grounds herself in connection with the *'āina* that her Hawaiian identity is reclaimed and restored.

Not only is *kuleana* a value for the self, it also expands to the community. Once Native Hawaiians understand our own role within the culture, we have a responsibility to pass on that knowledge to the next generation. This is apparent in *Moana.* In sailing past the reef, finding Maui, and returning Te Fiti's heart, not only does Moana rescue her people and the land, she also saves them in terms of their lost identity. The heart of Te Fiti is restored, and so are the hearts of the people of Motunui. The practice of voyaging is restored and passed along to the next generation.

Likewise, in *Waikiki,* responsibility to one's community and Native Hawaiian youth is of utmost importance. In one powerful scene, Kea is at her third job as a teacher at a Hawaiian immersion school. She teaches the students the term "*he ali'i ka 'āina, he kauwā ke kanka*" ("the land is the chief and the people are its servants"). She writes this phrase on the board and has the following discussion with her students:

Kea: *Alright, somebody remind me what does this mean?*
Student 1: *It means that the land is the chief and the people are its servants.*
Kea: *Yes, but that is a literal translation, what does this mean to you guys [sic] specifically?*
Student 2: *We must care for the land because if there is no land there are no people.*
Kea: *Maikai (good), that was so good! We all must take care of the 'āina because it will in turn take care of us.*

This scene shows the strong connection that Hawaiians have to the land, that of a culture–nature relationship. Kea is carrying out her *kuleana* and her legacy to the Kānaka Maoli community by teaching her students this lesson about our connection to *'āina.* She is also doing what her grandmother did, leading by example in teaching the students about Hawaiiana, *'āina*, and *'ōlelo.*

Discussion and Conclusion

Two diametrically opposed themes dominate the current onscreen representation of Pacific and Native Hawaiians: amnesia and militarization.

The former is rooted in escapist fantasy and white melodrama, negating any historical accountability on the part of the United States to its colonization of Hawai'i. Instead, Hawai'i figures as a wholesome ecosystem that restores broken relationships, induces new romances, or produces escapist self-awakening (Konzett 2017). The white hegemonic universe that fantasizes Hawai'i as a home away from home appears benign, but gives little voice to those living in Hawai'i who have been socioeconomically displaced by settler colonialism, tourism, and an extremely high cost of living. In contrast to these fantasy scenarios, films with a dose of realism view Hawai'i as a battleground for global conflicts and the maintenance of geopolitical dominance through military power. The necessary (re)militarization of Pacific culture is made acceptable to audiences via action plots (Kajihiro 2009). Once again, the reality of contemporary Hawai'i falls through the cracks in such scenarios that indulge in the ever-growing enlargement of the military-industrial-entertainment complex (Miyose and Grimshaw 2019). This strengthens the need to counter such tropes by allowing Pasifika and Kānaka Maoli to speak using postcolonial filmmaking.

Disney's *Moana* attempts to provide a more culturally accurate portrayal of the Pacific Islander, and specifically the Native Hawaiian experience, by using an advisory board of Pacific Islander elders and cultural specialists in the form of the OST, as well as by having a cast of Pacific Islander–identified voice actors and actresses. Also, Disney translated *Moana* into Hawaiian and Māori, making it the first Disney movie to be translated into these languages. The Hawaiian version of *Moana* is being used in Hawaiian immersion schools to help students learn *'ōlelo*. Furthermore, in 2023, it was announced that live-action iterations of Disney animated films *Lilo and Stitch* and *Moana* were forthcoming, bringing even more optimism for the future of Pasifika representation. A sequel to the first animated *Moana* was released in 2024. *Moana 2* made box office records with the largest ever five-day gross, which included the biggest Thanksgiving debut ever (Yang 2024).

Waikiki is a positive first step as the first feature-length film to be written and directed by a Native Hawaiian. Director Christopher Kahunahana was asked in a CBC radio interview why he wanted to produce the film. He responded that it was his *kuleana* to create this film (Shantz-Hilkes and Goodyear 2020):

> to actually show a fuller picture, you know, not just the one that we see every day in the tourist ads. . . . It's the image of what happens when she stops dancing and stops being performative and she has to go back to normal

> life. . . . Kea, our protagonist, has to navigate a world where intergenerational violence, abuse and poverty and mental illness are daily battles. So she has to deal with this diametrically opposed need to survive in modern society, and at the same time, the calling of our ancestors and their culture.

Kahunahana's statement that he felt it was his *kuleana* to provide a more accurate depiction of the Native Hawaiian experience in a colonized and tourist-driven land makes him the very definition of a postcolonial filmmaker.

Organizations that focus on conservation and sustainability can learn from traditional practices of Pacific Islanders. *Moana* and *Waikiki* show the importance of the finely tuned relationship between natural resources and culture. The actions and forces that resulted in a breaking of that interrelationship have contributed to the current global conservation crisis. Consequently, the reestablishment of those relationships represents a way to build a sustainable society. Cultural identity, knowledge, and practice are rooted in this reciprocal relationship with the land. As the *Moana* song "Where You Are" states:

This tradition is our mission
And Moana, there's so much to do (make way!) . . .
Consider the coconuts
The trunks and the leaves
The island gives us what we need

But this only happens when we take care of the land as well. Our life is connected to the land.

Discussion Questions

1. What are the cultural and environmental challenges faced by Pacific Islander communities due to settler colonialism, globalization, and tourism?
2. How does the stereotyping of Hawaiian culture by the tourist industry affect the representation and agency of Kānaka Maoli (Native Hawaiians)?
3. In what ways does postcolonial filmmaking decolonize or indigenize misrepresentations of Indigenous communities? In what ways can it be empowering for Indigenous media producers?

14

"We're the Original Storytellers"

Interview with Taietsarón:sere Leclaire

Taietsarón:sere Leclaire, a.k.a. Tai Leclaire, is a Native American director, writer, and actor from the Mohawk Nation of Kahnawà:ke. Tai's latest project, writing and directing an adaptation of the classic movie *The Prince and the Pauper* for Warner Bros. Studios, is available to stream on MAX. His previous short film, *Headdress*, which he wrote, directed, and starred in, premiered at the 2023 Sundance Film Festival. He's a former writer and actor on the NBC comedy series *Rutherford Falls* by Sierra Teller-Ornelas, Mike Schur, and Ed Helms. He wrote on the Will Arnett animated comedy series, *Super Team Canada.*

Please introduce yourself.

My name is Taietsarón:sere Leclaire. Everyone calls me Tai. I am Kanyen'kehà:ka, which is Mohawk, and Mi'kmaq. I am from the Mohawk Nation of Kahnawà:ke. I'm based on the Chumash Tongva lands of Los Angeles.

Describe your work. What compels you to do it?

I got into media when I was a kid, and I just happened to be Indigenous. I've made movies since I was eleven. I was always working in the creative field, performing in local theater as a kid. Then, I think it was only in college, I studied photography, and I studied communication design at Parsons School of Design in New York.

I grew up in Kahnawà:ke. It's a Mohawk Nation in south Montreal. I'm Mohawk and Mi'kmaq. I'm American and Canadian. I'm Native and First Nations. I'm very much in this in-between place. I grew up with APTN [Aboriginal People's Television Network] in Canada, which was sort of a big push [for me]. So I never grew up without there being a Native network on TV.

When I finished college, I went into fashion and advertising, mostly because it was storytelling. I was an art director at J.Crew. I was coming

Fig. 14.1. Taietsarón:sere Leclaire. Author photo.

up with narratives around seasonal campaigns and it was a creative, fun job. The entire time, I was still doing comedy. I was having my 9 to 5, and then I'd have my 5 to 9, which was very much my heart and my love. I'd be doing stand-up shows, sketch comedy, a lot of improv comedy. Eventually I got on *Characters Welcome*, which is a daunting task to get as a performer in this really nerdy comedy, improv scene. But I loved it.

When I was at UCB [Upright Citizens Brigade], I made this original character called Cheyenne Winters. Cheyenne was a Native American shaman who dealt exclusively with white ghosts. And it was really stupid, which is kind of my love language. I love stupidity.

Around 2019, I found an old journal entry that said something like, "A Native media renaissance is about to happen, and I want to be a part of it." A couple months later, the showrunner for *Rutherford Falls* saw me at a live show, DM'd [direct messaged] me on Twitter, asked if I had any samples. Then I got staffed on *Rutherford Falls*, and then I moved to LA. It was so insane to be on a TV show, to be in a writer's room. It was my first ever formal writer's gig, and it was the first time in a long time that

I had Native coworkers, and that was really fun. I feel so spoiled to have been in *Rutherford Falls*. It was part of my life from 2020 to 2023, even though it was only two seasons.

I was in the Sundance Native Lab in 2022 with a very stupid script inspired partially by Cheyenne, but it was more about a ghost dealing with systemic racism. Everything I do is in that comedic semi-horror space. I was always obsessed with things that were "the other" and that's mostly because, as a queer/gay person, but also as a Native person, I know what it is to be an outsider. I wrote, directed, and acted in my first short film, *Headdress*, and it got into the Sundance Film Festival in 2023. I felt okay. I thought, *Shit is starting to get a little more real now. Headdress* was my first taste of really being the director and facilitating an entire show. I had a fifteen-year journey to get to where I am now. I picked up so many things in the mediascape that helped me on the way.

What does Indigenous media mean to you?

It means everything to me. I'm a part of it. I support it, I watch it. I live and breathe for it. *Reservation Dogs* got nominated for an Emmy for best comedy series, and I think that's the first time an all-Native show has been nominated at the Emmys. I know everyone over there and I think it's groundbreaking. I'm just so excited that the world's catching up to Natives; it's not Natives catching up to media. Indigenous media is simply media created by Indigenous people, but it doesn't mean that it needs to involve an Indigenous narrative. Who's at the wheel is very much my point of view on it all.

My next short film is called *The Prince and The Pauper*. It's a remake of the 1937 classic and the Mark Twain novel as well. It was a really fun program because it was me and five other BIPOC directors, and they were kind of just "reimagine it however you want." I got to shoot on the Warner Bros. lot, and my budget increased. Bird Runningwater was my executive producer on this project. I don't know if anything's ever been shot on this lot that had a Native director, a Native actor, and a Native executive producer.

What does the future hold, in your view?

This "media renaissance" is happening, and now we're about to be in that wonderful space where we can skip the Indian 101 of it all and just start making the stupid stories that we want to make. I have a feature film

I'm working on, that I've been working on for the last two years, that's inspired by the character Cheyenne. I was so worried about the script for it because I thought, *God, I'm gonna have to do so much more explaining. What's a shaman? What's this?* I don't really have to anymore. I think I just kind of lean in to the stupid, do the thing that makes me laugh, and have fun with it. I'm grateful for *Reservation Dogs*, grateful for *Rutherford Falls*, grateful for *Dark Winds*. I'm grateful for *Frybread Face and Me*. I'm grateful for *Fancy Dance*—everything that came out in the last four or five years only helps. My dream is to just make more feature films.

Why is it important to have Indigenous people tell their own stories?

We're the original storytellers. We always like to say that. There's specificity in our culture that I/you can't bring unless you're in the culture, and I think it's that specificity that leads to commonality, so people start saying, "Oh, you guys do that at your house? We do something similar." If you have someone at the wheel who's not Native trying to do those things, it's going to feel inauthentic. Because it will be inauthentic. I think authenticity is the secret sauce to any of this stuff. I think that specificity is key.

My dream outside of all this is to have Indigenous people in positions of power outside of the creative side. I really do hope there will be more Native people on the executive side, more Native people on the studio side, and more Native people overall, because I've seen the instruments of change.

What should the next generation consider? Why is this work important?

That's what makes me so grateful for this moment now. All these leaders that we have right now understand that, as Indigenous people, community is key. Without community, you can't make this thing. As Indigenous people, we understand the power of community and we lean on it heavily for everything. I mean, I wouldn't be where I am today if it wasn't for community, without the support of fellow Indigenous people. To have that sort of structure that didn't quite exist before is groundbreaking on its own.

I was always a bit of an outcast growing up. I was too gay for the rez, but I was too rez for the city. It was one of those things where I never really found my footing, and it was sort of in these specific pockets of my career in life where I found my community. And it's still Native, it's still queer. I genuinely hope we get to the place where it's less a conversation around "there's one Native show happening," to where the story and the narrative become the centerpiece, rather than the assets around it.

Rutherford Falls, *Reservation Dogs*, *Dark Winds*, they're all in that place where they're standing on their own. They're part of the ecosystem of this natural evolution that happens once diverse voices finally get into a position of some power. I'm very optimistic because there's no other choice. I'm not even entertaining the idea that they're going the other way.

Is there anything else you would like to add?

Whatever career, company, or thing you're interested in, it has a program you can apply to be a participant in. Every year, I try to get at least one hundred professional rejections, because you only need two good ones. These companies want these voices, and they want to hear these stories. So search and you will find.

—Interviewed by Cristina L. Azocar

15

The Power of Positionality in Indigenous Nonfiction Film

Tsanavi Spoonhunter

Indigenous culture is no stranger to depiction on the big screen, especially in nonfiction films, but more often than not this depiction is to the detriment of Indigenous communities. An example that illustrates this is the feature-length documentary *Reel Injun* (2009) by Cree filmmaker Neil Diamond. This film spans decades of Indigenous American misrepresentation in Hollywood and shows how those portrayals have created harmful stereotypes. Positionally refers to the idea that a filmmaker's cultural standpoint—especially in relation to Indigenous identity and community—shapes how stories are told in nonfiction film.

We can trace negative trajectories of Native American representation over more than a century. It all began at the dawn of ethnographic documentary filmmaking with Robert J. Flaherty's *Nanook of the North* (1922). Ethnographic films are nonfiction films and visual media, rooted in anthropology, that depict non-Western or colonial cultures and societies (Hasty et al. 2022). *Nanook of the North* is a black-and-white picture that is widely regarded as having been the first documentary. It resulted in Indigenous peoples finding themselves at the center of exclusively colonialist depictions of who they are, how they live, and how they behave. *Nanook of the North* doesn't truly encompass or reflect the actual experiences of Indigenous peoples.

Nanook of the North staged Inuit life that was not reflective of the realities they had to navigate. In fact, neither should be promoted for profit, but rather used as tools for understanding and connection. Flaherty's commodification of the Indigenous experience is a point of controversy and contention. Therefore, to frame this discussion, I will share a ceremonial experience from my life, to contrast with the fictional story of the Inuit ways of life that Flaherty constructed.

When I was growing up, every Sunday my family would practice what we called "Sweat." In preparation, my father would take my brothers to the banks of the canal that ran along our backyard to pick tule plants that we would later comfortably sit on in the Sweat Lodge. My father and brothers would then go to gather lava rock. Before Sweat began, my mother, sisters, and I would cook meals based on the staple foods of our people. This food would be offered to everyone involved for their sacrifice and prayers.

My brothers would build a fire to heat the lava rocks before the ceremony, and as soon as the rocks were at a smoldering temperature, the women would enter the Sweat—a circular dome made of cloth and branches—followed by the men. The heated stones would be placed in the center of the Lodge by men not participating in the ceremony, and then they would leave, softly closing the door behind them as the proceedings began. The leader of the Sweat Lodge—my father, in this case—would sing traditional songs. My people convened in front of the hot embers to pray with each other for ourselves and our communities. The Lodge was a space where I went to experience a rebirth of the spirit alongside family and friends. Afterward, we would go about our lives in our homes. It is a warm, familiar communal space such as this that *Nanook of the North*'s igloo is supposed to symbolize. However, Flaherty constructed a communal space and directed those in the film in a way that wasn't authentic to the realities of Inuit life (Essner and Ruby 1987).

As much as I have committed my career and life to capturing images and telling intimate personal stories, I would not build or show a reproduction of the Sweat or stage any Indigenous way of life. The Sweat is an experience that is uniquely and exclusively tied to my culture and people. It is a transformative experience so exceptional that it simply cannot and should not be displayed for the world's entertainment. Most Indigenous people would agree with me, which is why Flaherty's depiction of an intimate experience is an affront to our beliefs, varied as they may be.

The need to respectfully and accurately represent Native American traditions and customs is evident and necessary. Seeing the film was when I encountered my first dilemma as an Indigenous documentary filmmaker. On the one hand, outsiders try to understand and document the reality of us; on the other, this so often involves betraying the very essence of being Native American—the privacy of such traditions. By paralleling the story and production of America's first documentary, *Nanook of the North*, with the modern nonfiction film landscape of Native American storytelling and existence, it becomes immediately evident how fallible filmmakers are (and have always been) in their attempts to capture the ineffable experience of Indigenous life, and how we, the Indigenous, are still overcoming the consequences of a film that is over one hundred years old.

A Background of the Foundation of Documentary Based on the Indigenous Experience

Nanook of the North is a silent, black-and-white picture that profiles an Inuit hunter and his family as they build igloos and hunt seals using centuries-old Inuit methods. Even if we set aside the fact that the entire plot of this nonfiction film was staged—those who appeared in the film (including Nanook) invented the scenes, rehearsed some of the scenes, and even shot on professional film sets—we cannot ignore the fact that the film resulted in harmful and inaccurate depictions of an entire race of people. The immeasurable tragedy of *Nanook* is that, from that point on, the mold of the typical Indigenous American peoples leaned into the shape of the mythical, fictional "Nanook" caricature—a mold created and put in place by non-Natives. We are still fighting that caricature vigorously.

Robert Joseph Flaherty (figure 15.1) is widely considered to be the first ever documentary filmmaker. He was born the son of Robert Henry Flaherty, a prospector who made his money by extracting iron ore from the mines he had acquired during his explorations (Essner and Ruby 1987). Having an explorer for a father influenced Flaherty Jr., who also chose to become an explorer, albeit of the arts. Both were frontrunners in their field, and they both accomplished this by extracting or exploiting the resources of their adopted lands to the detriment of the locals.

Flaherty started down his filmmaking path as an explorer. He embarked on expeditions to the northernmost parts of the Americas to find areas with bountiful resources that he could extract or document. He began his documentary work by collecting moving pictures during his expeditions in what settlers described as "unchartered territory" between 1913 and 1916 (Christopher 2005). His early showings of the films inspired by these excursions were well received, as one spectator detailed: "Mr. Robert J. Flaherty of Toronto . . . has a most interesting series of ethnological moving pictures of Esquimo life, which show the primitive existence of a people in the way they lived before being brought in contact with explorers" (Barnouw 1993, 35).

Flaherty quickly found stardom through his explorations. He worked in a Michigan copper mine, and with the Grand Trunk Pacific Railway prospecting for marble on Vancouver Island and iron ore at Lake Huron and the Mattagami River (Christopher 2005). He started filming his expeditions

Fig. 15.1. Portrait of Robert J. Flaherty. Courtesy of the Library of Congress, Prints and Photographs Division, Washington, DC. LC-DIG-agc-7a17021.

and soon found his calling in motion pictures. He continued north until he reached Baffin Island, in what is now the territory of Nunavut, Canada. He combined his early moving pictures into one reel and began early screenings in 1922, which were incredibly well received by the public.

I remember watching this mandatory "classic," *Nanook of the North*, as the only Native American student in a documentary history class while at the University of California, Berkeley Graduate School of Journalism. It struck a chord that the only film about Native Americans we watched was by a filmmaker who was himself as far as you could get from being an Indigenous American. I recall asking myself why I was being put in a position where I had to admire a film that created and perpetuated incredibly damaging narratives about my community, and forever stained how Indigenous peoples are portrayed in the media. Why, instead, were we not celebrating Indigenous filmmakers like Neil Diamond, who have managed to reclaim the narrative of their people and thereby reshaped the future of their communities?

Nanook of the North (figure 15.2) is celebrated in the industry because, through it, Flaherty created a new form of film: the ethnographic documentary. In this context, positionality means that filmmakers possess their own beliefs, biases, and viewpoints when portraying the lives and cultures of others—it serves as a reminder that Flaherty's work is not that of a neutral observer, but represents merely one interpretation of Inuit identity.

Over the years, many critics have consistently questioned Flaherty's motives and the accomplishments that arose out of his deeply unethical style of storytelling (Brave NoiseCat 2020). However, in 2022, documentarians worldwide happily observed the one-hundredth anniversary of the release of *Nanook of the North*. It has never stopped being celebrated as the first documentary feature film ever made by an American.

Flaherty was undoubtedly motivated by his perception of what being Inuit *should* mean, not what it actually was. He orchestrated his vision through Allakariallak, the actor who portrayed Nanook, as well as the actor's family (Zimmermann and Zimmermann Auyash n.d.). In the early 1900s, Native American tribes across the continent were being assimilated by the colonial governments. As a result, they lost for decades many of their traditional lifeway practices and were aggressively forced to conform to Western lifestyles. Flaherty staged scenes in an igloo and outfitted the participants in traditional clothing they would not otherwise have worn. For instance, at this point in history, Allakariallak and other members of his community would have hunted animals in the wilderness with modern tools, such as guns. However, Flaherty insisted they hunt seals and other beasts with spears (Laman 2023).

Have YOU said "If I could get THE PICTURE I can get the crowds?" Here is THE picture!

REVILLON FRÈRES
presents

"NANOOK OF THE NORTH"

Produced by
ROBERT J. FLAHERTY F.R.G.S.

SUCH a picture comes once in a lifetime. It is just such a picture as you have been looking for during the dull days of the past twelve months.

You know that *if you've got the picture you can get the crowds.*

Your chief worry has been that big pictures are so scarce. Here is as big a picture as this business has ever seen, different, absolutely different from any other ever made.

It's a picture that offers immense opportunities for exploitation.

Pathepicture

Fig. 15.2. Movie poster for Nanook of the North. *Courtesy of the Library of Congress, Motion Picture, Broadcasting and Recorded Sound Division, Washington, DC. LC-USZ62–116710.*

It was not until 1978, when the American Indian Freedom of Religion Act (AIFRA) was passed, which meant that Native Americans were once again allowed to practice their religions freely without violating the law. The Act protected the rights of Native Americans to honor their traditions by ensuring access to sacred sites, the use and possession of sacred objects, and the freedom to worship through ceremonies and traditional rites (Harjo 2004). Up until then, and especially in the 1910s, Native Americans could be sent to court and put in jail for practicing their traditions. From 1883 to 1934, the federal government established the Courts of Indian Offenses to criminalize Native American traditions (Harjo 2004). More specifically, Secretary of the Interior Henry M. Teller called for the creation of these courts, urging that actions that appeared to deviate from Christian norms, such as polyamory, "medicine man" practices, or ritual gift-giving, should be prosecutable offenses (National Geographic n.d.)

The outlawing of Indigenous religions is one of the most historically documented practices of cultural genocide (Kanu 2022). In retrospect, it is shocking that Flaherty was able to sell the world on the idea that Native Americans were actually free to live within their own communities, speak their language, and practice their religion, when in fact the behavior of colonists was brutish, inhuman, and effectively kept Indigenous people prisoners on their own land. For instance, in 1988, the AIFRA statute was tested in *Lyng v. Northwest Indian Cemetery Protective Association*. The Forest Service's plan to construct a logging road through sacred Native American lands was initially halted due to its potential disruption of tribal religious practices. However, the Supreme Court later allowed the construction of the road.

The Realities for Those Practicing Traditions That Documentary Film Ignores

In a cultural sense, my siblings and I are privileged. My parents always observed our traditional religious practices even before the AIFRA passed. Their decision to raise us as Paiute and Arapaho people cultivated a sense of pride in me, even though, to my shame, I spent a long time rejecting that pride and being embarrassed by my race. However, having a foundation of tribal knowledge and family traditions not only enabled me to accept my Native American identity wholeheartedly, but also instilled a way for me to harness my experiences creatively.

In the second year of my graduate degree, I made a short documentary film titled *Crow Country: Our Right to Food Sovereignty* about food deserts on a Native American reservation. Yet, even as I was making it and screening each new cut weekly in front of my class for feedback, I experienced hurtful tokenism. My journalism skills and efforts to build relationships with my protagonists didn't matter to the other students. They assumed that I would have an easier time with the stories I was telling simply because I am Native American. In fact, this was not the case because I'm not from the Crow tribe, so I had to be just as diligent than any outsider telling the story I told. A "pretendian" is a colloquial term used to describe an individual falsely claiming Indigenous identity exclusively through self-identification as a citizen of a Native American or Indigenous tribal nation, or by proclaiming descent from a distant Native American ancestor (Associated Press 2022). Historian Philip J. Deloria observes that European Americans have a history of "playing Indian," a phenomenon that can be traced back to at least the 1773 Boston Tea Party (Deloria 1998).

The "pretendian" movement is yet another consequence of the Flahertian tradition of showing from a non-Native's perspective what an Indigenous person should look like and how they should behave based on very stereotypical knowledge of a culture they in no way comprehend. In truth, a non-Native person's approach to storytelling can never align with the realities of Indigenous lived experiences. For instance, Heather Rae is known throughout the film industry as a titan of Indigenous content production. However, Rae fabricated an Indigenous Cherokee identity during the production of her first film, *Trudell*, to win a bidding war for the rights to the story of Santee Dakota activist John Trudell (Aratani 2023). Rae was eventually outed as a non-Indigenous person, yet amazingly she continues to garner accolades and maintain a lucrative high status in the film industry.

Realistically, being a tribal citizen results in many Native American filmmakers and academics feeling like imposters in their chosen professions (Chakraverty 2022). This perspective is understandable given how often both academia and film have been used as tools against Indigenous people, especially in attempts to erase and replace tribal origin stories with ones more convenient for the settler identity (Smiles n.d.).

Indigenous Storytelling as an Oral Storytelling Approach

My father was the first person to confront me about my understanding and belief in the veracity of the Bering Land Bridge Theory during a road trip to a conference to which he was invited. I know now that he brought it up because scientists at the time were loudly spreading the theory that Native Americans themselves had emigrated to North America—only before the white settlers did. My father didn't believe it, but he asked me if I did. I didn't really know anything about it until he explained it to me. I felt hurt that, by explaining the theory, he'd even suggest that we were from somewhere else. During my upbringing he instilled in us that this is where we were from, and he solidified that with creation stories specific to the locations that surrounded us. I guess he just wanted to hear my thoughts on the matter, even though he already had his own. Unfortunately, many Indigenous children were forced to learn this theory as fact in the public school system, and not all children were as lucky as I was to have parents who taught my siblings and I the tribal stories of creation, reinforcing from an early age that we belong to this land. It's a place we were meant to steward and take care of—instructions passed down through generations.

Payahuunadü has always been home to my ancestors and me. The Paiute, my people, call the Owens Valley "the place of flowing water" after the Owens River, which flows right through it and gives the valley its shape. To the north of several Paiute reservations stands the Sierra Nevada mountain range, while the White Mountains and the Inyo Mountains are to the south. To the west is the Mojave Desert. My name, Tsanavi, is a Paiute word that means "desert peach"—a flower indigenous to the area—and my last name is a surname found frequently in the local Arapaho community.

Looking back on that car ride with my father, in that moment I felt angry and hurt that he could even suggest we weren't from a place my people had belonged to for a long time. I remember firmly saying to my father, "Creator put us here just like he put people everywhere else around the world." In my mind, that was that. We were not brought here. This land, its beauty, and its ruggedness have been ours since the beginning.

Of course, this was a test, and my father knew perfectly well the illegitimacy of the Bering Land Bridge Theory. When I was young, he would take my siblings and me to a place sacred to the Paiute people not for generations but for millennia: Coso Paya, or "Hot Water," in the Mojave Desert. My people believe that precious life-healing plants and medicines can be found there, so we would go there to collect clay for ceremonies and dance rituals. My father was the first to advocate for our Paiute tribal members to have access to re-enter this sacred land after centuries of not being allowed passage to this place of healing. It was also a place where my mom would always pull over, when driving past, to give an offering as gratitude and proof to the Creator that we understood and appreciated the power of the life He gave us.

We were always taught that everything on earth belongs to the Creator and always will, just as our ancestors before us had been taught. My father wanted to continue his traditional ways of life and further strengthen our tribal government's sovereignty, so he went to school at the University of California. But he dropped out after one semester when he realized that the settler education system would in no way prepare him for his chosen lifestyle on the reservation. He went there hoping to learn how best to lead his tribal government, but he found that there were no classes in the University of California system that encouraged the strengthening and growth of the reservation system—a system of erasure that had essentially enabled the creation of the university itself.

Instead, my father returned home and founded the Bishop Paiute Environmental Management Office in 1996 in order to promote Indigenous environmental stewardship of the Bishop Paiute reservation and its neighboring communities (Bishop Tribe Environmental Office n.d.). After his passing, my father's strong ideals and belief system fueled our community's spirit and growth. Today, there is a gymnasium named after my father in dedication to his work advancing our tribe.

With all this multigenerational lore and history under my belt, I made my cautious foray into both the University of California school system and nonfiction filmmaking. Like my father, I consider myself a storyteller; unlike my father, who chose to turn his attention to the community ward, I decided to bring my community to the world through the art of visual storytelling.

When my brothers and I were integrated into the public school system, we were easy targets for stereotypical racist taunts such as "bloodthirsty savage," "noble warrior," and the all-time favorite "redskin." The latter is tough to stomach since it refers to the scalps white settlers took from the heads of the Native American men, women, and children who refused to let the federal government take over their lands. Government officials would give people cash in exchange for the scalps as punishment for Native Americans not vacating their tribal lands. The scalp was proof that a bounty hunter had killed an Indian. Such was the federal policy implemented in order to seize lands that rightfully belonged to Native Americans.

In order for Indigenous media to thrive in any shape or form, it is imperative that we as a society dismantle painful systemic stereotypes and resensitize people to offensive, racist terminology so that the next generation of Native Americans will be able to grow up in an environment free of judgment. No more teasing for having long hair, traditional "Indian" profiles, and stereotypical Native American noses—long with a hump. Worryingly, many young Native Americans have internalized these caricatures. Indigenous children only learn stereotypes in the public school system when tribal history and traditions are entirely absent from the curriculum.

The lived experience of being an outcast in my own Native land made it especially difficult for me to enter the film industry. This industry is not easy to access regardless of your socioeconomic status, but it is especially hard for a Native American who grew up on a reservation. I survived the casual racism of the American public school system. However, I knew that if I wanted to further my education, I would need to find an institution that did not make me feel like an outsider or a token. I also needed a school that I could afford. Cost is often the most prohibitive barrier to young Native Americans pursuing higher education. I decided to attend Haskell Indian Nations University, a four-year institution dedicated to teaching federally recognized citizens of American Indian Nations. It was here that I first saw the film *Reel Injun* by Cree filmmaker Neil Diamond, in my first journalism course.

Reel Injun was the first film I had ever seen that addressed, point blank, the stereotypical portrayals of Native Americans in films. Diamond perfectly showcased the evolution of such stereotypes in Hollywood filmmaking—the Indian as the strong silent warrior, the dimwitted drunk, or the helpless maiden—all of which were insults used against me in some shape or form throughout my childhood.

However, it was also while watching *Reel Injun* that I began to wonder: How can we Native Americans tell authentic stories about ourselves? Flaherty and his replicators showcased an inauthentic environment full of fictitious people with stories devoid of any cultural significance and not reflecting any actual issues. In other words, Flaherty bisected a fake igloo to reveal what life there was inside. The result was fantastical because capturing even the essence of Indian Country on film was (and for the most part, still is) beyond Hollywood's magic tricks and the genre of ethnographic film. The igloo, just like my father's Sweat Lodge, cannot and should not be portrayed on film. It is ineffable, the moral equivalent of filming a documentary inside a Catholic confessional.

Film can be devastatingly more potent than the written word. A century later, my community and I still feel the ramifications of Flaherty's work; the echoes of *Nanook of the North* reverberate through any graduate school filmmaking degree program, such as the one I enrolled in at UC Berkeley. In spite or maybe because of this, I settled on a career in nonfiction film, largely because doing so would allow me to try to represent my ethnicity and my people authentically. I wanted to help end the ingrained systemic stereotypes that started with Flaherty.

Inevitably, that naivete wore off quickly when I began to see how all major outlets knowingly overlooked even basic reporting on Indian Country. I found myself having to defend Native American dignity regularly, even while working with award-winning journalists. I begged my journalism classmates to move away from the four Ds—dancing, drums, drinking, and death—but to no avail. These were the only stories world-renowned journalists and filmmakers were willing to entertain telling (McCue 2014). To me, it felt like journalists could not help themselves in a society where no one expects them to. Much blame for this stereotypical representation is owed to a lack of knowledge of Indian Country that permeates all levels of education in the United States. It is the main reason Indigenous peoples are still unable to divorce themselves from the effigy of Nanook—myself included.

During my graduate degree program, I produced a story about Alcatraz and the since-broken 1868 Treaty of Fort Laramie that illegally deprived the Indigenous people of their land. The Treaty of Fort Laramie was signed by several Native Nations (including my people, the Arapaho) and the federal government. It was intended to end Chief Red Cloud's War in the west, but it also included a clause that would allow Native Americans to reclaim federal lands that were abandoned, retired, or out of use. However, the government did not allow Native Americans to reclaim their land, breaking not only a promise but a federal treaty. This is what caused the American Indian Movement to occupy Alcatraz Island for nineteen months in 1971 (Johnson 2008). Sixty years later, I decided to produce a short film based on the anniversary of this heart-wrenching protest. My protagonist, an American Indian Movement member, allowed me to film him preparing to paddle a canoe out to the island on the anniversary of its occupation.

My academic supervising producer, as well as my classmates, insisted—nay, demanded—that I remove any reference to the 1868 Treaty of Fort Laramie from my story. As a young, inexperienced filmmaker struggling with imposter syndrome, I caved. The story I ended up producing portrayed my protagonist as yet another sad Native American attempting to relive an era forever lost to history. I was not able to show that my protagonist had every right to remind the audience what exactly was taken from Indigenous people. Thus, in the first year of my filmmaking career, Flaherty's negative impact on my people had stopped being academic and become a reality. Distorting or completely removing historical facts—whether it is that Nanook always hunted with a gun rather than a spear, or that my protagonist was grieving the loss of a past movement rather than commemorating an anniversary—dilutes not only people's understanding of Indian Country, but eventually the realities of Indian Country itself.

We Native Americans learn about our lifeways, creation stories, and tribal history through oral storytelling. My choice to pursue a career in journalism and documentary filmmaking is a direct reflection—or maybe a continuation—of the oral storytelling traditions of my ancestors. I feel that making nonfiction film is the best way to sustain the cultures of Indigenous American tribes both externally with settler communities and within the tribes themselves. Furthermore, the media coverage in and of Indian Country (what little there is of it) is not only necessary, but in dire need of individuals who can cover issues that Indigenous communities face with understanding, empathy, and intimate knowledge. Unfortunately, that has rarely been the case so far. More often than not, Native Americans are shown exclusively from an outsider's perspective because the vast majority of media coverage in the United States today is created by non-Native Americans.

And yet, storytelling is in my people's blood.

That canal that ran through our land when my father led Sweat ceremonies, a waterway that my people had devised and constructed centuries before, has since been taken over by the Los Angeles Department of Water and Power to enable the government to take water from our Owens Valley River and divert it to Los Angeles. Three years after my father passed away, the Department decided it needed even more land and took it from Indian Country, even though Indian Country only makes up approximately 5 percent of the United States (Ramsey 2023). This new government-enforced border around our already tiny reservation cut directly through my father's Sweat Lodge, forcing my family to take the Lodge down. It has yet to be rebuilt in the exact place it was created. All that remains of my father's Sweat Lodge is our stories.

The only way to move away from the legacy of *Nanook of the North* is for Native Americans to become tellers of our own stories. There are stories that have been passed down through our communities, generation to generation, for thousands of years, but there are also modern-day histories that speak of the injustices being done to Indigenous peoples in North America today, every day. These stories must be told and listened to by the world for Indian Country to begin to heal. That evolution can start by focusing on Indigenous stories authored by Indigenous peoples.

Discussion Questions

1. Aside from *Nanook of the North*, what other anthropologic ethnographic films have been motivated by non-Indigenous perceptions of what being Indigenous means?
2. Find at least three current nonfiction films made by an Indigenous person or people. Describe the themes of these films.
3. How does removing historical facts from films dilute people's understanding of Indian Country?

16

"One of the First Images Captured Was of Native People"

Interview with Colleen Thurston

Colleen Thurston is a documentary storyteller, educator, and film curator from Tulsa, Oklahoma. Colleen has produced for the Smithsonian Channel, Vox, PBS, and federal, tribal, and non-profit organizations. Her work has screened at international film festivals and on national broadcasts, receiving support from Firelight Media, the Sundance Institute, Patagonia, the Independent Television Service, the Redford Center, and Creative Capital. Colleen founded the Indigenous Moving Image Archive and has curated film programs for the Momentary, the National Gallery of Art, UCLA Film and Television Archive, Vidiots, and numerous film festivals. She is a citizen of the Choctaw Nation of Oklahoma.

Please introduce yourself.

I am a filmmaker, nonfiction storyteller, and film curator from Tulsa, Oklahoma. I'm a citizen of the Choctaw Nation of Oklahoma. My work really focuses on Indigenous stories from within Oklahoma, and also examines human interconnectedness with land and place.

What does Indigenous media mean to you?

Indigenous media is any media created by Indigenous people. I think oftentimes Indigenous media gets pigeonholed into a space that it has to be *about* Indigenous people, cultures, subject matters, or history. But the fact is that if it's made by an Indigenous person, it's Indigenous media. I think there's another view of the term that can be applied to tribal media, or more generally, media that is made for Indigenous audiences, such as tribal television, tribally produced newspapers, or independent news that is made for Indigenous folks. But overall, I define Indigenous media as any media that is made by Indigenous people.

Fig. 16.1. Colleen Thurston. Author photo.

Describe your work. What compels you to do it?

I've been working in Indigenous, or Native, films since about 2009, 2010. Really, I feel like I fell into it a bit. I was in graduate school in Montana, at a predominantly white institution, yet I was on Native land and surrounded by Indigenous communities and reservations. I was really struck by the lack of knowledge that my colleagues and other students had of Native people. I found that this was being reflected in media. I found myself saying, "Oh, well, I'm learning to be a documentarian." I got into documentary work because of its ability to educate. Then I realized, well, I have a voice, I have a platform, and I have a lot of privilege here that I can use. I became passionate about the work of other Native storytellers, too. Because our stories have been silenced and erased for so long, we've come into this time and place where the American public is going, "Oh, wait, we need to know this history. We need to include Indigenous people in the conversation." Now there is work available to tell Indigenous stories. There is funding available because of centuries of erasure. And now there's a reckoning happening around inclusion.

Why is it important to have Indigenous people tell their own stories?

It's important because of that silencing. Not only was there physical genocide in this country, there was cultural genocide. That's where my love of curation and of film programming comes in, creating opportunities to showcase those stories that other people are telling as well.

A lot of cultural knowledge and a lot of history from our land bases was lost during relocations. Cutting us off from our traditional knowledge, through boarding schools and forced removals, was abuse, but it was also systemic. That loss has also been part of our education system—and that was by design.

For example, the first semester I was teaching, I had a student tell me that she didn't know Indigenous people still existed. Yeah. That was a student in Fayetteville, Arkansas, which is maybe fifty miles from the border with Oklahoma, which is also right at the border between the Cherokee, Creek or Muskogee (Mvskoke), and Choctaw Nations, which are three of the largest Indigenous nations on this continent. The population of Indigenous people in that area is probably 500,000 to one million.[1]

I told that student, "I'm really sorry that you have been failed and that nobody has taught this to you." The media is incredibly effective. I don't even need to get into that, right? Even the best-intentioned media creators can make problematic material or reinforce stereotypes because they can't speak from experience. If Indigenous people have a voice in the media, that is the most effective way to platform ourselves and our stories and our cultures. If we don't speak for ourselves, if we're not allowed to speak for ourselves, then we are completely erased, and that is another form of genocide.

What does the future hold, in your view?

I'll speak personally to the evolution of my work, but I'll ground it in context first—that is, in the medium of film. Native people have been involved in filmmaking since the very beginning. Some of the first film ever created was by Thomas Edison's studios, and one of the first images it captured was of Native people dancing. Some of the first films made in America were made here in Oklahoma. There were some really influential silent filmmakers who were Native from Oklahoma or with ties to Native tribes, such as the Fox Brothers and Will Rogers, who was Cherokee, and who was one of the most famous men in America in his time. In a lot of ways, what I do cannot be spoken about without speaking about the rich history of filmmaking that comes from this, that comes from the land I come from. Our tribes and our nations are so rich with this deep storytelling culture and this deep filmmaking culture. I think what's really cool is that Sterlin Harjo[2] insisted upon creating *Reservation Dogs* here, because he knew the story was not separate from the land.[3]

As for the future, in both education and industry, there's a lot of conversation going on now about technology, and specifically about AI. I can only imagine that it will continue to influence my art. For example, I produced a short educational documentary in 2023, and I did one of the interviews completely over Zoom. When it comes to AI, I don't know that there's a lot of black and white there—it's a big gray area. Do I personally think it's right that Anthony Bourdain's voice should be recreated so that he can narrate his own autobiographical documentary? No, I don't. But do I think AI is incredibly useful if you have terrible sound in a documentary and you can have that sound recreated? Yes, I think that's wonderful. For me it is more a matter of ethics than benefit.

What should the next generation consider? Why is this work important?

I think, from an Indigenous film perspective, there has been this "Indian 101" approach. Like, "Okay, if we're going to tell a story about our people, we really have to start at square one because people don't know anything, because the American public doesn't know anything." I think, now, Indigenous people are becoming more empowered and saying, "I'm not going to tell you the '101' stuff. If I say 'Indian Removal' and you don't know what that means, that is your responsibility as an engaged active consumer of media, an active audience member, to research that. It is no longer our responsibility to fill in the gaps where you have been failed."

That's really what I'm excited about—getting into, like, "Indian 201" maybe, where Indigenous filmmakers, storytellers, and media makers will not conform to a Western idea of how things should be made. When you go through film school, or any storytelling curriculum, you're often taught "standards" like the "three-act structure" or the "hero's journey," right? Those are Western versions of storytelling. Now I'm seeing stories that are more nonlinear, more cyclical, that maybe have a five-act structure instead of a three-act structure. I'm excited about seeing more creators lean into Indigenous traditional storytelling ways and forms.

Is there anything else you would like to add?

Yes! The working title of my film research project is the Indigenous Moving Image Archive. The purpose of the archive is several-fold, but it will be a "one-stop shop" for information about a film, on where you can find a film, as well as a platform for our rich history of Indigenous filmmaking. Another aim is to combat misinformation about Indigenous cultures. It's not a physical archive, but a digital repository and interactive database. This project is inspired by many things, but among those is the work of Maya S. Cade, the director of the Black Film Archive online.[4]

—Interviewed by Meta G. Carstarphen

Notes

1. Although Thurston reflected that this estimate represented "quite a range," she nevertheless believes the actual number of Tribal citizens residing on the reservations in Oklahoma is "likely within that number." For context, according to a 2023 updated report by the Annie E. Casey Foundation, the total American Indian (Alaska Native) population, including those who identify as "AI/AN in combination with another race [is] significantly larger and growing." As an example, the report pointed to 2021 estimates that the number of people of all ages who identify as "AI/AN in combination with another race was . . . 8.75 million," which represents an increase of "73 percent from 5 million in 2010."

2. For more about Sterlin Harjo's work in film, see the Hungry Man Productions website: https://hungryman.com/directors/sterlin-harjo/.

3. See Gross (2022) for an interview with Sterlin Harjo and context for this award-winning TV series.

4. See the Black Film Archive at: https://blackfilmarchive.com/.

PART THREE

PERSUASION

17

Lights, Camera, Activism!

How Three Tribal Teens Helped Stop a Mine

Patty Loew

The Maricopa teen was a compelling kaleidoscope of piercings, ink, and a two-toned rez 'fro—blond on one side, ebony on the other. All I could think was, *Please, oh please, say something nice*. The three Bad River Ojibwe[1] teenagers I was chaperoning had traveled nearly 2,000 miles to show their documentary film about a proposed mine that threatened their community's wild rice beds. The screening at an all-Native charter school in Scottsdale, Arizona had just finished and the principal's request for comments and questions had produced nothing but awkward silence until the Maricopa teen stood up. Given that this was the first time the Bad River teenagers had shown their film to an audience of their peers, it was obvious that my three charges were petrified, afraid of being ridiculed by teens from this Salt River Pima–Maricopa community. I cursed myself for putting them in this situation (and later scolded myself for my old-school attitudes about body piercing and tattoos). "Yo dude," the Maricopa teen said. "That was, like, super powerful. What can we do to help?"

Protect Our Future, a thirty-minute film screened at the 2014 Human Rights Film Festival in Tempe, Arizona and at the charter school in Pima–Maricopa, is one of dozens of multimedia projects produced between 2005 and 2023 by Native youth under the auspices of Tribal Youth Media (TYM) workshops. Middle and high school teens learned scriptwriting, video and audio editing, photojournalism, and digital music composition at one- to four-week summer camps held on rural reservations throughout the country—an experience intended to help them better understand themselves and their place in their community (Pyles 2016, 13). Visual storytelling for Native youth in particular is an "empowering" and "sovereignty-affirming experience" (Tynan and Loew 2010, 8–9) and one that can help mobilize Native youth and address current climate-related crises on rural reservations for the betterment of future generations (Braithwaite and Warner 2023, 14).

Twenty years ago, a film like *Protect Our Future*—the film produced by the three Ojibwe teens—would not have been possible. High-quality cameras were not available to fourteen-year-old kids from a remote Indian reservation like Bad River in northern Wisconsin. The nearest editing facility would have been eighty miles away in Duluth, Minnesota, and at $150 an hour, cost prohibitive. But today, in a time when you can upload, download, and edit video on your smartphone, anything seems possible.

Do a quick Google search using keywords like "Native American documentary" and you'll get nearly seventy-five million results! It's clear that at least *some* of Indian Country is plugged in and accessible to a mass audience. I say "some" because according to the latest US Federal Communications Commission Report on Broadband Deployment in Indian Country, development of broadband on tribal lands "continues to lag behind other areas." Only 65 percent of the homes on rural tribal lands have fixed broadband access, compared to 99 percent of households in urban areas (Bureau of Indian Affairs 2021, 1–3).

From Pictographs to the *Cherokee Phoenix*

It's not as if Native peoples have ever been cut off from the rest of the world. Since the dawn of time, Indigenous communities have shared news and advocacy through songs, dances, and stories when tribal peoples have come together for ceremonies and social encampments or have encountered people from other cultures. In the summer of 1855, for example, the self-styled German ethnographer Johann Kohl visited the village of my great-great-grandfather, Mangusid (Loon-foot), near present-day Duluth, Minnesota. Communicating in French, the lingua franca of trade and a language they both spoke, Kohl asked Mangusid about his relatives (Kohl 1860, 146–48). My great-great-grandfather produced "an old, venerable, smoky, and dirty birch bark on which a number of strokes, crosses and points were engraved." Essentially, it was my family tree, a genealogical record of our ancestors. Loon-foot, Kohl wrote, recited nine generations of names:

> Although they were not written on the bark, Loon-foot could remember every one accurately by looking at the signs, crosses, and dots. Each cross reminded him of a person, and the points and strokes indicated the age each person had reached.

While the Ojibwe and other woodland nations often used to communicate via scrolls, eastern nations such as the Haudenosaunee delivered political news via wampum belts.[2] In the west, tribes like the Shoshone-Bannock created petroglyphs and pictographs along the Columbia River Gorge to warn visitors about rapids and dangerous eddies. In the Pacific Northwest, the Tlingit and Haida carved totem poles to memorialize events and people. Nonprint communication is the hallmark of an oral culture.

Print journalism in Indian Country is generally thought to have begun in 1828 with the publication of the *Cherokee Phoenix*, the first Native American newspaper published in the United States. The *Phoenix* chronicled the Cherokees' removal from their ancestral lands in the State of Georgia to the Indian Territory of Oklahoma. It criticized white land-grabbers, offered practical advice to tribal members about how to adjust to their new lands, and expanded its coverage to include the events of other tribes facing government reprisals.

Native Media in Wisconsin

Since its establishment in 1848, Wisconsin—a state with more federally recognized Native American nations than any other state east of the Mississippi River—has seen more than sixty tribal newspapers publish the news and events of the twelve Indigenous communities located within its physical borders.[3] Most of these periodicals have been tribally owned operations, but a few, including *News from Indian Country* and *Ojibwe Akiing*, have been published by Native entrepreneurs outside tribal governments. During the 1990s, Native journalism in Wisconsin experienced a period of unprecedented growth, attributed in part to a "heightened sense of tribal sovereignty" and enabled by dollars generated from casino revenues (Loew and Mella 2005, 130). Gaming dollars allowed Native communities to invest in their own newspapers and newsletters, and more recently in broadcast media.[4]

For thirty-five years, radio has had a presence in Indigenous Wisconsin. Promising to bridge the cultural gap between Natives and non-Natives in northern Wisconsin, in 1982, WOJB FM began broadcasting "100,000 watts of Anishinaabe power" from the Lac Courte Oreilles Ojibwe Reservation (Seyler 2018). As a member of the NPR network, WOJB offers news, public affairs, and music that appeal to a diverse group of listeners. In 2003, the Red Cliff Ojibwe began broadcasting on a low-powered radio station licensed to the First American Prevention Center. However, the license was revoked ten years later when station operators failed to file paperwork to renew it. In 2008, Paul DeMain, the publisher of *News from Indian Country* launched the web channel IndianCountryTV.com, which streamed news and public affairs and offered "recorded and edited general interest programs from the powwow circuit, concerts, presentations, rebroadcast of mining programs, etc." (*News from Indian Country* website n.d.b). Sadly, the paper and web channel went dark in 2019 when DeMain retired (see chapter 8).

Mining Becomes Front-Page News

The emphasis on mining news by Native media in Wisconsin is not surprising. Since the mid-1970s, nine of the twelve Native nations in Wisconsin have been directly affected by proposed or actual mineral extraction projects,[5] including a massive copper mine proposed but never built near the Sokaogon Chippewa Community, and an open-pit copper mine that was permitted and built despite the objections of the Lac Courte Oreilles Band of Ojibwe.

More recently, the intensification of hydraulic fracturing to expand natural gas production in the United States has had a dramatic impact on members of the Ho-Chunk Indian Nation in western Wisconsin. Although there are no shale oil or natural gas deposits located in this Midwestern state, in 2014, Wisconsin became the number one producer of finely grained sand, a necessary component in the fracking process (Midwest Environmental Advocates website n.d.). In just five years, the number of frac sand mines in Wisconsin exploded from a handful in 2009 to more than 140 by 2016, many of them in Ho-Chunk country, where tribal members worried about the degradation of sacred sites and the impact on water quality. They were also concerned about health issues, including silicosis and other pulmonary conditions associated with sand mining.

In 2011, yet another form of mining made its way into the headlines. Gogebic Taconite (GTAC) announced plans to build a massive open-pit taconite mine in the Penokee Hills. The mine site was a few miles upstream of the Bad River Reservation, in an area where the Ojibwe held treaty-based hunting, fishing, and gathering rights upheld by the US Supreme Court in a landmark 1999 case.

In the years before GTAC announced its intentions to mine in northern Wisconsin, Native communities throughout the United States and First Nations in Canada had organized water walks, largely ignored by mainstream media, to draw attention to mining and other industrial threats to water. In June 2011, in a show of solidarity with the Ojibwe, Indigenous women carried water from four directions—from the Pacific Ocean, the

Atlantic Ocean, the Gulf of Mexico, and Hudson Bay—to Bad River, where they comingled it and returned it to Lake Superior. Water walks continue to this day.

Although taconite mining was commonplace in northern Minnesota and the Canadian province of Ontario in the mid-1950s to mid-1960s, most Wisconsin residents were unfamiliar with it. Some equated it with the small-scale shaft mining their grandfathers had done—the kind of mining on which Wisconsin had been founded. However, taconite, a low-grade form of iron, requires mining on a mass scale in order to be cost effective. While local mainstream media reports focused on job creation and the perceived economic boost from mining, Indigenous activists using social media questioned the long-term environmental effects of mountaintop removal on both Native and non-Native inhabitants of the region.

After the company announced that the mine would create 800 jobs (a figure opponents refuted), the Wisconsin legislature moved to ease the state's mining laws in order to fast-track GTAC's permit process. The legislature's decision to hold just one public hearing on the bill 350 miles away from the affected area drew more than 1,100 people, all but twenty-five of whom registered in opposition to the legislation.

Despite the poor publicity and dwindling local public support, little more than a month after the public hearing, the governor signed the bill into law. The Bad River Band responded by setting up a legal defense fund and laying the groundwork for a court challenge to the mine. Environmental groups prepared lawsuits over endangered species and wetland rules violations. Hunting, fishing, and recreational groups mobilized their members for a fight.

And three tribal teenagers decided to produce a documentary.

Tribal Youth Media

Jordan Principato and Shania Jackson (both fourteen years old) and fifteen-year-old Ahpahnae Thomas were veterans of the TYM workshops. In 2005, a grant from the University of Wisconsin–Madison Morgridge Center for Public Service supported the launch of a digital storytelling program on the Lac Courte Oreilles Reservation, in which we taught middle and high school students how to design web pages, operate cameras, tell stories, and find their voices. Three years later, we moved TYM to Bad River, where I am an enrolled member. In 2017, the Medill School of Journalism at Northwestern University took over the project, enabling us to continue our work.[6]

In early 2013, I successfully received grants for a good-quality camera, laptop editors, and funds to support three internships at Bad River, where I intended to spend a summer sabbatical. In June, I met with Jordan, Shania, and Ahpahnae and asked them what kind of documentary they wanted to produce. All three wanted to focus on the mine. “All we hear about is jobs,” one told me. “Nobody ever talks about what it will mean to the *manoomin* or to us.”[7]

“Manoomin” is the Ojibwe word for wild rice. Actually an aquatic grass, wild rice is at the center of Ojibwe history, culture, ceremony, and survival. It is a superfood with high nutritional value. It was the food that allowed the Ojibwe to survive long, frigid winters, and a staple over which wars were fought with the Dakota Sioux. One of the largest ancient beds of wild rice in North America is in Bad River’s Kakagon Sloughs, a 10,000-acre wetland on the south shore of Lake Superior located downstream from the proposed mine site. In 2012, the Sloughs were added to the United Nations’ Ramsar list of internationally renowned wetlands (Ramsar Wetlands Convention 2012).

Manoomin figures prominently in the Ojibwe migration narrative, a story the three teens wanted to include, along with information about treaty rights and the effects of mining on air and water, and concerns about the scale of the project—four and a half miles long in its initial phase and perhaps as large as twenty-two miles long in its final phase.

The fledgling filmmakers began by agreeing that, while they would all share the writing, shooting, editing, and music composition duties, Jordan would take the lead on videography, Shania would write the script and do the on-camera narration, and Ahpahnae would create the original score. They began with cloud planning, in which they identified major themes and “experts” who they could speak to. These included elders, relatives, Native and non-Native scientists, the tribal chair, the tribe’s historic preservation officer, and non-Native neighbors who opposed the mine. The pro-mining perspectives had come out at the public hearing in Madison. The teens were adamant that their documentary would become a vehicle for the voices that were silenced at the hearing and ignored by mainstream media—especially those of Bad River tribal members who were not given an opportunity to speak.

The teens spent the first few weeks of preproduction researching tribal treaties and treaty rights, learning the geology and history of mining in the area, identifying interviewees, and formulating questions. They also found and secured permission to use historic photographs of mining from the Wisconsin Historical Society’s archives, reasoning that their viewers needed to see the difference between historic small-scale shaft mining that was part of the state's legacy and mountaintop removal, which GTAC was proposing. Much of their preproduction was pretty standard, with one exception. Intending to conduct their project *gwayako bimaadizi*—"in a good way"—the teens prepared *asema*, or ceremonial tobacco ties, which they offered to tribal members when they requested interviews. Gifting ceremonial tobacco is a cultural protocol among the Ojibwe.

One of the guiding cultural principles of the Ojibwe is Seventh Generation philosophy. It's a worldview that reminds tribal members to think about how a decision they make today will affect people seven generations into the future. Ironically, the teens learned that *they* were the seventh generation after the chiefs who had signed three cession treaties in the 1800s, securing for tribal members a perpetual right to hunt, fish, and gather on the lands the Ojibwe were forced to cede. The young producers decided to call themselves "We Are the Seventh Generation Productions," and Seventh Generation became an organizing theme in the documentary, established in the opening sequence with elder Edith Leoso, Bad River's tribal historic preservation officer.

The way that our ancestors thought was to look at the bigger picture of everything—not only what was directly in front of and around them, but far into the future. Part of that is looking at the seventh generation ahead. Every generation does that. My generation will do that. Your generation will do that. The past generations have done that for me.

Edith Leoso Interview in *Protect Our Future*

Whereas mainstream media had focused on the purported economic benefits of the mine and had used company-supplied figures about job growth and tax revenue, *Protect Our Future* focused on the environmental threats to air and water and explored cultural threats to the Ojibwe way of life. The late Joe Rose, former director of Native American studies and a professor emeritus of environmental sciences at Northland College, recounted the Ojibwe migration story about the "food that grows on water."

When our people, the Anishinaabe, migrated from the east coast and came back to their original homelands, they were told to look for signs. And one of those signs was the food that grows on the water. They sent their scouts out over there through the cut in Long Island, there in the Kakagon Sloughs, and they found the manoomin growing more profusely than they had ever seen it. And it was declared sacred and plays a very strong role in the feasts and ceremonies that we do today.

Many of the individuals included in the documentary were related to the teens. Joe Rose, for example, was Jordan's great-uncle. Shania interviewed her father, who at the time was the band's education director. Ahpahnae interviewed his non-Native neighbor for whom he often did chores. The teens themselves appeared in the video. Shania and her brother demonstrated traditional methods of gathering wild rice.

Jordan videotaped a five-mile hike to the mine site and then recorded his own observations about the experience. All three interviewed each other about what they had learned through the process of making the documentary. Their comments served as a kind of epilogue to the film. In all, seventeen individuals appeared in the thirty-minute documentary. Because the teens were known to everyone in the community, they had no difficulty in persuading people to talk to them. Tribal members took them out in boats, invited them into their homes, and gave them total access to the arena at Bad River's annual manoomin powwow.

In a typical news documentary, journalists do not allow interviewees to comment on or suggest edits in advance of screening. The approach the teens took was to be collaborative. They viewed *Protect Our Future* as a community-based, inclusive project. The young producers gave each interviewee a copy of the rough cut and asked for permission to use the clips that were chosen. None of the participants requested changes. Many commented on how professional it looked and how surprised they were that teenagers were capable of such expertise.

The Impact of *Protect Our Future*

Protect Our Future premiered at the Tales from Planet Earth Film Festival in the state capital of Madison, Wisconsin, where debate about the taconite mine issue was particularly heated. A standing-room-only crowd of about 300 gathered to watch the film and participate in a question-and-answer session with the teens and Bad River tribal chair Mike Wiggins, who introduced the film. It was the first of dozens of screenings at film festivals and environmental conferences throughout the country. The film's northern Wisconsin premiere was at the Big Water Film Festival in Washburn, Wisconsin, where it played to another standing-room-only audience and won the Young Filmmaker's Award. The teens collected a Youth Achievement Award at the Green Bay Film Festival. The success of the film prompted Wisconsin Public Radio to do a live interview with the teens, which was broadcast statewide.

The interview generated numerous requests from news media for preview copies, which we didn't have. Fortunately, the Nelson Institute for

Environmental Studies at the University of Wisconsin-Madison underwrote the costs of making several hundred DVDs of the documentary, which the tribe provided to the news media and educational institutions. The buzz surrounding the teens' project reached its apex when Arizona State University selected the film for screening at its 2014 Human Rights Film Festival, and also arranged for it to be shown at the aforementioned Native charter school in Scottsdale. Arizona State University offered to provide travel funds for one of the teens to introduce their film. Within a week, we had raised enough money to send all three to the festival.

Bolstered by Great Lakes Indian Fish and Wildlife Commission scientists who gathered data, wrote technical reports, and spoke publicly about the impact of mining, support for Bad River's fight against the mine continued to build.[8] Other Native nations in Wisconsin also expressed their opposition to the mine. The Ho-Chunk Nation sent Bad River's legal defense fund a $25,000 check. Delivering the 2012 State of the Tribes Address, Ho-Chunk president John Greendeer told Wisconsin legislators that the Native nations of Wisconsin stood in solidarity with Bad River, describing environmental assaults on air and water as "a call to action" (Greendeer 2012).

Opposition to the taconite mine and support for Bad River's defense of the Penokee Hills grew exponentially. Progressive groups, including Midwest Environmental Advocates, Madison Action for Mining Alternatives, the Sierra Club, and the Wisconsin Network for Peace and Justice, registered their opposition to the project, as did the National Wildlife Federation and its Wisconsin chapter, representing 195 hunting, fishing, and trapping clubs. High-profile environmental activists, including Winona LaDuke, made appearances in Wisconsin to speak out against the mine.

Between 2013 and 2015, *Protect Our Future* screened at more than thirty film festivals and environmental conferences. It was a powerful public relations tool in Bad River's fight to protect itself from what tribal members believed would be the destruction of their way of life. In question-and-answer sessions after *Protect Our Future* screenings, audience members often reacted with outrage to the proposed mine. The film moved people to contribute to Bad River's legal defense fund and write letters to their legislators and local newspapers. When Gogebic announced in March 2015 that it was withdrawing from the project, the filmmakers experienced deep satisfaction in knowing that their project had helped make a difference.

Protect Our Future resonated with many different audiences—from the Maricopa teen and his peers at the Native charter school in Scottsdale, Arizona, to Native communities throughout Wisconsin, to mainstream viewers throughout the country. It is not unlike what happened in North Dakota with the Dakota Access Pipeline protests, albeit on a much smaller scale. In North Dakota, thousands of "water protectors" representing more than 300 tribes established Sacred Stone Camp near the construction site for the pipeline to support the Standing Rock Sioux. The pipeline was originally designed to run north of the state capital in Bismarck, but it was rerouted because of fears that it could compromise the city's water supply. Instead, company officials redesigned it to cross under the Missouri River—the sole source of water for Standing Rock—just half a mile upstream from the reservation, on land where the Sioux have treaty rights (Dalrymple 2016). The notion that Indigenous communities should become "sacrifice zones"[9]—unwilling hosts for polluting industrial projects white Americans won't allow in their neighborhoods—offends the sensibilities of many individuals.

A frequent complaint expressed by the water protectors at the Sacred Stone Camp was that mainstream media largely ignored the Dakota Access Pipeline issue until the protests turned violent and involved non-Native celebrities, including movie actress Shailene Woodley, Green Party presidential candidate Jill Stein, and *Democracy Now* reporter Amy Goodman. Woodley was arrested and briefly jailed on charges of criminal trespass and engaging in a riot. Arrest warrants on similar charges were issued for Stein and Goodman. The charges against Goodman followed a riveting report, which included Goodman's video of private security guards unleashing dogs on the protesters and using pepper spray and mace. The images, horrifying and compelling, eventually made their way from social media to mainstream media. However, many Native observers were disappointed when the story's focus then shifted away from water and Indigenous rights to the First Amendment and whether Goodman's rights as a journalist had been violated.

If there is a lesson to be learned from the *Protect Our Future* documentary and the Dakota Access Pipeline protests, it is that the best opportunity for Native communities to amplify their environmental concerns and promote solidarity is most likely through social media and video-sharing sites like YouTube and Vimeo, not mainstream media. "They didn't learn about it off CNN or NBC," a water protector responded when asked why so many different tribes were represented at Sacred Stone. "They learned about it through social media" (von Oldershausen 2016). Indeed, when pipeline opponents create their own stories on social media, they are free to frame themselves as "water protectors," not "protesters."

The danger, of course, is that anyone with a smartphone can call him or herself a journalist and upload unvetted and sometimes untrue information and call it "news." This is why programs like the TYM initiative are so important. We teach our Native youth not only how to master media equipment and techniques, but also how to apply their newfound skills responsibly. This does not mean that TYM stories must conform to mainstream media structure and protocols (e.g., ten-second soundbites). However, we do insist that the reports be ethical.

Tribal Youth Media Today

In the years since the premiere of *Protect Our Future*, TYM workshops have continued on reservations in northern Wisconsin. In 2016, the TYM workshop at Bad River coincided with northern Wisconsin's "flood of the century," which inundated highways, washed out bridges, and destroyed more than forty homes on the reservation. For nearly a week, Bad River was an island. Things were so dire that tribal members needing kidney dialysis relied on National Guard helicopters to airlift them to an Ashland, Wisconsin clinic. Because of bridge washouts, the clinic, normally a ten-minute drive away, became a five-hour trip. TYM participants documented the damage, videotaped interviews with flood victims, and produced inspiring stories about how the community had pulled together to take care of each other. The reservation hotel, which had closed, was one of the few buildings with an emergency generator and access to the internet. That allowed our young reporters to upload video for television stations in Duluth, Wausau, and Madison, and a packaged report for Wisconsin Public Television. Their work also became video evidence in a successful application for a federal disaster declaration, which brought relief money to the tribe in the form of grants, not loans.[10]

While many environmental threats to Native communities remain, including mining and pipelines, the technology documenting these threats has changed. TYM participants now produce their stories using the high-definition cameras on their smartphones. They plug lavalier mics into the phone's audio jack or USB input, use handheld gimbals[11] to steady their shots, and illuminate their subjects with candy bar–sized LED lights. The equipment is kid-friendly, portable, and relatively inexpensive.

In testament to the broader impact of these youth-produced documentaries, in 2024, file footage and archived TYM interviews were featured in the critically acclaimed film *Bad River*,[12] which was screened nationwide in AMC Theatres. In 2025, four TYM-produced short documentaries about climate change were shown in science museums across the country. They included videos produced by teenagers on the Quinault Reservation in Western Washington, the Poarch Band of Creek Indians

Reservation in Alabama, the Onondaga Nation in New York, and Bad River in Wisconsin. The teens framed their documentaries as empowering and hopeful.

We want the stories of our Native youth to be compelling and to reflect their communities' traditional values of honesty and integrity. Working collaboratively with their elders and tribal leaders, we aim to inspire Native youth to connect with their natural and cultural landscapes. In this way we hope to help grow the next generation of Indigenous land stewards and storytellers whose voices and stories can be amplified to a global audience.

Discussion Questions

1. How is digital storytelling compatible with Indigenous oral tradition?
2. How can student-produced documentaries be used in positive youth development?
3. How can storytelling amplify youth voices?

Notes

1. Historically, scholars have used the words "Ojibwe," "Ojibwa," "Ojibway," "Chippewa," and "Anishinaabeg" (which includes the Ojibwe, Potawatomi, and Odawa) to identify the bands of the Lake Superior Tribe of Chippewa Indians. I use the name preferred by the three young filmmakers from the Bad River Reservation.

2. Wampum belts were made of purple and white beads made from quahog clam shells. The beads were sometimes strung together to form a pictographic message and often used for monetary exchange.

3. Wisconsin is home to six bands of Ojibwe—Bad River, Red Cliff, Lac du Flambeau, Lac Courte Oreilles, Sokaogon, and St. Croix—Menominee; Forest County Potawatomi; Ho-Chunk Nation; Oneida, Stockbridge–Munsee Band of Mohican Indians; and Brothertown, a Native nation that lacks federal acknowledgment.

4. In its 1987 decision in *California v. Cabazon Mission Band of Indians*, the US Supreme Court ruled that states did not have the legal authority to regulate Indian gaming within their borders. The following year, the US Congress passed the National Indian Gaming Regulatory Act, which established a regulatory framework for gaming on Native lands and limited the scope of it. By the early 1990s, all of the federally recognized Native nations in Wisconsin had opened at least one casino.

5. The following mining projects have either operated or been proposed in the following communities: sulfide mining—Mole Lake Ojibwe, Forest County Potawatomi, Menominee, Oneida, Lac Courte Oreilles Ojibwe; iron mining—Bad River Ojibwe and Red Cliff Ojibwe; frac sand mining: Ho-Chunk Nation and St. Croix Ojibwe.

6. The move to Northwestern occurred after I moved there to direct Northwestern's Center for Native American and Indigenous Research. The core team from 2015 to

2023 included University of Wisconsin-Madison faculty associate Don Stanley (Oneida descendant), Fawn Youngbear Tibbets (White Earth Anishinaabe, Sac & Fox), and me (Mashkiiziibii–Bad River Ojibwe). Through the years, we have been joined by various Native and non-Native graduate and undergraduate students from both University of Wisconsin-Madison and Northwestern University. We have tried to maintain a ratio of one instructor for every three to four youth participants.

7. Ahpahnae Thomas, author interview, Bad River Reservation, Odanah, WI, June 17, 2013.

8. The Great Lakes Indian Fish and Wildlife Commission was established in 1984 by eleven bands of Ojibwe in Minnesota, Wisconsin, and Michigan (signatories to the 1837, 1842, and 1854 treaties) to provide "natural resource management expertise, conservation enforcement, legal and policy analysis, and public information services in support of the exercise of treaty rights during well-regulated, off-reservation seasons throughout the treaty ceded territories." Great Lakes Indian Fish and Wildlife Commission, accessed March 31, 2023, https://glifwc.org/.

9. A sacrifice zone is an area that is permanently affected by destructive environmental activities or economic disinvestment. The term was first used in a 1974 government report about coal mining. See US National Research Council, 1974, "Study Committee on the Potential for Rehabilitating Lands Surface Mined for Coal in the Western United States," in *Rehabilitation Potential of Western Coal Lands* (Cambridge, MA: Ford Foundation Energy Policy Project/Ballinger Pub. Co.), 85–86.

10. A chronology of the flood and TYM's documentation of it is available in this twelve-minute video: https://www.youtube.com/watch?v=jy7Jo7-xVPY.

11. A gimbal is a miniature stabilizer that allows the user to shoot steady video.

12. 50 Eggs Films, 2024, *Bad River*, directed by Mary Mazzio, https://www.50eggs.com/films/bad-river-film/.

18

Promoting *Bad Press*

A Documentary Film from Indian Country and a Model for Public Relations

Sarah Liese, Shondiin Silversmith, Benjamin LaPoe, Victoria LaPoe, and Taylor Orcutt

Audiences rarely witness academia embracing Indigenous stories. One engaging story on social media altered that pattern. The 2023 documentary *Bad Press* won award after award and then began attracting attention on social media; the story of *Bad Press*' success was even covered by an international and local streaming service (TVGuide.com 2023). So why did festivals worldwide understand this story and make space for it to be told when typically so few Indigenous stories receive such a positive reaction?

The documentary's director, Rebecca Landsberry-Baker, is also the executive director of the Indigenous Journalists Association (IJA). The protagonist of the documentary, Angel Ellis, is an IJA board member who focuses on free press initiatives. This documentary contains all the elements taught in narrative writing: a protagonist, a narrative arc, and a storyline. In this case, the documentary told the story of those fighting for press freedom and social justice rights. It was understood that these rights could be taken away instantly by officials behind closed doors.

Bad Press engaged viewers locally and internationally, pulling them into the story through its use of natural sound and slow pacing, a documentary style that mimics real life. This story about a "bad press"—that is, a tribal press shut down by the Muscogee Nation's leaders—now uses public relations to help maintain newly established press freedom and even grow Mvskoke Media's independence, and therefore empower the voices of Muscogee (Creek) Nation citizens. This story shows the power of public relations organizations. We live in two worlds, news and marketing, under one media newsroom. But news can often only exist alongside marketing, social media, and influencer distribution. This chapter explores how public relations and *Bad Press* elevated voices and gained attention within Indian Country.

Writing press releases may seem simple because they have a formulaic composition and writers can get assistance from artificial intelligence (Suciati et al. 2021). However, the news media does not use all the press releases it receives. They must be well written and relevant to the audiences they serve (Bollinger 2001; Williams 1994). "Understanding worldviews of both the targeted [communities] and ourselves is imperative if we are going to do more good than harm" (Bishop et al. 2002, 611). Storytelling is a fundamental part of Indigenous communities, and Indigenous people use it to keep traditions, culture, and communities alive (LaPoe and LaPoe 2017). Press releases are a form of storytelling.

Many scholars posit a need to investigate the intersections between activism and public relations (e.g., Holtzhausen 2012; Weaver 2018). "Critical, postmodern, postcolonial, and decolonial public relations, in their various forms, encourage the examination of power within the profession, critique its Western and capitalist concepts of organizational public relations, and engage with notions of public relations' benefits to society" (Clark et al. 2022, 1). Studying press releases authored by Indigenous advocates and organizations provides plenty of opportunities to amplify decolonization of knowledge, activism, and public relations (Mohammed 2022).

Indigenous Journalism, Sovereignty, and Self-Determination

There are 575 federally recognized tribes today. Each is a sovereign nation with a government-to-government relationship with the United States. Because tribal nations are independent and sovereign, constitutional provisions determining federal and state powers, including the First Amendment, do not always apply to Indigenous communities. Therefore, the press laws applied at a federal and state level do not always apply at a tribal level (Cappetta and Matthews n.d.; see chapter 7 of this book).

Indigenous journalism is essential for supporting tribal sovereignty and self-determination within Indigenous communities (LaPoe and LaPoe 2017). It holds the powerful accountable and allows for the sharing of stories of cultural significance that nontribal media outlets often overlook. Having a free and independent Indigenous press promotes the objectives of tribal nations through a platform that allows community voices to be amplified (NAJA Director 2018[1]). Providing well-sourced journalism can be challenging for journalists reporting anywhere. Two of the most significant threats to tribal media, as identified by journalists, are a lack of financial resources and editorial control (NAJA 2018). Tribal journalists have reported how tribal nations' economies often affect their media outlets' ability to provide quality journalism, which hinders outlets' financial independence; also, government officials or political interests often determine media content (NAJA 2018).

There are tribal nations that include language about freedom of the press in their constitutional provisions. Many of them adopted language from the Indian Civil Rights Act, which includes many of the civil rights protected by the Bill of Rights, including freedom of the press (Cappetta and Matthews n.d.). However, the Muscogee (Creek) Nation in Oklahoma (Mvskoke Media 2023) is the only known tribal nation that has amended its constitution to add press protections for its independent media outlet, Mvskoke Media. The Muscogee Nation's story captured the attention of many different audiences when the film *Bad Press* documented its recent free press crisis. Awareness of this crisis started spreading thanks to online and social media press releases, illustrating the power of the packaged message for the free press.

Press Releases and the Free Press

In 2018, the Muscogee (Creek) Nation National Council voted quietly behind the scenes—and shockingly to its media—to repeal the tribe's Free Press Act. In doing so, the Nation placed its independent tribal media outlet, Mvskoke Media, under the control of the tribe's Department of Commerce. The repeal also dissolved the three-member editorial board at the outlet and placed the staff under the direction of the secretary of the nation and commerce (Mvskoke Media 2023).

The impact of the repeal did not end there. Staff members reported that they were required to send all future content to the executive branch for approval (NAJA 2018). NAJA's board of directors wrote several press releases—and did not let up as the story unfolded—calling the requirements direct tribal censorship of Mvskoke Media and a restriction on reporters' abilities to seek truth and report on stories of importance to Muscogee (Creek) citizens (NAJA 2018). Additionally, several media organizations condemned the Muscogee (Creek) Nation for repealing its free press laws, calling the move "alarming." NAJA disseminated five press releases through social media and also published an opinion piece to notify international audiences about the attack on press freedom in Indian Country, with the goal of getting the Nation to reinstate its law (NAJA 2018).

Documenting the Bad Press Beyond Press Releases

The independent film *Bad Press* chronicled the repeal of the Free Press Act through the eyes of Angel Ellis. One of the film's directors, Rebecca Landsberry-Baker (also Muscogee), is a former Mvskoke Media editor and the current executive director of IJA, which gave her a unique perspective from which to tell the story. *Bad Press* traces the events from the repeal into 2020, when Muscogee (Creek) citizens voted to enact the Independent Muscogee (Creek) Press Act, a law that provides legislative-level free press protections and keeps Mvskoke Media coverage free from influence by the tribal government (NAJA 2020). Some of the policies established through the Act included independent funding designated for staff salaries and news production, re-establishment of the requirements for the media director and editorial board, and elimination of oversight by the Muscogee (Creek) Nation secretary of the nation and commerce (Gray 2021).

Though the film concluded before showing Ellis's promotion to Mvskoke Media director, it highlighted her fight for a free press and her dedication to telling the truth to her community. Following the Act's passing, Ellis stated that she hopes the work done in the Muscogee (Creek) Nation—that is, Indigenous people claiming their roots by writing their own stories—catches on for every Indigenous nation in the country (Gray 2021).

Bad Press follows one community and one journalist for multiple years as they build connections, trust, and context. Newsrooms can learn from this approach. The film privileges Indigenous voices, perspectives, and the idea of ethical storytelling despite the threat from tribal government. It covers a timely topic that made waves in one community and revealed a hidden truth about Indigenous media to many US citizens. NAJA recognized the importance of the situation in Muscogee (Creek) Nation by issuing press releases and statements about the event. It understood the importance of shedding light on a decision made in the dark, and how this could resonate among other tribes. The organization held a roundtable about the film and how Rebecca Landsberry-Baker and co-director Joe Peeler collaborated to provide other tribal media and journalists with information to help them understand the issue within Indian Country.

Press releases have the power to inform, engage, and promote ideas. Because of their implicit influence on the communities they involve, we wanted to learn more about the themes they convey and the sources they employ. Specifically, in our study, we examined press releases written by Indigenous authors or appealing to Indigenous communities to understand how releases can help define an organization's character and core values over time. Essentially, we asked: How is Indigenous-related content promoted?

We focused on the narrative of *Bad Press* because it was driven by press releases and discussed in Indian Country and internationally, which provided the impetus to look at how stories like this can be amplified for both Indigenous and non-Indigenous audiences. We reviewed, through the lens of Indigenous Standpoint Theory (IST), press releases both submitted and published by the subscription-based public relations distribution service PR Newswire. The service's costs depend on local or national distribution and the number of languages in which a press release appears. The site reports 39,000 active monthly users and reaches more than 170 countries in forty languages, including nearly 10,000 websites and 3,000 newsrooms (PR Newswire n.d.). For each press release, we noted the date, headline, genre, theme, Indigenous source, non-Indigenous source, organization sponsoring the release, and contact information, if given. We color-coded each press release according to whether an Indigenous or non-Indigenous organization authorized it, and we classified Indigenous sources into community members and officials.

IJA developed its own version of a bingo card to combat frequent stereotypes used in mainstream news coverage of Indigenous communities (LaPoe et al. 2021). The card listed the storytelling approaches those outlets should avoid using. Reporters and editors could refer to the card when working on a story about Indigenous people or communities; if they "scored" too many tropes or stereotypes, they had to rethink their story. The hope with our analysis is to build a bingo card that attempts to amplify positive content in Indian Country.[2]

We examined each release and found the majority of the data sample did not privilege or individually cover Indigenous voices and issues. Instead, the press releases combined Indigenous people with other minority groups and only occasionally quoted Indigenous people. We therefore decided only to gather press releases specifically about Indigenous communities and organizations, and to search for press releases by organizations that specifically partnered with at least one Indigenous organization or individual. This ensured the sample would focus on an Indigenous topic, community, or idea relevant to Indigenous people or a particular tribal nation.

Our search uncovered 699 press releases. Of these, only thirty-eight included the terms "Indigenous" or "Native American." Therefore, we added the terms "aboriginal," "First Nation," "tribal," and "tribe." We also reviewed previously published press releases from PR Newswire from 2018 to 2022, authored by NAJA board members. The 108 press releases from PR Newswire allowed us to identify common themes and sub-themes from which to create a positive bingo sheet, and we reached a saturation point where no more new themes could be found. We analyzed sixty-one press releases by Indigenous organizations and forty-seven by non-Indigenous organizations. We found 139 articles published by Indigenous media outlets correlated with press releases published by Indigenous-run and non-Indigenous organizations. A single press release might have multiple corresponding articles, depending on how meaningfully the topic resonated in Indian Country.

As shown in Table 18.1, press releases by Indigenous organizations featured more Indigenous (81) than non-Indigenous sources (56). They also referenced more Indigenous officials (72) than community members (9). Press releases written by non-Indigenous organizations also contained a notable number of Indigenous officials (42). The more Indigenous officials are used as sources, the more Indigenous people are seen as decision-makers who are leading efforts to better their communities.

More Indigenous officials than community members were identified as sources in both types of press release, but neither type mentioned the Indigenous sources' tribal affiliations. According to the NAJA Reporting and Indigenous Terminology Guide (2018), "Failing to use the actual name of the tribe you are reporting on is neither accurate, fair or thorough and undermines diversity by erasing the tribe's identity." Additionally, as shown in Table 18.1, press releases written by Indigenous organizations tended to use contact information more than those written by non-Indigenous organizations.

Table 18.1. Press release findings related to sourcing and contact lists.

	Press releases by Indigenous organizations	Press releases by non-Indigenous organizations	Total
Total	61	47	108
Indigenous sources	81	47	128
Indigenous community members as sources	9	5	14
Indigenous officials as sources	72	42	114
Non-Indigenous sources	56	47	103
Use of contact list	43	18	61
No use of contact list	18	29	47

Table 18.2. Indigenous news stories in relation to topics of press releases.

	Press releases by Indigenous organizations	Press releases by non-Indigenous organizations	Total
All Indigenous media articles	62	34	95
Indigenous media with two or more corresponding articles	15	8	23
No articles corresponding with press release	18	24	42

We found 96 articles related to the 108 press release topics in our datasheet. We only analyzed articles published by Indigenous media outlets. Eleven of the Indigenous media outlets in our datasheet were particular to one tribe or region, whereas fifteen publications were reporting on multiple Indigenous nations. *Indian Gaming*'s articles accounted for the highest number in our analysis, with *Indian Country Today* in second place and *Tribal Gaming and Hospitality* in third. This suggests that those news organizations tune into PR Newswire for news information, and that hospitality and gaming information are also commonly released through PR Newswire. Additionally, most articles by *Indian Gaming, Indian Country Today*, and *Tribal Gaming and Hospitality* republished the press releases verbatim on their websites, while local news publications tended to write original articles about the topics.

Indigenous outlets the *Navajo-Hopi Observer, Red Lake Nation News*, and Indianz.com published fourteen news articles before PR Newswire released its press releases. Thus, we inferred that local media has more access to follow up on a news topic with the citizens of a particular region or nation. Additionally, local media is in the heart of where the news is taking place, and such outlets only sometimes need a press release to inform them about what is occurring in their communities. At the same time, national media outlets such as *Indian Gaming, Indian Country Today*, and *Tribal Gaming and Hospitality* cover all of Turtle Island. Thus, they need more access, resources, and time to send reporters to the scene to create an original news story, especially if the topic is not a hot-button issue.

Often, more than one theme or positive bingo word would emerge in a press release. For example, in the press release titled "Native American Basketball Invitational (NABI) to be Honored by Phoenix Suns and Phoenix Mercury for 20-year History" (PR Newswire 2022), the two main themes were partnership and support. The Indigenous organization NABI, in partnership with Phoenix Suns, supports young Indigenous basketball players. We frequently observed organizational partnerships that were aimed at achieving a common goal. However, it is essential to highlight that the press releases published by non-Indigenous organizations continually showed themes of partnership because those releases needed to involve a partnership with an Indigenous person or organization in order for us to perform an analysis on them. Therefore, we recognize how our data collection decisions significantly affected the theme of partnership.

Indigenous Leadership

The Indigenous leadership theme emerged via awards, recognition, promotions, and service. Leadership themes often interconnected with those of partnership and supporting Indigenous communities. While the themes were generally evident in the overarching ideas and concepts, we were also able to attach the themes to individual words. This detailed approach enabled us to create a positive word association bingo sheet. We identified ten positive bingo terms: "support," "community," "leader," "environment" or "land," "protect," "preserve" or "preservation," "future," "education," "scholar," and "partner." Press releases that used the term "environment" referenced it only in terms of Mother Earth, not in terms of other environments.

"Support" was the most used word in Indigenous releases, while non-Indigenous releases used "community," as did organizations that were not tribally affiliated but actively covered Indigenous communities in their releases. Other words found included "preservation," "protection," "education," "scholarship," "support," and "partner." Frequent theme combinations included "environment" and "leadership," "future" and "scholar," and "land" and "protection."

Another key finding was that more Indigenous than non-Indigenous organizations implemented the positive bingo words. Two hundred bingo words were deployed by non-Indigenous press releases and 251 by Indigenous press releases.

Power of the Press Release: Valuing Sources

It is not impossible, especially for non-Indigenous reporters and storytellers, to do stories, good stories, and good coverage of Indian Country. However, it takes much effort. Recognizing that it

> *takes extra time to build trust between sources and participants is crucial for practical and ethical coverage of Indian Country.*
>
> —*Landsberry-Baker (2023)*

The depth of information highlighting the importance of having a free press in Indian Country engenders multiple honors for Landsberry-Baker. The award-winning film *Bad Press* illustrated the importance of press freedom, and tensions around the question of Indigenous identity in Indigenous media. NAJA documented through press releases the repeal of the free press for Mvskoke Media before the film's creation, and those stories built the public script found in the film. NAJA's press releases gave citizens and Indigenous journalists a powerful voice as the government attempted censorship. We encourage readers of this chapter to visit IJA's website to see how the story unfolded through the press releases.

Bad Press received distinguished honors for its integrity, heart, and willingness to share truth in all forms—no matter the cost. The film won the Sundance Film Festival's US Documentary Special Jury Award for freedom of expression and was screened at additional festivals from March to May 2023 (Seattle International Film Festival, Milwaukee Film Festival, Independent Film Festival, Independent Film Festival Boston, Sun Valley Film Festival, San Francisco Film Festival, True/False Film Festival). Landsberry-Baker received requests from multiple university public relations and journalism departments to screen the film for its educational value, given that the issue of free press in Indian Country is a topic rarely discussed in American schools.

"It behooves the fields of media studies and communication studies, academic departments, conferences, journals, etc., to support the decolonization of knowledge and the legitimization of marginalized ways of knowing to support the self-determination of Global South communities" (Mohammed 2022, 21). Indigenous media and Indigenous social media privilege Indigenous life experiences, emphasize Indigenous contexts, honor Indigenous social mores, amplify Indigenous voices, and incorporate Indigenous worldviews (Azocar 2022).

Future scholars interested in examining storytelling within public relations may want to explore how Indigenous organizations use press releases to promote their specific stories and brands as models for community storytelling. Future research might consider conducting interviews with Indigenous news organizations, as well as with community members, to understand whether they believe public relations serve their respective goals.

Discussion Questions

1. In what ways is Indigenous-related content promoted?
2. How does this promotion speak to gaining attention?
3. In the spirit of publicity, what can we learn from a tribal news event that became the storyline of a popular documentary that captured screens internationally?

Notes

1. The Native American Journalists Association changed its name to the Indigenous Journalists Association in 2023.

2. The positive bingo card is an instructional tool for educators, journalists, and public relations professionals. Benjamin LaPoe came up with this idea while teaching a political communications course in communication studies at Ohio University. Students on his course had a hard time thinking of ethical words associated with Indian Country. The idea was shared by Victoria LaPoe with Rebecca Landsberry at NAJA. Sarah Liese helped bring the vision to life.

19

"The Struggle of the Freedmen Is Part of Tribal History"

Interview with Marilyn K. Vann

Marilyn K. Vann founded two Oklahoma-based organizations dedicated to advocacy for and education about Freedmen, or African Indian peoples. Nationally renowned for her leadership, Vann has been featured in numerous media stories and has been an invited speaker at universities including University of California, University of Indiana, and Michigan State University Law School. Her presentations discuss the history, culture, and political rights of Freedmen. Vann is the first Freedman to receive a Cherokee Nation board appointment. A retired engineer, Vann has received numerous awards for her service, including a 2018 Statesmanship Award by the Cherokee Nation.

[INTERVIEWER'S NOTE]

Concepts of Indigenous identity are central to the theme of this book, and each contribution offers important nuances and emphases. This interview spotlights "Freedmen" communities: people of African descent who also claim Indigenous heritage through blood, kinship ties, and/or the enslaved status of their ancestors.[1]

A little-known part of the colonization experience in the United States was the involvement of some Indigenous tribal nations as slaveholders. This interview highlights the experiences and reflections of Marilyn K. Vann, a Freedman descendant who is also an enrolled member of the Cherokee Nation,[2] *headquartered in Tahlequah, Oklahoma. As tribal history shows, colonial and settler violence realigned the Cherokee Nation's tribal governance structure from its traditional unitary structure into three individual entities: the Cherokee Nation, the Eastern Band of Cherokee Indians,*[3] *and the United Keetoowah Band of Cherokee Indians in Oklahoma.*[4] *A comprehensive history of the Cherokee Nation shows how forced removals and a succession of treaties contributed to these changes, as well as to the sometimes contradictory views held within the Cherokee Nation about the modern-day rights and privileges of Freedmen descendants.*[5]

Fig. 19.1. Marilyn K. Vann. Author photo.

Please introduce yourself.

My name is Marilyn Vann. I am the president of the Descendants of Freedmen of the Five Civilized Tribes Association and the African Indians of the Five Civilized Tribes Foundation, both nonprofits.

I am a retired engineer. I worked for more than thirty years in the US government, and I retired as an engineering team leader. I've lived in Oklahoma basically my entire life. I am married, with a family, and I am an enrolled member of the Cherokee Nation with Freedman status.

My father was an original enrollee on the Dawes Rolls made by the federal government, which listed all tribal members recognized by both the tribe and the US government.[6]

What does Indigenous media mean to you?

It's complicated. I've encountered media folks who don't want to run stories about people they think can't buy their ads. You have some members of tribal media whose attitude is, "Well, you're creating problems for all Indians. Go sit down and just be a Black person." Or some have said, "Let the chiefs handle it. We already fought for sovereignty. Don't do anything to try to limit it." So you have these different attitudes, different voices.

During those early years of establishing the status of Freedmen, one former chief would tell some media person, or even a member of Congress, that Freedmen were really "just some Black people that snuck in on some land runs across the border from Arkansas and their ancestors were just squatting on tribal lands. So the federal government just gave it to them." These are ideas that not only the Cherokee chiefs were putting out, but the chiefs of other tribes. But if you got a chance to sit down with a media person and show them the treaty, show them different census rolls, including where Freedmen were listed on tribal rolls, it was a different story.

Within the Cherokee Nation, we've had people who've served in the US Senate and in the House of Representatives. There have been some very wealthy citizens. A former chair of Phillips Petroleum was also a former principal chief.[7] The Cherokee Nation, being the second largest tribe in the country,[8] gets more publicity than a smaller tribe that isn't as well known nationally. So when news of the tribal election where the Freedmen were removed from the tribe hit,[9] it wasn't just local news. All of that blew up. I mean, Al Jazeera, the BBC, Fox, some national papers like *The New York Times*, *The Washington Post*, *The LA Times*, *The Wall Street Journal*, CNN . . . everybody was covering this. To a lot of people, the tribe throwing these Black people out—a lot of whom were their own blood relatives—really didn't sit right with a lot of people.

Describe your work. What compels you to do it?

It began when I wanted to register for tribal membership in 2001. I was in a pretty good place with my career. I thought, *Maybe there's something I can do for the tribe*. I got an application, sent it in, and was very surprised to be rejected. I didn't know anything about what they were calling "Freedmen roll number" or "degree of blood."

I'm not a person to see a wrong and do nothing. I'm a deacon's daughter, and faith has always been a very important part of my life. I didn't know *exactly* what to do, but it seemed the thing to do was to try to gather people and organize to do *something*. Eventually, I was a litigant on two lawsuits dealing with Cherokee Freedmen.[10]

So who are the Freedmen? They are people of African ancestry who received rights to tribal membership in 1866 treaties. Although the Cherokee National Council ended slavery in 1863, the nation initially fought against the United States during the Civil War, in large part to continue slavery, which was an important part of the tribe's economy. At the end of the war, the United States did not want any areas where slavery was still practiced, so emancipation was part of the 1866 treaty between the tribe and the United States.

Not everyone with African ancestry was enslaved before 1863; some "mixed Negroes" were freed earlier by their Cherokee fathers in their wills. Also, the 1839 Cherokee constitution allowed tribal membership to "mixed Negroes" with Native mothers, but not those with Native fathers and Black mothers.[11] The 1866 treaty guaranteed citizenship to former slaves, free Blacks, and their descendants.

Ironically, from 1839 to 1866, people of other nationalities could receive citizenship through their mother, their father, or through marriage. I'm talking about Cubans, Puerto Ricans, Armenians, Germans, Irish, whatever—but not persons of African descent.

At the end of the Civil War, there was no requirement to call someone a "freed man," or to set up blood quantum, or anything like that. This only came because of the US government policies for land allotments, which were established to steal the lands of the tribal members, especially the Blacks.

As I said earlier, I've lived in Oklahoma nearly my whole life. One of my first memories as a small schoolchild was having a boy ask me, "What kind of Indian are you?" I went home and asked my dad. He said, "Well, we're Cherokee Indians, but we also have colored blood."

All tribes had some kind of slavery before 1492,[12] generally through war captives. Later, when tribes began to purchase Africans, slaves could still eventually be freed, married, or adopted into the tribe, just like anyone else. But as Southern whites began to marry into the tribes and get more power, this antiblackness became more important. Cherokees who were getting big plantations in Georgia, Alabama, and other places brought chattel slavery and plantation economies into what is now Oklahoma.

Why is it important to have Indigenous people tell their own stories?

Freedmen's history and tribal history are linked. For instance, I read that about 80 percent of the Lakota [Sioux] and some other tribes perished during the nineteenth century,[13] but I've also read that 25 percent of the

Cherokees perished on the Trail of Tears. Well, maybe Cherokees didn't perish at the same rate as these other tribes because there were other people doing the hard, dirty work. After everybody walked, who built those fires? Who cooked while others rested? Maybe there were slave babies who died because there wasn't enough milk since the slave had to feed someone else's baby. Maybe that Cherokee baby became a tribal leader later because of the African woman who nursed him. People don't think of these things as possibilities.

Literature about the Freedmen and their ancestors is just not there, because by law they couldn't read and write before 1863. Yes, later there were some schools that Freedmen could attend. Yes, some were able to go to schools with other tribal members. But as a class of people, the Freedmen were not well educated and were not able to write the stories about their ancestors on the Trail of Tears, and how they survived. Still, some history is in the slave narratives recorded in the 1930s,[14] because there were some elderly people who were able to give their stories, or those of their parents and grandparents.

What does the future hold, in your view? What should the next generation consider? Why is this work important?

In recent years, media coverage has been more positive, but I think the Freedmen issue is important for future generations because these enrollment issues still exist where treaties come into play. The struggle of the Freedmen for their tribal rights is part of tribal history.

Is there anything else you would like to add?

It is very important to have media coverage, just like in the days of the civil rights movement, to cover whatever injustices still exist. Some are more difficult to fix because they don't directly involve treaties, like the Pamunkey Tribe in Virginia that got incentives to remove persons of African ancestry from their previous rolls.[15] More recently, I learned about a racial incident down in Tishomingo, Oklahoma,[16] which used to be the capital of the Chickasaw Nation. But I just want to re-emphasize that those tribal governments that are discriminating against Freedmen could change things if they followed the treaties their ancestors signed.

—Interviewed by Meta G. Carstarphen

Notes

1. See Linda Reese, 2010, "Freedmen," in *The Encyclopedia of Oklahoma History and Culture*, last updated July 29, 2024, https://www.okhistory.org/publications/enc/entry?entry=FR016.

2. See the Cherokee Nation's official website: https://www.cherokee.org/about-the-nation/history/.

3. See the Eastern Band of Cherokee Indians website: https://www.ebci.gov/. According to the website, enrolled members must have "a direct lineal ancestor . . . who appears . . . on the 1924 Baker Roll of the Eastern Band of Cherokee Indians" (Strickland 2010).

4. See the United Keetoowah Band of Cherokee Indians in Oklahoma website: https://www.ukb-nsn.gov/. According to the website, these members were known originally known as "Old Settlers . . . as many . . . were already moving west to avoid U.S. encroachment before the Trail of Tears began."

5. See Rennard Strickland, 2010, "Cherokee (Tribe), an Extensive Historical Overview," in *The Encyclopedia of Oklahoma History and Culture*, last updated November 13, 2024, https://www.okhistory.org/publications/enc/entry?entry=CH014.

6. Historian and award-winning author Tiya Miles published *The House on Diamond Hill: A Cherokee Plantation Story* in 2010, which highlighted the story of nineteenth-century Cherokee chief and entrepreneur Joseph Vann, who is part of Marilyn Vann's ancestry. The Dawes Severalty Act of 1887 "ushered in the allotment era but it did not pertain to the Five Tribes." In 1893, Dawes led a "three-member commission to the Five Tribes to negotiate agreements with the leaders of the Cherokee, Choctaw, Chickasaw, Creek and Seminole," establishing Individual land ownership as opposed to tribal land ownership. See Kent Carter, "Dawes Commission," *The Encyclopedia of Oklahoma History and Culture*, https://www.okhistory.org/publications/enc/entry?entry=DA018.

7. William Wayne Keeler (1908–87). See "Keeler, William Wayne (1908–1987)" in *The Encyclopedia of Oklahoma History and Culture*, https://www.okhistory.org/publications/enc/entry?entry=KE002.

8. According to the US Census Bureau, the Cherokee Nation has the second largest "share of the American Indian alone population," behind the Navajo Nation. See Ana I. Sánchez-Rivera, Paul Jacobs, and Cody Spence, "Detailed Data for Hundreds of American Indian and Alaska Native Tribes," Census.gov, October 3, 2023, https://www.census.gov/library/stories/2023/10/2020-census-dhc-a-aian-population.html.

9. This took place on March 3, 2007, in a special election. See Will Chavez, February 1, 2021, "A Timeline for the Cherokee Freedmen," *Cherokee Phoenix*, updated September 25, 2024. See also Murray Evans, "Cherokees Vote to Revoke Membership of Freedmen," Associated Press, March 12, 2007, published in *Indian Country Today*, https://ictnews.org/archive/cherokees-vote-to-revoke-membership-of-freedmen/.

10. See *Vann et al. v. Norton, The Cherokee Nation of Oklahoma et al.* (2006) and *The Cherokee Nation v. Nash et al., Vann et al. and Zinke* (2017).

11. See Article III Section 5: "The descendants of Cherokee men by all free women, except the African race, whose parents may have been living together as man and wife, according to the customs and laws of this Nation, shall be entitled to all the rights and privileges of this Nation as well as the posterity of Cherokee women by all free men." This difference also reflects the Cherokee Nation's history as a matrilineal society. See Phoenix Archives, February 10, 2006, "The Cherokee Clan System," *Cherokee*

Phoenix, https://www.cherokeephoenix.org/education/the-cherokee-clan-system/article_a88fcc42-f3f8-5f33-b575-8cff7d3bffd2.html.

12. See William G. McLoughlin, 1974, "Red Indians, Black Slavery and White Racism: America's Slaveholding Indians," *American Quarterly* 26, no. 4: 367–85. https://doi.org/10.2307/2711653. See also William Christie MacLeod, 1928, "Economic Aspects of Indigenous American Slavery" in *American Anthropologist* 30, no. 4: 632–50.

13. See the two-volume Daniel F. Littlefield and James W. Parins, eds., 2011, *Encyclopedia of American Indian Removal*, for narratives, records, and documents from each tribe about removal and relocation experiences.

14. See Monroe Billington, Spring 1982, "Black Slavery in Indian Territory: The Ex-Slave Narratives," Oklahoma Historical Society: The Gateway to Oklahoma History, accessed September 27, 2024, https://gateway.okhistory.org/ark:/67531/metadc2031424/.

15. Jeremy M. Lazarus, February 28, 2020, "Blood Feud: Descendant Pushes to be Recognized by Pamunkey Tribe Despite vestiges of 'Black Laws,'" accessed October 11, 2024, https://richmondfreepress.com/news/2020/feb/28/blood-feud/. For additional context on the Pamunkey Tribe, see also Cristina L. Azocar, 2002, *News Media and the Indigenous Fight for Federal Recognition* (Lanham: Lexington Books), 17.

16. See Elizabeth Caldwell and Zach Boblitt, September 20, 2024, "Tishomingo Grapples with Racist Incident at High School," KWGS Public Radio Tulsa.

20

Flipping the Script

How Deb Haaland Used Instagram to Question Indigenous Stereotypes

Newly Paul

In March 2021, when Deb Haaland was sworn in as US secretary of the interior, the first picture she posted from her new Instagram account, @SecDebHaaland, was of herself at the ceremony, where she wore a ribbon dress. The skirt was decorated with motifs such as corn stalks, which represented her membership in the Pueblo of Laguna Tribe, and butterflies, which symbolized hope (Kunze 2021). The post mentioned her gratitude at being appointed to the position and expressed her desire to work hard to ensure that future generations could enjoy public lands and waters for years (@SecDebHaaland, March 18, 2021). The account had about 71,000 followers, and the post received more than 15,000 likes. Followers expressed pride at seeing a Native American woman serving in an important position.

As the first Native American to serve as Secretary of the Interior and one of the first Native American women to serve in Congress, Debra Anne Haaland was a unique politician. She was an Indigenous woman in a predominantly white and male field. She held public office at a time when political polarization and white supremacy have become a part of mainstream politics (Maxim and Akee 2020). This chapter explores how Haaland used her personal and official Instagram accounts (@DebHaalandNM and @SecDebHaaland) to construct her identity and communicate with audiences. The framework used to analyze the themes that emerge from Haaland's communications on Instagram will be Hallahan's (2011) typology of strategic framing.

Making History as a Fierce Leader

Deb Haaland was born in Winslow, Arizona on December 2, 1960. She is a thirty-fifth-generation New Mexican. Her mother, Mary Toya, was a navy veteran, and her father, J. D. "Dutch" Haaland, served thirty years in the US Marines. As a military child, Haaland and her three siblings moved often, and she attended thirteen different schools while she was growing up. She graduated in 1994 from the University of New Mexico with a bachelor's degree in English, and in 2006 she received her JD from the University of New Mexico School of Law (Rielly 2022).

Haaland's life as a young adult was filled with challenges. Her daughter, Somáh, was born four days after Haaland completed her undergraduate degree. As a single mother attending law school, Haaland struggled financially, and at one point she started a small business selling salsa. Her family of two struggled to find stable housing, and she relied on food stamps to feed her child. Haaland later acknowledged that her paycheck-to-paycheck existence had shaped her career as a legislator (McGrady 2019). She posted on her Twitter and Facebook accounts when she was nominated for the cabinet secretary position: "A voice like mine has never been a Cabinet secretary or at the head of the Department of Interior. Growing up in my mother's Pueblo household made me fierce. I will be fierce for all of us, our planet, and all of our protected land. I am honored and ready to serve" (@SecDebHaaland, December 17, 2020).

Haaland began her political career in 2008 as a volunteer for Barack Obama's campaign, and worked her way up to become the Democratic Party chair for New Mexico in 2015. In 2018, she was elected to the US House of Representatives. As a congresswoman, she supported raising the minimum wage, expanding Medicare, improving access to voting, and protecting national parks. Although she was elected to a second term in Congress, Haaland decided to accept the position of secretary of the interior, where her duties were to conserve the environment, manage public land, national parks, and wildlife refuges, and manage the federal trust to tribes by protecting Indigenous lands and resources (Rielly 2022).

Haaland's congressional campaign was noteworthy because she ran openly as a Native American woman and embraced discussions about her identity (Steinhauer 2021). Although she knew that her constituency consisted of people from diverse cultures and backgrounds, Haaland emphasized the special "importance of her role to tribe members" (195). Her social media accounts provide a snapshot of how she constructed her identity as a Native American politician who would fight for the welfare of all her constituents.

Social Media and Women in Politics

Social media is an important campaign tool for politicians (Fujiwara et al. 2023), especially those from marginalized communities (Evans and Clark 2016; Wagner et al. 2023). It offers candidates a cost-effective means of communicating with their followers. Candidates use text and images to shape their public persona (Owen 2010), raise funds, discuss issues, attack opponents, publicize accomplishments, and mobilize voters (Jungherr 2016).

Political messaging strategies on social media vary based on race and gender (Fountaine 2017). Women tend to post negative messages and attack-based posts to counter gender-stereotypical perceptions of them being weak and unsuited to public office. Men, on the other hand, tend to highlight their family and personal relationships to create a relatable image (Evans and Clark 2016; Meeks 2016). Black politicians often use social media to discuss their stance on racial issues (Tillery 2021).

Women of color, such as Haaland, occupy an intersectional position wherein their identities are shaped by both race and gender (Crenshaw 1991). In addition to gender stereotypes, there are also racialized stereotypes against women of color; Native Americans are stereotyped as alcoholic, uncivilized, unreliable, and mysterious (Erhart and Hall 2019), and women in particular have been negatively stereotyped as overly sexual and lacking in intelligence (Merskin 2010).

Women of color navigate the race and gender dynamic by strategically using racial and gender messaging. Women candidates emphasize their gender, uniqueness, and religious beliefs in their social media posts and interact more frequently with people on social media (Meeks 2016). Female candidates of color tend to emphasize racial issues in their campaigns (Zilber and Niven 2000) and present themselves as neutral to Washington politics, rather than as insiders or outsiders (Gulati 2004). These tactics intend to humanize women candidates, while portraying them as feminine yet capable of handling political issues, which are typically perceived as a masculine domain (Huddy and Terkildsen 1993).

Given the small number of Native American politicians holding elected office in US governmental structures (Center for American Women and Politics 2023), the majority of politicians from other backgrounds have yet to understand how this group communicates with Indigenous constituents and other voters, and if there are specific issues and frames that Indigenous politicians use more than others. An examination of Haaland's social media accounts could help answer these questions.

Strategic Framing of Political Messages

Strategic communication scholar Kirk Hallahan (2011) identified three levels of framing and valuable analysis in political contexts: framing by sources, framing by intermediaries (including the news media), and framing by message recipients and audiences. This case study discusses framing by political candidates. According to Hallahan (2011, 179), political candidates "act as framing strategists . . . by choosing which aspects of a candidate, issue, or cause to emphasize or deemphasize" across a wide range of contexts. His typology of applications consists of framing the following: attributes, risks, arguments supporting actions, issues, responsibility, and stories. Candidates frame situations such as encounters with other politicians, public meetings with voters, speeches, press conferences, and debates to highlight words, actions, and visuals that help curate an image of the candidate in voters' minds.

Framing of attributes involves using language to "focus attention on particular aspects of objects, people, and ideas" (Hallahan 2011, 183) to promote the candidate's positive qualities, differentiate them from others, and establish a broad appeal. Risk framing involves messages that highlight the candidate's stability, issues, and positions, and frames their decisions as nonrisky. Framing of arguments supporting actions includes messages that stress urgency and encourage people to take action in order to avoid a catastrophic outcome. The framing of issues involves discussing issues in terms of identifying a problem, outlining a solution, or encouraging action. Responsibility is framed by taking credit for policy or legislative successes and ascribing blame for failure to circumstances or people. Lastly, framing stories involves "the telling of complex narratives that explain an idea or situation" (193) and uses culturally familiar meanings and values. Political actors seek to establish shared frames across these approaches to build relationships with constituents. These shared frames or mutual perspectives are based on common beliefs and traditions (Hallahan 2011).

Images, videos, and words from Haaland's two Instagram accounts, @SecDebHaaland and @DebHaalandNM, provide a picture of Haaland's political career, first as a congresswoman and later as a cabinet secretary. The content published on these accounts between January 1, 2020 and May 31, 2023 was analyzed; the hashtags and phrases used in the individual Instagram posts, and the visuals and videos accompanying the posts, were also examined. Five main themes arose across 320 posts: a strong advocate of Native communities and a voice of change, elevating Indigenous experiences, connecting the personal with the public, a leader for all constituents, and a solutions-oriented leader.

A Strong Advocate for Native Communities and a Voice for Change

Haaland prominently expressed her identity as a member of the Pueblo of Laguna Tribe and a thirty-fifth-generation New Mexican in her social media posts. She wore clothing and jewelry that reflected her Native culture and celebrated the multiple Indigenous cultures in the United States. Haaland was often photographed wearing turquoise jewelry and Pueblo clothing while performing her official duties. Brown and Lemi (2021) argue that women politicians' hairstyles, clothing, and self-presentation are strategic because they are judged against Eurocentric beauty standards that are especially restrictive for women of color.

Haaland posted videos that showed her Indigenous origins, spoke in Keres, her Pueblo language, and shared memories of growing up in her mother's Pueblo household. Pictures taken in her office showed paintings, photographs, and sculptures in the background that highlighted her heritage and presented an alternative to the established white, male norms of politics. Referring to Haaland's choice of wearing the ribbon skirt to the inauguration and using Native artifacts to highlight her Pueblo culture, the designer of the piece, Agnes Woodward, wrote in a post: "Wearing it [the ribbon skirt] in this day and age is an act of self-empowerment and reclamation of who we are, and that gives us the opportunity to proudly make bold statements in front of others who sometimes refuse to see us" (@Reecreeations, March 18, 2021).

Haaland's posts show her to be a strong advocate of Indigenous issues. She discussed topics of intersectional Indigenous concerns, including violence against women and environmental issues. Her use of language in these posts shows that she strongly identifies with Native communities and their members' concerns. For example, in a post criticizing the US Department of Justice for its lack of prosecutions in cases involving missing and murdered Native women, Haaland said: "Today I stand with the Native community and all who are fighting to provide equitable protection of Indigenous women" (@DebHaalandNM, May 5, 2020). Her use of "I" and her solidarity with the cause indicates her concern about the issue.

Another post showed an image of Haaland draping a red shawl over her chair at the office of the US Department of the Interior. The post read: "On Red Shawl Day, we bring attention to the relatives who are impacted by the missing and murdered Indigenous peoples' crisis. It's a day of remembrance and of commitment to continue our quest for justice. . . . Today, I wear my red shawl as a symbol of my deep commitment to addressing the root causes of the violence in Indian Country that has plagued us for far too long" (@SecDebHaaland, November 19, 2022). The post used words and phrases such as "we," "our," and "my deep commitment" to indicate Haaland's personal connection with Indigenous issues, and showed the authenticity of her desire to address them.

Her issue-centric posts had a positive tone and focused on progress and solutions. In the post about Red Shawl Day, Haaland noted how the Department of the Interior had investigated more than 500 missing and murdered persons cases and solved about seventy-five such cases in 2022. "Though I know this is a small step, I also know this is progress we can be proud of," her post said (@SecDebHaaland, November 19, 2022). Another post showed a photo of a file system. It explained that the files contained "thousands and thousands of records" associated with American Indian boarding schools, and that staff members of the Bureau of Trust Funds Administration had digitized them. "These boxes of files represent ancestors—children who were taken away from their families by the U.S. government," Haaland's post said, documenting the work to memorialize the history of the American Indian boarding school system (@SecDebHaaland, May 21, 2023).

Another post on the same topic echoed this tone of hopefulness and progress: "In Washington State today, Assistant Secretary Newland and I heard from survivors of federal Indian boarding schools. The stories are heartbreaking, and the day was heavy, but this work needs to be done in order to heal from the intergenerational trauma we carry. As our country learns more of this history, we can build a better future for the generations that come after us" (@SecDebHaaland, April 23, 2023). As is evident in this post, Haaland acknowledges the traumatic past of Indigenous people, but instead of expressing anger at past events, she adopts a forward-looking approach that uses instances from the past to inform the future.

Elevating Indigenous Experiences

Haaland's posts elevated Native American stories and experiences; she shared the community's lived experiences and collective knowledge while explaining the work done by the Department of the Interior. For example, Haaland posted a picture of a yellow poppy at Castner Range in New Mexico to commemorate President Biden designating Castner as a National Monument (@SecDebHaaland, March 26, 2023). Her post explained that the flower was significant to the nearby communities of El Paso and Las Cruces, and was used in *quinceñeras*, graduations, engagements, and weddings. With the federal government's new designation, the area would be "protected for future generations and will be the backdrop for the lives of future generations," Haaland's post said. This post emphasized the connection of Indigenous people to the environment. It highlighted the progressive actions that the federal government and Haaland's Department of the Interior had taken to reduce risks to future generations.

Another post on a similar topic celebrated the return of 1,000 acres of unceded Onondaga lands and waters of the Tully Valley in Central New York. "As the original stewards of the land, the Onondaga Nation will use Indigenous knowledge to manage the area's wildlife and habitat," Haaland's post said. "This is another step forward for @potus' America the Beautiful initiative: we all have a role to play when it comes to preserving our shared natural resources" (@SecDebHaaland, June 29, 2022).

Yet another post celebrated the efforts to aid the recovery of the American bison (@SecDebHaaland, March 7, 2023):

> The bison is inextricably intertwined with Indigenous culture, grassland ecology, and American history. While the overall recovery of bison over the last 130 years is a conservation success story, significant work remains to not only ensure that bison will remain a viable species but also to restore grassland ecosystems, strengthen rural economies dependent on grassland health and provide for the return of bison to tribally-owned and ancestral lands. New historic funding from the Inflation Reduction Act will help support @usinterior's efforts to restore this iconic species and integrate Indigenous Knowledge into our shared stewardship goals.

In early 2024, the Department of the Interior's Bureau of Indian Affairs earmarked $1.5 million for distribution among three tribal-led bison expansion and ecosystem restoration projects. The programs include one run by the Cheyenne and Arapaho Tribes in Oklahoma, while others occurred in North Dakota and Idaho (Pope 2024). The tone of Haaland's posts celebrated Native knowledge and expertise and portrayed Indigenous people as responsible stewards of the world they inhabit.

Other instances of Haaland using her social media account to advocate for Indigenous communities include posts that promoted Indigenous politicians and business owners. For example, she posted a picture praising the designs of Quannah ChasingHorse, whose Indigenous ancestry is Hän Gwich'in (from Alaska and Canada) and Oglala Lakota (from South Dakota). Haaland also posted a picture with Sharice Davids, a member of the Ho-Chunk Nation and congressional candidate from Kansas, with a caption saying that Congress needs new voices like hers. More broadly, Haaland's posts often showed visuals of herself surrounded by members of diverse Native American communities. These members appeared in various roles—as constituents, leaders, and subject matter experts—which helped people visualize Indigenous people in nonstereotypical roles.

Her posts also discussed her efforts to reduce discrimination against Native communities. An example was her campaign to remove the word "squaw" from federal use. When this change went into effect, she posted: "Words matter, particularly in our work to ensure our nation's public lands and waters are accessible and welcoming to people of all backgrounds. This is a big moment. We're showing why representation matters and charting a path for an inclusive America" (@SecDebHaaland, January 12, 2023). Her post also explained that the slur had been used historically for Indigenous women and was used to delegitimize and silence them.

Lastly, Haaland used stories to connect US Indigenous communities with other communities worldwide. An example was a post where she shared a picture of a tree carving that she noticed on her trip to Australia, accompanied by the text: "Aboriginal communities in Australia use the bark of trees to build canoes, bowls, and other tools. Instead of cutting down the whole tree for their use, they only take the piece that they need, and the tree remains alive, but a scar is left behind" (@SecDebHaaland, May 14, 2023). She explained that, on her trip, she had attended a tree-scarring ceremony and described it as "a beautiful tribute to the tree that provided something for the community and transformed it into a piece of art." Haaland said that the "ceremony and reverence for what the Earth provides us is how we should all live and is an example of how Indigenous Knowledge can help us restore nature and bring balance back to our world."

This story highlights the existence of common beliefs within Indigenous communities regardless of international boundaries. The stories we hear about these communities often relate to hardship and persecution, but Haaland's stories highlight the ingenuity and interconnected nature of Native American cultures.

Connecting the Personal with the Public

Haaland used stories from her personal life to inject authenticity into her posts and create a connection with her constituents. Her posts tied various family members' life stories to America's history, reiterating that

Indigenous people have been integral to American history for centuries. On Veterans Day, she posted a picture of her uncle Paul, who had served in the army during the Korean War. "Today, I'm thinking of him, my father, and so many other veterans that have served our nation," her post said. "Happy Veterans Day, and if you see a veteran, thank them for their service" (@SecDebHaaland, November 11, 2022). Another post commemorating the day featured a picture of Haaland's parents in their military uniforms. The post read: "These are my parents. I salute them and all our veterans and active-duty service members. Far too many Americans have paid the ultimate sacrifice for this country. The President's view of our POWs and fallen service members is sickening. Our service members have more courage and leadership than Trump could ever hope to have" (@DebHaalandNM, September 4, 2020).

While Haaland's posts generally avoided directly criticizing the statements and actions of members of the Republican Party, posts such as these were the exception. Despite adopting an attacking tone, Haaland's post used a story from her personal life to explain why she was criticizing then-president Trump. As Hallahan (2011, 193) argues, stories use "culturally resonating meanings, norms, and values" and depict characters in identifiable roles. Haaland's personal stories depicted her family members as quintessential Americans who are brave and patriotic, in contrast with Trump.

Haaland's other stories demonstrated her personal connection with her work as a cabinet secretary. For example, to commemorate fee-free days at national parks, she told the story of her days as a young mother: "When I was raising my child Somáh, I didn't have a lot of money, so I relied on free opportunities to offer them experiences in the outdoors. Many of our adventures were to public parks or free refuges," she wrote, adding that fee-free days help make public lands accessible to all (@SecDebHaaland, February 6, 2023). Another post noted her personal struggles, such as living paycheck to paycheck and relying on food stamps, which she said helped her understand the struggles of everyday Americans. These stories humanized her and portrayed her as a politician whose work was informed by her life experiences, which overlapped with those of average Americans.

Other posts drew parallels between her life and more significant political issues. For example, one post celebrated President Biden's signing into law of the Respect for Marriage Act, which requires federal and state governments to recognize same-sex marriages performed in other states. "It means people like my child will have the same rights as everyone else," Haaland wrote, referencing her daughter, who is queer and uses they/them pronouns. She wrote that she was proud to be Somáh's mom in another post celebrating LGBTQ Families Day: "They inspire me every day to use my platform to lift others and to be fierce for those who are targeted because of who they are and who they love" (@SecDebHaaland, June 1, 2022).

Haaland's stories had a familiar arc of resilience against all odds, and they featured brave characters who embody progressive values. She used personal stories and images from her family album to explain her position on various political issues, which helped constituents understand her and identify with her.

A Leader for All Constituents

Haaland's posts and visuals painted her as a politician interested in representing all her constituents. Her posts expressed her desire to work collaboratively with all stakeholders by emphasizing commonalities between her background and that of other Americans. When she was nominated for the cabinet secretary post and was going up for confirmation, she posted the following on her Instagram accounts: "I believe we all have a stake in the future of our country, and I believe that every one of us shares a common bond: Our love for the outdoors and a desire and obligation to keep our nation livable for future generations" (@SecDebHaaland, March 4, 2021). The use of terms such as "all," "our," and "every one of us" indicates Haaland's collectivist rather than individualistic approach to policy making.

The visuals on her account also emphasized this point. The pictures showed her surrounded by diverse people and participating in various activities. Haaland appeared in the company of other Democratic leaders, such as vice president Kamala Harris, or engaging with constituents in their spaces, such as talking with them at a café, visiting a small business, volunteering at a food bank, and giving speeches to crowds. Other pictures, such as those of her holding a birthday cake or wishing her daughter a happy birthday, served to humanize her. These images portrayed her as an accessible politician who was tuned in to the needs of her community and actively involved with all her constituents.

Another way in which Haaland signaled her identity as a representative for all her constituents was by highlighting events and issues that are intersectional and have a broader impact on the community. "It was an honor to join the National Menorah lighting ceremony this week," she said in a post celebrating Hanukkah. "During the holiday season, may we work toward a future that embraces our diverse traditions and backgrounds"

(@SecDebHaaland, December 20, 2022). Another post documented her efforts related to gun control: "I voted YES on background checks for every gun sale. I got an 'F' from the NRA. I'm immensely proud of both. #ProudOfMyF" (@SecDebHaaland, April 26, 2022). On Labor Day, she posted a picture of herself with Dolores Huerta, Albuquerque mayor Tim Keller, New Mexico governor Michelle Lujan Grisham, and others using the hashtags #sisepuede, #laborstrong, and #justice. Posts such as these tackled intersectional issues and increased her appeal to a broader range of people in the community.

Haaland also used her platform to highlight racial issues and express solidarity with movements such as Black Lives Matter. For example, she posted content featuring fellow politicians of color, such as Black Congresswoman Ayanna Pressley (D-MA). She also posted an image with the text: "Right now my heart is with George Floyd's daughter and with his family, and with many others. I want so badly for things to change. Justice must be a reality for people who haven't ever known it. #BlackLivesMatter" (@SecDebHaaland, April 20, 2021). Another example is her post expressing disagreement with the Trump administration's immigration policies, specifically the creation of the border wall. Haaland argued that Trump's immigration policy rested in indignity and inhumanity.

Thus, Haaland used a variety of frames to discuss pressing political issues. She framed issues as moral and rooted in inequality and injustice, rather than as controversial or purely political. She used social justice, equality, and human rights frames to discuss various societal problems. Her posts highlighted the impact of a given issue on humans regardless of their identity, instead of focusing on conflict. Her social media presence portrayed her as an advocate for the New Mexico's most vulnerable people, and showed that her efforts aligned the interests of disparate groups by highlighting the commonalities among them. Thus, Haaland bridged disparate elements and created coalitions within the community.

A Solutions-Oriented Leader

Haaland's posts frame her as solutions-oriented and invested in environmental and socioeconomic issues. Her posts encouraged people to take action to solve problems. Instead of blaming a particular person or group, Haaland framed her posts to ascribe collective responsibility for finding and implementing solutions. Several posts from her Instagram accounts echo this theme. For example, a post about orphaned oil and gas wells explained that these structures contaminate the land, air, and water. Haaland noted that she had toured the Deep Fork National Wildlife

Refuge in Oklahoma, which has nearly 1,000 wells, and learned about clean-up efforts funded by investments from President Biden's Bipartisan Infrastructure Law. Haaland portrayed Democrats as a solutions-oriented party and the law as correcting past wrongs for the betterment of all. Another example is a post that mentioned how the infrastructure law would help combat climate change by investing in water resources and building climate resilience. These posts used concrete examples and images to help demystify federal laws that might otherwise appear distant, abstract, and unrelated to people's lives.

The posts that used this theme framed Haaland as a leader interested in learning from experts, understanding the community's problems, and finding solutions. For example, in a post about climate change worsening fire seasons, she said that she had visited a training center for firefighters in New Mexico and toured a burn scar, which gave her important insights. Another picture that demonstrated her willingness to learn and troubleshoot with community members showed her at a workshop in the University of Oregon. "Outdoor recreation and conservation go hand in hand, and they have invaluable economic benefits for local communities," the post read. "Today, I hosted a roundtable in Bend, Oregon, to learn how to continue to invest in the outdoors, now and for the future" (@SecDebHaaland, March 17, 2023). Another post praised farmers' knowledge and innovative efforts to conserve water, and emphasized the need for collaboration between the Department of the Interior and community stakeholders.

Overall, Haaland's social media presence indicates that our society bears a collective responsibility for solving issues with help from the government. Her posts credit people who work together to find solutions, and portray the government as an entity invested in the greater good of all Americans. The visuals accompanying these posts echo the same theme of focusing on solutions: images show Haaland surrounded by people from various fields, such as business and politics, listening actively, participating in activities with community members, or speaking to them—thus strengthening her image as an action-oriented leader.

Implications

This analysis of Haaland's posts shows that she framed herself as a leader who spoke against white supremacy and racism, built diverse coalitions, and upheld Native voices. Her social media style overlaps with more significant trends in the campaigns of women of color. Haaland avoided negativity or attacking her opponents, instead highlighting her family ties in ways that portrayed her as a capable and sensitive leader. Though most women of color do not discuss racial issues or identities on social media (Wagner et al. 2023), Haaland emphasized her Pueblo of Laguna roots. By highlighting commonalities between her Indigenous life experiences and those of broader American life, she flipped the script on Native Americans as mysterious and "un-American."

Haaland's posts do not frame issues as being particularly relevant to women, and neither do they highlight her gender. Instead, she framed issues as affecting all community members regardless of their identity. Visually, though, her posts showed her interacting with a large number of women and amplifying women's voices. Though her posts praised the policies enacted by a Democrat president, she avoided pandering to Washington and emphasized the need to build partnerships between multiple communities and the government. Her posts reframed Indigenous people as productive and honest stewards of the land, as people who are patriotic, knowledgeable, and invested in the country's future.

These findings are important to the literature on how women of color, particularly Native American women, use social media for political campaigns. The findings indicate that women of color are not a monolithic group and that their strategies vary depending on their racial identities and life experiences. This chapter also documented how Haaland used imagery and words to appeal to Indigenous audiences and her broader constituency. Women of color are sometimes limited by the "double jeopardy" (Beale 1970) of gender and racial stereotypes, but Haaland's strategy allowed her to have a wider reach, which made her appealing to a broad swath of voters.

Discussion Questions

1. This chapter discusses how racial and gender stereotypes shape the campaign messages of women politicians of color. Media coverage is another important part of campaigns. How does the media cover minority women running for high-profile public offices? What factors shape media coverage?
2. How do social media messages affect voters and their opinions about issues? Thinking about your own voting behavior, discuss how social media campaigns have affected your choice of candidate or likelihood to vote.
3. Do candidates' social media messages differ depending on the type of platform? How do campaign messages differ between Facebook, Instagram, and TikTok?

21

"We Prayed and Danced in Our Own Ways"

Interview with LiL Mike and Funny Bone

LiL Mike & Funny Bone are two award-winning Native American recording artists, dancers, actors, and motivational speakers, as seen on *America's Got Talent* and *Reservation Dogs*. The hip-hop duo, born and raised in Oklahoma City, aim to entertain and inspire by making music and performing at venues of all kinds, from arenas to public schools and everything in between. They've dedicated their lives to entertaining crowds with good music, good medicine, and unforgettable performances.

Please introduce yourself.

Funny Bone: Well, we are LiL Mike & Funny Bone. Together, we are known as Mike Bone. We're recording artists and actors. We do a little motivational speaking and comedy. What else?

LiL Mike: We grew up, born and raised, in Oklahoma City, in the urban areas.

Funny Bone: So we didn't really get in touch with our culture until our late teens.

LiL Mike: Yeah, late teens.

Funny Bone: So there's that. But we're Pawnee and Choctaw.

LiL Mike: They call me "LiL Mike" 'cause I started out dancing like Michael Jackson, and they called me "Little Michael Jackson." It just stuck.

Funny Bone: I would get on stage in between his songs and tell a joke, do something funny, and make the crowd laugh. Now my name is an acronym. It stands for "Fully United, Newly Nourished, Young Brother of Noble Essence." Also, we play Mose and Mekko on three seasons of the TV show *Reservation Dogs*. Our

Fig. 21.1. LiL Mike and Funny Bone. Author photo.

characters are the neighborhood . . . what would you call it?

LiL Mike: I don't want to say gossipers, but we're the instigators.

Funny Bone: Yeah, we spread the word on the street of what's happening with him, her, and them. We also play rappers, which is funny 'cause we actually rap!

LiL Mike: And then we'll go around hustling CDs on the show.

Funny Bone: We basically play ourselves.

LiL Mike: Besides all the gossiping.

Funny Bone: Right!

What does Indigenous media mean to you?

Funny Bone: As Indigenous people, you know, we try not to make or create things with bad energy. So we try to do that in our music.

LiL Mike: Not a lot of rappers do that. They just get all in their feelings and get in the studio and share that energy. And some people will listen to the songs and be like, "I feel depressed now." It's probably 'cause that artist had a spirit of depression, and now it's like contagious. That was my thing. I was attracted to that aggressive, angry music, and it kept getting me in trouble. Then I had a lightbulb go off. I was like, "Man, words have power!" Creator spoke to me and said, "You need to burn all your CDs that are holding you back." That was the hardest thing to do 'cause I had like 350 CDs.[1]

Funny Bone: We had a collection!

LiL Mike: And I had some classics in there too, girl! I was like, "God. I'll get rid of everything except Michael Jackson."

Funny Bone: Yeah, can't burn Michael Jackson! He already got burned once.

LiL Mike: Seriously, we just want to leave a good legacy.

Funny Bone: Like in our recent album, *VIBIN.* It's an anthem for Indigenous issues, whether it's the missing and murdered women movement . . .

LiL Mike: . . . or to raise awareness about the boarding schools issue, or the fight to protect natural resources, like water.

Funny Bone: Yeah. And the police brutality song as well, 'cause all people of color definitely face a lot more of that.

Describe your work. What compels you to do it?

LiL Mike: Like I said, we want to be the other side of an industry that's flooded heavily with depressing music, drug addiction, and substance abuse.

Funny Bone: Yeah, and on top of that, people already try to stereotype Native Americans, so we break that stereotype. We don't smoke. We don't drink. We party harder than others, but we can remember what happened the next day. We wake up with no regrets, no tattoos, and no babies we didn't ask for.

LiL Mike: Not only that, we're Christ followers. We did start off as Christian rappers. We believe in Christ, but we also believe in our traditional practices. We prayed and danced in our own ways. We believe we should use those practices too, and not forget about them, because Creator gave them to our ancestors for a reason.

Why is it important to have Indigenous people tell their own stories?

Funny Bone: It humanizes us. Here's an example. I remember thinking while we were shooting *Reservation Dogs* during the pandemic, *Y'all aren't even ready!* I was like, *Oh man, when audiences see this, they're gonna be like, "Oh, snap!"* They still are!

LiL Mike: Disney didn't even sign it originally. It was, like, a small-budget project at first.

Funny Bone: Yeah, so once it got picked up by Hulu and Disney, I'm like, this is going to be big! I knew it was going to be big in Indian Country. I did not know it was going to be as big as it was all over.

LiL Mike: Yeah. We didn't think the world was going to grab on to it like it did, even people overseas. But *Reservation Dogs* shows that we're dealing with the same issues that a lot of other communities are facing. We all have the same type of people that are in the show.

Funny Bone: And it sparked interest in the Indigenous lifestyle and traditions. It showed how we are, right now.

LiL Mike: Not all of us have reservation accents. Not all of us have teepees.

Funny Bone: Not all of us dress the same or talk the same. Not all of us are the same shade.

LiL Mike: Right. Sterlin Harjo[2] knew what he was doing when he created that series, and especially when he was telling all the different actors to speak like they were from Oklahoma, but not to change their accent too much because Oklahoma is the middle. Everybody comes from all over just to live here, and he wanted to express that.

Funny Bone: Yeah. That was beautiful 'cause when I heard "reservation," I thought of the movie *Smoke Signals*, and I was trying to have a rez accent like that. Sterlin was like, "Don't ever do that again," and I was like, "Oh, my bad. Was it that bad?" He said, "Yeah."

LiL Mike: But that was the beauty of it. It just showed our variety, and it was real.

Funny Bone: Including my Oklahoma country–urban accent.

What does the future hold, in your view?

LiL Mike: Family-friendly content opens way more doors. Definitely, for us. We're going to continue to keep it clean and positive.

Funny Bone: We do all kinds of events: youth events, school events, night clubs, casinos—you name it. Public festivals, TV shows, news shows, church events.

LiL Mike: We don't have to make an edited "clean" version of our music. They just automatically play it on the radio.

Funny Bone: Boom! That's opened so many more doors.

What should the next generation consider?
Why is this work important?

Funny Bone: I will say some knowledge for anybody who wants to get into the industry: be cautious, especially with contracts.

LiL Mike: Oh yeah, be cautious. If you don't understand it, have somebody else read it.

Funny Bone: And network. That's another thing we did, and we still do—find people in the industry who you want to be like. Don't be afraid to ask other artists questions. Don't think that everybody is trying to hide their resources.

LiL Mike: Definitely. And if you're looking to get into this industry or any industry, whether it be modeling, acting, or whatever, learn what you can learn. Use what you got to your best ability. Because when we first started, we recorded on a computer that had a five-dollar microphone, added a hanger and a sock, and we just used the beats that Bone made. We did the best that we could with what we had.

Is there anything else you would like to add?

LiL Mike: We didn't really talk about why we got into acting. It was kind of forced on us with COVID.

Funny Bone: Yeah, definitely forced! COVID shut down everything, as you know, and our tour dates all got canceled, and we were just sitting at home—broke. We needed some income. Acting was the only thing on the table.

LiL Mike: So by the grace of God, we found the *Reservation Dogs* opportunity, and there was a small role for two little guys. It was supposed to be eleven-year-old twins.

Funny Bone: But we're like, "Hey, we look like we're eleven, right? Let's just audition for the practice." We didn't think they were gonna call us back, but they said they loved it! We were exactly what they were looking for.

LiL Mike: Just having an Indigenous peoples' show is historic, and for us to be a part of it is a major blessing.

Funny Bone: Super grateful for that. Now we're getting contacted by different movies and producers to be on different projects in the future. We get a lot of requests from artists, like, "Let's do a collab. Let's do a collab." We tell them the rules first: can't be about drinking, no smoking, no sexual activity. And no cussing.

LiL Mike: Yeah, *no* cussing.

Funny Bone: And then they go, "Well dang, what's the song gonna be about?" And we're like, "See, if you can't even think of the possibilities, you can't qualify."

LiL Mike: Yeah, can't qualify. We have standards, and we're not going against our beliefs or our standards.

Funny Bone: So it's just like if you really want to work with us, listen to our music first. I think part of our Indigenous side is that integrity.

—Interviewed by Meta G. Carstarphen

Notes

1. Compact disc: an "optical disc used to store and playback digital data." See History of Information, "The Compact Disc (CD) Is Developed," https://www.historyofinformation.com/detail.php?id=949.

2. Sterlin Harjo, co-creator and showrunner for the *Reservation Dogs* series, which debuted on Hulu.

22

Still Buying into Racism

Beyond Using American Indian Icons in Product Marketing

Victoria E. Sanchez

As part of the "racial reckoning" of 2020, that year was tumultuous for consumer products that featured Indigenous mascots and imagery. Americans grappled with issues of race, racial inequity, and structural racism in the midst of a pandemic. Race-based healthcare inequalities came to light as communities of color were hardest hit by the pandemic. The Black Lives Matter movement gained strength in the wake of news coverage of a string of police killings of Black individuals, most visibly Breonna Taylor, Ahmaud Arbery, and George Floyd. This tumult was generally recognized within the United States as potentially perspective- and trajectory-altering on a societal level.

The hallmark of what came to be called the "summer of racial awakening" was also a reckoning—a call for antiracist actions and substantive change. Ibram X. Kendi's book *How to Be an Anti-Racist* (Kendi 2019) was wildly popular. A central tenet of Kendi's message is that there is no such category as "not racist"; an action is either racist or antiracist. The "middle ground" of "not racist" actually functions as complicity in maintaining the racist status quo, rather than actively countering it with antiracism.

At that time, antiracist actions included changing long-familiar product icons and renaming sports teams whose names and mascots had long been embroiled in controversy for their offensive portrayal of American Indians. However, there is still much work to be done in eliminating American Indian imagery in the marketplace and in raising the level of understanding about the harm done to Native people through cultural appropriation and pervasive stereotyping.

This chapter examines instances of misappropriation of American Indian identity that have been corrected and identifies some examples that still remain; looks back at the historical use of American Indians as symbols in advertising and branding; examines how product symbols contribute to stereotypes, prejudices, and discrimination; discusses how such use may adversely affect American Indian people and render American mainstream culture less able to recognize important issues facing American Indian communities today; and looks at alternatives that support Native people and businesses.

What Has Changed and What Has Stayed the Same

In the context of the "new" racial awareness, many brands reviewed and updated or changed their packaging, and in some cases their product name. Many of these were popular products that used icons that were stereotypical portrayals of African Americans.

In June 2020, the Aunt Jemima brand led the charge by rebranding to Pearl Milling Company: "In June 2020, PepsiCo and The Quaker Oats Company made a commitment to change the name and image of Aunt Jemima, recognizing that they do not reflect our core values" (Pearl Milling Company n.d.a). Mars Inc.'s Uncle Ben's brand, which featured on its packaging an image of a smiling Black man in a bow tie (reminiscent of a Black servant or porter), rebranded as Ben's Original, without the image. In September 2020, B&G Foods announced that it would remove the image of the Black chef from its cream of wheat packaging: "While research indicates the image may be based upon an actual Chicago chef named Frank White, it reminds some consumers of earlier depictions they find offensive" (McEvoy 2020).

Amid the publicity around brands featuring African American product icons, significant but less publicized changes were made to brands featuring Indigenous people as product icons. In October 2020, Dreyer's Grand Ice Cream announced that its Eskimo Pie ice-cream bars would be rebranded as Edy's Pie, and that the caricature of an "Eskimo" child would be removed. The term "Eskimo," which had branded the product since the early 1920s, was a colonial term applied to the Indigenous peoples of the Arctic region: "We are committed to being a part of the solution on racial equality, and recognize the term is inappropriate" (Cramer 2020).

In February 2020, Land O'Lakes announced its new packaging ahead of its hundredth anniversary. The press release made no mention of the previous packaging—which featured a Native woman, "Mia the Butter Maiden," kneeling in a farm field holding a butter box (figure 22.1)—or of having removed this product icon, which it had used since 1928. Instead, the press release focused on the new packaging, which retains

Fig. 22.1. The "Butter Maiden" was featured on the packaging of Land O'Lakes' food products from the 1920s, until the corporation removed the image from its branding in 2020, as it celebrated its hundredth year in business.

the background landscape of the iconic shimmering blue lake, green trees, and butter-yellow sky in which Mia had appeared.

Especially in the context of the racial awakening and other corporate rebranding efforts, the co-op's silence on why it chose to retire its Native product icon caused some consternation, even as the change was welcomed by American Indian activists who had long opposed the use of the figure. Many felt Land O'Lakes had missed an opportunity to discuss the history of the image, including the fact that the original 1928 image had been updated by Ojibwe artist Patrick DesJarlait in the 1950s, and that now the image was recognized as being stereotypical and inappropriate. The visual void on the packaging was underscored by the void in communications. Paul Chat-Smith (Comanche), associate curator at the Smithsonian Institution's National Museum of the American Indian, said in a *Smithsonian Magazine* piece, "One wishes for an alternative besides stereotype or erasure" (Wu 2020). A common joke in Indian Country at the time was that, once again, the white people had removed the Indian and kept the land.

The awakening also gave momentum to the decades-long controversies around sports team names and mascots that appropriate American Indian identities and use stereotypical and offensive language and images. In July 2020, ten days after the Washington, DC football team said it would thoroughly review its long-controversial name, it announced that it would retire the name prior to the next season (Carpenter 2020); the team rebranded as the Washington Commanders. The team's owners had been under pressure to change the highly offensive team name for over fifty years. Despite high-profile protests from Native activists and allies, legal actions from Native groups, the 2014 loss of federal copyright on the name, and other efforts to elicit a name change, then-owner Don Snyder still steadfastly refused. The sudden re-examination and change in the context of 2020's racial awareness was forced by a number of major sponsors, such as FedEx, Nike, and PepsiCo, which demanded that the team change its name under threat of terminating their contracts with the team, and by elected officials in Washington, DC, who opposed the possibility of the team's home stadium being within the district without a name change. The change was welcomed by the Native community. A joint press release from the Morning Star Institute and the International Indian Treaty Council issued the following day noted that, after many years of engaging in this "intergenerational struggle," "today our voices were finally heard. We are not mascots for America's fun and games" (The Morning Star Institute and the International Indian Treaty Council 2020).

The Cleveland Indians baseball team changed its name to the Guardians and adopted a new logo at the end of the 2021 season, also after many years of protests about the offensive mascot image. These changes followed a slow stream of name and mascot changes by a number of sports teams, professional, college, and local. In 2007, faced with pressure from the National Collegiate Athletics Association (NCAA), the University of Illinois retired its "Chief Illiniwek" mascot. In 2015, the University of North Dakota replaced "Fighting Sioux" with "Fighting Hawks." Yet many teams still hold on to their American Indian mascots and names, including the Kansas City Chiefs, Atlanta Braves, and numerous local schools. Fans of teams with updated names still hold on to the nostalgia of the racist past.

Historical Context

The use of American Indian images in advertising is not a modern phenomenon. The practice of appropriating ethnic imagery, particularly that of American Indians and African Americans, was established in the late nineteenth century. At the same time, warfare and legislation against

American Indians sought to resolve the "Indian problem" in the United States (Berkhofer 1979; Steele 1996). Many advertising images used today are essentially similar to early ones, containing American Indian characters in caricature (often the image of a comely maiden or a brave warrior in a feathered headdress) and playing upon such stereotypes as stoicism, connection to nature, spirituality, bravery, and strength.

Many of the Native images used for marketing today convey a romanticized, often nineteenth-century or pre-European-contact ideal of the noble savage. Michael K. Green (1993) has identified three categories of stereotypical imagery that continue to portray American Indians in advertising contexts: the stoic noble savage, the civilizable savage (capable of redemption and education), and the fierce, bloodthirsty savage. Green's categories map onto the dichotomy between noble savage and savage Indian that has influenced notions of "the Indian" since first contact.

The practice of using images of the noble savage and savage Indian in sports and advertising began in the latter half of the nineteenth century, as America worked to be done with the "Indian problem" (Steele 1996). Ironically, the nobility of American Indians—this supposedly dying race—was to be honored and preserved even as American Indian people were forcibly annihilated and removed from their homelands. For example, the United States Treasury minted the first Indian Head penny in the same year as the slaughter of nearly 300 Lakota men, women, and children during the 1890 Massacre at Wounded Knee, South Dakota, by the US Army. At about the same time, Wild West shows played to large audiences and enacted the defeat and "taming" of "wild Indians" in theatrical settings. These forces served to link the notion of the authenticity of American Indians with the past, diffuse the sense of direct threat to white civilization, and minimize or eliminate consideration of American Indians within the contemporary social and political landscape (Berkhofer 1979; Morgan 1986).

Advertisements for common products that appropriated American Indian cultural images began to appear in America at the same time, depicting American Indians in demeaning postures and as caricatures. As a result, nineteenth-century trade cards, which merchants handed out to attract potential customers, remain to this day the most graphic examples of racial and ethnic stereotypes being used as marketing tools (Steele 1996, 47). These depictions provided the two basic ingredients of prejudice: denigration and gross overgeneralization (Allport 1954). In addition, this reaffirmed and helped mainstream American culture define itself by clearly showing that it could not possibly belong to the out-group.

American Indians were portrayed as homogeneous and lacking in variability (Fiske 1998; Merskin 2001; Staurowsky 1999).

In the nineteenth century, American Indians became a romanticized abstraction, with an exotic appeal suitable for use by the fledgling advertising industry (Jay 1987). American Indian advertising motifs were often set in nature, focused on stereotypical attire—such as beads, feathers, and fringed buckskins—and referenced specific treaties or American Indian wars. They fixed the image of "the Indian" in a historical context and created a people that were frozen outside the mainstream (Steele 1996, 53–54; Allport 1954).

One common depiction of American Indians was alongside vegetables, as in an image of the corned Indian (i.e. an Indian in the shape of or wearing an ear of corn) on an 1886 Diamond Lawnmowers trade card. Merging deeply rooted images of oral gratification, masculine sexuality, and racialized iconography, this motif represents the American Indian as a consumable product. In the face of white imperialism, this card suggests American Indian cultures could be absorbed at will (Steele 1996, 53–54).

Marketing imagery also employs an American Indian male archetype. Current and historical consumer products are associated with an image of the head of a male American Indian chief or warrior in a Plains-style headdress. For example, Money House Blessing air freshener promises the protection of the warrior in a full-feathered headdress. Tecumseh small engines employ the profile of an American Indian chief in a war bonnet and promise the strength and endurance of their namesake. Sioux Chief Manufacturing Co. (figure 22.2) chose its name and image because the founder "wanted to evoke the attributes that he believed a Sioux Chief represents: strength, fierce competitiveness, pride, respect, determination, and a trailblazing spirit" (Sioux Chief Manufacturing Co. 1999–2017). Calumet baking powder, Big Chief sugar, Cherikee Red pop, Indian Head corn meal, Crazy Horse malt liquor, the once-ubiquitous Big Chief writing tablet, Red Man chewing tobacco (rebranded as America's Best Chewing Tobacco in January 2022, without the image).

American Indian tribal names and individual names also proliferate—for example, the Winnebago Brave recreational vehicle, Pontiac (which formerly used the warrior-head image and had a line of cars known as the Star Chief), Mohawk carpeting (which formerly used the image of an infant warrior in feathers) and Chief Wenatchee apples. These appropriations can result in ironic unintentional meanings. "Winnebago," which translates to "people of the dirty water" (Milwaukee Public Museum 2022), makes an unsavory name for a motor home. The Pontiac Aztec (manufactured from 2001 to 2005) juxtaposed the Ottawa leader Pontiac

Fig. 22.2. A family-owned plumbing business, Sioux Chief Manufacturing, brands shower drain covers and other related products with a name that reflects the founder's collection of Native American artifacts.

from the French and Indian wars and the Siege of Detroit with a pre-Columbian Mexican civilization. Crazy Horse, a much-admired Lakota chief and warrior who adamantly opposed drinking alcohol, made an ironic symbol for malt liquor (figure 22.3).

The Power of Stereotypes, Prejudice, and Symbolic Annihilation

Although the American Indian population is small, there is great diversity within it. As of April 12, 2025, there were 575 federally recognized tribes (United States Department of the Interior n.d.) in which many Indigenous languages are still spoken, although today there are fewer than 200 in active use (Bureau of Indian Affairs 2017).

Simplistic stereotypes of American Indians are constructed and reinforced by recurrent portrayals of American Indians in the mass media, particularly in movies (Mihesuah 1996). The dominant culture comes to expect American Indian nations to be like the artificial and inaccurate portrayals of them that are presented to consumers. These stereotypes are often powerful enough to be self-confirming, even when an individual is faced with evidence that contradicts a deeply held stereotype. Indeed, one may interpret the evidence to favor the stereotype, because "in addition

Fig. 22.3. Founded in 1992, this brand renamed its product Crazy Stallion after settling a lawsuit in 2000, led by the Rosebud Sioux Tribe and descendants of the renowned Lakota leader.

to facilitating access to confirmatory material, stereotypes inhibit access to stereotype 'disconfirmatory' material" (Disjksterhuis and Kippenberg 1996). Meanwhile, American Indian cultures remain almost invisible in the American public consciousness. Their voices and self-representations are overshadowed by the pervasive and monolithic images perpetuated and reinforced by media companies.

This symbolic annihilation of American Indian people (Strinati 1995), accomplished in large part through the mass media, has very real implications for such people today. As in the early days of advertising with American Indian imagery, a stylized reality is created that bears little resemblance to the actual lives of American Indian people.

Tribal governments and Native organizations, including the National Congress of American Indians, have passed resolutions denouncing the use of American Indian mascots. Activists have helped the public understand the harm. Charlene Teeters (Spokane) has insisted, "Indians are people, not mascots" (Rosenstein 1997). Suzan Shown Harjo (Cheyenne and Hodulgee Muscogee) spent decades explaining to mainstream America that such images caricature American Indian peoples and place them in the past tense, thus implying that it is acceptable to American Indian cultures to appropriate their images, names, and identities to sell a product (Harjo 1992). "These uses of such images are not morally acceptable because they depend upon an underlying conception of Native Americans that denies to them the status of human being. By so doing, it also denies to them any moral standing and thus any claim to moral consideration and treatment" (Green 1993, 323).

William Mendoza (Oglala and Sicangu Lakota), executive director of the White House's Initiative on American Indian and Alaska Native Education (2011), notes that (Field 2016):

> What we are seeing is gaps of information about Native Americans, misinformation that confuses students, and in many instances harmful information—information that stops in the eighteenth century, and never speaks to anything other than resistance and activism. That is certainly part of our history, but not all of it. This leaves the population nearly invisible. . . . If there is stereotyping in resources and content, so is there in imagery and symbolism—in dehumanizing mascots and logos. Research tells us that this has an effect on all learners and a compounding effect on Native students. These harmful images and symbols speak for our youth, for our tribal nations, long before they get an opportunity to speak for themselves. They render individuals incapable of recognizing that we are still here, that we have a vibrant, living society that is not stuck in an eighteenth century existence.

Proponents of using American Indian imagery as a free and common practice argue that American Indians actually enjoy a positive stereotype as a result of this use. The use of caricatures and other devices to invoke American Indian cultures is justified by the argument that they pay homage to the positive attributes of Native cultures, and thus American Indians should feel honored by such treatments. A majority of American Indian cultures resent this notion, and nationwide demonstrations have demanded that American Indian imagery end. "The arrogance of telling any ethnic group what is important," says one commentator, "how it should interpret insults, that all members of the community must feel exactly the same way and how it 'should' feel is mind-boggling . . . and racist" (Metz 1995, 15).

These pervasive stereotypes contribute to an institutionalized ethnic prejudice against American Indian cultures and are commonly interwoven into the fabric of American consciousness (Berkhofer 1979; Deloria 1998; Mihesuah 1996). They are so ubiquitous that mainstream that America has simply come to normalize them. In his seminal work on prejudice, Gordon Allport (1954) described ethnic prejudice as a category resulting in "disparagement" of an ethnic "group as a whole," not necessarily based on defining attributes, but often including various "nonessential" and "false" attributes, such as those defined through stereotypes. Prejudice results from a perceived threat to one group by a different group and is often colored by self-confirming stereotypes (Fiske 1998). Stereotypes form the cognitive component; prejudice, the affective component; and discrimination, the behavioral component of group category–based responses (Fiske 1998).

The Impact on American Indian People

The effects of stereotyping, prejudice, and stigma contribute to a chronic experience of discrimination that can affect multiple areas of an individual's life, including their physical and mental health. Research shows that "racism increases the volume of stress one experiences and may contribute directly to the physiological arousal that is a marker of stress-related disease" (Harrell 2003, 247). Research also shows that discrimination is associated with multiple indicators of poorer physical health, including higher rates of cardiovascular and other disease (Williams et al. 2003). In April 2021, at the height of the COVID-19 pandemic, the Centers for Disease Control and Prevention declared racism a serious public health threat and announced efforts to address it as a fundamental driver of racial and ethnic health inequities in the United States (Centers for Disease Control and Prevention 2021). The disjuncture between traditional American Indian values and identities and imposed Euro-American values and identities forces American Indian individuals into a position commonly termed as "walking in two worlds." This cultural schizophrenia "has caused untold confusion and misery as well as social and personal dysfunction among Indian people" (Cajete 1994, 144). The struggle to maintain traditional American Indian identities in the modern mainstream context and the resulting sense of disempowerment is symptomatic of what Gregory Cajete (1994, 189) refers to as "ethnostress": "Ethnostress is primarily a result of a psychological response pattern that stems from the disruption of a cultural life and belief system that one cares about deeply . . . Its initial effects are readily visible, but its long-term effects are many and varied, usually affecting self-image and an understanding of one's place in the world."

Dispossessed of the right to self-representation and self-determination, and faced with the prescribed notion of what an American Indian should be, the individual afflicted with this syndrome experiences "a range from total rejection of the perceived controllers to an attempt to actually identify with the inaccurate perception and become the same" (Cajete 1994, 190). In other words, American Indian individuals may react to the psychological stress of pervasive stereotyping in a range of ways. Some may completely reject modern, non-American Indian life and strive to live as completely within their Native culture as possible; for others, the reaction may be to assimilate into the dominant culture and reject Indian-ness; for others still, the confusion of ethnostress may lead them to internalize the stereotype and try to conform to the prescribed notion of Indian-ness (Allport 1954; Cajete 1994). Not measuring up to a prescribed identity can result in a crisis of self-identity and self-worth. It is these feelings of low self-worth that contribute to the alarming rates of suicide among American Indian and Alaska Native people, which are by far the highest of any racial or ethnic group in the United States (Stone et al. 2022).

Changing Practices

The path that eventually led to the highly visible changes seen in 2020 was long and frustrating, and there was little progress until the 1990s. In 1999, Crayola's "Indian Red" color was changed to "Chestnut" because teachers reported that children wrongly perceived the color to be that of Native Americans, when in fact the name had its roots in a pigment from India (Crayola n.d.).

The American Indian Mental Health Association of Minnesota issued a position statement in 1992 specifying the negative impact of the use of American Indian advertising and marketing icons and mascots, and called for their elimination from schools (Pewewardy 1998). On April 13, 2001, the US Commission on Civil Rights issued a statement calling for an end to use of American Indian team names and images by non-Native schools (US Commission on Civil Rights 2001).

The American Sociological Association (2007) issued a statement on "Discontinuing the Use of Native American Nicknames, Logos and Mascots in Sport" on March 6, 2007. Similar resolutions were passed by a number of institutions, including tribal organizations, educational boards, professional associations such as the Modern Language Association and the National Education Association, and civil rights groups such as the NAACP and the Southern Poverty Law Center.

In the early 1990s, two newspapers banned the use of American Indian nicknames and pictures of mascots in their coverage of the teams. *The Oregonian* (Portland) was the first, in 1992, followed by the decision by the *Minneapolis Star Tribune* in January 1994; shortly after, the *Kansas City Star* decided to no longer run pictures of the Cleveland Indians "Chief Wahoo" mascot. In 2002, the NAJA (now the IJA) urged the news media to stop using American Indian mascots and nicknames; few had adopted the policy in the intervening years. As it became more widely recognized that the Washington, DC football team name was a serious racial slur, and pressure to rename the team mounted, most news outlets simply referred to "the Washington Football Team," rather than using the slur.

The NCAA's Minority Opportunities and Interests Committee conducted an eighteen-month study, and in October 2002 released the document "Report on the Use of American Indian Mascots in Intercollegiate Athletics." Among its recommendations, which were adopted in August 2003, were that member institutions with American Indian mascots "complete a self-analysis checklist to determine if the depiction of the mascot, nickname, logo, or behaviors can be viewed as offensive" and stated that the NCAA would continue to monitor the use of American Indian mascots by member institutions (National Collegiate Athletics Association 2005). Following this study, the NCAA issued a ruling "prohibiting colleges or universities with hostile or abusive mascots, nicknames, or imagery from hosting any NCAA championship competitions," effective February 1, 2006.

The NCAA's bold stance pushed change at the collegiate level and did much to raise awareness of the issue and the negative impact of mascots on Native individuals and communities. It also helped highlight the contradiction of using stereotypical and racist team names in educational settings that otherwise strive to affirm and nurture students' abilities and belonging—strategies that may mitigate stereotype threat (Cohen 2002). Over the years, some sports teams changed their names or mascots because of these initiatives. Two highly contentious and high-profile examples were the University of Illinois's "Chief Illiniwek" mascot (Wolverton 2007) and the University of North Dakota's "Fighting Sioux" (Bosslett 2002; Biemiller 2011). Most schools and teams have been reluctant to break with the "tradition" of using American Indian imagery, and efforts to do so have often torn fan bases and local communities apart.

All the while, some familiar old products using American Indian identities remain on the market (Figures 22.4 and 22.5). Newer products with similar American Indian motifs continue to be introduced, including American Spirit cigarettes, Pocahontas fruit snacks, Big Chief imitation vanilla, AriZona iced tea, Liz Claiborne's Crazy Horse clothing line for JCPenney and the Jeep Gladiator Mojave.

The efforts to block cultural appropriation that picked up media attention were often those that turned to litigation. One example was a 1993 lawsuit brought by the family of revered Oglala Lakota warrior and spiritual leader Crazy Horse against the Hornell Brewing Company, producer of Crazy Horse malt liquor, which was introduced in 1992. The family contended that the use of his name and the image of a warrior in a headdress to represent him was especially offensive because Crazy Horse "strongly opposed the use of liquor and encouraged his people to abstain from alcohol" (Metz 1995, 15). In 1992, Congress passed a bill prohibiting the use of the name "Crazy Horse" on alcoholic beverage products. The Supreme Court eventually overturned the law based on the Hornell Brewing Company's free speech arguments. The Stroh Brewing Company (which had owned Crazy Horse malt liquor before it sold the product line to Hornell, and which remained a producer of the beverage) formally apologized in a 2001 ceremony (Johansen 2001), but federal and state suits continued to be filed against Hornell Brewing Company until it stopped using the name in 2021.

Urban Outfitters' line of "Navajo" clothing and accessories, launched in 2001, drew criticism from Native people and the Navajo Nation, and reached mainstream media in 2012 after the Navajo Nation filed a lawsuit. Especially egregious items were the Navajo Print Fabric-Wrapped Flask and the Navajo Hipster Panties. As one designer familiar with the Navajo Nation's opposition to the products said in an interview: "A

Fig. 22.4. Women's apparel at large chain stores often reflects Native motifs, but not those made by Indigenous creators.

'Navajo' flask is 'extremely insensitive' considering the long history of alcohol abuse among Native tribes, many of which ban the sale and consumption of alcohol on their reservation. . . . The Navajo Nation is among them. And branding underwear as 'Navajo' goes against the tribe's spiritual beliefs of modesty and avoidance of indecency" (Fonseca 2011). The Navajo Nation filed a copyright infringement suit in 2012, and registered the name "Navajo" in 1943 (Woolf 2016). The suit also referenced the American Indian Arts and Crafts Act of 1990, under which it is "illegal to offer or display for sale, or sell, any art or craft product in a manner that falsely suggests it is Indian produced, an Indian product, or the product of a particular Indian or Indian tribe or Indian arts and crafts organization, resident within the United States" (US Department of the Interior 1990). The parties settled in 2016, reaching an agreement that included an undisclosed amount and a plan for a partnership to collaborate on a line of jewelry (Wolf 2016; Schwartz 2016).

Fig. 22.5. Native themes are pervasive in many standard clothing designs.

The Power of Social Media

The Urban Outfitters "Navajo" clothing and accessory line entered public consciousness in 2011 when a Santee Sioux woman posted an open letter to the company with a request for the line to be pulled and an apology issued (Ng 2011). Her letter was picked up by mainstream media outlets and went viral. "The smart thing she did was she put it online on Columbus Day and a lot of newspapers were looking for some kind of story to go along with Columbus Day and that worked perfectly" (Donovan 2012).

In 2012, Gap launched a black T-shirt with the slogan "Manifest Destiny," a phrase that, as one journalist put it, "is drawn from the racist rhetoric of American history" (Mackay 2012). Manifest destiny was the doctrine underlying America's westward expansion, in which Native peoples were seen as an impediment to be removed, per God's will; today, the phrase evokes white supremacy and continued oppression. Almost immediately, American Indians and organizations denounced the T-shirt and encouraged followers to call for its removal on social media (Lutz 2012). An online petition to remove the product and issue an apology garnered more than 5,000 signatures on Change.org. Initially reluctant, designer Mark McNairy eventually apologized via his Twitter account, and Gap issued an apology on its Facebook page. The T-shirt was pulled from the Gap website before it could reach store shelves.

Perhaps the best-known example is Victoria's Secret, which has been called out for cultural appropriation a number of times. Its 2012 fashion show featured model Karlie Kloss dressed in leopard print–fringed bra and panties, fringed boots, large Southwestern-style turquoise jewelry on her neck, wrists, fingers, and hips, and a Plains-style feathered headdress that reached the floor and dragged behind her. The highly sexualized mash-up of Native stereotypes was immediately controversial. The next day, online publication *HuffPost* noted, "we're sure that one of Kloss' looks is sure to cause controversy" and asked readers to respond to a poll: "Check out the pics below and tell us . . . is this offensive?" (Misener 2017). *HuffPost* had an integrated social media presence on Twitter, Facebook, Tumblr, Pinterest, and Instagram, which helped increase visibility.

Victoria's Secret received thousands of comments on its Facebook site (USA Today 2012) and three days after the show issued an apology on Twitter and on its Facebook page: "We are sorry that the Native American headdress replica used in our recent fashion show has upset individuals. We sincerely apologize as we absolutely had no intention to offend anyone. Out of respect, we will not be including the outfit in any broadcast, marketing materials, nor in any other way." Kloss also apologized on Twitter the following day, writing: "I am deeply sorry if what I wore during the VS Show offended anyone. I support VS's decision to remove the outfit from the broadcast." These apologies were widely reported in both the online and mainstream press. Several outlets wondered why no one at Victoria's Secret had recognized the inappropriateness of the outfit, noting similar recent missteps by Paul Frank Industries' "Dream Catchin' with Paul Frank" party theme and pop band No Doubt's "Looking Hot" music video. Both apologized for their misappropriation of American Indian culture.

Despite the attention drawn by these three controversies, just five years later in the 2017 fashion show for Victoria's Secret, model Nadine Leopold dressed in an outfit featuring feathered jewelry, shoes with beaded rosettes reminiscent of American Indian beadwork, a jacket with ribbon appliqué reminiscent of American Indian ribbon work, and a feathered bonnet. Victoria's Secret was criticized "for the exact issues that were present in 2012, when Karlie Kloss walked the runway" (Matera 2018).

Holidays such as Thanksgiving and Halloween provide perennial examples, from grade school reenactments of "the first Thanksgiving" with "Pilgrims and Indians," to odd advertisements for a tanning salon, and any number of Halloween costumes drawn from stereotypes.

In 2022, a non-Native family posted photos of themselves on Instagram in their Halloween costumes—the father wore a leather vest, arm bands with geometric shapes, and a Plains-style feather headdress; the mother was in a fringed leather spaghetti-strap top with geometric designs, matching headband, and plastic "bone" choker; and the infant was in a fringed leather top with a headband that matched the mother's, with feathers standing in front. All three had stripes of "war paint" beneath their eyes. The image drew immediate backlash from the Native community and others. In response, the family updated the message to clarify that their intent was not to be disrespectful but to show their "respect and admiration" for Native Americans. They did not remove the photos, but stated: "We do see that our intention was not received or interpreted this way by everyone who saw our post." They indicated that they appreciated the dialogue but did not have to agree with those who were "in contrast" (Watts 2022). Their obstinacy resulted in continued controversy. One heavily circulated response was a repost on Twitter, which noted: "Nothing literally infuriates me more than white people trying to tell my people we should feel honored by their costumes. We don't! We've been saying this. Stop pretending to dress up like us. They say they value us then continue to disrespect us by leaving the post up" (Terra 2022). The response received more than 7,000 retweets. While packaged "Indian" Halloween costumes are no longer on the shelves of many stores, they are still available online.

What Are the Alternatives?

Is it possible for products with a Native motif to be marketed in an appropriate and responsible way? In contrast to vehicles such as the Jeep Cherokee and Pontiac Aztec, the Mazda Navajo (1991) used the name with the consent of the Nation and a promise to use it with dignity. Mazda unveiled the model by presenting a vehicle to the Navajo Nation for the government's use (Deseret News 1990; Donovan 2012).

The Faherty Brand clothing company partners with Native designers whose brands offer high-quality and sustainable fashion. These partnerships are an effort to "end appropriation in fashion and offer authentically designed clothing that benefits Native communities" (Faherty Brand n.d.). The company also extends its inward- and outward-facing efforts by hosting Native interns, including Native representation on its board of directors, featuring Native art and performances in its stores, and working with Native-led nonprofit organizations.

There are numerous other examples. The Oneida Nation's white corn soup jar uses the motif of an ear of corn, not a "corned Indian." Beyond Buckskin Boutique began in 2009 as a blog and soon became an online shop featuring fashion, jewelry, and accessories from Native designers and small businesses. It is known for selling apparel and accessories that counter stereotypical big-box store fare. The Native American Tea Company was founded in 1987 by a Turtle Mountain Chippewa family on the Crow Nation, and its products are widely available, including at the Smithsonian Institution's Museum of the American Indian. Turtle Mountain Chippewa author Louise Erdrich founded the independent bookstore Birchbark Books in Minneapolis in 2001, which offers an extensive selection of books by Native authors, including children's books, and also includes items for sale from local Native artisans. Native American Natural Foods, the producer of Tanka Bars, "the only nationally-distributed Native American packaged snack brand in the natural foods industry," was founded in 2006 on the Pine Ridge reservation by Oglala owners using traditional recipes for buffalo-based products that promote the wellness and restoration of Native communities by sourcing from Native-owned herds. The company's foundation, the nonprofit Tanka Fund, works to "revitalize Native American buffalo populations, ecosystems, and economies" and reintroduce buffalo into Native food systems by restoring buffalo populations to Native lands using a regenerative agriculture model (Native American Natural Foods n.d.; Ganje 2023).

Appropriation and Appreciation

It can be difficult to discern the difference between appropriation and appreciation. Recognizing when stereotypes are being used is one way to differentiate between the two; another is to determine whether permission, consent, and approval have been given by the Nation depicted in relation to the product. Have Native individuals, businesses, organizations, or nations directly benefited from the product in question, or do the profits go to non-Natives? Perhaps the best way is to ensure that the product is Native-made.

Resources such as "Moving from Cultural Appropriation to Cultural Appreciation" offer suggestions for how to recognize and avoid cultural appropriation that reinforces stereotypes (Han 2019). Ohio University's My Culture Is Not a Costume project focused on recognizing and avoiding culturally inappropriate Halloween costumes. The Native American comedy troupe the 1491s created a video to a remix of the song "I'm an Indian, Too" (from the 1946 musical *Annie Get Your Gun*), poking fun at non-Natives who appropriate Native identity. The video features a "hipster in a headdress" (who is actually a Native member of the troupe), dancing in outlandish ways among non-Native people who are wearing Native-themed clothing and jewelry, while Native people in regular street clothes look on, subtly mocking them with their heads bouncing to the beat of the music. Interspersed are images of pop-culture appropriations, such as sports team mascots, covers of romance novels, cigar store American Indian statues, and Halloween costumes. The comedy group has a popular YouTube channel.

Change from Within

It is notable that Debra Anne Haaland (Laguna Pueblo) was the first Native secretary of the interior in the history of the department, and her appointment in 2021 also made her the first Native cabinet secretary in US history. The Department of the Interior oversees US relations with American Indian nations. Early in her term as secretary of the interior, Haaland announced a formal process to remove derogatory names from federal lands and declared "squaw" to be derogatory. "Racist terms have no place in our vernacular or on our federal lands. Our nation's lands and waters should be places to celebrate the outdoors and our shared cultural heritage—not to perpetuate the legacies of oppression" (US Department of the Interior 2021b). The work of the Reconciliation in Place Names Committee is ongoing. The removal of derogatory place names will contribute greatly to removing the accompanying stereotypical images.

The Smithsonian Institution's National Museum of the American Indians exhibition *Americans* (on display in Washington, DC and online) features hundreds of objects, historical and contemporary, that use American Indian images to advertise products, serve as sports team mascots, identify fraternal orders and summer camps, and have many other uses. The exhibition asks how American Indians can be so invisible in American society while their names and images are all around us. For those who want to become more active allies to Native nations and peoples, *Changing the Narrative About Native Americans: A Guide for Allies* (Reclaiming Native Truth 2018) is an extensive guide to help people unlearn false and harmful narratives and learn positive ways to offer support.

Conclusion: Mass Media, American Indian Cultures, and Change

The voices of American Indian people alone have not been sufficient to effect widespread change in the pervasive cultural appropriation of American Indian identities and the perpetuation of stereotypes and misinformation. A significant paradigm shift will be required to create change. Business owners, communications ethicists, practitioners, and the general public must reconsider the use of American Indian imagery as a marketing tool and recognize the consequences and broader implications of such use. The issue is ultimately one of representation and self-determination. Any appropriation of American Indian images or cultural imagery to sell a product amounts to perpetuation of institutionalized racism and is a contributing factor to insensitive stereotypes, prejudice, discrimination, and stigmatization—all of which result in tangible harm to American Indian people. Sustaining significant progress is difficult. By its nature, mass media is in a position to help bring about a change in attitudes and beliefs concerning American Indians. The racial awareness of the summer of 2020 added momentum in this direction, but it remains to be seen whether that movement marked a true turning point or was just a momentary awakening from which we may sink back into continued slumber.

Discussion Questions

1. Prior to the "racial reckoning" of 2020, were you aware of the many products that used American Indian images and/or names, and their historical context? Did you purchase any such items? In what other ways might you be "buying into racism" without realizing it?
2. Why do companies continue to use American Indian images and motifs as product icons? What are they "selling" when they do so? Why do these items remain popular?
3. Do you think that the "racial reckoning" of 2020 marked a true turning point? Do you think there will be a further decrease in products using American Indian images and/or names? Will there be an increase in support for Native companies and artists?
4. What can you do to contribute to sustaining progress on this issue—as an individual, a consumer, a media consumer, and/or a media practitioner?

23

"Indigenous Media . . . Are Our Acts of Resistance"

Interview with Candace Hamana

Candace Hamana serves as director of tribal relations at Arizona State University (ASU), championing initiatives that uplift Indigenous voices and foster inclusive partnerships. With more than fifteen years' experience in communications and PR—including twelve in Indian Country—she has held impactful roles, including as tribal liaison at the Arizona Commerce Authority and public affairs specialist with the Indian Health Service. Candace is also the founder of Badger PR, a boutique agency amplifying diverse, hyper-local communities. A proud member of the Hopi Tribe and a military mom, she is dedicated to building culturally rich, inclusive spaces and empowering Indigenous narratives.

Please introduce yourself.

Nukwang Talöngva, nu Candace Hamana yan Hopimatsiwa, nu hunongwuwa, nu Munganaqsino.

Good morning, my Hopi name is Candace Hamana. I am of the Badger Clan and I am from the village of Mungapi.

My mom is Hopi, my dad is Navajo. Hopis are a matrilineal society. Therefore, since my mother is Hopi, that is how I identify and introduce myself. I am a public relations and strategic communications practitioner and have been so since 2009.

Presently, I am the director of tribal relations at ASU, which is a new position that I accepted in May 2024. I am also an entrepreneur and have been since September 2018. I own Badger PR, and it's been a wonderful journey. To take on this new role at the university just adds more depth to the type of media relations and stakeholder management I do, including fostering connections that create impact for our tribal communities.

Fig. 23.1. Candace Hamana. Author photo.

What does Indigenous media mean to you?

I feel Indigenous media has definitely grown over the years. As Native Americans, we are exercising our power to tell our stories in our own voices. In doing so, we instill that sense of identity about who we are, because we bring that lived experience to the forefront, you know, and that gets embedded in the storytelling itself.

I also feel that Indigenous media is about increasing visibility. Now there are so many ways that we can tell these stories. I listen to Indigenous podcasts and attend Indigenous poetry nights and book signings, for example. We have newscasts and online media, like *Indian Country Today*.

I've been in media relations for a while, and on scale, these can seem very small. But collectively, Indigenous media forms a small but mighty storytelling channel. Our Indigenous media is so powerful because we can add complexity, fight back against stereotypes, and celebrate our true selves in our storytelling. It's really about exercising that ability to celebrate our sovereignty in storytelling.

Describe your work. What compels you to do it?

Quite interestingly, one of my favorite movies is *The Wizard of Oz*. I've always related to the Wizard—that person who's in the background helping manage things, put things together, and make things run smoothly. Being behind the curtain has always sort of been my forte.

I just enjoy being able to amplify good work that is challenging old narratives and old stereotypes of who Indigenous people are and what they bring to the richness of our stories in society. If my work can affect and elevate those stories, then I consider that a job well done.

I'll give you a good example. I just finished up my contract with Netflix, and we did a lot of earned media[1] and publicity for the movie *Rez Ball*. *Rez Ball* is based off a book called *Canyon Dreams*.[2] The author basically embedded himself as a reporter into a tribal community to cover a basketball season and then wrote a book about it. But *Rez Ball* itself is based on a fictional high school team and how it goes from tragedy to triumph. The complexity of the characters and what they have to navigate, both on and off the court, told a story that resonated with a lot of our Indigenous people. *Rez Ball* gave us something to celebrate—that resilience, that grit, and that determination to push forward.

Also, I was able to elevate the actors and honor their traditional languages, and also their creativity. For me, to have been a tiny piece of that effort to amplify them to a global audience makes me feel good about the work that I'm doing at the end of the day. *Rez Ball* was produced by the Spring Hill Company,[3] which was co-founded by LeBron James. To have significant support from an icon in basketball and a superstar like him is a very exciting story. I was happy, blessed, and honored to do media pitching, monitor earned media, and assist in planning for events we hosted and screened for our tribal communities.

As director of tribal relations at ASU, I work very closely with the vice president on tribal affairs. Our work doesn't just align with what the institution wants to do—to be in service of communities and to be inclusive—but also makes sure that our students feel seen and have a sense of belonging when they come to ASU. That also brings in higher education and is very thrilling. This will be something to watch as my work unfolds.

Why is it important to have Indigenous people tell their own stories?

In PR, the work varies from things that are more fun and celebratory to things that are more like "crisis communications." In that realm of public relations, you really have to look at exercising diplomacy. A lot of reverence and regard needs to come into consideration. You can move across the spectrum from something that is fun to something that requires a lot of tact and transparency, especially when tribal communities are adjacent to major metropolitan areas. Those relationships, government to government, are paramount when it comes to crisis communications. Tribes have sovereignty that they can exercise to negotiate on their terms to self-govern.

We have twenty-two tribal nations here in Arizona, and I'm on the road a lot because I am traveling to those communities. The number one most effective way to foster those relationships is to be in the community, with the community. This helps you really understand how they want to create a future for their tribal members.

What does the future hold, in your view?

I'm encouraged by the ability of some of our younger storytellers to really adapt to technology and tell our stories. It excites me that we can have Indigenous youth who use technology to tell stories, whether that's through a podcast or a social media app like TikTok.

The downside, I think, is that not all of our stories might be able to be condensed down to a fifteen- or thirty-second reel or video. I think that while it's beautiful that we can celebrate ourselves, it's harder to get those longer-form stories out. It's not impossible, but it's definitely a challenge, especially if you're a content creator. I think it's a particular challenge for Indigenous folks, because we're moving the needle on how people see us and how we see ourselves.

What should the next generation consider? Why is this work important?

I've had a lot of youth and young adults reach out to me asking, "How can I do this? I want to be a part of this." I advise them to seek an internship or shadow someone in the field for a day to find a mentor. When you shadow somebody at their office or workplace, you get a real understanding of all the writing, rewriting, and revising that goes into what they do. People often see the "forward-facing" side of social media—attending events and having fun—but behind all of that are late nights, copy editing, writing, sending emails, and pitching to the media.

I'd also recommend continuing to write; you can't get better at writing unless you actually sit down and do it. So my best advice is to find mentors, seek internships, shadow someone, and keep practicing your writing skills.

Is there anything else you would like to add?

Yeah, something that I want to imprint on this interview is that our ability to influence the mainstream narratives really helps give us control over our identities and how we envision ourselves for the future. When you think of the amount of power that we hold, that is in our hands and in our voices as we share these stories, it's really Indigenous media and Indigenous storytelling that are our acts of resistance.

They are also acts of solidarity, because we're all in this together. We're a small but a mighty group, and I think we just need to continue to press forward. As long as we don't lose control over telling our own stories, we can shape the future we want to see for ourselves and for the generations to come.

That feels so very good at the end of the day.

—Interviewed by Meta G. Carstarphen

Notes

1. Earned media is "publicity your brand earns through word-of-mouth, content sharing or media coverage without directly paying for it." *PRNewsWire*, "What Is Earned Media? Definition, Benefits and Examples," October 15, 2024, https://www.prnewswire.co.uk/resources/articles/what-is-earned-media-definition-benefits-and-examples.

2. Michael Powell, *Canyon Dreams: A Basketball Season on the Navajo Nation*, 2021 (Blue Rider Press/Penguin Random House Canada). Powell was a former reporter for *The Washington Post.*

3. The Spring Hill Company was founded in 2020 by LeBron James and Maverick Carter and describes itself as "an entertainment development and production company."

Bibliography

Ablavsky, Gregory, and Elizabeth Hidalgo Reese. 2022. "The Supreme Court Strikes Again—This Time at Tribal Sovereignty." *The Washington Post*, July 1. https://www.washingtonpost.com/opinions/2022/07/01/castro-huerta-oklahoma-supreme-court-tribal-sovereignty/.

Act of Union Between the Eastern and Western Cherokees. 1838. https://tile.loc.gov/storage-services/service/ll/llscd/28014172/28014172.pdf.

Alia, Valerie. 2010. *The New Media Nation: Indigenous Peoples and Global Communication*. Anthropology of Media. Vol. 2. New York: Berghahn Books.

Allport, Gordon W. 1954. *The Nature of Prejudice*. Reading, MA: Addison-Wesley.

Alphonse, Lylah M. 2012. "Gap Pulls 'Manifest Destiny' T-Shirt, Gets History Lesson from Outraged Consumers." *Yahoo*. https://www.yahoo.com/lifestyle/tagged/health/fashion/gap-pulls-manifest-destiny-t-shirt-gets-history-025900453.html.

American Psychiatric Association. 2013. *Diagnostic and Statistical Manual of Mental Disorders: DSM-5*. 5th ed. Washington, DC: American Psychiatric Publishing.

American Sociological Association. 2007. "Statement by the Council of the American Sociological Association on Discontinuing the Use of Native American Nicknames, Logos and Mascots in Sport." http://asanet.org/about/Council_Statements/use_of_native_american_nicknames_logos_and_mascots.cfm.

Ann, Virginie. 2021. "First Nations Leaders, Quebec Teachers Press for Indigenous History to Be Taught Differently." *CBC News*. Accessed June 4, 2021. https://www.cbc.ca/news/canada/montreal/information-missing-quebec-teachers-indigenous-history-taught-differently-1.6084182.

Antinora, Sarah. 2017. "The Rhetoric of the Hawaiian Sovereignty Movement: Resistance Against Commodification, Consumption." *The Quint* 30: 31–60.

Aratani, Lauren. 2023. "Hollywood Producer Accused of Faking Cherokee Ancestry." *The Guardian*, March 27. https://www.theguardian.com/us-news/2023/mar/27/heather-rae-hollywood-producer-accused-faking-cherokee-ancestry.

Ardill, Allan. 2013. "Australian Sovereignty, Indigenous Standpoint Theory and Feminist Standpoint Theory." *Griffith Law Review* 22, no. 2 (January): 315–43. https://doi.org/10.1080/10383441.2013.10854778.

Argo Inc. n.d. "About Us." ACH Food Companies. Accessed July 17, 2023. https://www.argostarch.com/about_us.html.

Ark, M., and D. Fiddler. 2022. "On Petition for a Writ of Certiorari to the Supreme Court of Minnesota. Counsel for Petitioners." The Supreme Court of Minnesota.

Aronson, Joshua. 2002. "Stereotype Threat: Contending and Coping with Unnerving Expectations." In *Improving Academic Achievement: Impact of Psychological Factors on Education.* Edited by Joshua Aronson. New York: Academic Press (an imprint of Elsevier Science), 279–301.

Associated Press. 2022. "US Identifies More Than 50 Native American Boarding School Burial Sites." *The Guardian*, 11 May. https://www.theguardian.com/us-news/2022/may/11/native-american-children-schools-abuse-burial-sites.

Association on American Indian Affairs. 2023. "Indian Child Welfare Act."

Audi, R. 1998. *Epistemology: A Contemporary Introduction to the Theory of Knowledge.* New York: Routledge.

Auld, Mary. 2020. "COVID-19 Restrictions Put Tribal Sovereignty to the Test." *Montana Public Radio*, October 30. https://www.mtpr.org/montana-news/2020-10-30/covid-19-restrictions-put-tribal-sovereignty-to-the-test.

Austen, Ian. 2023. "More Evidence of Children's Graves Is Found at Former Indigenous School." *New York Times.* https://www.nytimes.com/2023/01/19/graves-indigenous-school-canada.html.

Azocar, Cristina L. 2022. *News Media and the Indigenous Fight for Federal Recognition.* Lanham: Lexington Books.

———. 2023. Interview with Martin Nakata, June 23.

———, Victoria LaPoe, Candi S. Carter Olson, Benjamin LaPoe, and Bharbi Hazarika. 2021. "Indigenous Communities and COVID-19: Reporting on Resources and Resilience." *The Howard Journal of Communications* 32, no. 5: 440–55. https://doi.org/10.1080/10646175.2021.1892552.

Bad Press Film. n.d. "Bad Press." Accessed 2023. https://www.badpress.film.

Bailey, L. E. 2021. "Standpoint Theory." In *Encyclopedia of Queer Studies in Education.* Brill, 676–82.

Baker, Twyla (@Indigenia). 2022. "I am not a legal expert by any means, just a Tribal citizen. I do believe though, that decisions like todays are a continued chipping away of Tribal sovereignty." Twitter, June 29, 3:14 p.m. https://twitter.com/Indigenia/status/1542224922889621509.

Barnouw, Erik. 1993. *Documentary: A History of the Non-Fiction Film.* 2nd ed. Oxford University Press.

Bauder, Harald, and Rebecca Mueller. 2021. "Westphalian vs. Indigenous Sovereignty: Challenging Colonial Territorial Governance." *Geopolitics* 28, no. 1 (May): 156–73. https://doi.org/10.1080/14650045.2021.1920577.

Beale, Frances. 1970. "Double Jeopardy: To Be Black and Female." In *The Black Woman: An Anthology*. Edited by Toni Cade. New York: New American Library, 109–22.

Beavert, Virginia. 2017. *The Gift of Knowledge/Ttnúwit Átawish Nch'inch'imamí*. Edited by Janne Underriner. 1st ed. Seattle and London: University of Washington Press.

Bennett, W. Lance. 1990. "Toward a Theory of Press-State Relations in the United States." *Journal of Communication* 40, no. 2 (June): 103–27. https://doi.org/10.1111/j.1460-2466.1990.tb02265.x.

———, Regina G. Lawrence, and Steven Livingston. 2008. *When the Press Fails: Political Power and the News Media from Iraq to Katrina*. University of Chicago Press.

Ben's Original. n.d. "About Us." Accessed July 9, 2023. https://www.bensoriginal.com/rice-and-health/about-us.

Berkes, Fikret, Johan Colding, and Carl Folke. 2000. "Rediscovery of Traditional Ecological Knowledge as Adaptive Management." *Ecological Applications* 10, no. 5 (October): 1251–62. https://doi.org/10.1890/1051-0761(2000)010[1251:ROTEKA]2.0.CO;2.

Berkhofer Jr., Robert F. 1979. *The White Man's Indian: Images of the American Indian from Columbus to the Present*. New York: Vintage Books.

Beyond Buckskin Boutique. n.d. "Beyond Buckskin." Accessed August 21, 2023. https://shop.beyondbuckskin.com/.

Bhabha, Homi K. 2012. *The Location of Culture*. Philadelphia: Routledge.

Biemiller, Lawrence. 2011 "North Dakota's 'Fighting Sioux' Law Won't Prevent Penalties, NCAA Says." *The Chronicle of Higher Education*, April 19. http://chronicle.com/blogs/ticker/north-dakotas-fighting-sioux-law-wont-prevent-penalties-ncaa-says/32279.

Billington, Monroe. 1982. "Black Slavery in Indian Territory: The Ex-Slave Narratives." *Oklahoma Historical Society: The Gateway to Oklahoma History*, Spring. Accessed September 27, 2024. https://gateway.okhistory.org / ark:/67531/metadc2031424/.

Bishop, Anne, Mark Cousins, Lorna Evans, and Suzanne Gatenby. 2002. "Understanding the Worldviews of Both the Targeted and Dominant Groups Is Imperative If We Are Going to Do More Good than Harm." *Social Work Education* 21 (6): 611–17. https://doi.org/10.1080/0261547022000024254.

Bishop Tribe Environmental Office. n.d. "Welcome to the Bishop Paiute Tribe Environmental Management Office." Accessed June 30, 2023. https://www.bishoptribeemo.com/.

Biswas, Masudal. 2022. "New Book: News Media and Indigenous Fight for Federal Recognition: Interview with Dr. Cristina Azocar." *Media Diversity Forum*.

https://www.mediadiversityforum.lsu.edu/azocar-news-media-indigenous-fight.html.

BlackDeer, Autumn A. (@DrBlackDeer). 2022. "All of y'all who were so vocal about Native Nations being a loophole for abortions, where's the same outrage as the Supreme Court just took another swing at." Twitter, June 29, 10:50 a.m. https://twitter.com/DrBlackDeer/status/1542173726715924481?s=20.

Blaeser, Kimberly. 2013. "Wild Rice Rights: Gerald Vizenor and an Affiliation of Story." In *Centering Anishinaabeg Studies: Understanding the World Through Stories*. Edited by Jill Doerfler, Niigaanwewidam James Sinclair, and Heidi Kiiwetinepinesiik Stark. American Indian Studies Series. East Lansing: University of Manitoba Press, 237–58.

Blei, David M., Andrew Y. Ng, and Michael I. Jordan. 2003. "Latent Dirichlet Allocation." *Journal of Machine Learning Research* 3: 993–1022. https://www.jmlr.org/papers/volume3/blei03a/blei03a.pdf.

Bollinger, Lee. 2001. "A New Scoring Method for the Press Release." *Public Relations Quarterly* 46, no. 1: 31–35. https://proxy.library.ohio.edu/login?url=https://search.ebscohost.com/login.aspx?direct=true&db=bth&AN=4435249&site=eds-live&scope=site.

Bosslett, Lindsay. 2002. "NCAA Treads Warily in North Dakota, Critics of Fighting Sioux Mascot Say Tournament Should Not Be Held on the Campus." *The Chronicle of Higher Education*, November 22. https://www.chronicle.com/article/ncaa-treads-warily-in-north-dakota/.

Braithwaite, Jeremy, and Linda Sue Warner. 2023. "The Feather and the Pen: An Evaluation of the Tribal Youth Media Workshop." EvaluACT, Inc. Unpublished evaluation for "Ice Worlds: A Giant Screen Film and Outreach Project," National Science Foundation AISL Award (Innovations in Development).

Braun, Ashley. 2022. "Treaty-less Tribes Struggle to Have Their Rights Recognized: A Five-Year Fight over a Few Dozen Clams in Washington Highlights the Inconsistent Rights of Indigenous Tribes." *High Country News*, October 27. https://www.hcn.org/articles/treaty-less-tribes-struggle-to-have-their-rights-recognized.

Brave Heart, Maria Yellow Horse. 1995. "The Return to the Sacred Path: Healing from Historical Trauma and Historical Unresolved Grief Among the Lakota." PhD dissertation. Smith College for Social Work, Northampton, MA. ProQuest Dissertations Publishing.

———, Josephine Chase, Jennifer Elkins, and Deborah B. Altschul. 2011. "Historical Trauma Among Indigenous Peoples of the Americas: Concepts, Research, and Clinical Considerations." *Journal of Psychoactive Drugs* 43, no. 4: 282–90.

Brave NoiseCat, Julian. 2020. "How Indigenous Filmmakers Are Shaping the Future of Cinema." *Aperture*, October 6. https://aperture.org/editorial/how-inuit-filmmakers-are-shaping-the-future-of-cinema/.

Brown, Jennifer. 1999. "Crayola Crayons Break with 'Indian Red' Label." *Centre Daily Times*, March 10.

Brown, Marie Alohalani. 2016. "Mauna Kea: Hoʻomana Hawai'i and Protecting the Sacred." *Journal for the Study of Religion, Nature & Culture* 10, no. 2: 150–69.

Brown, Nadia E., and Danielle C. Lemi. 2021. *Sister Style: The Politics of Appearance for Black Women Political Elites.* Oxford: Oxford University Press.

Bucko, Raymond A. 2006. "Native American Families and Religion." In *American Religions and the Family: How Faith Traditions Cope with Modernization and Democracy.* Columbia University Press, 70–86.

Budd, Brian. 2021. "Representation in the Era of Reconciliation: Media Framing of Indigenous Politics in Canada." PhD dissertation. University of Guelph.

Bureau of Indian Affairs. n.d.a. "Frequently Asked Questions." Accessed May 30, 2023. https://www.bia.gov/frequently-asked-questions.

———. n.d.b. "Tribal Leaders Directory." Accessed September 10, 2023. https://www.bia.gov/service/tribal-leaders-directory.

———. 1967. "Indian Adoption Project Increases Momentum." Press release, April 18. https://www.bia.gov/as-ia/opa/online-press-release/indian-adoption-project-increases-momentum?utm_source=chatgpt.com.

———. 2017. "Do All American Indians and Alaska Natives Speak a Single Traditional Language?" August 19. https://www.bia.gov/faqs/do-all-american-indians-and-alaska-natives-speak-single-traditional-language..

———. 2021. "National Tribal Broadband Strategy." January 5. https://www.bia.gov/sites/default/files/dup/assets/as-ia/doc/2020.%20December.%20National%20Tribal%20Broadband%20Strategy%20FINAL-cover%20change.pdf.

Byers, Lisa. 2010. "Native American Grandmothers: Cultural Tradition and Contemporary Necessity." *Journal of Ethnic & Cultural Diversity in Social Work* 4 (November): 305–16.

Cabas-Mijares, Ayleen. 2022. "In Feminism We Trust! On How Feminist Standpoint Epistemologies Shape Journalism Practices in Two Argentine Digital Newsrooms." *Journalism* 24, no. 8 (April): 1615–33. https://doi.org/10.1177/14648849221090741.

Cajete, Gregory. 1994. *Look to the Mountain: An Ecology of Indigenous Education.* Durango, CO: Kivaki.

———. 2000. *Native Science: Nature Laws of Interdependence.* Santa Fe, NM: Clear Light Publishers.

Caldwell, Elizabeth, and Zach Boblitt. "Tishomingo Grapples with Racist Incident at High School." KWGS Public Radio Tulsa, aired on September 20, 2024. https://www.publicradiotulsa.org/local-regional/2024-09-20/tishomingo-grapples-with-racist-incident-at-high-school.

Callison, Candis, and Mary Lynn Young. 2000. *Reckoning: Journalism's Limits and Possibilities.* New York: Oxford University Press.

Canadian Broadcasting Corporation. n.d. "Mandate." Accessed June 26, 2023. https://cbc.radio-canada.ca/en/vision/mandate.

Cappetta, Annie, and Sarah Matthews. n.d. "Press Freedom on Tribal Lands." Reporters Committee for Freedom of the Press. Accessed June 3, 2023. https://www.rcfp.org/resources/press-freedom-on-tribal-lands/.

Carpenter, Les. 2020. "Washington Redskins to Change Name; New Name to Come Later." *The Washington Post*, July 13. https://www.washingtonpost.com/sports/2020/07/13/redskins-change-name-announcement/.

Carstarphen, Meta G., and John P. Sanchez, eds. 2012. *American Indians and the Mass Media*. Norman: University of Oklahoma Press.

Carter, Kent. 2010. "Dawes Commission." *The Encyclopedia of Oklahoma History and Culture*, January 15. https://www.okhistory.org/publications/enc/entry?entry=DA018.

Carter Olson, Candi S., Benjamin LaPoe, Victoria LaPoe, Cristina L. Azocar, and Bharbi Hazarika. 2022. "'Mothers Are Medicine': U.S. Indigenous Media Emphasizing Indigenous Women's Roles in COVID-19 Coverage." *Journal of Communication Inquiry* 46, no. 3: 289–310. https://doi.org/10.1177/01968599221083239.

Caruso, Carmela. 2023. "Film Documents Muscogee (Creek) Nation Newsroom's Fight for Press Freedom." *Voice of America News*, April 20. https://www.voanews.com/a/film-documents-muscogee-(creek)-nation-newsroom-s-fight-for-press-freedom/7058407.html.

Casimir, Rosanne. 2021. "Remains of Children of Kamloops Residential School Discovered." Tk̓emlúps te Secwépemc, May 27. https://tkemlups.ca/wp-content/uploads/05-May-27-2021-TteS-MEDIA-RELEASE.pdf.

CBC Kids News. 2021. "751 Unmarked Graves Found at Former Saskatchewan Residential School." *CBC Kids News*, June 24. https://www.cbc.ca/kidsnews/post/751-unmarked-graves-found-at-former-saskatchewan-residential-school.

CBC News. 2021a. "Flags on Federal Buildings Lowered in Memory of Kamloops Residential School Victims." *CBC News*, May 30. https://www.cbc.ca/news/politics/flags-lowered-residential-school-victims-1.6046152.

———. 2021b. "Kahnawake Residents Create Memorial for 215 Children Found Buried at B.C. Residential School Site." *CBC News*, May 30. https://www.cbc.ca/news/canada/montreal/kahnawake-residents-create-memorial-for-215-children-1.6046193.

———. 2021c. "'Help Them to Understand': A Yukon Chief's Plea for the Catholic Church." *CBC News*, June 1. https://www.cbc.ca/news/canada/north/yukon-chief-bill-catholic-bishop-kamloops-1.6048823.

———. 2021d. "Survivor Let Down by Winnipeg Archbishop's Response to Residential School Calls for Action." *CBC News*, June 5. https://www.cbc.ca/news/canada/manitoba/residential-school-survivor-gerry-shingoose-archbishop-richard-gagnon-1.6054841.

———. 2021e. "Indigenous Artist Uses Painting to Heal from Residential School Trauma." *CBC News*, June 21. https://www.cbc.ca/news/canada/toronto/indigenous-artist-freddy-taylor-painting-trauma-residential-school-1.6073119.

———. 2021f. "N.W.T. Community Built Memorial to Name Its Residential School Victims. It Was Just a Start." *CBC News*, July 4. https://www.cbc.ca/news/canada/north/fort-providence-nwt-memorial-gravesite-residential-schools-indigenous-kids-1.6088159.

———. 2022. "Pope Francis Apologizes for Forced Assimilation of Indigenous Children at Residential Schools." *CBC News*, July 25. https://www.cbc.ca/news/canada/edmonton/edmonton-pope-alberta-apology-1.6530947.

CBS Philadelphia. 2012. "Gap Pulls Controversial 'Manifest Destiny' T-Shirt." *CBS News*, October 18. https://www.cbsnews.com/philadelphia/news/gap-pulls-controversial-manifest-destiny-t-shirt/.

Center for American Women and Politics. n.d. "Native American/Alaska Native/Native Hawaiian Women in Elective Office." https://cawp.rutgers.edu/native-americanalaska-nativenative-hawaiian-women-elective-office.

Centers for Disease Control and Prevention. 2019. "Racial and Ethnic Disparities Continue in Pregnancy-Related Deaths." Press release, September 6. https://www.cdc.gov/media/releases/2019/p0905-racial-ethnic-disparities-pregnancy-deaths.html.

———. 2021. "Media Statement from CDC Director Rochelle P. Walensky, MD, MPH, on Racism and Health." Press release, April 18. https://www.cdc.gov/media/releases/2021/s0408-racism-health.html.

———. 2022. "Pregnancy-Related Deaths in the United States." November 16. https://www.cdc.gov/hearher/pregnancy-related-deaths/index.html.

Chakraverty, Devasmita. 2022. "A Cultural Impostor? Native American Experiences of Impostor Phenomenon in STEM." *CBE Life Sciences Education* 21, no. 1 (February): 1–15. https://doi.org/10.1187/cbe.21-08-0204.

Chambers, David M., and Kendra Zamzow. 2009. "Report on Groundwater and Surface Water Contamination at the Flambeau Mine." Center for Science in Public Participation, June. http://www.wrpc.net/court/Docs/5aa%20Final%20Surface%20Water%20Summary_Chambers%20and%20Zamzow.pdf.

Chang, Jonathan. 2024. *lda: Collapsed Gibbs Sampling Methods for Topic Models*. R package version 1.5.2. https://cran.r-project.org/web/packages/lda/lda.pdf.

Change.org. n.d. "Discontinue the 'MANIFEST DESTINY' T-shirt and Issue a Formal Apology." Accessed July 31, 2023. https://www.change.org/p/gap-discontinue-the-manifest-destiny-tshirt-and-issue-a-formal-apology.

Changing Woman Initiative (@ChangingWomanIntiative). 2022. "Reclaiming our Indigenous medicine and teachings around health and wellness is our human right." Instagram, December 16. https://www.instagram.com/p/CmP4dL0rsdM/.

Chavez, Will. 2021. "A Timeline for the Cherokee Freedmen." *Cherokee Phoenix*, February 1. Updated September 25, 2024.

Cherokee Nation. n.d. "The History of the Cherokee Nation." https://www.cherokee.org/about-the-nation/history/.

Cheu, Johnson. 2013. *Diversity in Disney Films: Critical Essays on Race, Ethnicity, Gender, Sexuality and Disability*. Jefferson: McFarland.

Child, Brenda J. 2018. "The Boarding School as Metaphor." *Journal of American Indian Education* 57, no. 1 (Spring): 37–57. https://doi.org/10.5749/jamerindieduc.57.1.0037.

Choctaw Nation of Oklahoma. 2021. "Claims and Immunities Act of the Choctaw Nation of Oklahoma (CB-87-21)." https://www.choctawnation.com/sites/default/files/CB-87-21.pdf.

Choy, S., and J. Woodlock. 2007. "Implementing Indigenous Standpoint Theory: Challenges for a TAFE trainer." *International Journal of Training Research* 5, no. 1: 39–54. https://doi.org/10.5172/ijtr.5.1.39.

Christian Alliance of Indian Child Welfare. 2022. "Brackeen and State Petitioners Counsel for Amici Curiae." Court document. Supreme Court of the United States.

Christopher, Robert J. 2005. *Robert and Frances Flaherty: A Documentary Life, 1883–1922.* McGill-Queen's Indigenous and Northern Studies. McGill-Queen's University Press. https://doi.org/10.2307/j.ctt7zw7v.

Clark, Treena, Shannan Dodson, Nancia Guivarra, and Yatu Widders Hunt. 2022. "'I Want to Create Change; I Want to Create Impact': Personal-Activism Narratives of Indigenous Australian Women Working in Public Relations." *Public Relations Review* 48, no. 1 (March). https://doi.org/10.1016/j.pubrev.2021.102135.

Clements, Ron and John Musker, dir. 2016. *Moana.* DVD. Walt Disney Studios Motion Pictures.

Coates, Sarah Kim, Michelle Trudgett, and Susan Page. 2022. "Indigenous Institutional Theory: A New Theoretical Framework and Methodological Tool." *The Australian Educational Researcher* 50 (May 25): 903–20. https://doi.org/10.1007/s13384-022-00533-4.

Cohen, Geoffrey L., and Claude M. Steele. 2002. "A Barrier of Mistrust: How Negative Stereotypes Affect Cross-Race Mentoring." In *Improving Academic Achievement: Impact of Psychological Factors on Education.* Edited by Joshua Aronson. New York: Elsevier/Academic Press, 303–27.

Comfort, Ryan N. 2022a. "Exploring Environmental Communication in the U.S. Indigenous Diaspora." *Environmental Communication* 16, no. 5 (October 10): 1–14. https://doi.org/10.1080/17524032.2022.2130388.

———. 2022b. "Political Macroenvironments & Cultural Information Protection: The Challenge of Communication in Native American Environmental and Natural Resource Management." *Society & Natural Resources* 35, no. 12 (August 26): 1–18. https://doi.org/10.1080/08941920.2022.2113846.

Cook-Lynn, Elizabeth. 2007. *New Indians, Old Wars.* Champaign: University of Illinois Press.

Coombs, W. Timothy, and Sherry J. Holiday. 2012. "Privileging an Activist vs. a Corporate View of Public Relations History in the U.S." *Public Relations Review* 38, no. 3: 347–53. https://doi.org/10.1016/j.pubrev.2011.11.010.

Cox, Alex. 2021. "N.B. First Nation Hosts March in Memory of Children Buried at Former B.C. Residential School." *CBC News*, June 2. https://www.cbc.ca/news/canada/new-brunswick/first-nation-indigenous-1.6050935.

Cox, G. R., P. FireMoon, M. P. Anastario, A. Ricker, R. Escarcega-Growing Thunder, J. A. Baldwin, and E. Rink. 2021. "Indigenous Standpoint Theory as a Theoretical Framework for Decolonizing Social Science Health Research with American Indian Communities." *AlterNative: An International Journal of Indigenous Peoples* 17, no. 4: 460–68.

Cramer, Gary M. 2023. "'Free Press Supports Tribal Sovereignty': The Muscogee Reporter Fight Against Tyranny in 'Bad Press.'" *Salon*, January 17. https://www.salon.com/2023/01/17/press-muscogee-mvskoke-media/.

Cramer, Maria. 2020. "Maker of Eskimo Pie Ice Cream Will Retire 'Inappropriate' Name." *New York Times*, June 20. https://www.nytimes.com/2020/06/20/business/dreyers-eskimo-pie-name-change.html.

Crayola. n.d. "Crayola Crayon Chronology." Accessed June 21, 2011. http://www.crayola.com/colorcensus/history/chronology.cfm.

Crenshaw, Kimberle. 1991. "Mapping the Margins: Intersectionality, Identity Politics, and Violence Against Women of Color." *Stanford Law Review* 43, no. 6: 1241–99.

Curran, J., and M. J. Park, cited in Antje Glück. 2018. "De-Westernization and Decolonization in Media Studies." In *Oxford Research Encyclopedia of Communication.* Oxford: Oxford University Press, 1. https://doi.org/10.1093/acrefore/9780190228613.013.898.

Dados, N., and R. Connell. 2012. "The Global South." *Contexts* 11, no. 1: 12–13.

Dalrymple, Amy. 2016. "Pipeline Route Plan First Called for Crossing North of Bismarck." *The Bismarck Tribune*, August 18. http://bismarcktribune.com/news/state-and-regional/pipeline-route-plan-first-called-for-crossing-north-of-bismarck/article_64d053e4-8a1a-5198-a1dd-498d386c933c.html.

Danius, Sara, Stefan Jonsson, and Gayatri Chakravorty Spivak. 1993. "An Interview with Gayatri Chakravorty Spivak." *Boundary* 2, no. 20.2: 24–50.

Deloria, Philip. 1998. *Playing Indian.* New Haven: Yale University Press.

———. 2003. *Indians in Unexpected Places.* Lawrence: University of Kansas Press.

Demetrious, Kristin. 2013. *Public Relations, Activism, and Social Change: Speaking Up.* New York: Routledge.

Denetclaw, Pauly. 2022. "Supreme Court Could Halt Access to Safe Abortions, Indigenous Activists Say." *Indian Country Today*, May 3. https://ictnews.org/news/supreme-court-could-halt-access-to-safe-abortions-indigenous-activists-say.

———. 2023a. "Another Legal Challenge to Indian Gaming." *Indian Country Today*, April 3. https://ictnews.org/news/another-legal-challenge-to-indian-gaming.

———. 2023b. "Left Out of Truth and Reconciliation." *Indian Country Today*, May 9. https://ictnews.org/news/left-out-of-truth-and-reconciliation.

Deseret News. 1990. "Mazda Unveils Navajo Sport Vehicle and Donates 1 to Tribe in Arizona." September 16. https://www.deseret.com/1990/9/16/18881470/mazda-unveils-navajo-sport-vehicle-and-donates-1-to-tribe-in-arizona.

Diamond, James (@Jim_Diamond). 2022. "Just when #McGift gave #IndianTribes a sliver of hope, the new conservative majority retrenches. The Federal Courts have historically protected #Indigenous." Twitter, June 29, 12:32 p.m. https://twitter.com/Jim_Diamond/status/1542184303974440961.

Diamond, Neil, dir. 2009. *Reel Injun.* Rezolution Pictures.

Dickson, Courtney. 2021. "Victoria Cancels Scheduled Canada Day Programming in Wake of Kamloops Residential School Discovery." *CBC News*, June 10. https://www.cbc.ca/news/canada/british-columbia/victoria-canada-day-1.6061687.

Dippie, Brian W. 1982. *The Vanishing American: White Attitudes and U.S. Indian Policy.* Middletown, CT: Wesleyan University Press.

Disjksterhuis, Ap, and Ad van Knippenberg. 1996. "The Knife That Cuts Both Ways: Facilitated and Inhibited Access to Traits as a Result of Stereotype Activation." *Journal of Experimental Social Psychology* 32: 271–88.

Donovan, Bill, and Michel Martin, host. 2012. "Navajo Nation Sues Urban Outfitters Over Trademark." *Tell Me More*, NPR, April 5. https://www.npr.org/2012/04/05/150062611/navajo-nation-sues-urban-outfitters-over-trademark.

Dudley, Michael Kioni, and Keomi Kealoha Agard. 1993. *A Call for Hawaiian Sovereignty.* Vol. 2. Honolulu: Na Kane O Ka Malo Press.

Duran, Eduardo, Bonnie Duran, Heart, Maria Yellow Horse Brave, and Susan Yellow Horse-Davis. 1998. "Healing the American Indian Soul Wound." In *International Handbook of Multigenerational Legacies of Trauma.* Boston, MA: Springer US, 341–54.

Eastern Band of Cherokee Indians. n.d. https://www.ebci.gov/.

Edwards, Lee. 2011. *Public Relations, Society & Culture: Theoretical and Empirical Explorations.* Edited by Caroline E. M. Hodges. Routledge.

Elliott, Caitlin. 2016. "You Will Be Punished: Media Depictions of Missing and Murdered Indigenous Women." *Theses and Dissertations (Comprehensive)* 1863. https://scholars.wlu.ca/etd/1863.

Elliott, Sarah K. 2020. "Understanding the Origin of American Indian Boarding Schools." *Antiques Roadshow*, PBS, April 13. https://www.pbs.org/wgbh/roadshow/stories/articles/2020/4/13/early-years-american-indian-boarding-schools.

Eneas, Bryan. 2021. "Sask. First Nation Announces Discovery of 751 Unmarked Graves Near Former Residential School." *CBC News*, June 24. https://www.cbc.ca/news/canada/saskatchewan/cowessess-marieval-indian-residential-school-news-1.6078375.

Engel, Madeline H., Norma Kolko Phillips, and Frances A. DellaCava. 2012. "Indigenous Children's Rights: A Sociological Perspective on Boarding Schools and Transracial Adoption." *The International Journal of Children's Rights* 20, no. 2: 279–99.

Erhart, Ryan S., and Deborah L. Hall. 2019. "A Descriptive and Comparative Analysis of the Content of Stereotypes About Native Americans." *Race and Social Problems* 11, no. 3: 225–42.

Essner, Janis, and Jay Ruby. 1987. "Robert J. Flaherty (1884–1951)." *Arctic Profiles*: 354–55. https://journalhosting.ucalgary.ca/index.php/arctic/article/view/64848/48762.

Evans, Heather K., and Jennifer Hayes Clark. 2016. "'You Tweet Like a Girl!' How Female Candidates Campaign on Twitter." *American Politics Research* 44, no. 2: 326–52.

Evans, Murray. 2007. "Cherokees Vote to Revoke Membership of Freedmen." Associated Press, March 12. Published in *Indian Country Today*. https://ictnews.org/archive/cherokees-vote-to-revoke-membership-of-freedmen.

Eveleigh, Ana Adamandia. 2023. *Child Removal and Religious Conversion: Toward a Religious Liberty Defense of the Indian Child Welfare Act*. Barnard College of Columbia University.

Fable, Alessandra. 20112021. "Intersectionality Amongst Disproportionate and Forgotten Numbers Within the Child Welfare System." *Senior Capstone Projects* 1113. https://digitalwindow.vassar.edu/senior_capstone/1113.

Faherty Brand. n.d. "About Us." Accessed August 6, 2023. https://fahertybrand.com/pages/about.

Fanon, Frantz. 2008. *Black Skin, White Masks*. New York: Grove Press.

Fast, Elizabeth, and Delphine Collin-Vézina. 2010. "Historical Trauma, Race-Based Trauma and Resilience of Indigenous Peoples: A Literature Review." *First Peoples Child & Family Review* 5, no. 1: 126–36.

Ferris, Melanie. 2021. "Intergenerational Survivor Finds Comfort in Community at Ceremony for 215 Children Buried in Kamloops." *CBC News*, June 5. https://www.cbc.ca/news/canada/manitoba/first-person-melanie-ferris-kelowna-215-children-1.6053412.

Field, Kelly. 2016. "'Stereotypes Are at the Center': A White House Official on Why Native Students Often Struggle." *The Chronicle of Higher Education*, July 16. https://www.chronicle.com/article/stereotypes-are-at-the-center-a-white-house-official-on-why-native-students-often-struggle/.

Fisher Liu, Brooke, and J. Suzanne Horsley. 2007. "The Government Communication Decision Wheel: Toward a Public Relations Model for the Public Sector." *Journal of Public Relations Research* 19, no. 4: 377–93.

Fiske, Susan T. 1998. "Stereotyping, Prejudice, and Discrimination." In *The Handbook of Social Psychology*. Edited by Susa T. Fiske Gardner Lindzey and Daniel T. Gilbert. Boston: McGraw-Hill, 357–411.

Flaherty, Robert J., dir. 1992. *Nanook of the North*. Revillon.

Fletcher, M. L. M., and Winona Sengel. 2022. "Lawyering the Indian Child Welfare Act." *Michigan Law Review*, June. https://michiganlawreview.org/journal/lawyering-the-indian-child-welfare-act/.

Fodder, Torivio. 2012. "A Libertarian Framework for Indian Rights." SJD dissertation, April 10. University of Arizona College of Law, Indigenous Peoples Law & Policy Program. http://dx.doi.org/10.2139/ssrn.2089533.

Foley, Dennis. 2003. "Indigenous Epistemology and Indigenous Standpoint Theory." *Social Alternatives* 22, no. 1: 44–52.

———. 2006. "Indigenous Standpoint Theory: An Acceptable Academic Research Process for Indigenous Academics." *International Journal of the Humanities* 3, no. 8 (January): 25–36. https://doi.org/10.18848/1447-9508/CGP/v03i08/41775.

Fonseca, Felica. 2011. "Urban Outfitters Line Sparks Protest from Navajo." *Today*, October 17. https://www.today.com/news/urban-outfitters-line-sparks-protest-navajo-wbna44929941.

Fort, Kate. 2023. "In the Matter of S.J.W." *Turtle Talk*, April 26. https://turtletalk.blog/2023/04/26/icwa-jurisdiction-case-out-of-the-oklahoma-supreme-court/.

Fort, Kathryn E., and Adrian Smith. 2023. "The Indian Child Welfare Act During the Brackeen Years." *SSRN Electronic Journal*. https://papers.ssrn.com/sol3/papers.cfm?abstract_id=4339489.

Fostering Media Connections. 2022. "The Imprint Launches National Indigenous Family Reporting Beat." September 20. https://www.prlog.org/12933554-the-imprint-launches-national-indigenous-family-reporting-beat.html.

Fountaine, Susan. 2017. "What's Not to Like? A Qualitative Study of Young Women Politicians' Self-Framing on Twitter." *Journal of Public Relations Research* 29, no. 5: 219–37.

Fraser, Sara. 2021. 2021. "How to Talk to Kids About Residential Schools and the Trauma They Caused." *CBC News*, June 4. https://www.cbc.ca/news/canada/prince-edward-island/pei-indigenous-residential-schools-ben-gould-1.6053325.

Fujiwara, Thomas, Karsten Müller, and Carlo Schwarz. 2023. "The Effect of Social Media on Elections: Evidence from the United States." *Journal of the European Economic Association* 22, no. 3 (October): 1495–539. https://doi.org/10.1093/jeea/jvad058.

Fuller, Steve. 19981988. *Social Epistemology*. Bloomington: Indiana University Press.

Funk, Cary, Jeffrey Gottfried, and Amy Mitchell. 2017. "Science News and Information Today." Pew Research Center. https://www.journalism.org/wp-content/uploads/sites/8/2017/09/PJ_2017.09.20_Science-and-News_FINAL.pdf.

Gageo, Daniele M. 2001. "Indigenous Knowledge and Epistemology." In *International Encyclopedia of the Social & Behavioral Sciences*. Edited by Neil J. Smelser and Paul B. Baltes. Oxford: Elsevier, 8148–51.

Gallichio, Christian. 2020. "Waikiki Review: An Assured Exploration of Hawaii's Cultural Trauma." *The Film Stage*, October 31. https://thefilmstage.com/waikiki-review-an-assured-exploration-of-hawaiis-cultural-trauma/.

Gamson, William A., and Andre Modigliani. 1989. "Media Discourse and Public Opinion on Nuclear Power: A Constructionist Approach." *The American Journal of Sociology* 95, no. 1: 1–37.

Ganje, Francie. 2023. "Makers of Tanka Bar Look to Support, Source Bison Meat from Indian-Owned Herds." *KBHB Radio*, February 7. https://kbhbradio.com/makers-of-tanka-bar-look-to-support-source-bison-meat-from-indian-owned-herds/.

Garrow, Carrie E., and Sarah Deer. 2015. *Tribal Criminal Law and Procedure.* Tribal Legal Studies Series. Vol. 2. AltaMira Press. https://www.ojp.gov/ncjrs/virtual-library/abstracts/tribal-criminal-law-and-procedure.

Gearon, Jihan. 2021. "Indigenous Feminism Is Our Culture." *Stanford Social Innovation Review,* February 11. https://ssir.org/articles/entry/indigenous_feminism_is_our_culture.

Geddert, Jeremy Seth. 2021. "Indigenous Sovereignty and the (Enlarged) Responsibility to Protect." *American Review of Canadian Studies* 51, no. 2 (September): 251–71. https://doi.org/10.1080/02722011.2021.1910425.

Gegeo, D. W., and K. A. Watson-Gegeo. 2001. "How We Know: Kwara'ae Rural Villagers Doing Indigenous Epistemology." *The Contemporary Pacific* 13, no. 1: 55–88. http://www.jstor.org/stable/23718509.

Ginsburg, Faye. 1991. "Indigenous Media: Faustian Contract or Global Village?" *Cultural Anthropology* 6, no. 1: 92–112.

Goldman, A.I. 1986. *Epistemology and Cognition.* Cambridge, MA: Harvard University Press.

———. 1999. *Knowledge in a Social World.* Oxford: Oxford University Press.

Gollom, Mark. 2021. "How Radar Technology Is Used to Discover Unmarked Graves at Former Residential Schools." *CBC News,* June 14. https://www.cbc.ca/news/canada/ground-radar-technology-residential-school-remains-1.6049776.

Gomez, Lauren. 2016. "Beyond Black and White: Native American Representation in Newspaper Media." Thesis. University of Oklahoma Graduate College.

Gray, Liz. 2021. "Citizens to Vote on Constitutional Free Press During Primary Election." *Mvskoke Media,* August 12. https://www.mvskokemedia.com/citizens-to-vote-on-constitutional-free-press-during-primary-election/.

Great Lakes Indian Fish and Wildlife Commission. 2025. https://glifwc.org/. Accessed March 5, 2026.

Green, Michael K. 1993. "Images of Native Americans in Advertising: Some Moral Issues." *Journal of Business Ethics* 12, no. 4: 32–330.

Greendeer, Jon. 2012. "State of the Tribes Address." Wisconsin State Capitol, March 13, 2012, 55:25. http://video.wpt.org/video/2209270397/.

Greene-Blye, Melissa. 2020. "Great Men, Savages, and the End of the Indian Problem." *Journalism History* 46, no. 1: 32–49.

———, and T. Finneman. 2023. "The Influence of Indigenous Standpoint: Examining Indian Country Press Portrayals of Native Women in Politics." *Newspaper Research Journal.* 44 (4): 390–408. https://doi.org/10.1177/07395329231155195.

Gross, Terry. 2022. "'Reservation Dogs' Co-Creator Says the Show Gives Audiences Permission to Laugh." NPR, September 19. https://www.npr.org/2022/09/19/1123452609/reservation-dogs-sterlin-harjo-Native-stories.

Grossman, Zoltán. 2017. *Unlikely Alliances: Native Nations and White Communities Join to Defend Rural Lands.* 1st ed. Seattle and London: University of Washington Press.

Gulati, Girish J. 2004. "Members of Congress and Presentation of Self on the World Wide Web." *Harvard International Journal of Press/Politics* 9, no. 1: 22–40.

Haig-Brown, Celia. 2002. *Resistance and Renewal: Surviving the Indian Residential School.* Vancouver: Arsenal Pulp Press.

Haight, Wendy, Cary Waubanascum, David Glesener, Priscilla Day, Brenda Bussey, and Karen Nichols. 2019. "The Center for Regional and Tribal Child Welfare Studies: Reducing Disparities through Indigenous Social Work Education." *Children and Youth Services Review* 100: 156–66.

Hallahan, Kirk. 2011. "Political Public Relations and Strategic Framing." In *Political Public Relations: Principles and Applications.* Edited by Jesper Strömbäck and Spiro Kiousis. New York: Routledge, 177–213.

Hammersley, Mia M., Adriana M. Orman, and Wouter Zwart. 2022. "Indigenous Erasure in Public Schools." *Arizona Attorney: Special Focus on Indian Law* (Summer). https://www.azattorneymag-digital.com/azattorneymag/library/item/20220708/4029128/.

Han, Hsiao-Cheng (Sandrine). 2019. "Moving from Cultural Appropriation to Cultural Appreciation." *Art Education* 72, no. 2: 8–13. https://doi.org/10.1080/00043125.2019.1559575.

Hargrove, Ermile, Kent Sakoda, and Jeff Siegel. 2014. "Hawaiʻi Creole." *Language Varieties.* Accessed February 20, 2023. https://www.hawaii.edu/satocenter/langnet/definitions/hce.html.

Harjo, Suzan. 1992. "American Indians." *The Oprah Winfrey Show*, November.

———. 2004. "American Indian Religious Freedom Act After Twenty-Five Years: An Introduction." *Wicazo Sa Review* 19, no. 2: 129–36. https://www.jstor.org/stable/i261474.

Harrell, Jules P., Sadiki Hall, and James Taliaferro. 2003. "Physiological Responses to Racism and Discrimination: An Assessment of the Evidence." *American Journal of Public Health* 93, no. 2: 243–48.

Hart, Michael A. 2010. "Indigenous Worldviews, Knowledge, and Research: The Development of an Indigenous Research Paradigm." *Journal of Indigenous Social Development* 1, no. 1A.

Harvard Project on American Indian Economic Development. 2020. "Harvard Project on American Indian Economic Development Releases Research on Allocation of COVID-19 Response Funds." Press release, April 13. https://ash.harvard.edu/articles/harvard-project-on-american-indian-economic-development-releases-research-on-allocation-of-covid%E2%80%9019-response-funds/.

Hasty, Jennifer, David G. Lewis, and Marjorie M. Snipes. 2022. *Introduction to Anthropology.* SAGE Publications Inc.

Hatch, John. 1992. "American Indian and Alaska Native Adult Education, and Vocational Training Programs: Historical Beginnings, Present Conditions, and Future Directions." In *Indian Nations at Risk: Listening to the People.* Edited by Patricia Cahape and Craig B. Howley. Charleston, WV: ERIC, 102–6.

Heath, Robert L., and Damion Waymer. 2009. "Activist Public Relations and the Paradox of the Positive: A Case Study of Frederick Douglass' Fourth of July Address." In *Rhetorical and Critical Approaches to Public Relations II*. Edited by Robert L. Heath, E. L. Toth, and Damion Waymer. New York: Routledge, 195–215.

Heckes, Hevyn. 2021. "Missing and Murdered Indigenous Women (and Children)—A Global Problem." *University of New Mexico Digital Repository*, December 8. https://digitalrepository.unm.edu/cgi/viewcontent.cgi?article=1019&context=ugresearchaward_2022.

Hellier, A., A. C. Newton, and S. O. Gaona. 1999. "Use of Indigenous Knowledge Thesis for Rapidly Assessing Trends in Biodiversity: A Case Study from Chiapas, Mexico." *Biodiversity and Conservation* 8, no. 7: 869–89.

Herald, Everett. 2023. "Deb Haaland Visits Tulalip to Hear from Boarding School Survivors." *Indian Country Today*, April 25. https://ictnews.org/news/deb-haaland-visits-tulalip-to-hear-from-boarding-school-survivors.

Herrera, Allison. 2023a. "Oklahoma Supreme Court's Opinion Challenging Parts of the Indian Child Welfare Act Is Flawed, Experts Say." *KOSU*, May 2. https://www.kosu.org/local-news/2023-05-02/oklahoma-supreme-courts-opinion-challenging-parts-of-the-indian-child-welfare-act-is-flawed-experts-say.

———. 2023b. "Two Candidates Will Face Off for Chairman of the Iowa Tribe of Oklahoma." *KOSU*, June 2. Accessed June 5, 2023. https://www.kosu.org/2023-06-02/two-candidates-will-face-off-for-chairman-of-the-iowa-tribe-of-oklahoma.

Hidalgo Reese, Elizabeth (@Yunpovi). 2022. "For those wondering, 'Why is it bad that states can prosecute too?' Three answers: 1- States/Tribes have a long history of animosity. Fair treatment isn't." Twitter, June 29, 10:57 a.m. https://twitter.com/yunpovi/status/1542160420877832197.

Hodison, Maya. 2022. "Abortion Bans Continue to Reinforce Colonization of Indigenous People, Community Leaders Say." *The Lawrence Times*, July 1. https://lawrencekstimes.com/2022/07/01/abortion-bans-colonize-indigenous-people/.

Hoerig, Karl. 2002. "Remembering Our Indian School Days: The Boarding School Experience." *American Anthropologist* 104, no. 2: 642–46.

Holtzhausen, Derina R. 2012. *Public Relations as Activism: Postmodern Approaches to Theory & Practice.* New York: Routledge.

House, Daisy. 2021. "A Message to Canada from a Cree Community Chief in Chisasibi, Que." *CBC News*, June 30. https://www.cbc.ca/news/canada/north/cree-residential-chisasibi-daisy-house-fort-george-1.6075601.

Hubner, Austin. "How Did We Get Here? A Framing and Source Analysis of Early COVID-19 Media Coverage." *Communication Research Reports* 38, no. 2 (2021): 112–20. https://doi.org/10.1080/08824096.2021.1894112.

Huddy, Leonie, and Nayda Terkildsen. 1993. "Gender Stereotypes and the Perception of Male and Female Candidates." *American Journal of Political Science* 37, no. 1: 119–47.

Hunter, Sandra. 2023. *Defining and Reclaiming Traditional Indigenous Child Rearing Practices.* Thesis, January 4. University of Manitoba.

ICT Staff. 2018. "Gap 'Manifest Destiny' T-Shirt Sparks Outrage in Indian Country: A T-Shirt Being Sold by the Gap Bearing the Words Manifest Destiny Has Struck Many Native Americans as Incredibly Insensitive." *Indian Country Today*, September 13. https://ictnews.org/archive/gap-manifest-destiny-t-shirt-sparks-outrage-in-indian-country.

IllumiNative. 2022. "The Time Is Now: The Power of Native Representation in Entertainment." June. https://illuminative.org/wp-content/uploads/2022/06/IllumiNative_industry-guide_June-2022.pdf.

——— (@IllumiNative). 2023. "'Native kids have been the tip of the spear in attacks on Tribal sovereignty for years,' journalist and activist Rebecca Nagle (Cherokee) explains on this week's episode of @NPRCodeSwitch. #ProtectICWA." Twitter, May 19, 5:01 p.m. https://twitter.com/IllumiNative/status/1659680722758639616.

Indian Country Today. n.d.a. "About Us." Accessed June 13, 2022. https://ictnews.org/about-us/.

Indian Country Today. n.d.b. "Our History." Accessed March 5, 2026. https://ictnews.org/about-us/#history.

——— (@IndianCountry). 2022. "OP-ED: The Supreme Court's decision in Oklahoma v. Castro-Huerta is not an application of the law. It is an outcome-determinative decision designed to satisfy." Twitter, August 4, 7:21 p.m. https://twitter.com/IndianCountry/status/1555348106589372418?s=20.

Indianz.com. 2013. "Radio: Baby Veronica Dispute Brings Up Blood Quantum Issue." August 23. https://indianz.com/News/2013/08/23/radio-baby-veronica-dispute-br.asp.

Indigenous Journalists Association. n.d.a. "Free Press Resources." Accessed October 25, 2023. https://najanewsroom.com/free-press-resources/.

———. n.d.b. "Red Press Initiative." Accessed October 25, 2023. https://najanewsroom.com/red-press-initiative/.

———. 2018. "NAJA Condemns Repeal of Muscogee (Creek) Free Press Act." November 9. https://najanewsroom.com/2018/11/09/naja-calls-on-the-muscogee-creek-national-council-to-protect-press-freedom-2/.

Ing, N. Rosalyn. 1990. *The Effects of Residential Schools on Native Child-Rearing Patterns.* Thesis. University of British Columbia.

Iseke, Judy. 2013. "Indigenous Storytelling as Research." *International Review of Qualitative Research* 6, no. 4: 559–77.

Jay, Robert. 1987. *The Trade Card in Nineteenth-Century America.* Columbia: University of Missouri Press.

Johansen, Bruce E. 2001. "Crazy Horse's Estate Reaches Settlement in Malt Liquor Case." *Native Americas* 18, no. 2 (August): 6.

Johnson, Rhiannon. 2021."Couple Uses Chalk Art to Talk to Their Daughter About Discovery at Kamloops Residential School." *CBC News*, June 5. https://www.cbc.ca/news/indigenous/chalk-hearts-talking-to-kids-about-kamloops-1.6052314.

Johnson, Troy. 2008. "The Alcatraz Indian Occupation." National Parks Service. Accessed June 30, 2023. https://www.nps.gov/alca/learn/historyculture/we-hold-the-rock.htm.

Jones, Alyse. 2023. "Oklahoma State Board of Education Terminates Contract with Indigenous Charter School." *KOCO News*, January 27. https://www.koco.com/article/oklahoma-state-board-of-education-terminates-contract-indigenous-charter-school/42692472.

Jungherr, Andreas. 2016. "Twitter Use in Election Campaigns: A Systematic Review." *Journal of Information Technology & Politics* 13, no. 1: 72–91.

Kaeding, Danielle. 2016. "Former GTAC President Fine in Connection with Spanish Mine Water Pollution Case." *Wisconsin Public Radio*, September 21. https://www.wpr.org/former-gtac-president-fined-connection-spanish-mine-water-pollution-case.

Kahunahana, Chris, dir. 2020. *Waikiki*. Perf. Danielle Zalopany and Peter Shinkoda. Hula Girl Productions and Island Film Group.

Kajihiro, Kyle. 2009. "Resisting Militarization in Hawai'i." In *The Bases of Empire: The Global Struggle Against US Military Posts*. Edited by Catherine Lutz and Cynthia Enole. New York: New York University Press, 299–331.

Kame'eleihiwa, Lilikalā. 1992. *Native Land and Foreign Desires: Pehea lā e pono ai*. Honolulu: Bishop Museum Press.

Kanahele, George. 1992. *Ku Kanaka Stand Tall: A Search for Hawaiian Values*. Honolulu: University of Hawaii Press.

Kanu, Hassan. 2022. "U.S. Confronts 'Cultural Genocide' in Native American Boarding School Probe." *Reuters*, May 18. https://www.reuters.com/legal/government/us-confronts-cultural-genocide-native-american-boarding-school-probe-2022-05-18/.

Kemper, Kevin R. 2002. "Land of the Free? Despite the Creation of Laws to Protect the Cherokee Free Press, the Control of the Press by Tribal Leaders has Garbled the Process." *IPI Global Journalist* 8, no. 3: 12–15.

———. 2010. "Who Speaks for Native Americans? Tribal Journalists, Rhetorical Sovereignty, and Freedom of Expression." *Journalism & Communication Monographs* 12 (Spring), 3–58.

———. 2012. "Sacred Spaces: Cultural Hybridity and Boundaries for Visual Communication About the Hopi Tribe in Arizona." *Visual Communication Quarterly* 19 (October/December): 216.

———. 2013. "You Have to EARN Access: A Case Study of Arizona Tribes and Reporting About Indigenous Religion Around the Pacific Rim." *Asia Pacific Media Educator* 23, no. 1: 1–21.

———., and Litzy Galarza. 2016. "More Than Ever, But Not Enough Yet: Protections of Freedom of Expression in Tribal Constitutions." NAJA and Excellence in Journalism Convention, New Orleans.

Kempton, W. 2001. "Cognitive Anthropology and the Environment." In *New Directions in Anthropology and Environment—Intersections.* Edited by Carole L. Crumley with A. E. van Deventer and J. J. Fletcher. California: Altamira Press, 49–71.

Kendi, Ibram X. 2019. *How to Be an Anti-Racist.* Random House Publishing Group.

Kessi, Shose, Zoe Marks, and Elelwani Ramugondo. 2020. "Decolonizing African Studies." *Critical African Studies* 12, no. 3: 271–82, https://doi.org/10.1080/21681392.2020.1813413.

Kohl, Johann Georg. 1860. *Kitchi-Gami: Wanderings Round Lake Superior.* London: Chapman and Hall.

Kloss, Karlie (@KarlieKloss). 2012. "I am deeply sorry if what I wore during the VS Show offended anyone. I support VS's decision to remove the outfit from the broadcast." Twitter, November 11, 2:20 p.m. https://twitter.com/karliekloss/status/267723529536036865.

Knopf, Kerstin. 2008. *Decolonizing the Lens of Power: Indigenous Films in North America.* Leiden: Brill Publishers.

Kohl, Johann Georg. 1985. *Kitchi-Gami, My Life Among the Lake Superior Ojibway.* St. Paul: Minnesota Historical Society Press.

Konzett, Delia Caparoso. 2017. *Hollywood's Hawaii: Race, Nation, and War.* New Brunswick: Rutgers University Press.

Krehbiel-Burton, Lenzy. 2018a. "Muscogee (Creek) Nation Votes to Repeal Free Press Act, Citing Need for 'More Positive' Coverage." *The Journal Record,* November 18. https://journalrecord.com/2018/11/08/muscogee-creek-nation-votes-to-repeal-free-press-act-citing-need-for-more-positive-coverage/.

———. 2018b. "Muscogee (Creek) National Council Votes to Reinstate Free Press Act." *The Journal Record,* December 17. https://journalrecord.com/2018/12/17/muscogee-creek-national-council-votes-to-reinstate-free-press-act/.

Kunze, Jenna. 2021. "Meet the Seamstress Who Designed Deb Haaland's Ribbon Skirt for Swearing-In Ceremony." *Native News Online,* March 19. https://nativenewsonline.net/currents/meet-the-seamstress-who-designed-deb-haaland-s-ribbon-skirt-for-swearing-in-ceremony.

LaCourse, Richard. 1998. "A Native Press Primer." *Columbia Journalism Review* 36, no. 51 (December). https://archive.org/details/sim_columbia-journalism-review_january-february-1998_36_5.

Laman, Lisa. 2023. "*Nanook of the North* at 100: How Documentaries Can Warp Reality." *Collider.* Accessed September 30, 2023. https://collider.com/nanook-of-the-north-100-anniversary-documentary-robert-flaherty/.

Landesman, C. 1997. *An Introduction to Epistemology.* Wiley-Blackwell.

Land O'Lakes. n.d. "Land O'Lakes History." Accessed June 14, 2002. http://www.landolakes.com/ourCompany/LandOLakesHistory.cfm.

———. 2020. "Farmer-Owned Cooperative Land O'Lakes, Inc. Unveils New Packaging Celebrating Farmers Ahead of 100th Anniversary." Press release,

February 6. https://www.landolakesinc.com/Press/News/new-butter-and-dairy-packaging.

Landsberry, Rebecca, and Joe Peeler, dirs. 2022. *Bad Press*. Sundance Film Festival (2023). Accessed June 2, 2023. https://festival.sundance.org/program/film/638a1ffad406b20f68f2e3f2.

Landsberry-Baker, Becca. 2023. Interview by Sarah Liese, April 14.

Langmia, Kehbuma. 2018. *Black/Africana Communication Theory*. Springer International Publishing.

———, and Agnes Lucy Lando. 2020. *Digital Communications at Crossroads in Africa: A Decolonial Approach*. Springer International Publishing.

LaPoe, Benjamin R. 2022a. "Amplifying Indigenous Standpoint Theory: Supporting Decolonizing Journalism and Mass Communication Theory." Presented at the 2022 AEJMC Conference: Theory Colloquium, Detroit, August 5.

———, Candi S. Carter Olson, Victoria L. LaPoe, Parul Jain, Allyson Woellert, and Aaron Long. 2022b. "Politics, Power and a Pandemic: Searching for Information and Accountability During a Twitter Infodemic." *Electronic News* 16, no. 1: 30–53. https://doi.org/10.1177/19312431211057488.

LaPoe, Victoria. 2020. "2020 NAJA Media Spotlight Report." Native American Journalists Association, February 10. https://najanewsroom.com/2020-naja-media-spotlight-report/.

———, and Benjamin R. LaPoe. 2017. *Indian Country: Telling a Story in a Digital Age*. American Indian Studies Series. East Lansing: Michigan State University Press.

———, Candi Carter Olson, and Stine Eckert. 2017. "'LinkedIn Is My Office; Facebook My Living Room, Twitter the Neighborhood Bar': Media Scholars' Liminal Use of Social Media for Peer and Public Communication." *Journal of Communication Inquiry* 41, no. 3: 185–206. https://doi.org/10.1177/0196859917707741.

———, Candi S. Carter Olson, Cristina L. Azocar, Benjamin R. LaPoe, Bharbi Hazarika, and Parul Jain. 2022c. "A Comparative Analysis of Health News in Indigenous and Mainstream Media." *Health Communication* 37, no. 9 (August): 1192–203.

———, Rebecca Tallent, Tristan Ahtone, and Benjamin R. LaPoe II. 2018. "Ethics and Reporting on Native Communities: Going Beyond the Parachute Story." In *Underserved Communities and Digital Discourse: Getting Voices Heard*. Edited by Victoria LaPoe, Candi S. Carter Olson, and Benjamin R. LaPoe. Lanham, Boulder, New York, London: Lexington Books, 185–203.

———, Sarah Liese, and Allyson Woellert. 2021. "2021 NAJA Media Spotlight Report." Native American Journalists Association, August 2. https://najanewsroom.com/2021-naja-media-spotlight-report/.

———, Sarah Liese, and Benjamin LaPoe. 2022b. "Evaluating Media Sources of Sovereignty Following U.S. Supreme Court Rulings." International Indigenous Research Conference: PĀTAI Puāwai, University of Auckland, New

Zealand, Virtual-Oral-Live, November 17. Ngā Pae o te Māramatanga. www.iirc.ac.nz/.

Lazarus, Jeremy M. 2020. "Blood Feud: Descendant Pushes to be Recognized by Pamunkey Tribe Despite vestiges of 'Black Laws.'" February 28. Accessed October 11, 2024. https://richmondfreepress.com/news/2020/feb/28/blood-feud/.

Lcrawfor. 2022. "James Monroe's Trail of Tears." James Monroe Museum and Memorial Library, November 28. https://jamesmonroemuseum.umw.edu/2022/11/28/james-monroes-trail-of-tears/.

Leary, J. P. 2018. *The Story of Act 31: How Native History Came to Wisconsin Classrooms*. Madison, WI: Wisconsin Historical Society Press.

Leavitt, Peter A., Rebecca Covarrubias, Yvonne A. Perez, and Stephanie A. Fryberg. 2015. "'Frozen in Time': The Impact of Native American Media Representations on Identity and Self-Understanding: Media & Self-Understanding." *Journal of Social Issues* 71, no. 1: 39–53.

Leslie, Carolyn. 2017. "Island Idols: Custom, Courage and Culture in Disney's Moana." *Screen Education* 86: 18–27.

Liles, Stinson. 2022. "Meet the Indigenous Social Workers Who Transformed Tribal Child Welfare." Alliance for Early Success. https://earlysuccess.org/icwa-champions-spotlight/.

Lindschouw, Camilla. 2024. "What Happens Now? Indigenous Nations Prepare for Increased Mobilization of Education About ICWA and Its Vitality for Native Children in Coming Debates." *Indigenous Policy Journal* 34, no. 2: 318.

Lindstrom, Geoffrey. 2010. "Oceania: Islands, Land, People." *Cultural Survival*, March 16,. https://www.culturalsurvival.org/publications/cultural-survival-quarterly/oceania-islands-land-people.

Lippman, Walter. 1922. *Public Opinion.* New York: Harcourt Brace.

Littlefield Daniel F., and James W. Parins, eds. 2011 *Encyclopedia of American Indian Removal*. Westport: Greenwood Publishing.

Loew, Patty. n.d. "Bad River Flood Chronology Final." https://www.youtube.com/watch?v=jy7Jo7-xVPY. Accessed March 5, 2026.

Loew, Patty, and Kelly Mella. 2005. "Black Ink and the New Red Power: Native American Newspapers and Tribal Sovereignty." *Journalism and Communication Monographs* 7, no. 3: 99–142. https://journals.sagepub.com/doi/abs/10.1177/152263790500700301?journalCode=jmoa.

Luo, Carina Xue. 2022. "Missing Children of Indian Residential Schools: On Discovery of Unmarked Graves at Former Indian Residential School Sites in Canada." ArcGIS Storymaps, Academic Data Centre, Leddy Library, September 6. https://storymaps.arcgis.com/stories/cfe29bee35c54a70b9621349f19a3db2.

Lutz, Ashley. 2012. "Gap Offended Customers with This 'Manifest Destiny' T-Shirt." *Business Insider*, October 15. https://www.businessinsider.com/gaps-manifest-destiny-t-shirt-2012-10.

Mackay, James. 2012. "Gap's 'Manifest Destiny' T-Shirt Was a Historic Mistake." *The Guardian*, October 16. https://www.theguardian.com/commentisfree/2012/oct/16/gap-manifest-destiny-t-shirt.

———, and Polina Mackay. 2020. "NDNGirls and Pocahotties: Native American and First Nations Representation in Settler Colonial Pornography and Erotica." *Porn Studies* 7, no. 2: 168–86.

MacLeod, William Christie. 1928. "Economic Aspects of Indigenous American Slavery." *American Anthropologist* 30, no. 4: 632–50.

Malone, Molly, and Libby Chisholm. 2016. "Indigenous Territory." In *The Canadian Encyclopedia*. Historica Canada. https://thecanadianencyclopedia.ca/en/article/indigenous-territory.

Maloney, Ryan. 2021. "Trudeau Flew to Tofino, B.C., with Family on 1st National Day for Truth and Reconciliation." *CBC News*, September 30. https://www.cbc.ca/news/politics/trudeau-tofino-national-day-truth-reconciliation-1.6195591.

Mannik, Lynda, and Karen McGarry. 2017. *Practicing Ethnography: A Student Guide to Method and Methodology*. Toronto: University of Toronto Press.

Mansoor, Sanya. 2022. "The 'Deplorable' History Behind the Pope's Apology to Canada's Indigenous Communities." *Time*, July 26. https://ictnews.org/news / left-out-of-truth-and-reconciliation.

Martin, Karen, and Booran Mirraboopa. "Ways of Knowing, Being and Doing: A Theoretical Framework and Methods for Indigenous and Indigenist Research." *Journal of Australian Studies* 27, no. 76 (2003): 203–14. https://doi.org/10.1080/14443050309387838.

Martin, Rachel. 2022. "South Korea Sets Up a Truth and Reconciliation Commission to Investigate Adoptions." NPR, December 20. https://www.npr.org/2022/12/20/1144311584/south-korea-sets-up-a-truth-and-reconciliation-commission-to-investigate-adoptio.

Matera, Avery. 2018. "5 Times Victoria's Secret Was Accused of Cultural Appropriation from Chinese Dragons to Native Headdresses." *Teen Vogue*, November 7. https://www.teenvogue.com/gallery/victorias-secret-fashion-show-cultural-appropriation.

Matthews, S. 2021. "Decolonising While White: Confronting Race in a South African Classroom." *Teaching in Higher Education* 26, no. 7–8: 1113–21.

Maxim, Robert, and Randall Akee. 2020. "What Deb Haaland's Historic Nomination as Interior Secretary Means for Indigenous Peoples." *Brookings*, December 18. https://www.brookings.edu/articles/what-deb-haalands-historic-nomination-as-interior-secretary-means-for-indigenous-peoples/.

Mazzio, Mary, dir. *Bad River*. 50 Eggs Films, 2024.

McCue, Duncan. 2014. "What It Takes for Aboriginal People to Make the News." *CBC News*, January 29. https://www.cbc.ca/news/indigenous/what-it-takes-for-aboriginal-people-to-make-the-news-1.2514466.

———. 2022. *Decolonizing Journalism: A Guide to Reporting in Indigenous Communities*. 1st ed. Don Mills, Ontario: Oxford University Press.

McEvoy, Jemima. 2020. "Black Chef on Cream of Wheat Packaging Will Be Removed in Rebranding." *Forbes*, September 24. https://www.forbes.com/sites/jemimamcevoy/2020/09/24/black-chef-on-cream-of-wheat-packaging-will-be-removed-in-rebranding/.

McGrady, Clyde. 2019. "Haaland Recalls Struggles as Single Mom, Thanksgiving and Being Homeless." *Roll Call*, September 16. https://rollcall.com/2019/09/16/haaland-recalls-struggles-as-single-mom-thanksgiving-and-being-homeless/.

McGuire, Tim. 1991. "Racism in Sports." Racism and Sports Conference, St. Paul, MN. Accessed July 11, 2011. http://www.naja.com/pr-mcguire.html.

McKie, David, and Debashish Munshi. 2007. *Reconfiguring Public Relations: Ecology, Equity and Enterprise.* Routledge.

McKinley, Catherine E., Jennifer Lilly, Jessica L. Liddell, and Hannah Knipp. 2021. "'I Have to Watch Them Closely': Native American Parenting Practice and Philosophies." *Journal of Child and Family Studies* 30, no. 12: 2952–65.

McLoughlin, William G. 1974. "Red Indians, Black Slavery and White Racism: America's Slaveholding Indians," *American Quarterly* 26, no. 4: 367–85. https://doi.org/10.2307/2711653.

Meeks, Lindsey. 2016. "Gendered Styles, Gendered Differences: Candidates' Use of Personalization and Interactivity on Twitter." *Journal of Information Technology & Politics* 13, no. 4: 295–310.

Merskin, Debra. 2010. "The S-Word: Discourse, Stereotypes, and the American Indian Woman." *The Howard Journal of Communications* 21, no. 4: 345–66.

Merskin, Debra. 2001. "Winnebagos, Cherokees, Apaches, and Dakotas: The Persistence of Stereotyping of American Indians in American Advertising Brands." *Howard Journal of Communications* 12, no. 3: 159–69.

Merton, Robert K. 1957. *Social Theory and Social Structure.* New York: Free Press.

Metz, Sharon. 1995. "Crazy Horse Malt Liquor Equals Racism." *Peace and Freedom* 55, no. 4: 15.

Meuers, Michael. 2021. "America's Real Longest War Was Against Indigenous Americans." *The Circle News*, September 2. https://thecirclenews.org/opinion/americas-real-longest-war-was-against-indigenous-americans.

Meyer, M. A. 2008. "Indigenous and Authentic." In *Handbook of Critical and Indigenous Methodologies*. Edited by N. K. Denzin, Y. S. Lincoln, and L. T. Smith. Los Angeles: Sage Publications, 217–32.

Midwest Environmental Advocates. n.d. "The Future of the Frac Sand Industry in Wisconsin." https://midwestadvocates.org/blog-future-of-frac-sand.

Migdal, Alex. 2021a. "182 Unmarked Graves Discovered Near Residential School in B.C.'s Interior, First Nation Says." *CBC News*, June 30. https://www.cbc.ca/news/canada/british-columbia/bc-remains-residential-school-interior-1.6085990.

———. 2021b. "Members of Tk'emlúps te Secwėpemc Nation Wonder Whether Trudeau Was Listening During His Apologetic Visit." *CBC News*, October 19.

https://www.cbc.ca/news/canada/british-columbia/trudeau-first-nation-appearance-1.6216129.

Mihesuah, Devon. 1996. *American Indians: Stereotypes and Realities.* Atlanta: Clarity.

Miles, Tiya. 2010. *The House on Diamond Hill: A Cherokee Plantation Story.* Chapel Hill: University of North Carolina Press.

Miller, Autumn, and Susan Dente Ross. 2004. "They Are Not Us: Framing of American Indians by the *Boston Globe.*" *Howard Journal of Communications* 15, no. 4: 245–59.

Miller, Korin. 2020. "Mrs. Butterworth Was Modeled After 'Gone With the Wind' Actress Butterfly McQueen." *Women's Health.* June 8. https://www.yahoo.com/lifestyle/mrs-butterworth-modeled-gone-wind-153700631.html.

Milwaukee Public Museum. 2022. "Ho-Chunk Culture." Accessed September 20, 2023. https://www.mpm.edu/content/wirp/ICW-52.

Mintzer, Jordan. 2023. "*Bad Press* Review: An Eye-Opening Expose on Democracy and Journalistic Freedom." *The Hollywood Reporter*, January 25. Accessed June 7, 2023. https://www.hollywoodreporter.com/movies/movie-reviews/bad-press-review-1235309510/.

Misener, Jessica. 2017. "Karlie Kloss Wears Native American Headdress at Victoria's Secret Fashion Show: See the Look That Caused All the Fuss." *HuffPost*, December 6. https://www.huffpost.com/entry/karlie-kloss-victorias-secret-headdress-fashion-show_n_2091958.

Miyose, Colby, and Eean Grimshaw. 2019. "Ua ma uke ea o ka 'āina i ka pono: Cultural Appropriation of the Hawaiian Language in Hawaii Five-0." *PRism* 15, no. 1: 1–17.

Miyose, Colby, and Rayna Morel. 2019. "Eh . . . You Hawaiian? Examining Hawaii Five-0's 'Hawaiian.'" *PRism* 15, no. 1: 66–80.

Mohammed, Wunpini F. 2021. "Decolonizing African Media Studies." *Howard Journal of Communications* 32, no. 2: 123–38. https://doi.org/10.1080/10646175.2021.1871868.

———. 2022. "Bilchiinsi Philosophy: Decolonizing Methodologies in Media Studies." *Review of Communication* 22, no. 1: 7–24. https://www.academia.edu/71044409/Bilchiinsi_philosophy_decolonizing_methodologies_in_medistudies. https://doi.org/10.1080/15358593.2021.2024870.

Monkman, Lenard. 2021. "Residential School Survivors Gather in Winnipeg to Grieve, Heal." *CBC News,* June 1. https://www.cbc.ca/news/indigenous/manitoba-legislature-residential-school-vigil-1.6047802.

Moreno Sandoval, Cueponcaxochitl D., Rosalva Mojica Lagunas, Lydia T. Montelongo, and Marisol Juárez Díaz. 2016. "Ancestral Knowledge Systems: A Conceptual Framework for Decolonizing Research in Social Science." *AlterNative: An International Journal of Indigenous Peoples* 12, no. 1: 18–31. https://doi.org/10.20507/AlterNative.2016.12.1.2.

Morgan, Hal. 1986. *Symbols of America.* New York: Viking Press.

The Morning Star Institute and the International Indian Treaty Council. 2020. "A Blow Against Racism: Washington D.C.'s Football Team Retires the 'R' word." Joint press release, July 15. https://www.iitc.org/a-blow-against-racism-washington-d-c-s-football-team-retires-the-r-word/.

Morton, Katherine. 2018. "Ugliness as Colonial Violence: Mediations of Murdered and Missing Indigenous Women." In *On the Politics of Ugliness*. Edited by Sara Rodrigues and Ela Przybylo. Springer Link, 259–89.

Muir, Nicole, and Yvonne Bohr. 2019. "Contemporary Practice of Traditional Aboriginal Child Rearing: A Review." *First Peoples Child & Family Review* 14, no. 1: 135–65. https://www.erudit.org/en/journals/fpcfr/2019-v14-n1-fpcfr05475/1071293ar/abstract/.

Mvskoke Media. 2023. "Live Wire with 'Bad Press.'" YouTube video, January 13, 34:59. https://youtu.be/0jdyKvIoHTw.

Nagle, Mary Kathryn. 2022. "Castro-Huerta Decision 'Flips Federal Indian Law on Its Head.'" *Indian Country Today*, August 2. https://ictnews.org/opinion/castro-huerta-decision-flips-federal-indian-law-on-its-head.

Nagy, Rosemary, and Emily Gillespie. 2015. "Representing Reconciliation: A News Frame Analysis of Print Media Coverage of Indian Residential Schools." *Transitional Justice Review* 1, no. 3: Article 2.

NAJANewsroom.com. n.d. "Muscogee Creek Nation." Accessed 2020. https://najanewsroom.com/tag/muscogee-creek-nation/page/2/.

Nakata, Martin. 1998. "Anthropological Texts and Indigenous Standpoints." *Australian Aboriginal Studies (Canberra)* no. 2: 3–12. https://search.informit.org/doi/10.3316/informit.151991702568013.

———. 2004. *Indigenous Australian Studies and Higher Education.* Wentworth Lecture, Australian Institute of Aboriginal and Torres Strait Islander Studies, Canberra.

———. 2007. "The Cultural Interface." *The Australian Journal of Indigenous Education* 36, Supplement: 7–14. https://doi.org/10.1017/S1326011100004646.

National Collegiate Athletics Association. 2002. "Report on the Use of American Indian Mascots in Intercollegiate Athletics to the NCAA Executive Committee Subcommittee on Gender and Diversity Issues." Report, November 1. http://www.ncaa.org/wps/wcm/connect/NCAA/Legislation%20and%20Governance/Committees/Assoc-wide/Moic/2003/Mascot%20Report/mascotreport.htm.

———. 2005. "NCAA Executive Committee Issues Guidelines for Use of Native American Mascots at Championship Events." Press release, August 5. http://fs.ncaa.org/Docs/PressArchive/2005/Announcements/NCAA+Executive+Committee+Issues+Guidelines+for+Use+of+Native+American+Mascots+at+Championship+Events.html.

National Conference of State Legislatures. 2016. "State Recognition of American Indian Tribes." October 10. https://www.ncsl.org/quad-caucus/state-recognition-of-american-indian-tribes.

National Congress of American Indians. 2022. "The Castro-Huerta Decision: Understanding the Case and Discussing Next Steps." YouTube video, July 7, 1:37:18. https://www.youtube.com/watch?v=TJkKoMrp47s.

National Constitution Center. n.d. "Roe v. Wade (1973)." Accessed May 17, 2023. https://constitutioncenter.org/the-constitution/supreme-court-case-library/roe-v-wade.

National Geographic. n.d. "Native Americans and Freedom of Religion." Accessed October 18, 2023. https://education.nationalgeographic.org/resource/native-americans-and-freedom-religion/.

National Indian Child Welfare Association. n.d. "Indian Boarding Schools." https://www.nicwa.org/boarding-schools/.

———. 2018. "Setting the Record Straight: The Indian Child Welfare Act Fact Sheet." https://www.nicwa.org/wp-content/uploads/2025/02/Setting-the-Record-Straight-2018.pdf.

———. 2019. "Tracing Native Ancestry: A Guide to Responding to Inquiries." December. https://www.nicwa.org/wp-content/uploads/2020/10/Tracing-Your-Native-Ancestry-2019-Final.pdf.

———. 2021a. "The Indian Child Welfare Act: A Family's Guide: Answers to Your Questions About ICWA." October. https://www.nicwa.org/wp-content/uploads/2020/10/Family-Guide-to-ICWA-2018.pdf.

———. 2021b. "Disproportionality in Child Welfare Fact Sheet: What Is Disproportionality in Child Welfare?" October. https://old.nicwa.org/wp-content/uploads/2021/12/NICWA_11_2021-Disproportionality-Fact-Sheet.pdf.

National Institute of Health. 2009. "President Grant Advances 'Peace Policy' with Tribes—Timeline—Native Voices." Native Voices: National Institute of Health. https://boardingschoolhealing.org/us-indian-boarding-school-history/.

National Native American Boarding School Healing Coalition. 2019. "US Indian Boarding School History." Accessed 2019. https://www.nlm.nih.gov/nativevoices/timeline/342.html.

National Research Council. 1974. Rehabilitation *Potential of Western Coal Lands: A Report to the Energy Policy Project of the Ford Foundation.* Cambridge, MA: Ballinger.

Native American Journalists Association. n.d.a. "NAJA Calls upon News Media to Stop Using Mascots." Accessed December 8, 2004. http://www.naja.com/pr-stopmascot.html.

———. n.d.b. "Mission." Accessed May 29, 2023. https://najanewsroom.com/mission/.

———. n.d.c. "So You Need an Indigenous Expert." Accessed May 22, 2023. https://najanewsroom.com/reporting-guides/.

———. 2018. "Reporting and Indigenous Terminology." https://najanewsroom.com/wp-content/uploads/2018/11/NAJA_Reporting_and_Indigenous_Terminology_Guide.pdf.

Native American Journalists Association Director. 2018. "Journalism Organizations Urge the Muscogee (Creek) Nation to Reinstate Its Free Press Act." November 21. https://najanewsroom.com/2018/11/16/journalism-organizations-urge-the-muscogee-creek-nation-to-reinstate-its-free-press-act/.

Native American Journalists Association Executive Director. 2018. "NAJA Condemns Repeal of Muscogee (Creek) Free Press Act." November 9. https://najanewsroom.com/2018/11/09/naja-calls-on-the-muscogee-creek-national-council-to-protect-press-freedom-2/.

Native American Natural Foods. n.d. "About Tanka." Accessed August 23, 2023. https://tankabar.com/pages/about-tanka.

Native American Tea Company. n.d. "Native American Tea Company—Our Story." Accessed August 21, 2023. https://www.nativeamericantea.com/the-native-american-tea-company-our-story/.

Navajo Times. n.d. "Contact Us." Accessed June 13, 2022. https://navajotimes.com/contact-us/corporate/.

Nesper, Larry. 2002. *The Walleye War: The Struggle for Ojibwe Spearfishing and Treaty Rights*. Lincoln: University of Nebraska Press.

Nesterak, Max. 2019. *The 1950s Plan to Erase Indian Country*. American Public Media Reports. https://www.apmreports.org/episode/2019/11/01/uprooted-the-1950s-plan-to-erase-indian-country.

Newland, Bryan. 2022. "Federal Indian Boarding School Initiative Investigative Report." Bureau of Indian Affairs. May. https://www.bia.gov/sites/default/files/dup/inline-files/bsi_investigative_report_may_2022_508.pdf.

Ng, Christina. 2011. "Urban Outfitters Under Fire for 'Navajo' Collection: A Native American Woman Criticized the Company in an Open Letter to the CEO." *ABC News*, October 11. https://abcnews.go.com/US/urban-outfitters-fire-navajo-collection/story?id=14721931.

Noble, Marilyn. 2018. "Bison Bars were Supposed to Restore Native Communities and Grass-Based Ranches. Then Came Epic Provisions." *The Counter*, November 27. https://thecounter.org/tanka-bar-general-mills-epic-provisions-bison-bars/.

Norman-Hill, Rosemary. 2019. "Australia's Native Residential Schools." In *Residential Schools and Indigenous Peoples*. Routledge, 66–94.

Office of the United Nations High Commissioner for Human Rights. 2023. "China: UN Experts Alarmed by Separation of 1 Million Tibetan Children from Families and Forced Assimilation at Residential Schools." February 6. https://www.ohchr.org/en/press-releases/2023/02/china-un-experts-alarmed-separation-1-million-tibetan-children-families-and.

Oglesby, C. 1969. "Vietnamism Has Failed. The Revolution Can Only Be Mauled, Not Defeated." *Commonweal* 90: 11–12.

Ohio University. n.d. "My Culture Is Not a Costume." Accessed September 21, 2023. https://www.ohio.edu/diversity/diversity-leadership-ambassadors-program/cultural-appropriation.

Olivas, Kaylee. 2023. "Overreach of the State Government: Senate Passes Bill Limiting Reading Materials in Schools, Public Libraries." *KFOR*, March 8. https://kfor.com/news/oklahoma-legislature/senate-passes-bill-limiting-reading-materials-in-schools-and-public-libraries/.

Owen, Diana. 2010. "Media in the 2008 Election: 21st Century Campaign, Same Old Story." In *The Year of Obama: How Barack Obama Won the White House*. Edited by Larry Sabato. New York: Longman, 167–86.

Oyan, Katie. 2022. "Indigenous News Outlets, Nonprofits Drive Deeper Coverage." *Associated Press News*, January 11. https://apnews.com/article/business-media-journalism-phoenix-native-americans-6324ac76c0fca02e2e7f91cb80369bc1.

Pannett, Rachel. 2021. "Australia to Pay Hundreds of Millions in Reparations to Indigenous 'Stolen Generations.'" *The Washington Post*, August 5. https://www.washingtonpost.com/world/2021/08/05/australia-indigenous-school-reparation/.

Parker, B.A., Courtney Stein, and Christina Cala. 2023. "The Implications of the Case Against ICWA." NPR, May 17. https://www.npr.org/2023/05/09/1175041677/the-implications-of-the-case-against-icwa.

Pearl Milling Company. n.d.a. "Our History." Accessed July 10, 2023. https://www.pearlmillingcompany.com/our-history.

———. n.d.b. "P.E.A.R.L. Pledge." Accessed July 10, 2023. https://www.pearlmillingcompany.com/pearlpledge.

Pewewardy, Cornel. 1998. "Why Teachers Can't Afford to Ignore Indian Mascots." National Indian Education Association. Accessed September 19, 2002. http://earnestman.tripod.com/fr.education.htm.

Phillips, J. 2019. "Indigenous Australian Studies, Indigenist Standpoint Pedagogy, and Student Resistance." In *Oxford Research Encyclopedia of Education*. Edited by George W. Noblit. New York: Oxford University Press. https://doi.org/10.1093/acrefore/9780190264093.013.594.

Phoenix Archives. 2006. "The Cherokee Clan System." *Cherokee Phoenix*, February 10. https://www.cherokeephoenix.org/education/the-cherokee-clan-system/article_a88fcc42-f3f8-5f33-b575-8cff7d3bffd2.html.

Pinel, Elizabeth C. 1999. "Stigma Consciousness: The Psychological Legacy of Social Stereotypes." *Journal of Personality and Social Psychology* 76: 114–28.

Pope, A. 2024. "Cheyenne and Arapaho Tribes Receive Funds for Oklahoma Bison Herd Expansion." *KGOU*, January 12. https://www.kgou.org/indigenous-news/2024-01-12/cheyenne-and-arapaho-tribes-receive-funds-for-oklahoma-bison-herd-expansion.

PR Newswire. n.d. "Media Room, About PR Newswire." Accessed April 10, 2023. https://prnewswire.mediaroom.com/index.php.

———. 2022. "Native American Basketball Invitational (NABI) to Be Honored by Phoenix Suns and Phoenix Mercury for 20-Year History." November 23. https://www.prnewswire.com/news-releases/native-american-basketball

-invitational-nabi-to-be-honored-by-phoenix-suns-and-phoenix-mercury-for-20-year-history-301686505.html.

———. 2024. "What Is Earned Media? Definition, Benefits and Examples." October 15. https://www.prnewswire.co.uk/resources/articles/what-is-earned-media-definition-benefits-and-examples.

Pukui, Mary Kawena, and Samuel Elbert. 1986. *Hawaiian Dictionary: Hawaiian-English, English-Hawaiian.* Honolulu: University of Hawaii Press.

Pyles, D. G. 2016. "Rural Media Literacy: Youth Documentary Videomaking as a Rural Literacy Practice." *Journal of Research in Rural Education* 31, no. 7: 13. https://eric.ed.gov/?id=EJ1114833.

Quapaw Nation. n.d. "Ogahpah Constitution." Accessed June 7, 2023. http://quapawtribe.com.

Ramsar Wetlands Convention. 2012. *11th Conference of the Contracting Parties.* July 6–13, Bucharest, Romania.

Ramsey, Kelly. 2023. "Dear Los Angeles: You're Drinking Indigenous Water." *Sierra,* October 9. https://www.sierraclub.org/sierra/dear-los-angeles-you-re-drinking-indigenous-water.

Rao, S. 2011. "The 'local' in global media ethics." *Journalism Studies* 12, no. 6, 780–90. https://dx.doi.org/10.1080/1461670x.2011.614818.

Reclaiming Native Truth. 2018. *Changing the Narrative About Native Americans: A Guide for Allies.* Accessed August 23, 2023. https://e1.nmcdn.io/assets/rnt/wp-content/uploads/2018/06/MessageGuide-Allies-screen.pdf.

Reese, Linda. 2010. "Freedmen," *The Encyclopedia of Oklahoma History and Culture.* Last updated July 29, 2024. https://www.okhistory.org/publications/enc/entry?entry=FR016.

Reyhner, Jon. 2018. "American Indian Boarding Schools: What Went Wrong? What Is Going Right?" *Journal of American Indian Education* 57, no. 1: 58–78.

Rice, B. 2005. *Seeing the World with Aboriginal eyes: A Four Dimensional Perspective on Human and Non-Human Values, Cultures and Relationships on Turtle Island.* Winnipeg, Manitoba: Aboriginal Issues Press.

Rielly, Edward. 2022. *Native American Women Leaders: Fourteen Profiles.* Jefferson: McFarland & Company.

Rigney, Lester-Irabinna. 1997. "Internationalisation of an Indigenous Anticolonial Cultural Critique of Research Methodologies: A Guide to Indigenist Research Methodology and Its Principles." *Journal of American Studies* 14, no. 2: 109–22.

———. 1999. "The First Perspective: Culturally Safe Research Practices on or with Indigenous Peoples." 1999 Chacmool Conference Proceedings. University of Calgary. https://services.anu.edu.au/files/guidance/Foley_17Sept2019_Part2_0.pdf.

Riley, Angela. 2022. "The Ascension of Indigenous Cultural Property Law." *Michigan Law Review*, no. 121.1: 75.

Rix, E. F., S. Wilson, N. Sheehan, and N. Tujague. 2019. "Indigenist and Decolonizing Research Methodology." In *Handbook of Research Methods in Health Social Sciences*. Edited by P. Liamputtong. Springer Singapore, 253–67.

Rodriguez, Olga R. 2023. "Berkeley Professor Apologizes for False Indigenous Identity." *Associated Press*. May 5. https://apnews.com/article/berkeley-professor-false-native-identity-apology-dabc6d97dcb6f96aedc6c6c62b4975ee.

Rosenstein, Jay, dir. 1997. *In Whose Honor? American Indian Mascots in Sports*. New Day Productions.

Roth, Lorna. 2005. *Something New in the Air: The Story of First Peoples Television Broadcasting in Canada*. McGill-Queen's Native and Northern Series 43. Montreal: McGill-Queen's University Press.

Rothwell, N. 2001. "Noble Rot." *The Weekend Australian*. April 14.

Said, Edward. 1978. *Orientalism*. London: Routledge.

Sanchez, Victoria, Meta G. Carstarphen, and John P. Sanchez. 2012. "Buying into Racism: American Indian Product Icons in the American Marketplace." In *American Indians and the Mass Media*. Norman: University of Oklahoma Press, 153–69.

Sánchez-Rivera, Ana I., Paul Jacobs, and Cody Spence. "Detailed Data for Hundreds of American Indian and Alaska Native Tribes." Census.gov. October 3, 2023. https://www.census.gov/library/stories/2023/10/2020-census-dhc-a-aian-population.html.

Sasaki, Christen Tsuyuko. 2016. "Threads of Empire: Militourism and the Aloha Wear Industry in Hawai'i." *American Quarterly* 68, no. 3: 643–67.

Schmieding, Jana (@Janaunplgd). 2020. "Our power is and has always been in our love for each other, our love for this land and—through telling our own stories and pursuing autonomy—our love for ourselves." Instagram, December 29. https://www.instagram.com/p/CJZAF7UlNtn/.

———. 2022. "THANK YOU to beadwork buyers and abortion advocates and supporters for your participation in #BOBS beadwork drop today! We have collectively raised about $2500." Instagram, August 5. https://www.instagram.com/p/Cg5cHAvpUVw/.

Schneider, Lindsey, Joshua Sbicca, and Stephanie Malin. 2020. "Native American Tribes' Pandemic Response Is Hamstrung by Many Inequities." *The Conversation*, June 1. https://theconversation.com/native-american-tribes-pandemic-response-is-hamstrung-by-many-inequities-136225.

Schulman, Sandra Hale. 2023. "Writers Strike Hits Home for Indigenous TV Shows, Films." *Indian Country Today*, May 19. https://ictnews.org/news/writers-strike-hits-home-for-indigenous-tv-shows-films.

Schwartz, David. 2016. "Navajo Nation Settles Trademark Suit Against Urban Outfitters." *Reuters*, November 16. https://www.reuters.com/article/us-navajo-urbanoutfitters/navajo-nation-settles-trademark-suit-against-urban-outfitters-idUSKBN13D2QA.

Sciretta, Peter. 2016. "How Disney Formed the Oceanic Story Trust to Make Moana More Authentic." *Slash Film*, September 7. https://www.slashfilm.com/546367/moana-oceanic-story-trust/.

Scott, Henry. 2021. "Impeding the Free Press for Native Americans: Inside the Quest for Independent Journalism on Tribal Lands Across the Country." *Editor & Publisher*, December 3. https://www.editorandpublisher.com/stories/impeding-the-free-press-for-native-americans,210621.

Secretary Deb Haaland (@DebHaalandNM). 2020. "Violence rates against women and girls in Indian Country are 10x higher than the national average. Today is a National Day or Awareness for Missing & Murdered Native Women & Girls. Today I stand with the Native community and all who are fighting to provide equitable protection of Indigenous women. We can't ignore this #SilentCrisis we are #NotInvisible! #MMIW." Instagram, May 5. https://www.instagram.com/p/B_0jYerliGV/.

——— (@SecDebHaaland). 2020. "These are my parents. I salute them and all our Veterans and active duty service members. Far too many Americans have paid the ultimate sacrifice for this country. The President's view of our POWs and fallen service members is sickening. Our service members have more courage, and leadership than Trump could ever hope to have." Instagram, September 4. https://www.instagram.com/p/CEuv7KPF1P4/?img_index=1.

——— (@SecDebHaaland). 2020. "#BeFierce." Instagram, December 17. https://www.instagram.com/p/CI6xGPilf-K/.

——— (@SecDebHaaland). 2021. "I believe we all have a stake in the future of our country, and I believe that every one of us shares a common bond: our love for the outdoors and a desire and obligation to keep our nation livable for future generations. Thank you to the Senate Energy Committee for their vote of confidence." Instagram, March 4. https://www.instagram.com/p/CMAM7eNFy-O/.

——— (@SecDebHaaland). 2021. "Thank you @POTUS Biden and @VP Harris. I am honored and ready to work. I look forward to tackling some of the nation's most pressing issues with @USInterior so that future generations can enjoy our public lands and waters for years to come. Photo by Tami Heilemann, Department of the Interior." Instagram, March 18. https://www.instagram.com/p/CMkSEMfpf0p/.

——— (@SecDebHaaland). 2021. "Right now my heart is with George Floyd's daughter and with his family, and with many others. I want so badly for things to change. Justice must be a reality for people who haven't ever known it. #BlackLivesMatter." Instagram, April 20. https://www.instagram.com/p/CN6NxFGFN5i/.

——— (@SecDebHaaland). 2022. "I voted YES on background checks for every gun sale. I got an 'F' from the NRA. I'm immensely proud of both. #ProudOfMyF." Instagram, April 26. https://www.instagram.com/p/DMlLhnwtcFY/.

——— (@SecDebHaaland). 2022. "On this #LGBTQFamiliesDay and every day, I am so proud to be Somáh's mom." Instagram, June 1. https://www.instagram.com/p/CeRBUxErDEv/?hl=en.

——— (@SecDebHaaland). 2022. "Today, 1,000 acres of the Tully Valley in Central New York will be returned to the Onondaga Nation. It's a great day for locally led conservation and for the Onondaga people who have inhabited the area for centuries. As the original stewards of the land, the Onondaga Nation will use Indigenous knowledge to manage the area's wildlife and habitat." Instagram, June 29. https://www.instagram.com/p/CfZlPpJpVUU/.

——— (@SecDebHaaland). 2022. "To all veterans and the families who served alongside them, thank you. Happy Veterans Day, everyone." Instagram, November 11. https://www.instagram.com/p/Ck03akgD62V/.

——— (@SecDebHaaland). 2022. "On Red Shawl Day, we bring attention to the relatives who are impacted by the missing and murdered Indigenous peoples crisis. It's a day of remembrance and of commitment to continue our quest for justice. At U.S. Department of the Interior, we're making steady progress in pursuit of this work." Instagram, November 19. https://www.instagram.com/p/ClKUu5Wpbf6/.

——— (@SecDebHaaland). 2022. "During the holiday season, may we work toward a future that embraces our diverse traditions and backgrounds." Instagram, December 20. https://www.instagram.com/p/CmZt9fMJill/.

——— (@SecDebHaaland). 2023. "Words matter, particularly in our work to ensure our nation's public lands and waters are accessible and welcoming to people of all backgrounds. This is a big moment. We're showing why representation matters and charting a path for an inclusive America. I'm grateful to the members of the Derogatory Geographic Names Task Force and the Board on Geographic Names for their efforts to finalize the removal of this harmful word." Instagram, January 12. https://www.instagram.com/p/CnUufR9Bf3N/.

——— (@SecDebHaaland). 2023. "When I was raising my child Somáh, I didn't have a lot of money, so I relied on free opportunities to offer them experiences in the outdoors. Many of our adventures were to public parks or free @usfws refuges. @usinterior has a great list of Fee Free Days this year to help make our public lands accessible to all. It is my hope that the list of days offered at the link in my bio will help families experience the wonders of our public lands." Instagram, February 6. https://www.instagram.com/p/CoVF57CpbSu/.

——— (@SecDebHaaland). 2023. "The American bison is inextricably intertwined with Indigenous culture, grassland ecology and American history. While the overall recovery of bison over the last 130 years is a conservation success story, significant work remains to not only ensure that bison will remain a viable species but also to restore grassland ecosystem." Instagram, March 7. https://www.instagram.com/p/CpgOBLUJVQx/.

——— (@SecDebHaaland). 2023. "Outdoor recreation and conservation go hand in hand, and they have invaluable economic benefits for local communities. Today, I hosted a roundtable in Bend, OR to learn about how we can continue to invest in the outdoors, now and for the future." Instagram, March 17. https://www.instagram.com/p/Cp6UE-0Lw5D/.

——— (@SecDebHaaland). 2023. "As Secretary, I have the privilege to experience incredible places, visit our public lands, and bear witness to progress that is making our country better for future generations. I want to share some of that with you all. Each Sunday, I'll share a moment from my camera roll that made an impression on me." Instagram, March 26. https://www.instagram.com/p/CqRNxDZpDHP/.

——— (@SecDebHaaland). 2023. "In Washington State today, Assistant Secretary Newland and I heard from survivors of federal Indian boarding schools. The stories are heartbreaking and the day was heavy, but this work needs to be done in order to heal from the intergenerational trauma we carry. As our country learns more of this history, we can build a better future for the generations that come after us." Instagram, April 23. https://www.instagram.com/p/CrZKDuyJ68S/?img_index=1.

——— (@SecDebHaaland). 2023. "This 'Camera Roll Sunday,' I'm sharing this beautiful tree carving. Aboriginal communities in Australia use the bark of trees to build canoes, bowls and other tools. Instead of cutting down the whole tree for their use, they only take the piece that they need and the tree remains alive, but a scar is left behind." Instagram, May 14. https://www.instagram.com/p/CsPoXFspCg6/.

——— (@SecDebHaaland). 2023. "This 'Camera Roll Sunday' I'm sharing a photo of a file system. I know it doesn't seem significant, but this file system is leading to the digitization of records at the American Indian Records Repository. Staff at the Bureau of Trust Funds Administration are collecting, sorting, categorizing, and interpreting thousands and thousands of records associated with the Federal Indian Boarding School Initiative that we launched last year." Instagram, May 21. https://www.instagram.com/p/CshloekPXek/.

Sellars, Willie. 2021. "I'm Working Toward a Brighter Future for My First Nation Community—and I Need Canadians to Join Me." *CBC News*, September 30. https://www.cbc.ca/news/canada/british-columbia/national-day-for-truth-and-reconciliation-willie-sellars-1.6194824.

Selleck, Kristen L., Ashley M. Toland, and Joan M. Blakey. 2023. *From Denial to Disproportionality. Social Work, White Supremacy, and Racial Justice: Reckoning with Our History, Interrogating Our Present, Reimagining Our Future.* Oxford Academic.

Seyler, Lainey. 2018. "A small radio station helped fight racism in Northwoods. Now it's fighting for its life." *Milwaukee Journal Sentinel*, September 12. https://eu.jsonline.com/story/entertainment/2018/09/12/wojb-community-radio-fought-racism-wisconsin-but-its-future-unknown/1147418002/.

Shantz-Hilkes, Chloe, and Sheena Goodyear. 2020. "New Film Waikiki Shows Dark, Colonial Underbelly of Hawaii's Tourism Paradise." *CBC Radio*,

October 28. https://www.cbc.ca/radio/asithappens/as-it-happens-wednesday-edition-1.5780121/new-film-waikiki-shows-dark-colonial-underbelly-of-hawaii-s-tourism-paradise-1.5780518.

Shearer, Elisa, Katerina Eva Matsa, Amy Mitchell, Mark Jurkowitz, Kirsten Worden, and Naomi Forman-Katz. 2022. "Total Number of U.S. Statehouse Reporters Rises, But Fewer Are on the Beat Full Time." Pew Research Center, April 5. https://www.pewresearch.org/journalism/2022/04/05/total-number-of-u-s-statehouse-reporters-rises-but-fewer-are-on-the-beat-full-time/.

Sheehan, N. 2001. "Some Call It Culture: Aboriginal Identity and the Imaginary Moral Centre." In *Social Alternatives* 20: 29–33. Queensland: Sunshine Coast University.

Shoemaker, Pamela J., and Stephen D. Reese. 2014. *Mediating the Message in the 21st Century: A Media Sociology Perspective*. 3rd ed. New York: Routledge/Taylor & Francis Group.

Shohat, Ella, and Robert Stam. 1994. *Unthinking Eurocentrism: Multiculturalism and the Media*. Philadelphia: Routledge.

Siebert, Fred S., Theodore Peterson, and Wilbur Schramm. 1984. *Four Theories of the Press: The Authoritarian, Libertarian, Social Responsibility, and Soviet Communist Concepts of What the Press Should Be and Do*. University of Illinois Press.

Simpson, L. 2000. "Anishinaabe Ways of Knowing." In *Aboriginal Health, Identity and Resources*. Edited by J. Oakes, R. Riew, S. Koolage, L. Simpson, and N. Schuster. Winnipeg, Manitoba: Native Studies Press, 165–85.

Sioux Chief Manufacturing Co. n.d. "Sioux Chief History." Accessed July 31, 2023. https://www.siouxchief.com/about-us/history.

Slotnick, Elliot, and Jennifer Segal. 1998. *Television News and the Supreme Court: All the News That's Fit to Air?* Cambridge: Cambridge University Press.

Smiles, Deondre. n.d. "Erasing Indigenous History, Then and Now." *Origins*. Accessed October 18, 2023. https://origins.osu.edu/article/erasing-indigenous-history-then-and-now.

Smith, Linda Tuhiwai. 2012. *Decolonizing Methodologies: Research and Indigenous Peoples*. 2nd ed. Zed Books.

———. 2021. *Decolonizing Methodologies: Research and Indigenous Peoples*. 3rd ed. Zed Books.

Snodgrass, Erin. 2022. "Which Supreme Court Justices Voted to Overturn Roe v. Wade? Here's Where All 9 Judges Stand." *Business Insider*, June 24. https://www.businessinsider.com/which-supreme-court-justices-voted-to-overturn-roe-v-wade-2022-6.

Snyder, Mark. 1984. "When Belief Creates Reality." In *Advances in Experimental Social Psychology*. Edited by Leonard Berkowitz. Vol. 25. San Diego: Academic Press, 248–306.

Solomon, Michael. 2009. "Saving the 'Slaves of Kings and Priests': The United States, Manifest Destiny, and the Rhetoric of Anti-Catholicism." Thesis. Duquesne University. https://dsc.duq.edu/etd/1225.

Spears, Nancy Marie. 2022. "How a Chippewa Grandmother's Adoption Fight Ended Up in the U.S. Supreme Court." *The Imprint*, November 2. https://cheyennearapahotribaltribune.wordpress.com/2022/11/02/how-a-chippewa-grandmothers-adoption-fight-ended-up-in-the-u-s-supreme-court/.

———. 2023a. "What Our Kids Stand to Lose: Reporting on Children's Rights." SXSW Global Conference, Austin Convention Center, March 12. Audio recording, 1:03:25. https://schedule.sxsw.com/2023/events/PP1142587.

———. 2023b. "Supreme Court Upholds Indian Child Welfare Act." *The Imprint*, June 15. https://imprintnews.org/icwa/indian-child-welfare-act-stands-native-families-empowered/242263?utm_source=chatgpt.com.

———. 2023c. "ICWA Challenges Could Still Loom in State Courts." *The Imprint*, August 9. https://imprintnews.org/top-stories/supreme-court-upheld-icwa-but-challenges-could-loom-in-state-courts/243522.

Spencer, Steven J., Claude M. Steele, and Diane M. Quinn. 2002. "Stereotype Threat and Women's Math Performance." In *Readings in the Psychology of Gender: Exploring Our Differences and Commonalities*. Edited by Anne E. Hunter and Carie Forden. Needham Heights, MA: Allyn & Bacon, 54–68.

Spring, Joel. 2012. *The Cultural Transformation of a Native American Family and Its Tribe 1763–1995: A Basket of Apples*. Taylor Francis.

Srinivasan, A. 2004. *Local and Indigenous Knowledge (LINK) for Adaptation to Climate Change*. Japan: Institute for Global Environment Strategies.

Staurowsky, Ellen J. 1999. "American Indian Imagery and the Miseducation of America." *Questj* 4: 382–92.

Steele, Claude M. 1997. "A Threat in the Air: How Stereotypes Shape Intellectual Identity and Performance." *American Psychologist* 52, no. 6: 613–29.

———. 1998. "Stereotyping and Its Threat Are Real." *American Psychologist* 53, no. 6: 680–81.

———, and Joshua Aronson. 1995. "Stereotype Threat and the Intellectual Test Performance of African Americans." *Journal of Personality and Social Psychology* 69, no. 5: 797–811.

Steele, Jeffrey. 1996. "Reduced to Images: American Indians in Nineteenth-Century Advertising." In *Dressing in Feathers: The Construction of the Indian in American Popular Culture*. Edited by S. Elizabeth Bird. New York: Westview, 45–64.

Steinhauer, Jennifer. 2021. *The Firsts: The Inside Story of the Women Reshaping Congress*. Algonquin Books.

Sterritt, Angela. 2021. "Investigation at B.C. Residential School Only Just Beginning, Tk'emlúps te Secwépemc Chief Says." *CBC News*, June 4. https://www.cbc.ca/news/canada/british-columbia/kamloops-residential-school-remains-update-1.6053467.

Stone, Deborah, Eva Trinh, Hong Zhou, Laura Welder, Pamela End of Horn, Katherine Fowler, and Asha Ivey-Stephenson. 2022. "Morbidity and Mortality Weekly Report." Centers for Disease Control and Prevention, September 16. https://www.cdc.gov/mmwr/volumes/71/wr/mm7137a1.htm.

Strickland, Rennard. 2010. "Cherokee (Tribe)." *The Encyclopedia of Oklahoma History and Culture*, January 15. Last updated November 13, 2024. https://www.okhistory.org/publications/enc/entry?entry=CH014.

Strinati, Dominic. 1995. *An Introduction to Theories of Popular Culture.* London: Routledge.

Stuckey, Mary E. 2014. "Arguing Sideways: The 1491's I'm an Indian Too." In *Disturbing Argument: Selected Works from the 18th NCA/AFA Alta Conference on Argumentation.* Edited by Catherine Palcweski. New York: Routledge, 75–80.

Suciati, Pijar, Mareta Maulidiyanti, and Ngurah Rangga Wiwesa. 2021. "The Public Relations Acceptance Towards Press Release Application with Artificial Intelligence." *Communicare: Journal of Communication Studies* 8(1): 20–40. https://doi.org/10.37535/101008120212.

Supreme Court of the Muscogee (Creek) Nation. 1979. "Muscogee Constitution (Annotated)." Accessed June 2, 2023, http://www.creeksupremecourt.com/mcn-constitutiion/.

Supreme Court of the United States. 2013. "Adoptive Couple v. Baby Girl." SCOTUSblog.com, June 25. https://www.scotusblog.com/cases/case-files/adoptive-couple-v-baby-girl/.

———. 2023. "Brackeen v. Haaland Opinion." https://www.supremecourt.gov/opinions/22pdf/21-376_7148.pdf?utm_source=chatgpt.com. Accessed 2022.

Switters, J. R. (@TheOriginalVoice). 2022. "I think I've been locked into a shadow ban." TikTok, August 21. https://www.tiktok.com/@theoriginalvoice/video/7134440818370301230?_r=1&_t=8aoS4FuRJXS.

Tachine, Amanda and Z. Nicolazzo. 2022. "Introduction." In *Weaving an Otherwise: In-Relations Methodological Practice.* Edited by Z. Nicolazzo, Leigh Patel, and K. Wayne Yang. Sterling, Virginia: Stylus, 1–11.

Taekema, Dan. 2021. "Six Nations Calls on Ottawa to Provide Radar to Search Former Residential School Site." *CBC News*, June 1. https://www.cbc.ca/news/canada/hamilton/six-nations-mohawk-institute-1.6047349.

Tallent, Rebecca J., and Rubell S. Dingman. 2011. "Cherokee Independent Press Act of 2000." *Journal of Communication Inquiry* 35, no. 2 (July): 252–74. https://doi.org/10.1177/0196859911413.

Tamaira, Mārata Ketekiri, and Dionne Fonoti. 2018. "Beyond Paradise? Retelling Pacific Stories in Disney's Moana." *The Contemporary Pacific* 30, no. 2: 297–327.

Tandoc Jr., Edson C., and Andrew Duffy. 2019. "Routines in Journalism." In *Oxford Research Encyclopedia of Communication.* Edited by Edson C. Tandoc Jr. and Andrew Duffy. Oxford University Press. https://oxfordre.com/communication/display/10.1093/acrefore/9780190228613.001.0001/acrefore-9780190228613-e-870.

Tanner, Andrea, and Daniela B. Friedman. 2011. "Authorship and Information Sourcing for Health News on Local TV Web Sites: An Exploratory Analysis." *Science Communication* 33, no. 1: 3–27.

Teaiwa, Teresia. 2016. "Postscript: Reflections on Militourism, US Imperialism, and American Studies." *American Quarterly* 68, no. 3: 847–53.

Terra. 2022. "Why Ashley Hann and Gerard Adams Are Being Canceled." *Where Is The Buzz*, November 5. Accessed August 6, 2023. https://whereisthebuzz.com/why-ashley-hann-and-gerard-adams-are-being-canceled/.

Thambinathan, V., and E. A. Kinsella. 2021. "Decolonizing Methodologies in Qualitative Research: Creating Spaces for Transformative Praxis." *International Journal of Qualitative Methods* 20 (May): 1–9. https://doi.org/10.1177/16094069211014766.

Thornton, Russell. *American Indian Holocaust and Survival: A Population History Since 1492*. 1st ed. Norman: University of Oklahoma Press.

Tillery, Alvin. 2021. "Tweeting Racial Representation: How the Congressional Black Caucus Used Twitter in the 113th Congress." *Politics, Groups, and Identities* 9, no. 2: 219–38.

Tilsen-Brave-Heart, Kim. 2012. "The Uproar Over Gap's 'Manifest Destiny' T-Shirt." *HuffPost*, December 25. https://www.huffpost.com/entry/gap-manifest-destiny-shirt_b_2017487.

Tokuyama, Evelyn. 2021. "Discrimination Increases Risk for Mental Health Issues in Young Adults, UCLA-Led Study Finds." Press release, University of California Los Angeles, November 7. https://newsroom.ucla.edu/releases/discrimination-risk-mental-health-young-adults.

Toohey, P. 2001. "Jedda Star Fights Culture of Rape." *The Weekend Australian*, April 14.

———. 2021. "Sticks and Stones." *The Weekend Australian*, April 14.

Trask, Haunani. 1999. *From a Native Daughter: Colonialism and Sovereignty in Hawai'i*. Honolulu: University of Hawaii Press.

Tuck, Eve, and K. Wayne Yang. 2012. "Decolonization Is Not a Metaphor." *Decolonization: Indigeneity, Education & Society* 1, no. 1: 1–40. https://jps.library.utoronto.ca/index.php/des/article/view/18630.

TurtleTalk. 2024. "Comprehensive State ICWA Laws." https://turtletalk.blog/icwa/comprehensive-state-icwa-laws/.

TVGuide.com. 2023. "Bad Press." Accessed 2024. https://www.tvguide.com/movies/bad-press/2060117692/.

Tynan, Timothy, and Patty Loew. 2010. "Organic Video Approach: Using New Media to Engage Youth in Science." *American Indian Culture and Research Journal* 34, no. 4: 8–9, https://eric.ed.gov/?id=EJ913000.

UNESCO. 2025. *Indigenous Peoples and the Media.* Paris: UNESCO. https://unesdoc.unesco.org/ark:/48223/pf0000393487.

United Keetoowah Band of Cherokee Indians in Oklahoma. n.d. https://www.ukb-nsn.gov/.

United Nations Declaration on the Rights of Indigenous Peoples. 2007. https://www.un.org/development/desa/Indigenouspeoples/wp-content/uploads/sites/19/2018/11/UNDRIP_E_web.pdf.

United Nations Genocide Convention. 1948. “Genocide Convention Factsheet.” UnitedNations.org. https://www.un.org/en/genocideprevention/documents/atrocity-crimes/Doc.1_Convention%20on%20the%20Prevention%20and%20Punishment%20of%20the%20Crime%20of%20Genocide.pdf.

US Census Bureau. n.d. “Table P8.” Accessed September 10, 2023. http://factfinder2.census.gov/faces/tableservices/jsf/pages/productview.xhtml.

US Commission on Civil Rights. 2001. “Commission Statement on the Use of Native American Images and Nicknames as Sports Symbols.” Accessed June 27, 2011. http://www.usccr.gov/press/archives/2001/041601st.htm.

US Department of the Interior. 1990. “The Indian Arts and Crafts Act of 1990 (P.L. 101–644).” Accessed August 3, 2023. https://www.doi.gov/iacb/act.

———. 2021a. “Secretary Haaland Announces Federal Indian Boarding School Initiative.” Press release, June 22. https://www.doi.gov/pressreleases/secretary-haaland-announces-federal-indian-boarding-school-initiative.

———. 2021b. “Secretary Haaland Takes Action to Remove Derogatory Names from Federal Lands.” Press release, November 19. https://www.doi.gov/pressreleases/secretary-haaland-takes-action-remove-derogatory-names-federal-lands.

———. 2022. “Department of the Interior Releases Investigative Report, Outlines Next Steps in Federal Indian Boarding School Initiative.” Press release, May 11. https://www.doi.gov/pressreleases/department-interior-releases-investigative-report-outlines-next-steps-federal-indian.

US Government. n.d. “Federally Recognized American Indian Tribes and Alaska Native Entities.” Accessed April 6, 2023. https://www.usa.gov/indian-tribes-alaska-native.

US Government Accountability Office. n.d. “Investigation of Allegations Concerning Indian Health Service.” Accessed May 17, 2023. https://www.gao.gov/products/hrd-77-3.

USA Today. 2012. “Victoria’s Secret Apologizes for Using Headdress.” November 11. https://www.usatoday.com/story/life/people/2012/11/12/victorias-secret-apologizes-for-use-of-headdress/1701413/.

Vanian, Jonathan. 2023. “NBCUniversal Ad Chief Linda Yaccarino in Talks to Succeed Elon Musk as Twitter CEO.” *CNBC*, May 11. https://www.cnbc.com/2023/05/11/elon-musk-says-hes-stepping-down-as-twitter-ceo-will-oversee-product.html.

Victoria’s Secret (@VictoriasSecret). 2012a. “We are sorry that the Native American headdress in our fashion show has upset individuals. The outfit will be removed from the broadcast.” Twitter, November 10, 4:16 p.m. https://twitter.com/VictoriasSecret/status/267390293794512896.

———. 2012b. “We are sorry . . .” Facebook, November 12. Accessed August 6, 2023. https://www.facebook.com/victoriassecret/posts/we-are-sorry-that-the-native-american-headdress-replica-used-in-our-recent-fashi/10151263247814090/.

Vizenor, Gerald Robert. 2008. *Survivance: Narratives of Native Presence*. Lincoln: University of Nebraska Press.

Vogel, Verity Saige. 2022. *A Look at the Missing and Murdered Indigenous Women Crisis: Investigation of Potential Causes and Effects*. Portland State University.

von Oldershausen, Sasha. 2016. "Standing Rock Pipeline Fight Draws Hundreds to North Dakota Plains." *NBC News*, October 17. http://www.nbcnews.com/news/us-news/standing-rock-pipeline-fight-draws-hundreds-north-dakota-plains-n665956.

Wagner, Angelia, Karen Bird, Joanna Everitt, and Mireille Lalancette. 2023. "Holding Back the Race Card: Black Candidates, Twitter, and the 2021 Canadian Election." *The Journal of Race, Ethnicity, and Politics* 8, no. 2: 164–81. https://doi.org/10.1017/rep.2023.11.

Wagner, Jovonne, and Kolby KickingWoman. 2023. "Montana TikTok Ban Brings Questions About Digital Sovereignty." *Indian Country Today*, May 19. https://ictnews.org/news/montana-tiktok-ban-brings-questions-about-digital sovereignty.

Walker, D. H., F. L. Sinclair, and B. Thapa. 1995. "Incorporation of Indigenous Knowledge and Perspectives in Agroforestry Development." *Agroforestry Systems* 30, no. 1–2, 235–48.

Walking Bull, Alfred (@Hoyekiyapi). 2022. "If #SCOTUS says prayer in school is fine, I say: SAGE THE FUCK OUT OF EVERYTHING ANS CALL THOSE ANCESTORS INTO YOUR CLASSROOM TO DROP SOME #INDIGENOUS WISDOM." Twitter, June 28, 10:58 a.m. https://twitter.com/hoyekiyapi/status/1541812056705433600.

Walter, Maggie. 2021. *Indigenous Data Sovereignty and Policy*. Routledge Studies in Indigenous Peoples and Policy. Abingdon, Oxon, New York, NY: Routledge.

Watson, Bridgette, and Sterritt, Angela. 2021. "Taking Back Tk'emlúps." *CBC News*, September 30. https://newsinteractives.cbc.ca/longform/taking-back-tkemlups/.

Watts, Terra. 2022. "Why Ashley Hann and Gerard Adams Are Being Canceled." *Where Is The Buzz*, November 5. https://whereisthebuzz.com/why-ashley-hann-and-gerard-adams-are-being-canceled/.

Weaver, C. Kay. 2018. "The Slow Conflation of Public Relations and Activism: Understanding Trajectories in Public Relations Theorising." In *Protest Public Relations: Communication Dissent And Activism*. Edited by Ana Adi. Routledge, 12–28.

Weeks, Rose. 2021. "New Data Shows COVID-19's Disproportionate Impact on American Indian, Alaska Native Tribes." Johns Hopkin's University Hub, October 11. https://hub.jhu.edu/2021/10/11/map-covid-19-impact-american-indian-population/.

Weizhun, Mao, and Bu Yongguang. 2016. "Sovereignty as Responsibility: Intellectual Sources, Evolving Paths, and Theoretical Debates." *International*

Security Studies March: 95–119. https://www.researchgate.net/publication/299368050_Sovereignty_as_Responsibility_Intellectual_SourcesEvolving_Paths_and_Theoretical_Debates.imp.

Western Native Voice. n.d. "About Us." Accessed May 26, 2023. https://westernnativevoice.org/about-us/.

——— (@WNativeVoice). 2023. "Before ICWA, Native children were systematically separated from their families and communities by state and private adoption agencies without evidence of harm." Twitter, May 16, 10:56 a.m. https://twitter.com/wnativevoice/status/1658486667270057988.

Weston, Mary Ann. 1996. *Native Americans in the News: Images of Indians in the Twentieth Century Press*. Contributions to the Study of Mass Media and Communications, no. 49. Westport, CT: Greenwood Press.

Wilkinson, Charles F. 2005. *Blood Struggle: The Rise of Modern Indian Nations*. 1st ed. New York: Norton.

Williams, David R., Harold W. Neighbors, and James S. Jackson. 2003. "Racial/Ethnic Discrimination and Health: Findings from Community Studies." *American Journal of Public Health* 93, no. 2: 200–8.

Williams, Doug. 1994. "In Defense of the (Properly Executed) Press Release." *Public Relations Quarterly* 39, no. 3 (Fall): 5–7. https://search-ebscohost-com.proxy.library.ohio.edu/login.aspx?direct=true&db=bth&AN=9412092092&site=eds-live&scope=site.

Wilson, Pamela, and Michelle Stewart. 2008. "Indigeneity and Indigenous Media on the Global Stage." In *Global Indigenous Media: Cultures, Poetics, and Politics*. Edited by Pamela Wilson and Michelle Stewart. Durham: Duke University Press, 1–35.

Win, Wasuta W. 2021. "Sarah Deer: Finding Her Way to Justice." *Lakota Times*, April 15. https://www.lakotatimes.com/articles/sarah-deer-finding-her-way-to-justice/.

Winslett, G., and Phillips, J. 2005. "ICTs and Indigenous Pedagogy: Techniques of Resistance in Chat Rooms." *Balance, Fidelity, Mobility: Maintaining the Momentum?* Ascilite Conference, 729–34.

Wisconsin Federation of Tribes. 2014. "A Joint Letter from Six Bands of the Anishinaabeg Territory Watersheds Waters of Lake Superior." May 27. http://midwestadvocates.org/assets/resources/Penokee%20Hills /ChippewaFederation_404cNotice_27May2014_(5).pdf.

Wohling, M. 2009. "The Problem of Scale in Indigenous Knowledge: A Perspective from Northern Australia." *Ecology and Society* 14, no. 1 (June). http://www.jstor.org/stable/26268043.

Wolverton, Brad. 2007. "After Years of Debate, U. of Illinois Drums Out Its Controversial Mascot." *The Chronicle of Higher Education*, March 2. http://chronicle.com/article/After-Years-of-Debate-U-of/21707/.

Woodward, Agnes (@Reecreeations). 2021. "Wearing it [the ribbon skirt] in this day and age is an act of self-empowerment and reclamation of who we are, and that gives us the opportunity to proudly make bold statements in front of others who sometimes refuse to see us." Instagram, March 18. https://www.instagram.com/p/CMkpxMorb6v/?img_index=1.

Woolf, Nicky. 2016. "Urban Outfitters Settles with Navajo Nation After Illegally Using Tribe's Name." *The Guardian*, November 18. https://www.theguardian.com/us-news/2016/nov/18/urban-outfitters-navajo-nation-settlement.

Woolford, Andrew. 2021. *Did You See Us?: Reunion, Remembrance, and Reclamation at an Urban Indian Residential School*. Winnipeg, Manitoba: University of Manitoba Press.

World Affairs (@World_Affairs). 2022. "Tribal rights are guaranteed by the US Constitution, but the #ICWA #HaalandvBrackeen case currently before #SCOTUS is a reminder that #Indigenous sovereignty." Twitter, December 4, 8:00 p.m. https://twitter.com/world_affairs/status/1599584389649907716.

Wright, Amy L., Rachel VanEvery, David Johnson, Landon Martin, Clare McGall, Jennifer K. Cano, and Heather Burnside. 2022. "International Perspectives on the Role of Indigenous Fathers in Caring for Their Infants: A Scoping Study." *The International Indigenous Policy Journal* 13, no. 3. https://doi.org/10.18584/iipj.2022.13.3.14491.

Wu, Katherine J. 2020. "Land O'Lakes Drops the Iconic Logo of an Indigenous Woman from Its Branding: The Story Behind the Image, and Its Removal, Led to Mixed Reactions from the Public, Including Native Communities." *Smithsonian Magazine*, April 28. Accessed July 12, 2023. https://www.smithsonianmag.com/smart-news/mia-land-olakes-iconic-indigenous-woman-departs-packaging-mixed-reactions-180974760/.

Yang, Angela. 2024. "'Moana 2' Leads in Highest-Grossing Thanksgiving Weekend Ever at Box Office." *NBC News*, December 1. Accessed December 31, 2024. https://www.nbcnews.com/news/us-news/moana-2-thanksgiving-box-office-record-rcna182346.

Yin, Robert K. 2009. "How to Do Better Case Studies (With Illustrations from 20 Exemplary Case Studies)." *The SAGE Handbook of Applied Social Research Methods* 2, 254–82. https://doi.org/10.4135/9781483348858.n8.

Zilber, Jeremy, and David Niven. 2000. "Stereotypes in the News: Media Coverage of African-Americans in Congress." *Harvard International Journal of Press/Politics* 5, no.1: 32–49.

Zimmermann, Patricia R., and Sean Zimmermann Auyash. n.d. *Nanook of the North*. Accessed June 30, 2023. https://www.loc.gov/static/programs/national-film-preservation-board/documents/nanook2.pdf.

List of Contributors

Cristina L. Azocar is a citizen of the Upper Mattaponi Indian Tribe and a professor of journalism at San Francisco State University. She is the author of *News Media and the Indigenous Fight for Federal Recognition*. Her research focuses on the intersection of race and journalistic practice, particularly in the area of news coverage of Indigenous people. Azocar served as a past president of the Native American Journalists Association, was an editor of *American Indian Issues* for the Media Diversity Forum, and was an inaugural board member of the Women's Media Center.

Meta G. Carstarphen is professor emerita in the Gaylord College of Journalism and Mass Communication at the University of Oklahoma. Carstarphen's research explores media storytelling and public relations, especially through their portrayals of culture and communities. She has received twenty awards and distinctions for her research and leadership. Additionally, Carstarphen has authored, co-authored, and/or co-edited eight books and twenty-one book chapters, and has served on more than sixty-five invited national and international panels. Her forthcoming book, *Writing Home* (Peter Lang Publishers), explores the influences of nineteenth-century newspapers published in pre-statehood Oklahoma on race, culture, and statehood. Carstarphen also serves as editor-in-chief of *Communication Booknotes Quarterly* (Taylor & Francis), a journal that curates book reviews about media and society.

Ryan N. Comfort (Keweenaw Bay Indian Community) studies Indigenous science and environmental communication, while continuing to make pictures and take on media assignments related to these topics. He uses theories and frameworks from media sociology and media effects, often with a twist of Indigenous epistemology, to understand how we might increase both the prevalence and efficacy of Indigenous science and environmental media. His research has been published in academic journals including *Journalism and Mass Communication Quarterly*, *Science Communication*, and *Environmental Communication*. His photography and video work has appeared in local, national, and tribal media outlets.

Dennis Foung is a lecturer in the School of Journalism, Writing, and Media at the University of British Columbia, Canada. He holds a doctorate in language education and several academic qualifications in language studies, human resource management, vocational education, and data science. He has a keen interest in computational methods and explores their application across various disciplines, including education and journalism.

Litzy Galarza is an assistant professor in the Department of Communication at the University of Pittsburgh. Galarza's scholarship focuses on Latina/o/x labor, representation, and citizenship in popular media, including television, film, and advertising. Galarza's work has appeared in the journals *Communication and Race*, the *Howard Journal of Communications*, the *International Journal of Communication, The Routledge Companion to Advertising and Promotional Culture, Immigrant Generations, Media Representations, Audiences*, and *The Routledge Companion to Media and Class*. Galarza teaches courses in Latina/o/x media, media and consumer culture, television and society, race, class, and gender in popular media, and media law.

Kevin R. Kemper has taught at higher educational institutions like the Gaylord College of Journalism and Mass Communication at the University of Oklahoma. He is also a candidate for a Master of Liberal Arts in Extension Studies for Creative Writing and Literature with Harvard Extension School. His academic scholarship has focused on Indigenous peoples, civil liberties, media representation, and access to information. He now practices law full-time in state and federal courts in Oklahoma and numerous tribal courts around Oklahoma, Kansas, and Montana. No part of his chapter in this book establishes an attorney–client relationship or should be considered legal advice.

Benjamin LaPoe received his master's in journalism from West Virginia University and his Ph.D. in political communications from the Manship School at Louisiana State University. His research focuses on the intersections or intercultural communications, political communications, and social media.

Victoria LaPoe is a professor of journalism at the University of Cincinnati. LaPoe's research focuses on digital media, public relations, and media inclusivity. Previously, she served as overall broadcasting and film sequence coordinator at Western Kentucky University's School of Journalism and Broadcasting. LaPoe is a lifetime member of the Indigenous Journalists Association and was vice president of the (then) Native American Journalists Association (2017–2019). She has been on the Indigenous Journalists Association/Native American Journalists Association's education committee since 2015. LaPoe has published four books, including *Indian Country: Telling a Story in a Digital Age.*

Sarah Liese is Diné and an enrolled member of the Turtle Mountain Band of Chippewa Indians. She works as an Indigenous affairs reporter at KOSU Radio in Oklahoma City. Her previous work focused on Indigenous research, documentary film, public relations, and broadcast journalism. She has received multiple fellowships from the Indigenous Journalists Association and the Sundance Institute and was awarded the Outstanding Master's Student Award in 2022 from the E. W. Scripps School of Journalism.

Patty Loew is professor emerita in the Medill School of Journalism and inaugural director of the Center for Native American and Indigenous Research at Northwestern University (retired). A citizen of Mashkiiziibii, the Bad River Band of Lake Superior Ojibwe, Loew is the author of four award-winning books and dozens of documentaries for commercial and public television. Loew writes extensively about treaty rights, sovereignty, and the role of Native media in communicating Indigenous worldviews. She is a member of the American Academy of Arts and Sciences and a recipient of Wisconsin's Martin Luther King Jr. Heritage Award.

Colby Y. Miyose is associate professor at the University of Hawaiʻi at Hilo in the Department of Communication. Miyose is an Asian American/Pasifika scholar of media and its influence on hegemonic ideology and identity formation. Miyose was elected second vice chair for the Asian Pacific American Caucus and Communication Studies Division for the National Communication Association. Miyose's works include, "Eh . . . You Hawaiian?: Kānaka Maoli and ʻAina in Hawaii Five-0" and

"Unrealistic Weeds of Love and Romance: Galician's Loves Myths in 'Flower Boy' K-Dramas."

Taylor Orcutt is a journalism and political science student at Ohio University. She is an Indigenous media researcher mentored by Victoria LaPoe, and a non-Indigenous associate member of the Indigenous Journalists Association. Taylor's research comprises Indigenous press functions and media representations of Indigenous peoples from gender, historical, and political angles. Taylor is a news reporter for her local newspaper, the *Athens Messenger*, and co-founder of the Society of Athens Preservation. She dedicates her work to her parents, consistent supporters of her education and research.

Newly Paul is an associate professor of journalism at the University of North Texas in Denton. Her research interests include intercultural communication, media coverage of race and gender, and entertainment studies. She teaches various classes, such as principles of news, news reporting and writing, copy editing, mass communication and society, political reporting, and minorities in media. Her research has won grants and awards. Before joining academia, she was a journalist who covered city government, crime, education, and politics. She received her Ph.D. in media and public affairs from Louisiana State University and her master's degree in journalism from the University of Southern California.

Victoria E. Sanchez is associate dean for educational equity in the College of Earth and Mineral Sciences at Penn State. As part of the college's leadership team, she works with administrators, faculty, staff, students, and alumni to promote a culture of belonging and advance diversity, equity, and inclusion initiatives. She is assistant coordinator of the annual Penn State traditional American Indian Powwow, founded in 2004. Sanchez holds a Ph.D. in English from The Ohio State University and has been at Penn State for over twenty-five years. She has articles in *Communication Studies, Western Journal of Communication, Southern Folklore*, and other publications.

Nancy Marie Spears is a citizen of the Cherokee Nation. They work nationally covering Indigenous children and families, with a focus on the Indian Child Welfare Act and the impact of boarding schools. They earned their bachelor's degree in journalism with distinction from the University of Oklahoma and received top honors from the Native American Journalists Association, as well as two first-place awards and one second-place prize for their coverage of environmental, health, and elder issues in Indigenous communities. Nancy is former president of the Indigenous Media Freedom Alliance, and their stories for *The Imprint* are co-published with news outlets across the country.

Tsanavi Spoonhunter is a citizen of the Northern Arapaho Tribe and a descendant of the Northern Paiute Tribe. She is a nonfiction storyteller based in the Reno-Lake Tahoe area, and she serves as a director, producer, and writer. She holds a master's in journalism from the University of California, Berkeley, with a documentary film concentration. In 2023, she founded the independent multimedia company Mahebe Media. Currently, Spoonhunter is a fellow at Open Society Foundations, and is a Chicken & Egg Pictures (now Chicken & Egg Films) and Independent Television Service grantee.

Index

2015 Free Press Act, 74
2SLGBTQIA, 110. *See also* Two Spirit

Aboriginal Peoples Television Network in Canada (APTN), 31, 136
abortion, 104–6, 110. *See also* health care
activism, 177, 220
adoption, 21, 83–84, 93, 113–114
Adoptive Couple v. Baby Girl, 82, 86, 90
advertising: and African Americans, 213, 215; American Indian Arts and Crafts Act, 225; American Indian Mental Health Association of Minnesota on, 223; by American Spirit cigarettes, 224; by AriZona iced tea, 224; beginnings of use of Indigenous imagery, 217, 220; by Big Chief imitation vanilla, 224; by Big Chief sugar, 217; by Big Chief writing tablet, 217; by Indian Head cornmeal, 217; by Calumet baking powder, 217; characters in caricature, 216; copyright lawsuit, 225; by Cherikee red pop, 217; by Chief Wenatchee apples, 217; by Crayola, 222; by Crazy Horse Malt Liquor (Hornell Brewing Company), 217–18, 219, 224; criticism from Natives, 224; cultural appropriation, 229; by Diamond Lawnmowers, 217; by Eskimo Pie, 213; and ethnostress, 222; by Faherty Brand clothing, 228; and fetishization of women and girls, 84; by Gap, 226; by Jeep Gladiator Mojave, 224; by Land O'Lakes, 213–14; by Liz Claiborne and JCPenney, 224; male archetypes in, 217; by Mazda, 228; Mia the Butter Maiden, 213–14, 214; and mental health, 221; by Mohawk carpeting, 217; by Money House Blessing air freshener, 217; by the Native American Tea Company, 229; noble savage, 216; by Paul Frank Industries, 227; Oneida Nation's white corn soup jar, 229; by Pocahontas fruit snacks, 224; by Pontiac, 217; product symbols, 213; rebranding, 213–14, 217, 222; by Red Man chewing tobacco, 217; by Sioux Chief Manufacturing, 217, 218; Stroh Brewing Company apology, 224; by Tanka Bar, 226, 229; by Tecumseh small engines, 217; by Urban Outfitters, 226; by Victoria's Secret, 227; by Winnebago, 217
advertising and stereotypes: mascot, team names, 223. *See also* American Indian Mental Health Association of Minnesota

African Indians of the Five Civilized Tribes Foundation, 187
artificial intelligence (AI), 60, 82, 85, 158, 177
Al Jazeera, 188
Alcatraz, 152
Allakariallak, 145. *See also* Flaherty, Robert J.; *Nanook of the North*
allies, 3, 21, 119, 215, 230
American bison, 199
American Indian Arts and Crafts Act of 1990, 225
American Indian Freedom of Religion Act (AIFRA), 147
American Indian Journalists Institute, 25
American Indian Mental Health Association of Minnesota, 223. *See also* advertising and stereotypes; health care; mascots and team names
American Indian Movement (AIM), 152
American Sociological Association, 223
Anishinnaabe, 165, 169
anticolonialist media, 124–25
Arapaho: bison expansion and ecosystem restoration projects, 199; community, 149; constitution of, 75; Defamation Act for the Cheyenne and Arapaho Tribes, 72. *See also* Cheyenne
Arizona Mirror (newspaper), 26
Arizona Republic, The (newspaper), 26–27, 57
Arizona State University (ASU), 23, 171, 232, 234
Atlanta Braves, 215. *See also* mascots and team names
audiences, 2, 110, 113, 129, 134, 171, 176–78, 180, 193, 205, 216; framing by, 196; Indigenous, 1, 155; international, 17; tribal, 30
Bad Press (film), 63, 176–85. *See also* Ellis, Angel (reporter); Independent Muscogee (Creek) Press
Bad River, Mich., 21, 106, 163–64, 167–71, 173–74
Bad River Ojibwe, 21, 163
Bad River Reservation, 166
Badger Clan, 232
Badger PR, 232
Baffin Island, Canada, 145
BBC (British Broadcasting Company), 188
Bear Clan, 77
Bering Land Bridge Theory, 148–49
Bering Strait, 80
BIA (Bureau of Indian Affairs / Bureau of Indian Administration), 57, 86, 87, 199
Big Water Film Festival (Washburn, Wis.), 170
Bill of Rights: Thlopthlocco Tribal Town Constitution/Muscogee (Creek) Nation, 74; US Constitution, 178
Bishop Paiute Environmental Management Office, 150. *See also* environmental management
Black Film Archive, 159
Black Lives Matter, 203, 212
blood quantum, 90, 189
boarding school era, 83
boarding schools, 2, 82, 85–88, 93, 107, 120, 157, 198
body sovereignty, 103, 106
border wall, 203
Boston Tea Party, 148
Brackeen v. Haaland / Indian Child Welfare Act (ICWA), 82–95, 104, 107, 113–15
broadband, 3, 164
broadcast media, 165

Bureau of Indian Affairs / Bureau of Indian Administration (BIA), 57, 86, 87, 199
Bureau of Trust Funds Administration, 198

Campus Voice (newspaper), 24–25
Canadian Broadcasting Corporation (CBC), 47, 49–51, 53–56, 134
Canadian residential schools, 46–56; generational harm, 108
Canyon Dreams (book), 234, 235n2. *See also* Rez Ball
capitalism, 88, 91
Caribou, Sue (Canadian residential school survivor), 54
Casimir, Rosanne, 46–56. *See also*, Tk'emlups te Secwepemc
casinos, 17, 20
Castner Range National Monument, N. Mex, 198
Catholic Church (Catholicism): confessional, 151; as a news source, 53; residential schools, 108; Supreme Court justices, 92; vandalism of Canadian churches, 46; as a veil for abuse, 107
Canadian Broadcasting Corporation (CBC) / CBC Radio, 47, 134
Canadian government, 47
censorship, 28, 62, 71, 75, 178, 184
Changing Woman Initiative, 106. *See also* health care
Cherokee Freedmen, 188–90
Cherokee Nation, 60, 71, 76, 90, 111, 157, 186–88
Cherokee Nation Independent Press Act of 2009, 71
Cherokee Nation of Oklahoma, 64, 69
Cherokee National Council, 189
Cherokee Phoenix (newspaper), 51, 164–65
Cheyenne: bison expansion and ecosystem restoration projects, 199; constitution of, 75; Defamation Act for the Cheyenne and Arapaho Tribes, 72. *See also* Arapaho
Cheyenne Winters (character), 137–39, 199, 220
Chickasaw Nation, 72, 75, 190
Chickasaw government, 72
Crazy Horse: 218; Liz Claiborne clothing line, 224; malt liquor, 217, 219, 224. *See also* advertising
Chief Illiniwek, 215, 224
Chief Red Cloud, 152
Chief Wahoo, 223
Child Welfare League of America, 87
Choctaw Nation: Claims and Immunities Act of the Choctaw Nation of Oklahoma, 72; impact of boarding schools on family structure, 86
Christian missionaries, 85, 111, 117
Chumash Tongva, 136
citizen journalism, 109
civil rights movement, 190
Civil War, 189
Claims and Immunities Act of the Choctaw Nation of Oklahoma, 72. *See also* Choctaw Nation
Cleveland Indians: changed name to the Guardians, 215; and Chief Wahoo, 223. *See also* mascots and team names
climate and environmental studies, 14
climate change, 15, 99, 115, 173, 204. *See also* environment; environmental issues; environmental professionals
climate resilience, 15, 204. *See also* environment
CNN (Cable News Network), 172, 188
collective memory, 35
colonial government, 67
colonial trauma, 15
colonization, 13, 32, 35, 47, 66, 83, 86, 88, 121, 123, 186

Columbia River Gorge, Pacific Northwest, 165
Columbia River Inter Tribal Fish Commission (CRITFC), 37–38
Columbus Day, 226
Columbus, Christopher, 80
commercial TV, 98
Common Sense (newspaper), 41–42
Confederated Tribes of Grande Ronde, 64
Congress: boarding school and assimilation policies, 85; Haaland, Debra Anne, 193–94, 200; Indian Child Welfare Act (ICWA), 82, 87, 93, 113; Indian Civil Rights Act, 69, 178; Indian Reorganization Act of 1934, 67; National Indian Gaming Regulatory Act, 174n4; plenary power over tribes, 67–68; prohibiting the use of "Crazy Horse" on alcoholic beverage products; and the reservation boundaries of the Muscogee (Creek) Nation, 65
conservation, 14, 135, 199, 204
Constitution of the Cheyenne and Arapaho Tribes of Oklahoma, 75
Courts of Indian Offenses, 73, 147. *See also* federal government
COVID-19, 10, 17, 31, 44, 46, 64, 210, 221. *See also* pandemic
Creative Commons, 26
Creator, 149–50, 208
critical race theory, 66
Crow Country: Our Right to Food Sovereignty (film), 147
cultural appropriation, 212, 224, 227, 229–31
cultural context, 15
cultural genocide, 147, 156
cultural heritage, 19–20, 230
cultural survival, 32, 127

Dakota Access Pipeline protests, 2, 172. *See also* Standing Rock Sioux Tribe Reservation
Dakota Sioux, 168
Dark Winds (television series), 139, 140
Dawes Rolls, 187. *See also* federal government
decolonization, 9–10, 15–17, 88, 124, 177
decolonized health practices, 106. *See also* health care
Deep Fork National Wildlife Refuge, Okla., 203–204
defamation, 72
Defamation Act for the Cheyenne and Arapaho Tribes, 72
Delaware Tribe of Indians, 105
Department of the Interior, 194
Descendants of Freedmen of the Five Civilized Tribes Association, 187
Descendants, The (film), 122
DesJarlait, Patrick, 214
Diamond, Neil (filmmaker), 141, 145, 151. *See also* documentary filmmakers
digital age, 28
digital and data sovereignty, 105
digital news outlets, 17
Diné, 67
Diné bi Naltsoos, 20. *See also* Navajo Times
disinformation, 82
Disney, 126–27, 134, 209
distribution: film and media, 125; financial, 199; influencer, 177; newspaper, 28; press releases, 180; statistical, 51
documentary: autobiographical, 158; ethnographic, 141, 145; film, 163; filmmaking, 153; news, 170; Sundance Film Festival Special Jury award, 63, 184; work, 156. *See also* ethnographic filmmaking
documentary filmmakers: Diamond, Neil, 141, 145; Flaherty, Robert J., 141–143, 144, 145, 147, 151–52; Landsberry-Baker, Rebecca, 176,

179, 184; Rae, Heather, 48; Tribal Youth Media workshop (Jackson, Shania; Principato, Jordan; Thomas, Ahpahnae)
Dougie Kameāloha (television series), 123
DQ University, 41

economic restoration, 17
Edison, Thomas, 157
editorial independence, 31, 74
education: government trust responsibilities, 44; Hoopa Education Committee, 41; Indian Self-Determination and Education Assistance Act of 1975, 66; Indigenous leadership, 183; and Indigenous standpoint pedagogy, 15; around mascots, 223–24; National Education Association, 223; in news framing, 51; as news sources, 53; public, 29, 31; teacher, 29; United Nations Educational, Scientific and Cultural Organization, 1; vocational, 15; White House's Initiative on American Indian and Alaska Native Education, 220; Wisconsin Educational Communications Board, 29
Ellis, Angel (reporter), 176. *See also* *Bad Press*; Independent Muscogee (Creek) Press
environment: climate change, 15, 99, 115, 173, 204; concerns, 172; culture-nature relationship, 129; degradation of, 129; destruction, 3; domestic, 88; effects of climate change, 167; erosion, 126; governance, 32, 36; human impact on, 3, 14–15, 40, 99, 115, 126–27, 135, 167, 169, 171, 173, 175, 204; and Indigenous knowledge, 14, 40; issues, 28, 32, 127, 135, 171, 175, 197, 203; legislation, 30; media, 2, 26, 39; social, 150; stewardship of, 66, 150; threats, 169, 173. *See also* climate change
environmental journalism and news stories, 8, 28, 29–33, 35–39
environmental management, 29, 36, 150
environmental professionals, 30
environmental science, 29, 39, 40
environmental sovereignty, 32, 66
epistemologies, 10
epistemology, 11–12
Eskimo Pie, 213
ethnographic filmmaking: films, 141, 154; documentary, 141, 145; Flaherty, Robert J., 141–143, 144, 145, 147, 151–52; *Nanook of the North*, 141–143, 145, 146, 151, 153
ethnographic interviews, 5–6
ethnographic methodology, 33
ethnostress, 222

Facebook, 120, 205, 227
Fancy Dance (film), 139
Farmington Daily Times (newspaper), 25
federal government, 11, 35, 44, 73, 75, 85–86, 114, 150, 157, 187; and Dawes Rolls, 187; and Indian Adoption Project, 86; and legal issues, 65–66; and oversight of tribal nations, 66, 111; policy for land allotments, 189; and Treaty of Fort Laramie, 152; and treaties, 68. *See also* government
Federal Indian Boarding School Initiative Investigation Report, 107
federal recognition, 10, 90
feminist standpoint epistemologies, 15–16
fetishization of Indigenous women, 84, 91
Finding 'Ohana (film), 123
First Amendment, 58, 63–64, 74–75, 177
fish and wildlife, 37

fisheries, 3, 38–39
Flaherty, Robert J., 141–143, 144, 145, 147, 151–52. *See also* Allakariallak; documentary filmmakers; ethnographic filmmaking; *Nanook of the North*
food deserts, 147–48
forced sterilizations, 105
Fort McDowell Yavapai Nation, 98
Fort Peck Assiniboine, 57
Four Ds (dancing, drums, drinking, death), 152
Fox (news channel), 188
Fox Brothers (Indigenous filmmakers), 157
Framework of historical oppression, resilience, and transcendence, 88
framing, media, 88; political messages, 196; problematic, 31; process, 50; strategic, 193
free press, 62–64. *See also* freedom of the press; press freedom
Free Press Act, 62
Freedmen, 186–92
freedom of expression, 64–65, 68, 76
freedom of the press, 64, 178. *See also* free press; press freedom
French and Indian Wars, 218. *See also* Indian Wars
Frontline (television series), 96, 99
Frybread Face and Me (film), 139

gaming, 10, 17, 97, 98, 114, 165, 174n4
Gannett Co. Inc., 26
gender nonconforming people, 105. *See also* Two Spirit
generational harm, 46–56. *See also* Canadian residential schools
genocide, 67, 80, 86, 147, 156–57
Goldwater Institute, 94
Google search, 50, 164
government: balance of power, 112; communicators, 32; and Deb Haaland, 198–99, 204; distrust of, 105; oversight, 89; rights and responsibilities, 32; tensions, 17
Government Accounting Office, 105
Grand Trunk Pacific Railway, 143
Great Lakes Indian Fish and Wildlife Commission (GLIFWC), 171, 175n8
Great Lakes Indian News Bureau, 79
Green Bay Film Festival, 170

Haaland, Deb, 193–205, 230
Haida, 165
Han Gwich'in, 199
Harjo, Alexandria, 63
Harjo, Sterlin, 157, 159n2, 209, 211n2
Harjo, Suzan Shown, 220
Harris, Kamala, 202
Haudenosaunee, 165
Hawai'i International Film Festival, 129
Hawaiian Kingdom, 122
Headdress (film), 138
health care: abortion, 104–6, 110; American Indian Mental Health Association of Minnesota, 223; in boarding schools, 86; Changing Woman Initiative, 106; decolonized health practices, 106; disparity, 61; Dobbs decision, 106; as a human right, 106; Indian Health Care Improvement Act, 60; Indian Health Service, 114; Indigenous Women Rising abortion fund, 106; mental health, 221; options, 106; pregnancy, 106; race-based inequalities, 212; reproductive, 106; resources, 89; risks, 105; statistics, 61; system, 61; wellness, 106
Herrera v. Wyoming, 68
Hiawatha First Nation, 55
historical loss, 15
historical trauma, 6, 15, 48, 49, 55; framework, 55; theory, 49

Ho-Chunk Indian Nation, 166, 171, 174n3, 174n5, 199
Hodulgee Muscogee, 220
Hollywood, 122, 125, 141, 151
Hoopa Education Committee, 41. *See also* education
Hoopa Valley Tribe, 41
Hopi, 41, 96, 97, 98, 232
House, Daisy (Chief of the Cree Nation of Chisasibi), 51
Huerta, Dolores, 203
HuffPost, 227
Hulu, 209, 211n2
Human Rights Film Festival (Tempe, Ariz.), 163, 171
hunting and fishing taxation, 81
hunting, fishing, and gathering rights, 29–31, 34, 166–67, 169
hybridized film production, 126

IllumiNative, 114–15, 116n2
Imprint, The, 92
Independent Film Festival, 184
Independent Film Festival Boston, 184
Independent Muscogee (Creek) Press Act, 74, 179. *See also Bad Press* (film); Ellis, Angel (reporter)
Indian Adoption Project, 86–87, 93. *See also* [The US] federal government
Indian Boarding School Policy, 85
Indian Child Welfare Act (ICWA) / Brackeen v. Haaland, 82–95, 104, 107, 113–15
Indian Civil Rights Act of 1968, 73
Indian Civilization Fund Act of 1819, 85
Indian Country Today (*ICT*) (newspaper), 20, 57–60, 96, 109–10, 112, 119, 182, 233
IndianCountryTV.com, 166. *See also News from Indian Country*
Indian Gaming (magazine), 182
Indian Gaming Regulatory Act, 108, 174n4
Indian Head penny, 216
Indian Health Service, 105, 114. *See also* health care
Indian Health Care Improvement Act, 60. *See also* health care
Indian Removal Act of 1830, 85
Indian Reorganization Act (IRA), 67, 75. *See also* Wheeler-Howard Act
Indian Self-Determination and Education Assistance Act of 1975, 66. *See also* education
Indian Wars (American Indian), 84–85, 217; French and Indian Wars, 218
IndianCountryTV.com, 166
Indianz.com, 182
Indigenous African epistemologies, 18
Indigenous Africans, 18
Indigenous journalism, 16, 19, 58, 64, 177; journalist, 25, 54–55, 64; journalists, 4, 17–18, 26–28, 51, 56, 62–65, 76, 92, 184
Indigenous Journalists Association (IJA) / Native Journalists Association (NAJA), 4, 24, 63, 77, 100, 108, 185n1
Indigenous science, 28–29, 40
Indigenous Standpoint Pedagogy (ISP), 15. *See also* education
Indigenous Standpoint Theory (IST), 4, 10, 12–18, 21, 64, 76, 87, 180
Indigenous/tribal epistemologies, 11–12
Indigenous Women Rising abortion fund, 106. *See also* health care
Indiqueer, 111
influencer, 120, 177
Information-sharing value orientations, 35
Instagram, 103, 106
Instagram stories, 106

intellectual property, 3
intergenerational transfer of knowledge, 38
intergenerational trauma, 56, 88, 129, 198
International Indian Treaty Council, 215
internet, 44, 120, 173
interpretivist approach, 50
Inuit, 47, 141–43, 145
Inuit Circumpolar Council, 31
invasion of privacy, 72
Inyo Mountains, Calif., 149
Iowa Tribe of Oklahoma / Bah Kho-Je / People of the Grey Snow, 62

James, LeBron, 234, 236n3

Kamloops Indian Residential School, 46, 49, 55
Kānaka Maoli (Native Hawaiians), 122, 127, 131, 133–35, 279
Kansas City Chiefs, 215. *See also* mascots and team names
Kansas City Star (newspaper), 223. *See also* mascots and team names
Kialegee Tribal Town of Oklahoma, 74–75
Kohl, Johann (German ethnographer), 164
KOOL (CBS affiliate in Phoenix), 97
KWDR.org and.net (Wolf Den Radio), 43–44

La Duke, Winona, 171
Lac Courte Oreilles Community College, 80
Lac Courte Oreilles Ojibwe Reservation, 77, 79, 165, 167
Lac Courte Oreilles Journal American, 78
Laguna Pueblo tribe, 193, 197
Lake Huron (Canada), 143
Lakota (Sioux), 189, 216
land: allotments, 189, 191; caring for, 127; closed areas/tribally protected 34; decision makers, 109; and forced assimilation, 85; Indian / Native, 67, 111, 151, 156; Indigenous belonging and connection, 135, 149; jurisdiction, 112; as a living being/interconnected, 35, 127, 133, 135, 157; management, 89; protected, 35, 194; public, 194; reclamation, 152; removal, 214; sacred sites, 11, 149; and settler colonialism, 125; sovereignty, 106; stewardship, 174, 199, 205; stolen, 152, 189; and Treaty of Fort Laramie 152, 153; treaty rights, 122, 126, 172; versus state laws, 113
Land O'Lakes, 213–14, 214. *See also* advertising; Mia the Butter Maiden
Landsberry-Baker, Rebecca, 176, 179, 184. *See also* documentary filmmakers
LCO Community College. *See* Lac Courte Oreilles Community College
lda package in R, 50
Lewis and Clark, 118
LGBTQ, 84, 121, 202. *See also* Two Spirit
libertarianism, 66
Lilo & Stitch (film), 123, 134
Los Angeles Asian Pacific Film Festival, 129
Los Angeles Department of Water and Power, 153
Los Angeles Times / LA Times (newspaper), 188
Lyng v. Northwest Indian Cemetery Protective Association, 147

Madison Action for Mining AlterNatives (MAMA), 171
mainstream journalism, 16, 18, 64–65
mainstream media, 17, 31, 109, 167

Mandan-Hidatsa-Arikara, 63
Mangusid (Loon-foot), 164
Manifest Destiny, 107, 226
manual coding, 49–50
marketing, 176–77, 216–17, 223, 231
mascots and team names: American Indian Mental Health Association of Minnesota on, 223; American Sociological Association on, 223; Atlanta Braves, 215; change in names of, 215; Chief Illiniwek as, 215, 224; Chief Wahoo as, 223; and ethnostress, 222; Kansas City Chiefs, 215; and Kansas City Star, 223; and mass media, 220; and Minneapolis Star Tribune, 223; NAACP on, 223; National Congress of American Indians on, 220; and Native American Journalists Association (now IJA), 223; NCAA on, 215, 223, 230; NCAA Minority Opportunities and Interests Committee study, 223; negative impact of, 223; and newspapers, 223; Oregonian, 223; and the racial reckoning of 2020, 212, 231; resolutions against, 220, 223; stereotypes, 84, 220, 230; at University of Illinois, 215; at University of North Dakota (Fighting Sioux), 224; and Washington Red***** (Washington Commanders / Washington DC football team), 4, 215, 223
matriarchy, 17
matrilineal, 86, 232
Mattagami River, 143
Maverick Gaming LLC V. United States, 108
Maynard (The Maynard Institute), 68
Mazina'igan, 29
McGirt v. Oklahoma, 65, 112
media ethnography, 32
media literacy, 82–84, 91
media relations training, 30
medicine man, 147
Melanesians, 127
Mendoza, William, 220
Metis, 47
MHA Times, 63
Mia the Butter Maiden, 213–14, 214. *See also* advertising; Land O'Lakes
Micronesians, 127
Midwest Environmental Advocates, 171
militarization, 133–34. *See also* stereotypes
Milwaukee Film Festival, 184
mining, 166–69, 173, 174n5, 175n9
Minneapolis Star Tribune (newspaper), 223
Missing and Murdered: Indigenous peoples' crisis, 197; and government agencies, 91; Missing and Murdered Indian Women, 79; Missing and Murdered Indigenous Women (MMIW), 89, 91; Missing and Murdered Indigenous Women and Girls, 60; missing and murdered Indigenous People, 84; missing and murdered Native women, 197; missing and murdered persons cases, 198; and scholars, 91
missionaries, 85, 111, 117
Moana (film), 123–24, 126–29, 131–35
Modern Language Association, 223
Mohawk carpeting, 217
Mojave Desert, 149
Montana Senate Bill 419, 105
Morning Star Institute, 215
Moscow-Pullman Daily News (newspaper), 57–58; multimedia, 29, 120, 163
Muscogee Constitution of 1979, 62–63. *See also* Thlopthlocco Tribal Town
Muskogee (Creek) Nation, 62–65, 71, 74–76, 157, 176, 178–79
Mvskoke Media, 63, 74, 176, 178, 179, 184

NAACP (National Association for the Advancement of Colored People), 223
Nanook of the North (film), 141–143, 145, 146, 151, 153. *See also* Allakariallak; ethnographic filmmaking; Flaherty, Robert J
National Collegiate Athletic Association, 215
National Congress of American Indians, 111, 220. *See also* mascots and team names
National Education Association, 223. *See also* education
National Native American Boarding School Healing Coalition, 85
National Public Radio (NPR), 114, 117
National Wildlife Federation, 171
Native Hawaiian Recognition Bill, 122
Native Hawaiians (Kānaka Maoli), 122, 127, 131, 133–35, 279
Native Journalists Association (NAJA) / Indigenous Journalists Association, 4, 24, 63, 77, 100, 108, 185n1
Navajo Code Talkers, 27
Navajo Nation, 23–25, 59, 67, 224–25, 228
Navajo Nation Today, 57
Navajo Times (newspaper), 20, 24–25, 57, 59. *See also* Diné bi Naltsoos
Navajo-Hopi Observer (newspaper), 182
NCAA (National Collegiate Athletics Association), 215, 223
NCAA's Minority Opportunities and Interests Committee, 223
Netflix, 234
New York Times, The, 188
News from Indian Country (newspaper), 79. *See also* IndianCountryTV .com
newspapers, 19, 59, 171; and Columbus Day, 226; in the Great Lakes region, 79; and mascots, 223; tribal, 155, 165. *See also* specific newspapers
Nez Perce, 118
NFCB (National Federation of Community Broadcasters), 41
non-indigenous reporters, 17, 183
Nunavut, Canada, 145

Obama, Barack, administration, 92, campaign, 194
Oceanic people, 123
Oceanic Story Trust (OST), 124
Oglala Lakota, 199, 224
Ohio University, 185n2, 230
Ojibwe, 29–30, 165–66, 168, 174n1, 174n3, 175n8,
Oklahoma Revised Statutes, 72
Oklahoma v. Castro-Huerta, 65, 104, 108, 110–12, 116n1
Oneida Nation, 229
Onondaga Nation, 199
oral storytelling, 153
Oregonian (newspaper), 223. *See also* mascots and team names
Osage Nation, 64, 71–72, 76
Osage Nation's Civil Code, 71–72
Osage News (newspaper), 71
Ottawa Tribe of Oklahoma, 69
Owens River, Calif., 149
Owens Valley, Calif., 149
Owens Valley River, Calif., 153

Pacific epistemologies, 124
Pacific Islander, 123–24, 126, 131, 134–35. *See also* Pasifika culture
Paiute, 149
Pamunkey Tribe, 190, 192n15
pan-indigeneity, 19
pandemic, 17, 31, 46, 49, 209, 212, 221. *See also* COVID-19
parachute reporting, 17

Pasifika culture, 123, 132. *See also* Pacific Islanders
Pasifika people, 126–27. *See also* Kānaka Maoli / Native Hawaiians; Pacific Islanders; Micronesians; Polynesians; Melanesians
patriarchy, 88
patrilineal nuclear family, 86
Pawnee rappers, 5
Pawnee Nation of Oklahoma, 69
Payahuunadu, 149
paywalls, 27
Peace Policy of 1869, 85
Phillips Petroleum, 188
Phoenix Indian School, 96
photography, 120, 136
Pidgin Hawaiian, 126
Pinterest, 227
Poarch Band of Creek Indian Reservation, 173–74
Pocahontas paradox, 91
police brutality, 208
polyamory, 147
Polynesians, 127
Pope Francis, 46
post-traumatic stress disorder, 48
postcolonial film theory, 124–25
power dynamics, 33
press releases, 177–84
press freedom: and Cherokee Nation, 71; and constitutions, 28; and Mvskoke Media, 74; fight for, 65; in *Bad Press*, 176, 184; inconsistencies in, 64. *See also* free press; freedom of the press
pretendian, 121, 148. *See also* Rae, Heather
Prince and the Pauper, The (film), 138
Princess Kaiulani (film), 122–23
Princess Kaiulani, 122–23
Protect Our Future (film), 163–64, 169–73. *See also* Tribal Youth Media (TYM)

Quapaw Nation, 69
queer/gay, 138
Quinault Reservation, 173

racism: 16, 204, 212; antiracism, 212; casual, 151; and consumerism, 231; and Deb Haaland, 212; fetishization of Indigenous women, 84, 91; as "Imagined Moral Centre" of white people, 16; institutionalized, 321; in Lewiston, Idaho, 118; observed, 119; and stress, 221; structural, 91, 212; systemic, 138
Rae, Heather, 148. *See also* documentary filmmakers; pretendian radio, 3, 41, 43, 165
rappers, 207
Red Lake Nation News (newspaper), 182
Reel Injun (film), 141
Reporters Committee for Freedom of the Press, 65, 71
reproductive rights, 106
Reservation Dogs (television series), 106, 120, 138–40, 157, 206, 209, 211, 211n2
residential school. *See* Canadian residential schools
resilience, 3, 5–6, 15, 17, 38, 115, 202, 204, 234
Respect for Marriage Act, 201
Rez Ball, 234. *See also* Canyon Dreams
ridge runners, 45
ritual gift-giving, 147
Roe v. Wade, 104–5, 108–9
Rogers, Will, 157
Rutherford Falls (television series), 109, 120, 136–40

Sacred Stone Camp, 172. *See also* Dakota Access Pipeline protests
sacrifice zone, 175n9
Salt Lake Tribune (newspaper), 57

San Francisco Film Festival, 184
Santa Clara Pueblo v. Martinez, 73
Seattle International Film Festival, 184
Seattle Post-Intelligencer (newspaper), 58
Seattle Times (newspaper), 58
self-determination, 1, 126, 177, 184, 222
Sellars, Willie, 51
Seneca-Cayuga Nation, 69
settler colonialism, 125, 130, 134–35
sharing stories, 2, 28, 39, 44, 121
Sharp, Fawn, 111
Sho-Ban News (newspaper), 57–58
Sicangu Lakota, 108
Sierra Club, 171
Sierra Nevada Mountain, 149
Sin-Wit-Ki (newsletter), 36–37
Sioux Chief Manufacturing, 218
slave narratives, 190
Smithsonian Institution's National Museum of the American Indian, 229–30
Smoke Signals (film), 209
social isolation, 15
Sokaogon Chippewa Community, 166
Southern Poverty Law Center, 223
sovereign immunity, 72, 75
sovereignty: body, 103, 106; digital and data, 105; environmental, 32, 66; Indigenous, 39; inherent, 62; land, 106; storytelling, 2; tribal, 10; and US Supreme Court, 65, 73, 89–90, 92, 103–5, 110–15, 147; and Wisconsin Educational Communications Board, 29
sports teams. *See* mascots and team names
Spotted Bear, Jodi Rave, 63
Spring Hill Company, 234, 236n3
"squaw," 200, 230. *See also* women
Standing Rock Sioux Tribe Reservation, 2, 172. *See also* Dakota Access Pipeline protests
stereotypes: in advertising and marketing, 213, 216; and appreciation, 229; and appropriation, 229–30; breaking down, 125, 208; and ethnostress, 222; gender, 195, 205; harmful, 141; and Halloween costumes, 228, 229; in Hollywood filmmaking, 151; inaccurate, 9; insensitive, 231; internalization of, 151, 222; of limited free press in Indian Country, 69; negative, 88, 123, 195; and news media, 10; pervasive, 221; positive, 221; power of, 218; previous media perpetuations of, 87; in public school, 151; racial and gender, 205; racialized, 195; racist, 84; reinforcement of, 157; resisting, 6, 180, 234; representation: amnesia and militarization, 133; self-confirming, 218, 221; sexualized, 227; systemic, 152
stereotype threat, 224
sterilization, 105
structural violence, 15
substance abuse, 208
suicide, 222
Sun Valley Film Festival (Idaho), 184
Sundance Institute: Native Lab, 129; Sundance Film Festival, 63; Sundance Film Festival US Documentary Special Jury Award for Freedom of Expression, 63, 184
survivance, 32
systemic discrimination, 16. *See also* racism

Tales from Planet Earth Film Festival (Madison, Wisc.), 170
Taylor, Freddy (Canadian residential school survivor), 54
Teen Gazette, 96
Teeters, Charlene, 220
Telecommunications Corporation, 43

Teller, Henry M. (Secretary of the Interior), 147
text analytics, 49, 51
Thlopthlocco Tribal Town, 74–75. *See also* Muscogee Constitution of 1979
TikTok, 103, 105, 110, 116, 120, 205, 235
Tk'emlups te Secwepemc, 46. *See also* Casimir, Rosanne
Tlingit, 165
topic modeling, 51, 56
totem poles, 165
tourism, 122, 130, 134, 135
tourist gaze, 132
traditional cultural expressions, 19–20
Trahant, Mark, 5
Trail of Tears, 114
transmen, 104. *See also* LGBTQ
Treaty of Fort Laramie, 152. *See also* federal government
Tribal Gaming and Hospitality (magazine), 182
tribal government, 28, 43, 68, 71, 73, 78, 150, 179, 184, 190; officials, 31, 66, 71; policy, 29; sources, 33, 36; staff, 30; tribal governments, 31, 112, 220; and censorship, 66; and Freedmen, 190; and media, 71, 165; officials, 79
Tribal Youth Media (TYM), 163, 167, 173, 175n10. *See also* documentary filmmakers; Protect Our Future
Trudeau, Justin, 46
Trudell (film), 148
Trudell, John, 148
True/False Film Festival (Columbia, Mo.), 184
trust responsibilities, 44
Tumblr, 227
Twitter, 59, 105, 107, 110
Two Spirit, 105, 91, 121. *See* also 2SLGBTQIA; LGBTQ

United Nations Convention on the Prevention and Punishment of the Crime of Genocide, 86
United Nations Declaration of Human Rights, 66
United Nations Declaration on the Rights of Indigenous Peoples, 12, 19, 65
United Nations Permanent Forum on Indigenous Issues, 1
United Nations Educational, Scientific and Cultural Organization, 1. *See also* education
United States Treasury, 216
University of Illinois, 215, 224. *See also* Chief Illiniwek; mascots and team names
University of New Mexico School of Law, 194
University of North Dakota, 224. *See also* Fighting Sioux; mascots and team names
University of Oregon, 204
University of Wisconsin-Madison, 171, 175n6
unwritten editorial law, 38
unwritten law, 34, 36–37
US Centers for Disease Control and Prevention, 105, 221
US Commission on Civil Rights, 223
US Department of Justice, 197
US Federal Communication Report on Broadband Deployment in Indian Country, 164
US House of Representatives, 188, 194
US Senate, 68, 188
USA Today (newspaper), 26. *See also* Arizona Mirror

Vancouver Island, Canada, 143
veterans, 201
videography, 120, 168
Vimeo, 172
visual storytelling, 29, 150, 163

WASH movement (We Are Still Here), 83, 94n1
Wall Street Journal, The, (newspaper) 188
Wampanoag Tribe, 25
Washington Post, The (newspaper), 109, 112, 188, 236n2
Washington Red***** (Washington Commanders / Washington DC football team), 4, 215, 223. *See also* mascots and team names
watchdog journalism, 109
web radio, 43
Western Native Voice, 113
Wheeler-Howard Act, 67, 75. *See also* Indian Reorganization Act (IRA)
White House's Initiative on American Indian and Alaska Native Education, 220. *See also* education
White Lotus, The (television series), 123–114
White Mountains, N.H., 149
white savior, 83
white supremacy, 88, 193, 204, 226
wild rice, 163, 168, 170
Wisconsin Educational Communications Board, 29. *See also* education
Wisconsin Network for Peace and Justice, 171
Wisconsin Public Radio, 117, 170
Wisconsin Public Television, 29
Wizard of Oz, The (film), 234
WOJB-88.9 FM, 79, 165
women, 17, 83–84, 87, 110, 142, 166, 191n11, 205; in Congress, 193; fetishization of, 91; gender stereotypes, 195; politicians, 197, 204; rights, 104–6, 108; "squaw," 200, 230; violence against, 197; women's apparel, 225. *See also* Missing and Murdered

Yakama Nation, 37
Yakama Nation Aviary, 33
Yakama Nation Review (newspaper), 28–29, 36–37, 39
YouTube: 60, 119–20, 172; channel, 230

www.ingramcontent.com/pod-product-compliance
Lightning Source LLC
LaVergne TN
LVHW101636100826
845155LV00014B/30/J
9780806197180